ROSAMUND BARTLETT lectures in .... Durham
and is a Fellow of the Europear .... here she
lives. Her new Chekhov translat .... ished by
Oxford World Classics, and her .... appears
with Penguin Classics. Her previ .... *akovich
in Context*, and (co-authored with .... w edition
of which was published in 2004.

Further praise for *Chekhov: Scenes from a Life*

'Rosamund Bartlett takes an impressionist approach to Chekhov's life, and it pays
off, making for a hugely enjoyable book which is far more interesting than a
conventional biography and much more moving. You end up wondering again at
Chekhov's astonishing greatness – man and writer'

David Hare

'A woman writing on a man, excellent! . . . Rosamund Bartlett has come up with the
ingenious idea of basing [her biography of Chekhov] on the places he lived in and
visited. Consequently, *Chekhov: Scenes from a Life* brings freshness to a familiar story'

Sunday Times Books of the Year

'A fresh angle on this most enigmatic of Russian writers . . . Bartlett persuades the
reader that Chekhov's life was full of drama . . . Bartlett's efforts as translator and
biographer should be greeted with prizes and acclaim. She has renewed Chekhov
for twenty-first-century readers, and revealed him to be a brilliant story writer as
well as a playwright of genius. Thanks to Bartlett, we can now see that beyond the
cherry orchard there is a rich pasture of short fiction'

Scotland on Sunday

'Something glues [Chekhov's work] all together, a something that Rosamund Bartlett
nails beautifully in her new book. In a word, it is landscape . . . [Bartlett] puts us on
a tour bus and drives us through nineteenth-century Russia . . . She focuses on
recreating each place in devoted Chekhovian detail, animating her scenes with
human comedy . . . Delightful . . . Bartlett has succeeded in freeing the playwright
from the dead hand of conventional, what-happened biography. Because it is
structured by place, and not chronologically, the narrative dances about through
time . . . As something to dip in and out of, it's a treasure'

New Statesman

'Here is a wonder: a book that delivers more than it promises . . . The place studies
are sensitively done, yet what emerges is something bigger: a book that though
deliberately impressionistic, is more informative about Chekhov the man than a
conventional biography; and more instructive about the roots of his work than dry
literary criticism . . . Much of the book is atmospheric, and the interplay between
Chekhov, his surroundings and his work is cleverly done . . . Rosamund Bartlett
more than pulls it off'

Sunday Telegraph

'[Bartlett's] focus on Chekhov's background helps us to gain a clearer sense of the
surprising scope of his life and work . . . [Chekhov is] a writer Bartlett clearly
understands very well indeed'

Literary Review

Таганрогъ № 17.
У пристани фиумъ.

Крымъ.—Crimée. № 14.
Ялта. Молъ.—Jalta. Le môle.

Ялта.   Видъ съ юго-западной стороны.

Chekhov

SCENES FROM A LIFE

ROSAMUND BARTLETT

*f*P

FREE PRESS

First published in Great Britain by The Free Press in 2004
An imprint of Simon & Schuster UK Ltd
A Viacom Company
This edition published in 2005

Simon & Schuster UK Ltd
Africa House
64–78 Kingsway
London WC2B 6AH

www.simonsays.co.uk

Simon & Schuster Australia
Sydney

A CIP catalogue record for this book
is available from the British Library.

ISBN: 0-7432-3075-2
EAN: 9780743230759

Typeset by M Rules
Printed and bound in Great Britain by
Cox & Wyman Ltd, Reading, Berks

FOR A.P. AND R.P.

CONTENTS

LIST OF ILLUSTRATIONS

NOTE ON ABBREVIATIONS,
TRANSLITERATION AND DATES

All quotations from Chekhov's writings refer to the thirty-volume Academy of Sciences edition of his complete collected works, published in Moscow between 1974 and 1983: the works are published in eighteen volumes and the letters in twelve volumes. Notes to the works are preceded by 'W' and contain volume numbers followed by page references; in the case of references to letters, volume numbers are preceded by 'L'.

A simplified transliteration system has been followed in the body of the text, with a more accurate system employed in the notes.

The dates cited refer to the Julian calendar used in Russia before 1917, which was twelve days behind the Western calendar in the nineteenth century and thirteen in the twentieth century.

PREFACE

In a recent volume of articles about Chekhov, a prominent Russian scholar asked the question: 'Is it easy to be Chekhov's biographer?'[1] Despite hundreds of memoirs, twelve volumes of annotated letters, articles, monographs, and copious other sources, published and unpublished, not to mention a myriad clues contained in the works themselves, she had to conclude that it was not. Chekhov's letters, after all, are not always as straightforward as they appear, and memoirs can often be unreliable and even flatly contradictory: there is still a lack of agreement even on such rudimentary points, for example, as the colour of Chekhov's eyes (variously described as grey, blue, or brown). A major achievement in the late twentieth century was to remove the layers of distortion that had accreted over the decades of Soviet rule and make Chekhov human again. The Stalinist image of Chekhov as a personality without flaws proved remarkably resilient, but has now at last given way to a more balanced view. For this, we are indebted to the pioneering biographies based on detailed study of the available Russian sources by British and American Slavists such as Ronald Hingley and Ernest J. Simmons, and, in particular, to the recent exhaustive account by Donald Rayfield. Because of the lingering reverence with which writers are still held in Russia, a full-scale biography of Chekhov in Russian has yet to be written, but thanks to Donald Rayfield's meticulous research in newly opened archives, we now have a definitive account of Chekhov's day-to-day life, set in the context of his immediate environment. The fact that Chekhov was as inconsistent and as contradictory as the next person, however, suggests that we will thankfully never have a definitive interpretation of his life. The conventional image of Chekhov as someone self-contained and reserved in manner certainly tallies with the form and structure of his artistic works, yet he himself admitted at one point to having a fiery temper and a nervous disposition. Such anomalies encourage us to continue the process of interpreting Chekhov's life, rather than acting as a deterrent.

Of the many clichés which have clung persistently to Chekhov's biography (frail, bespectacled, gloomy Russian writer etc.), the most tenacious perhaps is that of his elusive character. Here is an aspect where most memoirs seem to concur: we read that Chekhov kept his distance, that he was solitary, silent, reticent, sober, and possessed of a certain coldness.[2] Even when he married, he preserved his autonomy, choosing not to live permanently with his wife. But there was one area of his life where he was unusually expansive, and that was in his relationship with the landscape. Chekhov's main subject as an artist may have been people's frailties and the complexities of human interaction, but human beings rarely inspired him to flights of lyricism in the way that the Russian landscape did. Chekhov hid his lyrical persona carefully, but it is there to find in his letters, and particularly in his short stories. It was the landscape which occasionally provoked him to utter the word 'poetic', the highest accolade in his vocabulary, and it was the landscape which was responsible for some of the happiest moments in his life. It also pervaded the unconscious world of his dreams and nightmares, as he intriguingly revealed in a letter he wrote to the writer Dmitry Grigorovich in February 1887, when he was twenty-seven years old:

When my blanket falls off at night, I begin to see in my dreams huge slithery rocks, cold autumn water and bare riverbanks – all of this is foggy and unclear, without a single patch of blue sky; in despair and melancholy, as if I have lost my way or have been abandoned, I look at the rocks and feel that for some reason I must cross the deep river; I see little tug boats, pulling huge barges, pieces of timber, rafts and so on floating by. Everything is unbearably desolate, raw and stark. When I run away from the river I come to fallen-down cemetery gates, a funeral, my school teachers . . . And am I filled during this time with the sort of nightmarish cold which is unconceivable when I am awake . . . I think if I had been born and lived permanently in St Petersburg, I would definitely dream about the banks of the Neva, Senate Square and massive pedestals . . .[3]

Chekhov was a writer who was profoundly sensitive to his environment. If it is difficult for us to penetrate Chekhov's character through his relationships with people because of his inscrutability and reserve, perhaps our emphasis should be shifted to his relationship with the places in which he lived?

This biography therefore takes as its point of departure Chekhov's physical environment: the provincial town of Taganrog among the steppes in which he grew up, the burgeoning city of Moscow where he trained as a doctor and made his home as an adult, the more formal St Petersburg where most of his literary work was based, the rural summer retreats where he was able to enjoy being idle (which he regarded as an essential ingredient of happiness), the empty wastes of Siberia which enabled him to fulfil his lust for adventure and also put into practice the ideals that he cherished, the country estate of Melikhovo where he planted trees and roses and enjoyed living on the land, the beautiful but alien French Riviera, where he spent lonely winter months trying to get well, and the Crimean resort of Yalta where he had the excruciating experience of seeing his life slowly ebb away. The aim of each chapter is to convey the texture of Chekhov's life in each of the places in which he lived or spent significant amounts of time, and in so doing shed light on different aspects of his character. This book is a biography of Chekhov, and more specifically his creative spirit, but it is also a biography of the places in which he lived and worked, and an exploration of how they relate to his short stories and plays.

As the subtitle of this book suggests, this biography takes an impressionistic approach: it is deliberately not intended to be comprehensive. Numerous events and people from the vast cast of characters in Chekhov's life are not discussed at all, while others are explored at length, and certain small details examined closely. Not all the places that he went to are included: the trips Chekhov made to the Caucasus, and his honeymoon in a remote provincial sanatorium are not covered, for example, because of their relative brevity and paucity of documentation. The length of each chapter does not necessarily correspond to time-span, furthermore: chapter eight explores Chekhov's time in the South of France, where he spent just a few months, while chapter seven describes his life at Melikhovo in the Russian countryside, where he spent several years. Although they have been put together in a roughly chronological manner, the chapters themselves do not always adhere to a strict chronological framework, but sometimes look both forwards and backwards in time, and it is for this reason that a simple chronology of Chekhov's life and works has been included.

CHRONOLOGY

1860   Anton Chekhov is born on 17 January in Taganrog, a town on the Azov Sea in southern Russia, the third son of the merchant Pavel Egorovich Chekhov (1825–1898) and Evgenia Yakovlevna Chekhova (1835–1919). Chekhov's parents married in 1854: of their seven children, five sons and two daughters, only the youngest, Evgenia (1869–71), did not live to survive infancy

1868   Chekhov accepted as a pupil at the Taganrog classical *gymnasium*, following an unsuccessful first year at the Greek Parish school.

1873   Attends the theatre for the first time

1876   Father is declared bankrupt and flees with his family to Moscow, leaving Anton behind in Taganrog to finish school

1879   Moves to Moscow and becomes a student in the Medical Faculty of Moscow University

1880   First story published in a St Petersburg comic journal; meets the artist Levitan, who becomes a close friend

1882   Invited to contribute to the leading Petersburg comic journal, *Fragments*, by its editor Nikolai Leikin

1884   Graduates from medical school; first signs of tuberculosis; writes seventy-six stories over the course of the year; publication of first book of stories, *Tales of Melpomene*; serialization of only novel, *Drama at a Shooting Party*, in a Moscow newspaper

1885   Invited to write for *The Petersburg Newspaper*; summer at Babkino; first visit to St Petersburg

1886   Invited to write for *New Times* by its owner Alexei Suvorin, who becomes a close friend; first story published in Suvorin's newspaper is also under his own name; letter from Dmitri Grigorovich exhorting Chekhov to take his writing more seriously; second summer at Babkino

1887   Travels back to Taganrog and the steppe landscapes of his childhood; third summer at Babkino; first performance of *Ivanov* in Moscow

1888   Publication of 'The Steppe' in *The Northern Messenger* – the first story to appear in a serious literary journal; awarded the Pushkin Prize by the Imperial Academy of Sciences; first summer at Luka; first visit to the Crimea (Feodosia)

1889   Second summer at Luka; death of brother Nikolai from tuberculosis there; first visit to Yalta

1890   Travels across Siberia to the island of Sakhalin, where over a period of three months and three days completes a census of its prison population; returns by sea via Hong Kong, Singapore, Ceylon and Odessa

1891   First trip to Western Europe with Suvorin: six-week tour to Vienna, Venice, Bologna, Florence, Rome, Naples, Nice and Paris; summer at Bogimovo; assists with famine relief

1892   Purchases small country estate at Melikhovo, fifty miles south of Moscow, and moves there with his parents. Works as doctor to prevent cholera epidemic; publishes 'Ward No. 6'

1894   Second visit to Yalta

1895   First meeting with Tolstoy; *The Island of Sakhalin* published as a book

1896   Builds the first of three schools in the Melikhovo area, and starts sending books to the Taganrog library. Disastrous first performance of *The Seagull* at the Imperial Alexandrinsky Theatre in St Petersburg

1897   Falls seriously ill; publishes *The Peasants*, whose unvarnished depiction of rural life causes a furore; spends winter in Nice and takes serious interest in the Dreyfus case

1898   Meets Olga Knipper; death of father; successful first performance of *The Seagull* at the Moscow Art Theatre; spends first winter in Yalta

1899   Moves into house built for him in Yalta; first performance of *Uncle Vanya* at the Moscow Art Theatre; publishes 'The Lady with the Little Dog'; spends summer in Moscow; last visit to Taganrog

1900   Elected an honorary member of the literary section of the Imperial Academy of Sciences; the first volumes of the Marx edition of his collected works are published; spends part of autumn in Moscow; second long stay in Nice

1901 First performance of *Three Sisters* at the Moscow Art Theatre; marries Olga Knipper later in the year in Moscow

1902 Spends summer in Moscow, partly at Lyubimovka

1903 Spends part of spring and summer in Moscow, partly in Nara; returns to Moscow to attend rehearsals of *The Cherry Orchard*

1904 Attends first performance of *The Cherry Orchard* at the Moscow Art Theatre; worsening condition of his health leads to decision to seek treatment in Germany; dies in Badenweiler on 15 July (2 July according to Russian calendar)

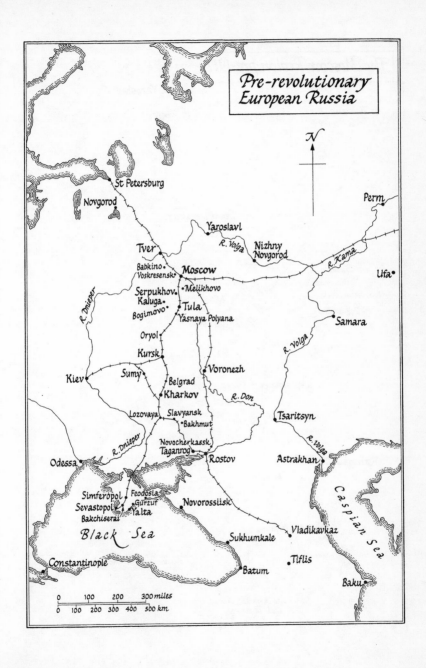

Pre-revolutionary
European Russia

N

St Petersburg

Novgorod

Perm

Yaroslavl

R. Volga

Nizhny
Novgorod

R. Kama

Ufa

Tver

Babkino
Voskresensk

Moscow

Serpukhov
Kaluga
Bogimovo

Melikhovo

Tula

Yasnaya Polyana

Samara

R. Volga

Oryol

Kursk

Voronezh

Kiev

Sumy

Belgrad

Kharkov

R. Don

Lozovaya

Slavyansk

Bakhmut

Tsaritsyn

Novocherkassk

Taganrog

Rostov

R. Volga

Astrakhan

Odessa

R. Dnieper

Simferopol
Sevastopol
Bakchiserai

Feodosia
Gurzuf
Yalta

Novorossiisk

Black Sea

Sukhumkale

Vladikavkaz

Tiflis

Caspian Sea

Constantinople

Batum

Baku

0   100   200   300 miles
0 100 200 300 400 500 km

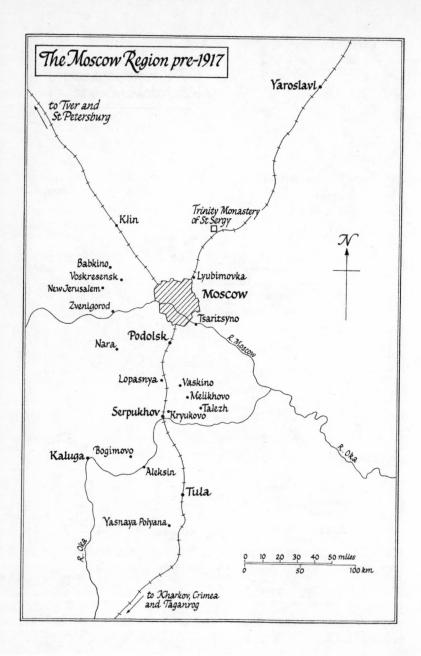

The Moscow Region pre-1917

to Tver and
St Petersburg

Yaroslavl

Klin

Trinity Monastery
of St Sergy

N

Babkino
Voskresensk
New Jerusalem
Zvenigorod

Lyubimovka

Moscow

Tsaritsyno

Podolsk

R. Moscow

Nara

Lopasnya
• Vaskino
• Melikhovo
• Talezh
Serpukhov • Kryukovo

R. Oka

Kaluga
Bogimovo

Aleksin

Tula

Yasnaya Polyana

R. Oka

0   10 20 30 40 50 miles
0   50   100 km

to Kharkov, Crimea
and Taganrog

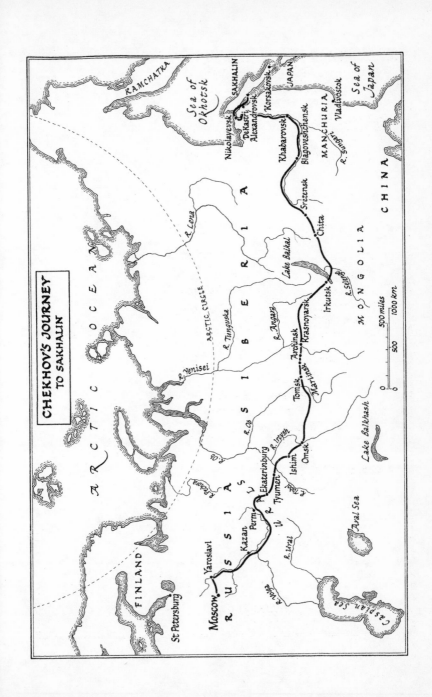

CHEKHOV'S JOURNEY
TO SAKHALIN

Chekhov was the kind of poet who sings like a bird – sings and rejoices.

Alexei Suvorin, 15 July 1904

PROLOGUE: CHEKHOV THE WANDERER

In the last months of his life, Chekhov pondered the subject of a new play he wanted to write. He told his wife, Olga Knipper, that the hero of the play would be a scientist who either suffers from unrequited love or who is betrayed by the woman he loves. Chekhov had set his previous plays in provincial Russia. As the Moscow Art Theatre director Vladimir Nemirovich-Danchenko rightly pointed out, this gave him more potential for lyricism. Chekhov was most inspired by the open spaces of his native landscape, and even if landscape and open spaces cannot easily protrude into the dramas themselves, they function as an important backdrop, providing both the author and his characters with room to breathe. In his projected last play, Chekhov planned to take this dimension one step further by having his scientist go on a journey to the far north. That is where the crucial third act would take place, and Chekhov imagined an icebound ship and the scientist standing alone on deck. Surrounded by silence and the majesty of the night-time sky, the scientist would suddenly see the shadow of his beloved flitting past against the backdrop of the northern lights.[1]

This embryonic idea is highly revealing. First of all it shows us Chekhov's creative mind in vibrant form even if the shell that housed it was gradually ceasing to function. One wonders what Stanislavsky would have made of a play in which there was no opportunity to introduce naturalistic detail. The constant swatting of mosquitoes that Stanislavsky introduced into his stagings in pursuit of atmosphere had led Chekhov to vow he would write a play in which the main character would specifically state how wonderful it was that there were no mosquitoes![2] More importantly, however, Chekhov's idea for his next play reveals a great deal about his own preoccupations. Apart from the obvious connection with the extraordinary journey he undertook to Siberia in 1890, it is clear that he was thinking about his contemporary,

the great Norwegian explorer Fridtjof Nansen, who had sailed his ship
to eastern Siberia in 1893 and waited until it was completely enclosed
by ice. Convinced that the ice of the polar sea drifted eastwards,
Nansen was going to let his icebound ship be carried back to Norway
by the currents – which it was, albeit three years later. Chekhov's plan
to go to Norway himself in autumn 1904 to research his idea was
perhaps delusional given the state of his health that year.[3] In the event,
his only journey abroad that year was to a spa town in the Black Forest
to die. But his undiminished thirst for adventure becomes even more
poignant seen in the light of events. He did not write an obituary of
Nansen as he had done for Nikolai Przhevalsky, the great Russian
explorer whom he admired equally, for the simple reason that Nansen
(who was just one year younger than he) was still fighting fit, and would
outlive him by twenty-six years. The fact that he named the Siberian
hunting dog he was given in 1897 Nansen, however, indicates how
much the explorer had caught his imagination. In 1898, Nansen was
presented with the Order of St Stanislav when he came to St Petersburg
(the same order that Chekhov received), and later had cause to become
directly involved with Russian affairs.

Chekhov's early contraction of tuberculosis forced him to adopt a
restricted lifestyle which has obscured the fact that he was a man with
a nomad's blood in his veins who longed for adventure, and to be free.
'Besides talent and material, other things are needed, no less vital,' he
wrote in January 1889; 'the first necessity is maturity, and after that *a
sense of personal freedom*; this feeling has only very recently begun to
grow in me.'[4] Even when he was already quite ill, he yearned to see the
Sahara, and then did his best to persuade his wife that they should
travel to the more unusual destination of Scandinavia rather than the
French Riviera. After the Russo–Japanese War started at the beginning
of 1904, he thought about going to the Far East to offer his services as
a doctor to the sick and wounded, but was himself dead by the time of
his planned departure. Even in his last few breathless days in
Badenweiler he dreamed of going to Como and seeing the Italian lakes.
It is characteristic of Chekhov that he once said that he felt terribly
cowardly when he was most successful and braver when he was
unlucky. But the bold and almost reckless streak in this self-effacing,
self-controlled man, which had led him to travel to Sakhalin, symbolizes
the contradictions and oddities of his life.

The contradiction between the image Chekhov projected of himself, whether consciously or not, and the reality of his personality is one we can find throughout his work. As with his characters, there was often a gap between the sentiments he professed and the feelings he actually experienced. Even during his lifetime Chekhov gained a reputation for being elusive, withdrawn and rather cold. Certain comments we find scattered in the thousands of letters he wrote over the course of his life, and his love of the empty steppe suggest that he was in some respects a loner in the mould of someone like Sir Wilfred Thesiger, who was also endowed with artistic gifts. Thesiger fell in love with the desert, exhilarated by its sense of space. Chekhov fell in love with the enormous expanses of the Russian landscape, particularly the steppe, and the area beyond Lake Baikal in Siberia. Thesiger wrote about feeling in harmony with the past, 'travelling as men had travelled for untold generations across the deserts, dependent for their survival on the endurance of their camels and their own inherited skills'.[5] The theme of continuity appears again and again in Chekhov's stories, and always connected with the landscape. The bishop in his penultimate story dies imagining that he is happily striding through the open countryside in bright sunshine, as free as a bird. Chekhov may have largely lost his religious faith as an adult, but in his own dream of wanting to leave home with just a bundle and set off to find the real life, he was following in the hallowed traditions of the *stranniki*, the religious wanderers from all walks of life who went on pilgrimages to visit holy places, walking great distances, usually barefoot, and who were such a distinctive feature of the life of old Russia.

The inscription engraved on the signet ring which Chekhov inherited from his father seems to sum up the creative tension which informs his life, that is to say, the desire to live in the community and contribute to it, and the desire to run away from it. 'Odinokomu vezde pustinya' after all can be interpreted both negatively: 'everywhere is a desert to the lonely person' – and positively: 'the desert is everywhere for the solitary person'. As Hugh Pyper has commented in *The Oxford Companion to Christian Thought*, the desert offers both asylum and threat: 'Life-threatening yet liberating in its unbounded spaces and solitudes, for the biblical tradition it stands in contrast to the orderliness of the city, which may represent security but also can be claustrophobic, violent and decadent . . . The desert is a liminal space where constraints of social life are stripped away and both destruction and transformation are possible.'[6] Chekhov loved being with his friends and family, but he always had an aching need to be on his own, on one occasion expressing a desperate desire to move to the North Pole to get away from his incessant visitors. Despite his sociability, several of his contemporaries described him as actually being quite unsociable, and he himself confessed to having a reclusive tendency.[7] It is not a coincidence that fishing was one of his favourite occupations, and that he had such a fondness for monks and people of the church. Even when he was in Siberia, he confessed that he found it 'far more interesting to sit in a carriage or in your room alone with your thoughts than to be with people'.[8] But he also referred to himself as a *pustynnik* – a man of the desert – during his years of exile in Yalta, when the solitude he experienced was not of his volition.[9]

In certain respects Chekhov was like a present-day St Antony, his namesake, and he was not always joking when he referred to himself as a monk or an archimandrite in his last years. He had as many sins on his conscience as the next man, but there was something ascetic about his personality which aligns him with his patron saint. Antony, the founder of Christian monasticism, abandoned the world to lead a life devoted to God in the solitary deserts of Egypt in the middle of the third century, but twenty years later left his life of asceticism to form his disciples into a community. It is no coincidence that Chekhov uses the word *podvig* in his obituary of Nikolai Przhevalsky, which denotes a heroic feat, but is related to the religious concept of *podvizhnichestvo* – asceticism. To lead an ascetic life, but also to carry out heroic feats to bring benefit to others, as he believed Przhevalsky did, was Chekhov's ideal, and what propelled him to write his book about the penal colony on Sakhalin. It extended to creative work too, though. 'If I was a landscape painter,' he wrote in 1895, having just visited his friend Levitan's studio, 'I would lead an almost ascetic life: I'd have sex once a year and eat once a day.' Painting landscapes was incompatible with self-indulgent living, he argued.[10] But, of course, Chekhov *was* a landscape painter – in prose. Levitan sat down to read Chekhov's stories again during a spell of bad weather in the summer of 1891 and then wrote to tell him how astonished he was by his friend's ability to paint landscapes in stories such as 'Fortune', which is set in the southern Russian steppe.[11]

Chapter 1

PRE-HISTORY: A PORT ON THE AZOV SEA

I

Greeks and Scythians

Taganrog... a narrow isthmus, defended by an entrenchment of ancient origin, but enlarged and fortified in later ages. It is in all probability the Τάφρον, or fosse mentioned by Herodotus; and *Kremni* Κρημνοί, the principal emporium of the Scythians in this quarter, must have been situated at or near *Taganrog*, where also some geographers place the village of *Koroia* (Κοροία κώμη), specified by Ptolemy.

E. Henderson, *Biblical Researches and Travels in Russia* (1826)

Chekhov returned only occasionally in later life to Taganrog, the southern town on the Azov Sea where he had spent the first nineteen and a half years of his life. It was a long way away from Moscow, where he had made his home, and it took two full days to cover the 800-mile journey by train. But there was also a more prosaic reason as to why he did not go back more often: he had grown accustomed to certain creature comforts, and in Taganrog there was no running water. With fears of encroaching illness, however, Chekhov sometimes succumbed to feelings of nostalgia for what he called the 'healthy air' of his home town in the 1890s, and these feelings intensified during his last years when he was ill and very bored living in Yalta in the Crimea. Like Taganrog, the Crimean peninsula finally became part of the Russian Empire at the end of the eighteenth century but had always been home to many nationalities, predominant among them Tatars. They were descendants of the Tatar-Mongols who had invaded Russia in the thirteenth century and had later converted to Islam. To Chekhov, it seemed like he was living abroad in Yalta, and he frequently complained of homesickness for Russia proper. He could hear the calls to prayer from the minaret near his house in Yalta, and it made him nostalgic for the sound of church bells being rung.[1] His marked susceptibility to the distinctive sound of Russian bells had been acquired growing up in a very religious family in Taganrog, where there were many churches. After he had been living in Yalta for two years, Chekhov informed a friend that as soon as Taganrog installed its own water supply, he would sell his house in Yalta and buy a 'lair' for himself right in the town centre, either on Petrovskaya, the main street, or on Grecheskaya – Greek Street – where all the smartest residences were located.[2]

Greek Street had acquired its name because of the illustrious role played in Taganrog's mercantile history by the traders from Greece who had been encouraged to settle in the town by Catherine the Great. Having seized the southern seaboard from the Ottoman Empire in the 1770s, in order to gain access to the Mediterranean via the Black Sea, Catherine had her sights set on Constantinople becoming once again the centre of a newly re-established Greek Empire. Potemkin was duly dispatched from St Petersburg to establish a fleet, and to found ports with Greek-sounding names, such as Sevastopol and Feodosia; the old Turkish fortress of Hadjibey was named Odessa, after Odysseus. Large numbers of Greek subjects, meanwhile, were lured to southern Russia with offers of land, and advantageous tax breaks, which enabled them to develop a lucrative shipping trade dealing in the export of grain.[3] At the time Chekhov was born in 1860, Taganrog was still the most important commercial port in Russia, the fortunes of its native traders in thrall to the Greek magnates who controlled the export of wheat out through the Sea of Azov and into the Black Sea and Mediterranean. As a small-time trader, Chekhov's father was part of this food chain. His poor business sense meant that he was one of the first to suffer when Taganrog lost its viability as a port in the 1870s, but he had ambition for his sons. Envious of one particular Greek who seemed to have the whole of Taganrog under his thumb, Pavel Egorovich decided to enrol Anton and his elder brother Nikolai in the preparatory class at the Greek school which was maintained by the expatriate community. He hoped that fluency in the language would be his sons' passport to wealth and prosperity, or at the very least a job as a clerk. Chekhov was seven years old.

The school stood, high on the cliff overlooking the Azov Sea, in the

The port at Taganrog

parish grounds of the Greek Orthodox Church of St Constantine, and was located in the middle of Greek Street (where the wealthier members of its congregation all lived). Unlike the richly adorned church, whose icons were covered with miniature gold and silver ships brought by grateful sailors who had prayed for the intercession of saints during storms at sea, the school was decidedly spartan. The rows of black desks in its one large room had to make do for all six classes, with seventy-odd pupils ranging in age from six to twenty, and ruled over by a tall, bearded Cephalonian with red hair.[4] When the school's unacceptably low standards and disciplinarian teaching methods were eventually uncovered, Nikolai and Anton were sent to join their elder brother, Alexander, at the Taganrog *gymnasium*. There they received a rigorous classical education, and Pavel Egorovich was forced to temper his naive idealization of all that Greece stood for. Chekhov later enjoyed sending it up obliquely in his popular one-act farce *The Wedding* (1889), in which the father of the bride, a retired collegiate registrar, asks increasingly ridiculous questions of his guest, Kharlampy Dymba, a Greek confectioner with poor Russian, a character reputedly based on a resident of Taganrog:

ZHIGALOV: Have you got tigers in Greece?
DYMBA: We have.
ZHIGALOV: And lions?
DYMBA: Lions too. It's Russia which has nothing, but Greece has
            everything. I have there father, uncle, brothers, but here I
            don't have nothing.[5]

The confectioner's uniform reply to enquiries as to whether Greece has whales, lobsters, particular kinds of mushrooms, and even collegiate registrars, led to the phrase 'Greece has everything' permanently entering the Russian language after a popular Soviet film was made of the play in the 1940s. In subsequent decades, as shops became emptier and emptier and the queues outside them ever lengthier, disaffected citizens jokingly used the phrase to refer ironically to the Soviet Union, parodying hyperbolic Communist propaganda.

As well as the disastrous year spent at the Greek school, Chekhov also had to endure several years of getting up in the small hours to sing at the Greek Monastery in Taganrog before he was ten years old. The Greek archimandrite in the Monastery's large white-walled church decided to introduce early morning services in Russian on Sundays in order to increase the income raised from collections, and Chekhov's

Petrovskaya Street, Taganrog

over-zealous father leaped at the chance to lead the choir. Apart from
attending the lunch at the Monastery's feast day every year, along with
Taganrog's most important Greek dignitaries, the only entertainment
for the three miserable young Chekhov boys, stuck in their *cleros* up on
the first floor, was watching birds feed their young in nests they had
made inside the grilles covering the church's round windows.[6]

At the end of his life Chekhov claimed to have no memory at all of
the modern Greek he once learned, and when he was fifteen he had to
stay down a class because he failed his end of year exams in ancient
Greek. Although his writings are sprinkled with occasional phrases in
Latin, a language which came in useful for his medical studies, there are
almost none in Greek, perhaps due to the unpleasant associations. And
it was perhaps to exorcize some ghosts that many years later he created
the character of the tyrannical Greek teacher Belikov in his famous
story 'The Man in a Case', for whom the classical languages are 'just
like his galoshes and umbrella really, hiding him from real life': "'How
resonant and beautiful the Greek language is!" he would say with a
sweet expression; and as if to prove the truth of his words, his eyes
would narrow and he would raise his finger and say "Anthropos!"' So
Chekhov was not exactly a Greek fan. But even he would have
probably been amazed by recent archaeological discoveries in his home
town, which suggest that Taganrog was the site of the oldest and most
northerly ancient Greek colony in the entire Black Sea area.[7]

Sometimes during particularly cold winters up north, Chekhov
started to dream of retiring to Taganrog so that he could spend his old
age sitting in the sun. He told his younger cousin Georgi that he wished
he could buy a little house by the sea, then he regretted not having the
money to build a castle by the flight of vertiginous stone steps which
descends from Greek Street all the way down to the shore.[8] Built in the
1820s in imitation of the famous Acropolis steps in Athens by one of
Taganrog's wealthy Greeks, they served as a model for the staircase in
Odessa later immortalized by Eisenstein in *Battleship Potemkin*.[9]
Chekhov was obviously thinking about the turreted mansion by the top
of the steps lived in by Tchaikovsky's brother, which had a fine sea view.
Ippolit Tchaikovsky was a retired naval officer with a shipping business,
and after he moved back to St Petersburg in 1894, Chekhov told Georgi
he would buy his house if he was rich. Tchaikovsky had been taken by
his brother out to sea and driven around town in his cabriolet on the

The Stone Steps

occasions when he had come to visit, and the Taganrog connection undoubtedly played a role in cementing the friendship that he formed with Chekhov in 1889; Georgi was later to work for Ippolit's shipping agency.

If Chekhov had not become infected with tuberculosis and had indeed been able to retire to his castle with the sea view in Taganrog, he would probably have still been around when the city began installing a proper sanitation system in the 1930s, following the belated provision of running water. It was when a sewage pipe was laid in the bay of Taganrog below Ippolit Tchaikovsky's house that fragments of pottery started washing up on the shore and were deposited at the foot of the stone steps. Perhaps if Chekhov had been able to understand the stories he had heard about Odysseus in his first year of school, he might have been interested to know that these fragments of pottery turned out to be Greek, and very old indeed – about seventh-century BC. Archaeologists took an immediate interest because there was no record of any ancient Greek settlement in the Taganrog area, but plans to carry out serious excavation were impeded first by the war, then by ideological problems. Finally they were forgotten about.

However, after recent study in more auspicious circumstances of the thousands of pieces of pottery which have washed up on the shore since those early finds, Russian and German archaeologists now believe that the ancient city that lies under the sea in the bay of Taganrog may be Cremni ('the Cliffs'), the city mentioned by Herodotus in his famous *History of the Persian Wars*. Taganrog is, after all, situated on a high peninsula with steep cliffs on either side. The relevant passage is in book four, where Herodotus talks about the nomadic Scythians who lived in these areas:

> On the opposite side of the Gerrhus is the Royal district, as it is called: here dwells the largest and bravest of the Scythian tribes, which looks upon all the other tribes in the light of slaves. Its country reaches on the south to Taurica, on the east to the trench dug by the sons of the blind slaves, the mart upon the Palus Maeotis, called Cremni (the Cliffs), and in part to the river Tanais.[10]

To the ancient Greeks, the area where Chekhov grew up was the end of the known world. Following in the footsteps of Odysseus, Greek settlers first set out to explore the unknown areas to the north of their empire at the end of the seventh century BC, while other colonists sailed east to Asia Minor and west to Italy. They called the Black Sea the Axine Pontus, or Inhospitable Sea, because of the dangers they faced both in navigating often stormy and uncharted waters and in encountering unfriendly nomadic tribes when they finally reached their destination. After the Black Sea littoral had become home to numerous new centres of Greek civilization, however, the Axine Pontus was renamed the Euxine Pontus, or Friendly Sea.[11] The next stage was to sail further north through the Kerch straits to conquer the even remoter Sea of Azov, which proved to be so shallow it was given the name of Palus Maeotis, or Maeotis Lake. Its waters also froze over in the winter, which posed an additional challenge to sailors accustomed to the warm seas of the Mediterranean.

It has been hitherto thought that the first Greek settlement on the Azov shores was Tanais, founded in the third century BC at the mouth of the River Don, just outside the present-day city of Rostov, some fifty miles to the east of Taganrog (Tanais was also the name the Greeks gave to the Don).[12] But it now seems that the Greeks had been more intrepid, and had established their most northerly colony several centuries earlier, at the very beginning of their first voyages to new lands. The Azov seabed has never before been excavated, and the underwater explorations to be started in the bay of Taganrog in 2004, the centenary of Chekhov's death, may yet yield sensational results, even prompting some journalists to speculate on the discovery of a Russian Atlantis. What is already clear is that archaeologists will have to revise prior perceptions about the Hellenization of the nomadic Scythian tribes who dominated the steppe territory north of the Black Sea between the Carpathian Mountains and the River Don. It now seems that the first contacts between the Scythians and the Ancient Greeks were probably made in the Taganrog area.[13]

II

Venetians, Turks and Russian Tsars

I have taken the Tanais River as the boundary between Europe and Asia.

Strabo, *Geographia*, Book XI

Taganrog has the strongest resemblance to a Levantine town, so much are its Greek and Italian inhabitants in a majority over the rest of the population.

Ignace Xavier Hommaire de Hell, *Travels in the Steppes of the Caspian Sea, the Crimea, the Caucasus*, 1847

Returning to Taganrog in 1887 for the first time since graduating from Moscow University opened Chekhov's eyes to how Asiatic his home town was. Just after Easter, three days into his stay, a postman had come to deliver a letter for him and then had calmly gone into the kitchen, sat down and drunk a cup of tea, not in the slightest bit worried about all the other letters he still had to deliver. 'It's Asia here!' Chekhov exclaimed when he sat down to reply to the letter the following day; 'Everything here is so Asatic I can hardly believe my eyes. There are 60,000 inhabitants who just eat, drink, and reproduce, but they have no other interests.' The friends and relatives Chekhov had been visiting had offered him Easter cake and wine, and they all seemed to have young babies, but none of them appeared to read newspapers or books. 'The town's location is superb in all respects, the climate is magnificent, there are fruits of the earth aplenty, but the inhabitants are ridiculously inert,' he commented. Their wit and imagination, their musical talents, their sensitivity were all wasted.[14]

Situated in a part of the empire as near to Tehran as to the Russian capital, and as close to Constantinople as to Moscow, Taganrog could indeed lay some claim to being at least geographically in Asia. Back in the first century the Greek historian Strabo had proposed the River Don, which lies just to the east of Taganrog, as the boundary between Europe and Asia. His contemporaries had been dissuaded from exploring the area back then because of 'the cold, the ice, the tumultuous tides which draw the waters miles away from the muddy shores, the mists and storms, the treacherous currents, the suffocating sultriness of summer and the swamps of mosquitoes'.[15] This meeting point of two continents became a vital trading area in the Middle Ages, however, since it lay directly on one of the main Silk Routes connecting Constantinople with China. By the time of the fall of the Roman Empire, the Greek town of Tanais at the mouth of the Don had been destroyed by marauding Goths and Huns, and the Scythian territories of south-eastern Europe invaded by the Iranian-speaking Sarmatians (it was they who gave the River Don – meaning water – its present name). In the thirteenth century a new city was founded at the mouth of the Don, but this time the colonists were Italians rather than Greeks: Tana was built by the Venetians. It was trade with the Byzantine Empire which had initially made Venice wealthy. After establishing themselves as an independent republic, the Venetians then used their power to bankroll the Fourth Crusade, which resulted not in the recapturing of Muslim Jerusalem but in the storming of Christian Constantinople in 1204. This victory struck for the Latin West over the Greek East was very much to the liking of the Venetians, because what they were really after was trade links with Asia. They now, at a stroke, obtained a monopoly in the area by acquiring strategic territories belonging to the once powerful Byzantine Empire and, more importantly, maritime access through the Bosphorus to the Black and Azov seas.

In 1260 two Venetian merchants, the father and uncle of Marco Polo, set out from Tana to journey overland across the steppe to the capital of the Mongol Empire. They became the first Europeans to visit the court of the great Kublai Khan, grandson and successor of Genghis Khan, and the ultimate conqueror of China. Tana became one of the most successful trading colonies founded by the Venetians in the Black Sea area.[16] A few decades earlier, another of Genghis Khan's grandsons had led the invasion of Europe by Turkic-speaking Tatars. Tana and the entire Azov Sea area had become part of the most westerly khanate of the now vast Mongol Empire. With its capital in Sarai, on the lower reaches of the Volga some way off to the east, it became known as the Golden Horde and accumulated much wealth via its annual tribute from the Russian lands under their dominion. The empire began to collapse at the end of the fourteenth century when Tamerlane's armies invaded on their way to India, having already conquered Iran, Mesopotamia and the Caucasus. And the oppressive 'Tatar yoke' was finally lifted from Russia in 1480 when Ivan III, Grand Prince of Moscow, decided he could afford to stop paying taxes to the Golden Horde. Thus ended two and a half centuries of Russia's subjugation to the Mongols.

It was, however, a long time before the territory around present-day Taganrog became part of Russia. The Golden Horde had been broken up into four independent khanates when it had disintegrated – Kazan, Astrakhan, Sibir and Crimea. Ivan IV, the first Russian leader to be crowned with the Byzantine title of Tsar (Caesar), conquered Kazan and Astrakhan in the middle of the sixteenth century, and conquest of Siberia soon followed. But the Tatars of the Crimean Khanate were able to resist invasion through collusion with the Turks, and were eventually subsumed into the mighty Ottoman Empire. Although the Turks did not really penetrate the steppe north of the Azov and Black Sea shoreline, their kingdom extended across the Crimean peninsula to encompass much of what is now southern Ukraine and Russia. Their main trading post and military stronghold was the fortress of Azov, built on the ruins of Tana, which was successfully occupied for a few years in the middle of the seventeenth century by fearless Don Cossacks aware of its strategic importance. It was not until the accession of Peter the Great, however, that a Russian tsar was successful in conquering the southern lands of the Crimean Khanate, thus gaining prized access to the Black Sea and the Mediterranean.

Intent on making Russia a naval power, Peter sailed a fleet down the Don and captured Azov from the Turks in 1696. His goal was to provide a harbour for his new navy on the Azov coast, and he chose nearby Tagan-Rog (Tatar for 'high promontory') as the most suitable location. In 1698 the first workmen were sent down from central Russia to build a fortress on the cape, to be equipped with hundreds of cannons and other munitions. Taganrog was the first purpose-built port to be constructed in the Russian Empire, and for a while Peter even considered establishing his new capital on the sea here, but changed his mind when land in the Baltic became available at the opposite end of his empire. By 1712, when Peter declared St Petersburg as his new capital, Taganrog could boast over a thousand dwellings and a population of about 8,000. The town's new residents had been forcibly settled here from towns on the Volga River, amongst them Kazan, Nizhny Novgorod, Samara, Saratov and Simbirsk. Other enforced colonists included exiles and convicts and Turkish and Tatar prisoners of war, as well as captured Swedes once the Northern Wars started. Peter also thought to station Cossacks in Taganrog to provide defence against attacks from the Crimea, which was still in the hands of the Ottoman Empire.[17]

Peter wanted to make Taganrog beautiful as well as functional. As well as issuing orders to plant oak trees along the shoreline for protection from the wind and sun, and willows in the most attractive areas, he ordered lemon and orange trees to be imported from Constantinople, which were planted in the newly ploughed soil along with vines, other fruit trees and medicinal herbs. Foreign gardeners were among the many specialists lured to Taganrog by promises of high salaries and other privileges.[18] Military personnel naturally made up the majority of the town's population in the early years, but trade was also developed. The prodigious quantity of fish of a great many varieties had always attracted travellers to the Azov and Black Sea areas, and Peter encouraged the development of a fishing trade. A century and a half later the young Chekhov would spend hot summer days fishing in the bay with his friends, and it bred in him a passion for fishing which remained with him for the rest of his life.

In 1711 the Turks decided to wrest their old territories back and declared war. Preoccupied with the protracted war with Sweden up in the north, Peter was unable to defend the Azov shoreline and ordered

The statue of Peter the Great in Taganrog by Antokolsky (1898)

his admiral, Count Apraksin, to withdraw from Taganrog after destroying its fortifications. It was not until the next war with Turkey, waged in the 1760s by Catherine the Great, that Taganrog once again became Russian territory. Despite the fifty-year hiatus in the middle of the eighteenth century when Taganrog returned to Turkish rule, the town celebrated its bicentenary in 1898, and Chekhov took a prominent role in honouring its illustrious founder by liaising with the sculptor Antokolsky who had been commissioned to produce a statue of Peter the Great. He also took especial care in recommending the best location for the statue in Taganrog, bearing in mind that Antokolsky had produced an imposing-looking Peter standing characteristically before the sea, the wind running through his hair.[19] His suggestions were ignored. Initially, the twenty-foot-tall statue was placed on a granite plinth on Taganrog's main street by the entrance to the municipal park, but in 1923, amid revolutionary fervour, it was inevitably replaced by a statue of Lenin. Tsar Peter was hauled with great difficulty off his plinth and left in the vestibule of the first Chekhov museum in Taganrog, housed in the former *gymnasium* where he had gone to school. Then, when Russia's tsars were automatically declared enemies of the people in the 1930s, orders were issued to melt the statue down. This was the fate meted out to the town's statue of Alexander I, but the statue of Peter miraculously survived. After being moved to the city museum it was boxed up and left outside in the yard. A few years later there was a move to restore the statue, and this was achieved in 1943 – by the Nazis occupying Taganrog during the Second World War. It was only after the war that the statue was moved to its final resting place by the fort at the edge of the promontory overlooking the sea – the place Chekhov had originally suggested back in 1898.[20]

As Russia's main naval base, Taganrog became a centre for ship-building under Catherine II, and the first ships of the Don flotilla were launched in 1771. But when Russia acquired first the rest of the Azov shoreline, then the Crimea in 1783, Taganrog immediately lost its strategic importance and Sevastopol was naturally chosen to become the headquarters of the newly formed Black Sea fleet. Taganrog now began instead to build up the international maritime trade for which it became famous in the nineteenth century, as witnessed by the fifteen foreign consulates established in the town. Merchants were ordered by the government to relocate there from other parts of Russia and, after the repeal of the Corn Laws in 1846, the amount of wheat exported to England significantly increased. Along with wheat and other grains, as well as ironware produced in the Urals, hemp, canvas and caviar were exported through Taganrog, while ships arrived in its port with cargoes of silk, fruit, nuts, wine and other colonial goods. The town's population inevitably became extremely cosmopolitan after Catherine began to entice large numbers of Greeks to the area; by the nineteenth century there was a population of about 30,000 expatriates, with their own weekly newspaper, *The Argonaut*.[21]

Taganrog flourished under Alexander I, with careful town planning influencing the building of rows of spacious streets radiating out in a grid along the peninsula from the fort. Churches and civic buildings appeared, as well as a public park – one of the oldest in Russia – which soon became the centre of the town's social life. The *gymnasium* founded in 1806, Chekhov's alma mater, was the oldest educational institution in southern Russia (the idea of the *gymnasium*, a state-controlled secondary school with an emphasis on the classics, had been adopted from Germany). Alexander I and his retinue visited Taganrog during his tour of Russia in 1818, and the Tsar decided to return to the town in 1825 when his sick wife Elizaveta was ordered to undertake an eight-month period of convalescence. The southern coastal climate, the town's peaceful lifestyle, and the freedom from court protocol all played a role in luring the Tsar back. By order from St Petersburg, the town governor was ousted from his unassuming single-storey mansion on Greek Street built in the early nineteenth-century Russian classical style, and 25,000 roubles were spent on redecorating the property. Three days of celebratory illuminations marked Alexander's arrival in September 1825. Within two months, however, he had died in mysterious circumstances, and his widow ordered that the room in which he had passed away should be turned into a chapel. Shortly afterwards, the building (now referred to as a palace despite the manifest inappropriateness of such a title) opened as Russia's first memorial museum, guarded by clean-shaven Cossacks with sabres. After the Revolution the palace chapel was closed and the rooms of the museum turned into communal apartments. Since 1963 the property has housed a children's sanatorium.[22]

Chekhov was very familiar with the palace of Alexander I. From childhood he had heard stories of how his grandmother had been given refuge, together with her two daughters, in the former town governor's house next door when they first arrived in Taganrog penniless in 1847. His mother was then twelve years old, and she later told stories to her children about how the custodian at the palace next door had knocked down part of the stone wall dividing the two gardens and built a gate so that she and her sister could play with his daughter Lyudmila. When *he* was twelve years old Chekhov, with his two elder brothers, was part of a choir which performed at the services held in the palace chapel during Easter and on Trinity Sunday. This was the last choir run by Chekhov's father. The Greek Monastery appointed for its main church a priest who spoke only Greek, and who had no interest in holding any services in Russian; then the new Church of St Mitrofan employed a paid choir when it was completed, so Pavel Egorovich was eventually forced to take his choristers elsewhere. The Taganrog aristocracy chose to attend the services at the modest palace chapel, with its faded carpets and flimsy linen iconostasis, and Chekhov's father clearly hoped its scions would be impressed with his ability to raise such delightful, God-fearing children. The boys invariably failed to live up to his unreal expectations, however, and usually misbehaved.[23]

Alexander I's widow herself died within a few months of her husband, as she was travelling back from Taganrog to St Petersburg. Before she left, she set aside some money for a bronze statue of her husband to be erected in the town. Since Alexander's body had been taken to lie in state at the Greek Monastery (lead for his coffin was so scarce it apparently had to be taken from the nearest available roof), Elizaveta decided that the statue should be erected in the square in front of it. The unveiling took place in 1831, to the accompaniment of a 101-gun salute, bell-ringing in all the town's churches, and municipal illuminations.

III

The British

The capture of Kertch and the occupation of the Sea of Azov will greatly cripple the operations of the Russians . . . with us it is merely a question of expense, with the Russians it is a question as to the limits of physical possibility.

Prime Minister Lord Palmerston, 1855

Just under a century before fragments of Greek pottery began to be washed up on the Taganrog shore, the stone steps near which Chekhov expressed a wish to own a house became the scene of an attempted assault by British sailors. The Crimean War clearly left a lasting impression on the town's inhabitants. When writing to a colleague about plans for a museum commemorating Taganrog's history in 1897, Chekhov mentioned as a possible exhibit a picture his aunt had on her wall depicting the British bombardment of the town.[24] One does not automatically associate Chekhov with the Crimean War, but his family became ineluctably caught up in its repercussions because they lived only a few hundred miles from the main battleground at Sevastopol, Russia's naval headquarters in the Black Sea. Taganrog came under attack for a whole summer by Her Majesty's Navy.

Chekhov's parents married six months after the start of the war on 29 October 1854 – the same week Florence Nightingale arrived to attend to the wounded in the British Military Hospital in Scutari across the Bosphorus from Constantinople – and the couple's first summer together in Taganrog as husband and wife was blighted by attacks from Royal Navy gunboats. Evgenia had become pregnant almost immediately after marrying Pavel, and it was a blessing that they eventually decided to leave Taganrog temporarily for safety reasons; also that the British naval officers took pains to prosecute their mission in as humane a way as possible.

The Sea of Azov was used as a vital supply route by the Russian army, and Taganrog was the most important trading port on its shores at that time. With an important grain store and coal and iron deposits nearby, the town was naturally drawn into the theatre of war when the Allies marshalled 15,000 troops and launched their campaign to take maritime control of the area. The success of the campaign was to lead directly to victory for the Allies over the Russians at Sevastopol a few months later. 'The Sea of Azoff is open to us,' reported William Howard Russell to *The Times* on 26 May 1855 after the strategically important capture of Kertch at the mouth of the Black Sea a few days earlier. 'And our flying squadron of steam gunboats is searching it from end to end,' he continued, 'burning and destroying the ships and trading vessels of the Russians, crushing their forts, and carrying terror and dismay along the seaboard of their inland lake.'[25] Together with his French counterpart, Captain Edmund Lyons, commander of the *Miranda*, sailed a flotilla of eighteen vessels into the Azov Sea immediately after Kertch had been taken. It was the first time that the flag of a British admiral was flown in these waters, and the Allies now started moving up the coast, bombarding first the ships, stores and government offices at Berdiansk, then doing the same at Genitchi when the town refused to surrender. By this time, 249 boats had already been destroyed, as well as the equivalent of two months of food rations for 100,000 Russian soldiers. The Russians helped in this effort by destroying enormous quantities of grain and flour themselves at Kertch.

Lyons then headed for Taganrog with twenty gunboats armed with howitzers and rockets, and on 1 June was obliged to anchor several miles outside the town, due to its shallow waters.[26] Two days later, he was able to send a lengthy dispatch to his father Rear-Admiral Sir Edmund Lyons, Commander-in-Chief of the Black Sea fleet, describing a successful campaign begun at three o'clock that morning on the *Recruit*, an ex-Prussian iron gunboat:

> ... so heavy a fire opened that although the enemy made repeated attempts to get down to the houses lining the beach, so as to save the long range of store houses from destruction, they never succeeded in doing so in sufficient numbers ... By 3pm, all the long ranges of stores of grain, plank and tar and the vessels on the stocks were in a blaze, as well as the custom house and other government buildings, and unfortunately but unavoidably the town in many places ... The loss of the enemy in men must have been severe, as many were seen to fall ... The only casualty in carrying out this service, was one private of the Royal Marine Artillery, severely wounded in the face by a musket-ball ... [27]

Lyons reported that a Russian sergeant, who deserted and gave himself up to a French boat, stated the number of (mostly Cossack) troops in the town to have been in the region of 3,200, of whom 800 had arrived the night before. The allies, on the other hand, had about 600 men on 43 boats. Similar procedures ensued at Mariupol and Eisk up the coast, not surprisingly leaving the whole coastline 'in a state of terror'.

Amongst the frightened inhabitants of Taganrog that early summer morning were Pavel and Evgenia Chekhov, Pavel's brother Mitrofan, and Evgenia's mother, sister and brother. Lyons took pains in his report to his father to note that civilian casualties had been expressly avoided insofar as it was possible: 'Many large buildings had the black flag hoisted, as a sign, I presume, of their being hospitals, these were most carefully respected by us, as were the churches, and as far as possible private houses.'[28] In fact there were eleven casualties and eighteen wounded.[29] Two hundred houses were also destroyed and a cannon ball remains lodged to this day in the belfry of the Church of St Nicholas, which stands close to the town harbour. The Russian version of events is, of course, somewhat different, war reportage being what it is. Their account maintains that, despite six and a half hours of bombardment, it was a combination of Taganrog's steep cliffs and the valour of its Cossack defenders which prevented 300 Allied infantry from entering the town via its Stone Steps. The Allies met unexpectedly strong resistance from the Russians, according to the diary of one British officer to whom it seemed that the spirit of perseverance had transferred from the defenders of Sevastopol.[30]

Commander Sherard Osborn of the *Vesuvius* now took over as senior officer in the Sea of Azov from Captain Lyons, who returned to join his father in Sevastopol. The admiral did not want his son to miss the next bombardment later that month, but was shocked when the *Miranda* was hit by a shell and its commander wounded in the leg. So well-liked was Captain Lyons that his unexpected death on 23 June at the age of thirty-five caused even Queen Victoria to commiserate with the admiral on the loss of his 'gallant and beloved son'.[31] The intrepid Commander Osborn, also thirty-five years old, with a trip to the Arctic already behind him, and equally competent, now impressed Lyons's grieving father with his reports of further successful sorties in the Sea of Azov. On 19 July he returned to reconnoitre Taganrog in the gunboat of Her Majesty's steam-vessel *Jasper*, and reported to the vice-admiral that 'every part of that town showed signs of the severe punishment it had received when we visited it under the late Captain Edmund Lyons of the *Miranda*'. Two shots were 'thrown into' the new battery being constructed on the heights near the hospital next to the harbour, but there had been no response. Osborn nevertheless ordered two gunboats to remain in the vicinity of the town, and requested Commander Craufurd on 20 July to continue to 'harass the enemy' and ensure that no munitions of war were able to reach Taganrog by water from the River Don.[32] There was no mention in British accounts of the capture of the *Jasper* at the end of July by Cossack troops, who handed over its flag to the cathedral in Taganrog; the ship's cannons to this day are kept in the basement of the city museum.

A few weeks later, Osborn reported to Vice-Admiral Lyons that he had returned to Taganrog on 5 August to discover 'signs of great activity in the garrison': batteries had been thrown across streets and roads leading from the water. Closer inspection revealed five heavy guns lurking beneath the cliffs, which were summarily destroyed. These turned out to have been old ship guns, which, as Osborn commented drily, would have actually posed a far greater danger to the Russian gunners than to their British targets.[33] Pavel Chekhov and Evgenia's brother Ivan had caught sight of the gunboats of the *Vesuvius*, the *Wrangler* and the *Beagle* that Sunday (24 July according to the Russian calendar) after leaving morning service in Taganrog's Cathedral of the Assumption, where Evgenia's mother, Alexandra, had remained to pray. Evgenia was by then eight and a half months pregnant with her first child, and now in great alarm at the prospect of further bombardments. She and Pavel abandoned the samovar boiling in the yard, and their lunch of chicken soup, and decided to flee forty miles or so inland to Krepkaya, where Pavel's parents lived, taking lodgings with the local priest. Chekhov's eldest brother, Alexander, was born there two weeks later on 10 August.[34]

The Chekhovs were not the only residents of Taganrog to take fright at this new offensive. Count Egor Petrovich Tolstoy, the Governor of Taganrog, had been so incensed by the Allied squadron's first attack that he sent a dispatch to the *St Petersburgh Gazette*, depicting it a cruel and unnecessary act, while at the same time apparently claiming a Russian victory (this was because the late Captain Lyons had been 'forbearing and merciful', according to Osborn). Then in July, John Martin, an English businessman resident in Taganrog, wrote a letter to the Admiralty condemning the behaviour of the British towards the civilian inhabitants of the town as excessively cruel, and alleging that Her Majesty's officers had been sighted 'dining under an awning on board the gunboat, and drinking toasts with brutal hilarity'. A letter from the former British Consul in Taganrog, J. P. Carruthers, subsequently revealed that Count Tolstoy had in fact persuaded Martin to write the letter, although Martin had animus enough of his own since his livelihood had been badly damaged by Allied operations in the Sea of Azov. When he was finally shown this letter, Osborn penned a robust but slightly tongue-in-cheek dispatch to Vice-Admiral Lyons in his defence. 'That the destruction of an enemy's resources must necessarily be a painful duty, I need not remind you, sir, and no doubt, individuals have occasionally suffered. The Cossacks have repeatedly drawn our fire upon places they could not defend: the blame must rest with them, not us,' he began. He acknowledged that his steamer had indeed fully succeeded in harassing the 'victorious' garrison of

Taganrog, as well as its gallant governor, 'and I dare say alarmed the inhabitants; the numbers of mothers and babes destroyed Mr Martin leaves to my imagination'. He found it hard to comprehend, however, that anyone could believe British naval officers to be capable of such brutality as to fire at women and children, and dismissed this as 'malicious falsehood'. Whether or not Count Tolstoy had given an order for his men not to fire on British troops at one point, he continued, it had not been obeyed, and even if it had, Lieutenant Hudson could not reasonably have been expected to be 'prepared for the humane eccentricities of the Governor of Taganrog'. He also remonstrated with the complaint about the Taganrog hospital being hit by pointing out that it was likely to suffer fire because of the earthen rampart pierced with embrasures a hundred yards in its rear, and the entrenchment parapet and guns standing in front of it. 'Humanity would suggest that the sick had better be in a safer spot,' he commented drily.[35]

The impressively moustachioed Count Tolstoy was governor of Taganrog from 1854 to 1856. A veteran of Russia's wars with Persia and Turkey, he was, according to his contemporary N. V. Sakharov, rather more negligent when it came to dealing with complaints that came to him and was always the last of the governors to submit his annual report. Despite his own personal honesty and strongly held religious views, his lackadaisical attitude to his civic duties led to the flourishing of bribery and corruption among his officials. Egor Petrovich was a distant relative of Count Lev Nikolaevich Tolstoy, then a young officer currently establishing his literary reputation with his war reportage from Sevastopol and later to become something of a paternal figure to Chekhov – he was three years younger than Chekhov's father. Many years later, the war would be a favourite topic of conversation for Chekhov and Tolstoy when they were both living in the Crimea for health reasons.

On 14 September 1855, a week after the Allies occupied southern Sevastopol, and Lev Nikolaevich had started his last of three outspoken indictments of the appalling conditions in the Russian army there, a jubilant Vice-Admiral Lyons telegraphed the Royal Navy headquarters in London to report that the Russians had burned their steamers in the harbour ('thus the late Russian Black Sea fleet is annihilated'). Meanwhile, Commander Osborn found the fortifications in the supposedly 'harmless commercial town' of Taganrog to be continually on the increase, despite its governor's protestations to the contrary. A large garrison, and uniforms belonging to nine separate infantry and five cavalry regiments, had been observed by the naval officer delivering letters and clothes to Allied prisoners of war held in the town, and nearly 20,000 troops were noted to have benefited from a stay in the town on their way to the Crimea. The governor could thus hardly be 'astonished at the occasional exchange of shots on the efforts of our gunboats to delay his proceedings'. The abominable conditions endured by rank-and-file soldiers in the Russian army under Nicholas I (mercilessly exposed by Tolstoy in his Sevastopol dispatches) meant that young men dreaded having to join up; being killed on duty was seen as far preferable to surviving. A revealing comment from Commander Osborn shows just how bad the situation really was:

> Mr Martin and Count Tolstoy seem to think Her Majesty's naval commanders are lost to all humane feelings. At any rate, the Russian inhabitants of the seaboard seem to think otherwise, for our greatest difficulty is to prevent ourselves being burdened with voluntary prisoners.[36]

It was understandably with an eye to avoiding conscription that Evgenia Chekhova pressed her husband to raise the money necessary to join the merchant class when the couple returned to Taganrog at the close of the Crimean War together with their baby son: one of the privileges was exemption from military service.[37]

Chapter 2

TAGANROG AND THE STEPPE

I

A Southern Childhood

There is in reality nothing to see at Taganrog beyond the house in which Alexander I died. The town is neat and tidy but the dust is terrific.
Murray's Handbook for Travellers to Russia, 1875

The south is your homeland; the south will always attract you.
Letter from Georgy Chekhov, 1889

Chekhov's last brief visit to his home town of Taganrog took place in the hot summer days of July 1899, and he arrived unannounced. He met with relatives and acquaintances whom he told about the circumstances of his father's death, he discussed plans for the statue of Peter the Great that had been commissioned for Taganrog's bicentenary, he gave advice on how best to cultivate conifers (a rarity in that part of the world), and then he headed back to Yalta. If Taganrog had been in Chekhov's mind a lot at that time, it was not only because his father had died the previous autumn. He had received the news just after he had reluctantly set off to spend his first winter in Yalta. Chekhov's move south to the Crimea had taken him back to his childhood: the memories of the years he spent growing up now came flooding back, and were intensified during his first Yalta spring by the sweet scent of blossoming acacia trees, which were foreign to Moscow but grew in profusion in Taganrog's warm climate. Chekhov's love of trees is well known, and it began early. Large numbers of poplars and lilac trees lined the streets of Taganrog along with the acacias, often planted in two rows to provide shade during the summer months.[1] When they were in full leaf, the rows of tiny cottages tended to disappear completely in the foliage, their diminutive size accentuated by the broadness of the streets they stood on. It was in one of those tiny single-storey houses with a low roof and shuttered windows that Chekhov was born in 1860. Located in one of the less well-appointed neighbourhoods of Taganrog, the squat whitewashed building was rented from a local merchant, and was one of hundreds of such buildings which still line the dusty back streets of the town. Like its neighbours, it was constructed with mud bricks and set a long way back from an unpaved road in a yard full of wild steppe grass, and trees with nesting boxes fixed to them. Before it was renamed in honour of its famous former resident, the

Chekhov's birthplace, Taganrog

street was imaginatively named Politseiskaya – Police Street, because there was a police station located there.[2]

The twenty-three square metres of the Chekhovs' house certainly did not provide much living space for a family of five. Apart from a minuscule kitchen with an earthen floor, there were just three low-ceilinged rooms. Chekhov's parents slept in one bedroom, and baby Anton joined his elder brothers, four-year-old Alexander and two-year-old Nikolai in the other. His aunt later recalled that he rarely cried as a baby, and learned to walk and talk early.[3] The third room, with four large windows, served as dining room, sitting room, and study for Chekhov's father. But the most important function of this room was as a place to pray. Pavel Egorovich took praying very seriously. The icon corner was as traditional a feature of Russian households as the brass samovar, but many families paid scant regard to the holy image that was there to help them pray. Many a family icon became obscured over the years with soot from the oil lamp supposed to burn continually beneath it as a symbol of God's constant grace. This was never the case in the God-fearing Chekhov family home: the main corner of their front room was covered with icons. Beneath the icons and the icon lamp stood a cabinet on which lay a prayer book, the family Bible and a tall brass candlestick. Pavel Egorovich would lead prayers without fail every evening, and before certain feast days would burn incense before the icons. On the eve of the Feast of the Transfiguration, celebrated in early August when the first fruits of the harvest were traditionally blessed, the Chekhovs would place honeycomb, apples and poppy seed underneath the icons. The next day they would take them to be blessed in church, and only then could the family break their fast and eat the fruit. Of all the members of his own family, Pavel Egorovich was particularly close to his brother Mitrofan, who was equally devout and served as an elder in one of Taganrog's churches. Whenever Mitrofan Egorovich came to visit, so his relatives liked to recount, he would go straight to the icon corner and start praying, crossing himself and bowing down to the floor. Pavel Egorovich would stand waiting to greet his brother with outstretched arms, but the praying would go on and on. And typically, by the time Mitrofan Egorovich had finished saying a prayer to each of the many icons, and was finally ready to meet his brother's embrace, Pavel Egorovich would have begun praying himself.[4]

Pavel and Mitrofan Chekhov and their families, 1874

Impecunious Russians did not tend to lead settled lives, and like the nomadic tribes who had once populated the southern steppe regions, the Chekhovs moved frequently from one rented property to another. They lived in six different places in Taganrog during Anton's childhood. Just before a fourth son, Ivan, was born to Pavel and Evgenia Chekhov in April 1861, they moved further out of the centre of Taganrog, but moved back to Politseiskaya Street to live in a house belonging to a local priest two years later (this was where their first daughter, Maria, was born). In 1864 they moved to the main street of Taganrog, Petrovskaya (or Piterskaya, named after the city's founder, Peter the Great), the year before the birth of their last son, Mikhail. This was another small one-storey house, with a red wooden roof, according to the memories of Nikolai Chekhov, surrounded by burdock, nettles and buttercups. Alexander, Nikolai, Anton and Ivan all shared a featherbed in the musty bedroom next to the kitchen with its acrid smell of burnt sunflower oil. The family lived here for five years before finally moving, in 1869, to much grander premises. Chekhov was nine years old in 1869, the year he became a pupil at the Taganrog *gymnasium*.

The family's new home, rented from a merchant, was a large, two-storey brick building at the crossroads of Monastery Street and Fair Lane on the edge of town.[5] Upstairs were the bedrooms and sitting room, with the kitchen and dining room downstairs, next to Pavel Chekhov's grocery store (advertised by a large black sign, with lettering in gold leaf, hanging over the door). Downstairs there were also quarters for Andriushka and Gavriushka, the two young boys apprenticed to work in the shop for five years, without salary but provided with food and clothes.

It was a full house. Chekhov's widowed aunt, Fenichka, later moved in with her son Alexei, also taking a room on the ground floor, while two young lodgers shared a room upstairs. One of these lodgers, Ivan Pavlovsky, was later arrested for political activities, and led a colourful life, having worked as a hairdresser in New York before being deported to Siberia. When he was finally amnestied, he left Paris where he had been supported by Turgenev, and came to visit Chekhov at his Melikhovo estate. Chekhov was very interested to meet Pavlovsky again, as he had written on the Dreyfus case, an affair in which he himself took a passionate interest.[6] The four windows of the upstairs

Pavel Chekhov's store, Taganrog

floor on one side of the building looked out to the sea less than a mile away. The Chekhov children and their cousin would spend hours watching the triangular-shaped sails of fishing boats on the horizon and steamships gradually emerging from the distance, identifiable first by the line of smoke from their chimneys. A relative of Chekhov's mother arrived by steamship once and the whole family was given lunch on board, where they watched sailors cutting open a sturgeon and taking out the caviar to serve with spring onions. Chekhov's father was something of a gourmand; he liked to make his own mustard and *zakuski*, and was apparently particularly fond of caviar (which reminds one of Chekhov's late story 'In the Ravine', which begins with a description of a village best known for a sexton who once ate four pounds of caviar during a funeral feast).[7]

Down the road from the Chekhovs' house was the majestic Alexandrovsky Square, designed by Campignoni in 1810 and built on a marshy area overgrown with rushes. A large, rectangular open space, framed at both ends by an elegant semi-circular arcade with Doric columns in empire style, it was built to provide the main trading area for the town. Behind the columns were the shops that made up the 'new bazaar', replacing the old one in the square next to the cathedral. St Mitrofan's Church (the church where Chekhov's father directed the choir for several years) was first built here, but had to be moved when its foundations collapsed. In 1960 a Socialist Realist-style statue of a pensive Chekhov, book in hand, sitting with his arm resting on his knee was erected in this square on a large black marble plinth to mark the centenary of his birth.[8] He might have balked at the site, for this was where executions were held during his childhood. The family could see condemned prisoners walking past their house to the scaffold, each wearing a board on his chest detailing his crime. Chekhov's mother would cross herself when prisoners passed the house, and would visit the prison every year on the holiday of the coronation of the Tsar. One prisoner had been sitting in the prison for sixteen years, and had been completely forgotten about. His crime had apparently been to collect money to build a church without permission.[9]

Taganrog was still a thriving port when Chekhov was born, with an array of foreign (British, French, Italian, Spanish, Turkish, Greek, German, Danish, Persian, American, even Paraguayan) consulates and a highly cosmopolitan population of about 20,000 that was dominated by Greeks and Italians. Taganrog wheat was considered the best in Europe and exported in huge quantities to make Italian pasta and British biscuits. The volume of its trade made it a serious rival to Odessa, and it was certainly more sophisticated and European than nearby Rostov-on-Don. There was a theatre (which boasted one of the oldest professional companies in Russia) and an orchestra which gave open-air concerts in the town park until midnight on summer evenings.[10] Once the wealthy foreign merchants had built their smart houses on the town's best streets, they wanted entertainment, and so they paid impresarios to bring in prima donnas. The foundation of an Italian opera company in 1863 led to the building of a new theatre a few years later, with the aid of Italian sponsorship.[11] Its red velvet interior, with the habitual cloud of mist above the chandelier, later came into Chekhov's mind whenever he described a provincial theatre in his stories.

Taganrog could also boast the oldest educational institution in southern Russia: Chekhov's alma mater, the Taganrog *gymnasium*, provided a rigorous education with a pronounced bias towards the classics. There were about 130 such schools in existence when Chekhov was a pupil, their highly conservative curriculum closely monitored to prevent any influx of dangerous political ideas. The study of Greek and Latin was actually increased by government decree while Chekhov was at school, and ended up occupying almost half of his weekly timetable. Pupils at the school had to wear the standard blue and grey uniform, with starched collars, and suffer inspectors peering in through the round observation windows in their classroom doors as they patrolled the corridors. Chekhov was probably more than once spotted daydreaming as his desk was at the back and closest to the window – not the one in the door, of course, but the one which faced outside.[12]

As long as Taganrog's trade flourished, Chekhov's father stood a chance of earning a decent living. His grocery shop sold everything from rhubarb to castor oil, and was open all hours. The hours of misery which Chekhov spent in his childhood serving behind the counter have become the stuff of legend, but he got to see a wide array of people. Perhaps the most colourful visitors to his father's shop were the two monks from Mount Athos, who came to Taganrog twice a year to send out icons printed on calico all over Russia in the hope that people would make donations to the island's Russian monasteries. Father Feodosy, a former peasant, and Father Filaret, a retired soldier, enjoyed the break from routine which their trips to Taganrog afforded them. They particularly enjoyed their visits to Pavel Chekhov's shop, during which they would talk in glowing terms about life on Mount Athos. Neither would drink in the presence of the other, but their strict vows were quickly suspended when they came into the shop alone. Chekhov got used to seeing drunk monks staggering around the shop when he was growing up. Far less amusing was the service conducted in the shop to bless the olive oil that a rat had fallen into. Pavel Egorovich set up an altar with the family icons on his shop counter, and ordered his children and the apprentices to attend while the local priest said the requisite prayers which would supposedly purify the oil. It was not the best exercise in public relations, and most of Pavel Egorovich's main clients vowed never to buy anything from him ever again.[13]

There was certainly enough justification for Chekhov's complaint that he had no childhood in his childhood, as he put it, having been made to work in his father's grocery shop like his brothers, sing at interminable church services and endure frequent beatings. Although he later forgave his father, the 'lies and despotism' of his childhood left an indelible mark. The death of his two-year-old sister Evgenia when he was eleven must also have been traumatic for the family. But there were also opportunities for Anton and his brothers to get up to various pranks, some of which have been recorded for posterity in the various memoirs that have been published. There were the hot air balloons made from large sheets of cigarette paper, for example, which would be filled with coal gas. This was a somewhat risky enterprise, since the source of the gas was the lamp that stood on the corner in front of the family's house. Until their activities were discovered and reported to the police, Chekhov and his brothers would gather at first light and fill their balloons with a rubber hose attached to the gas jet. Chekhov had a particular reputation for practical jokes. His cousin Alexei recalled him persuading the school janitor to let him borrow a human skull and some bones on one occasion. The plan was for Anton to give his sister Masha (Maria) a fright by putting them in her bed and covering them up with a blanket. When Masha came home, she was duly informed that a friend had come from Moscow and was in her bed resting; on discovering the bones she promptly fainted. Chekhov's devout Aunt

Fenichka was so horrified by this sacrilegious behaviour that she apparently went and buried the bones in the yard.[14] The Chekhov family was close-knit, and remained so, but they had a wide circle of acquaintances in Taganrog, including a well-to-do Polish family. 'To this day, the cakes and preserves I consumed in this family's house when I was a schoolboy arouse the most nostalgic memories,' Chekhov later recalled towards the end of his life; 'there was music and young ladies and liqueurs, and catching goldfinch in the big, wild garden . . .'[15] The best days of his childhood in Taganrog were undoubtedly spent outdoors. While the rest of his family was in Moscow during his teens, he was able to spend long summer days down on the shore, swimming and fishing. Many happy hours were also spent catching finches, which he then sold in the market.[16]

Chekhov retained a steadfast loyalty to his home town in his adult years, sending regular shipments of books to the Taganrog municipal library, and assisting with plans to found a town museum. Among the many people who made a positive impact on him during his childhood was Father Vasily Bandakov, the priest at St Michael's Church, where his Uncle Mitrofan was warden. Chekhov only ever wrote three obituaries in his life, so the fact that he chose to write a eulogy to Father Vasily is of some significance. His obituary appeared in *New Times* on 26 January 1890, eleven days after Bandakov's death in Taganrog.[17] Like the famous Russian explorer Nikolai Przhevalsky, and Dr Zinaida Lintvaryova, a family friend, Father Vasily was someone Chekhov particularly admired. The tall priest with the kind face and the flowing white beard was a frequent visitor to the Chekhov household, and on one occasion led an all-night vigil for the family in their home. Father Bandakov's great popularity stemmed from his sermons, which were always very short and simple, but extremely effective.[18] Delivered in his distinctive hoarse but dramatic voice, they drew enormous congregations. As Chekhov noted in his obituary, the number of sermons Father Vasily delivered during his lifetime ran into the thousands. The best of them were published in twelve volumes under the title *Simple and Short Sermons*. For Chekhov these volumes constituted a veritable encyclopaedia, with something to offer people from all walks of life: rich businessmen, officials, ladies, soldiers and convicts. Their enduring popularity can be judged from the fact that they were into their fifth edition by 1900. One sermon was given during the 'week of the prodigal son':

What is to be done when ruin faces us, when we do not want to give up our favourite sins and stick to the Lord who loves us? Cry? That is all right for those who have tears, but what about those who have no tears? . . . Fasting, prayer and humility help us cry. We should pray and fast and be humble until we receive tears to cleanse our sins.

Another sermon was read on the occasion of his return to Taganrog, on the topic of unhappiness:

What use is there in unhappiness? Unhappiness helps you learn humility, gives you understanding, cleans you of sins. What other wisdom does unhappiness give us? You should treasure friendship in sorrow and poverty, not be ashamed to chop firewood and dress in clothes you would have been ashamed to wear before.[19]

It was not just that Father Vasily preached at any available opportunity, no matter what time of day it was or wherever he happened to find himself, which impressed Chekhov. It was also that he possessed rare powers of observation, and an extraordinary knowledge of life and of human beings. As Chekhov pointed out in his obituary, Father Vasily did not like to get bogged down in abstract topics, but preferred to concentrate on the topical problems of the region in which he lived and worked. Chekhov's generous appreciation of Vasily Bandakov reveals a great deal about the values he cherished himself, both in his writing and in his personal life:

As a preacher, he was passionate, bold and often quite harsh, but always just and impartial. He was not afraid to speak the truth and he spoke it openly, without accusation; people do not like to be told the truth, and the deceased therefore suffered a great deal in his life. He died at the age of eighty-four, leaving behind memories of a kind, loving, selfless person.[20]

The fact that Chekhov admired the 'simplicity, strength and beautiful language' of Father Vasily's sermons points even more strongly to the fact that they had a great impact on his own writing, of which these very same qualities are hallmarks.

II

The Merchant Background

A doctor advised a merchant (one with education) to eat chicken and bouillon. The merchant took this ironically. First he dined on fish soup and pork, then he asked for bouillon and chicken, as if remembering the doctor's orders, and ate that up too, thinking it was very funny.

Chekhov, *Notebook No. 1*

Chekhov's father was thirty-two when he finally opened his first grocery business in 1857, as a merchant on the bottom tier of the Russian Guild system. He may have been one of the numerous impecunious Russian subjects who declared more capital than they possessed in order to avoid conscription, or perhaps he managed to scrape together sufficient funds. Initially his prospects were good. In December 1863, he put an advertisement in the local paper informing readers of the range of China tea he sold (black, red and fragrant), as well as 'colonial goods at a most reasonable price'.[21] Chekhov's aunt Marfa remembered boiled sweets on threads like coloured garlands, dried fish with an acrid smell, all kinds of sweet things imported from abroad such as halva, persimmons, turkish delight and currants, and tapers with different-coloured tips arranged in the shape of a star in circular red wooden boxes.[22] Pavel Egorovich was twice elected to join the Taganrog trade delegation by colleagues in the Society of Merchants who saw him as a pillar of the community, and in 1871 he was awarded the silver medal of St Stanislav for conscientious service. Life was all about medals for Pavel Egorovich, and he was proud to wear his St Stanislav on a ribbon round his neck. Later his son would write a story satirizing a career-minded official whose life revolves around winning medals and advancement, its punning title, 'Anna on the Neck', referring also to the protagonist's scheming wife. As far as Chekhov's brother Alexander was concerned, their father's obsession with medals had ruined their childhood. Pavel Chekhov was certainly ambitious, at one point embarrassing his sons by actually asking for a medal from the priest after they had sung at one set of Easter services. The priest was equally embarrassed, Alexander later recalled.[23] But Pavel Egorovich's ambition was not matched by his ability to make money, and in 1876 he went bankrupt. After almost two decades of precarious survival as a merchant, he suffered the indignity of being relegated to the ranks of the lower classes again and decided to flee with his family to Moscow, leaving sixteen-year-old Anton behind to finish his education.

Chekhov later drew directly on the wellspring of his own experience of growing up in a merchant's family when he came to write such stories as 'The Steppe', 'Three Years' and 'A Woman's Kingdom', and the play *The Cherry Orchard*. Indeed, after the publication in 1895 of 'Three Years', which depicts the life of a prominent Moscow merchant family, his friend Suvorin immediately assumed that the character of the despotic, pious patriarch, Fyodor Laptev senior, was a thinly veiled portrait of the author's father. Chekhov demurred, explaining that his father possessed neither Laptev's talent nor his vision, yet there were clearly some resemblances, particularly concerning questions of filial obedience and obsessive devotion to religious ritual. The description Alexei Laptev gives his wife about how he and his brother Fyodor were brought up contains distinct echoes of Chekhov's childhood:

> I remember my father starting to teach me, or to put it more simply, beat me before I was even five years old. He flogged me with a birch rod, boxed my ears, and hit me round the head and every morning when I woke up the first thing I would think about would be: was I going to get beaten? Fyodor and I were forbidden to play or lark about; we had to go to matins and early mass, kiss the hands of priests and monks and read *akathists* at home. You are religious and you love all of that, but I am afraid of religion and when I go past a church I remember my childhood and feel terrified. I was taken off to the warehouse when I was just eight; I worked like an ordinary apprentice, and it was not good for me, because I was beaten there almost every day. And then when I was sent to the *gymnasium* I studied until dinner, but from dinner I had to sit in that warehouse all evening, and it went on until I was twenty-two years old . . . [24]

This passage describes nothing out of the ordinary for the young sons of merchant households in Russia; in fact it was the classic model of a merchant childhood. Chekhov, too, was regularly beaten by his father, made to serve in his father's shop and repelled by religion, having been dragged to church so often as a child. Suvorin thought that the young

Laptev's irritation with religion struck a false note, but Chekhov retorted that it was far more plausible than the kind of paternalistic love for religion felt by some people, who were 'like those who love blizzards and storms while sitting in their study'. Since merchants inhabited a closed cultural world in which there was no literary culture to speak of beyond that of the Holy Scriptures, comparatively little is known about their way of life. The mid-nineteenth-century playwright Alexander Ostrovsky, who came from a wealthy merchant background in Moscow, had earlier created a series of largely unflattering portraits – almost caricatures – of people from that milieu in his plays, depicting them as uneducated and brutish. Chekhov was really the first great Russian writer to treat merchants as complex and sympathetic human beings in his stories and plays.

Ever since Peter the Great had sought to advance the interests of his empire by creating the hierarchical Table of Ranks in 1722, the Russian population had been rigidly stratified and controlled by the state. Unlike class systems in other countries, Russian social segregation was actually enshrined in laws, which dictated everything from educational rights to the clothes people were allowed to wear. The obsession with status that this inevitably produced (particularly among minor bureaucrats) was a frequent target of Chekhov's satire in many of the comic stories he wrote in the early 1880s, which betray a clear debt to his illustrious forebear Gogol. In 'Fat and Thin', for example, an official suddenly becomes obsequious when he discovers that an old school friend he has just met at a railway station has attained a much higher rank: 'The fat man wanted to say something, but there was so much awe, sycophancy and reverential sourness written on the thin man's face that the Privy Councillor started to feel nauseous.'[25] In the equally popular early story 'The Chameleon', a policeman's attitude to a white borzoi puppy, which has bitten the finger of a local goldsmith, changes several times according to whether or not he thinks it belongs to a general.

Until the very end of the nineteenth century in Russia there was no middle class as such: people who belonged neither to the rural peasant class of 22 million serfs (who finally acquired their freedom in 1861) nor to the noble class – the educated elite which controlled them – were either clergy, *raznochintsy* (non-noble educated), urban lower class, or merchants, but no one escaped classification in some form or other.

Approximately half of those who lived in towns were registered as *meshchanin*, or urban lower class, thus liable to pay a demeaning poll tax ('petty bourgeois' does not fully convey the word's meaning). Becoming a *kupets*, or merchant, offered the only viable path to social advancement, but to be able to call oneself a merchant it was necessary to join a guild, and to do that one had to possess a certain amount of capital. The tiered system of merchant guilds had been initially based by Peter the Great on the Western model, and was later reorganized by his successor Catherine, particularly in the provinces, in the hope of stimulating economic development (not to mention bringing in more state revenue). As well as adding a third guild, she gave freed serfs the choice of becoming either a meshchanin or a kupets, relieved merchants from paying the poll tax, raised their social status as 'valued' citizens, and granted them other generous privileges such as exemption from corporal punishment. People who paid for the annual guild certificate licensing them to engage in trade thus constituted a particular social class that had no equal elsewhere. Culturally, the Russian merchant class was the most subservient and static section of Russian society, but as it was determined solely by financial status, it was also the least stable, as demonstrated by the short-lived career of Chekhov's father.

Pavel Chekhov had spent the first sixteen years of his life as the personal property of Count Chertkov, a landowner with estates in the fertile area of central Russia south of Voronezh, half way between Moscow and Taganrog (his grandson later became Tolstoy's close associate). In 1841, twenty years before the abolition of serfdom, Pavel's enterprising father had managed to buy his family's freedom and moved south to the steppe, taking a job as an estate manager for another aristocratic landowner. His three sons were apprenticed to different businesses in different cities as they came of age, with both Pavel and his brother Mitrofan eventually becoming tradesmen in Taganrog, and thus members of the merchant class. Pavel's wife, Evgenia, was also not without ambition for social betterment, and the family's later relegation to the ranks of the lower-class meshchanin was a huge blow to her. A meek and mild-mannered person, ten years younger than her husband, she also came from a rural background, but her grandfather had bought freedom for himself and his son somewhat earlier, in 1817, and so she had never been a serf. Evgenia had also grown up in the Russian heartland, but further north, with relatives who were wealthy icon painters. Her father, Yakov Morozov, ran a fabric business, and when it went bankrupt he was fortunate in finding employment with General Papkov, the former governor of Taganrog, initially leaving his wife, Alexandra, and two daughters behind. When her father suddenly died from cholera in 1847 and the family home was destroyed in a fire, his widow and daughters were forced to take to the road. They also appealed to General Papkov for protection. Evgenia's elder brother Ivan (Chekhov's red-haired Uncle Vanya) had earlier been apprenticed to a merchant in Rostov-on-Don, where he worked under Pavel Chekhov's brother Mitrofan; both subsequently moved to Taganrog.

Merchants had traditionally represented the more Asiatic face of Russian society due to the fact that their trade links had initially developed with the Orient. During the two and a half centuries of the Tatar yoke, the Tatar-Mongols had exacted humiliating tributes from Russian principalities, but they also stimulated trade via the great caravan routes spanning the length of their enormous empire. Russian merchants profited from the trading opportunities that opened up with Persia, Central Asia and China, acquiring a Tatar-based commercial vocabulary along the way. *Tovar*, the Russian word for merchandise, for example, is derived from the Tatar term for possessions or cattle, as is *tovarishch* ('comrade'), which meant business partner long before it was commandeered by the Bolsheviks. The pro-Asiatic orientation of Russian trade continued long after the Mongols were expelled at the end of the fifteenth century. Of all the social classes in Russia, the merchant class was the most passive, and most supportive of the autocratic regime, and it was really only in the nineteenth century that it began to change its patriarchal ways and succumb to the processes of modernization. Due to the restrictive practices of the imperial government, which did its best to inhibit any activity that might threaten its authority (it took several years merely to decide which government department should pay for the replacement of kerosene with electricity at one police station in St Petersburg, for example), capitalism reached Russia late, but the Westernization of the merchant class finally began to accelerate in the 1860s, the era of the Great Reforms.

A new law passed in 1863 reduced the number of guilds from three to two. To compensate for the fact that the guilds were now open to all sections of the population following the Emancipation of the Serfs, merchants of the First Guild now acquired privileges that enabled them to be presented at court and wear the official green and red uniform of the regional government with sword and spurs (although they were not allowed to wear different colour cuffs and collars, like members of the nobility). If they had served for twelve years in the First Guild and were Orthodox Christians, merchants were also allowed to enrol their children as boarders in various educational establishments. Merchants had always been identifiable by their long beards and oriental style of dress, but the traditional uniform of kaftans and high boots with pointed toes had finally given way to Western-style frock-coats and top hats by the time Chekhov's father began trading.[26] Pavel Chekhov took pride in his appearance even when business was very poor, and the starched linen shirts dutifully ironed by his daughter were always spotless; his son Anton was to inherit his father's neatness, if nothing else.

Like every other social group in Russia, merchants had a distinct culture of their own, which the Chekhov family typified to a certain degree. Direct contact with foreign traders and their Western-style capitalist business practices meant that Taganrog was inevitably more cosmopolitan than most provincial towns in Russia, but its merchants still inhabited a relatively closed world, symbolized by the eternally closed shutters of their houses. It was something Chekhov noticed for the first time when he came back to his home town in 1887, and was in large measure due to the insecurity merchants felt with regard to their tenuous social status, segregated from the rest of society. With their lives ruled largely by financial concerns and the simple problem of survival, it was not surprising that merchants wanted to protect their businesses by keeping them within the family. Sons were expected to work long hours for their fathers from an early age, and merchants like Pavel Chekhov, who kept shops, would trade long hours every day, even on Sundays, closing only for the major religious holidays at Christmas and Easter. Pavel Chekhov opened his doors at five in the morning and would not shut them until at least eleven in the evening – later, if he liked the conversation of customers who had lingered. In the patriarchal family life of the Russian merchant, the father's word was law. This was certainly the case in the Chekhov family, and Evgenia always deferred to her husband, even if she disapproved of his harsh disciplinarian methods.

Chekhov's family was also typical in its religious devotion. The church was central to the life of Russian merchants, some of whom were so conservative that they clung to the Old Belief, dating from the church schism of the seventeenth century. The financial year for merchants began, significantly, in Easter week, and other dates in the commercial calendar were also timed to coincide with major religious holidays. Merchants regarded the family icons as their most treasured possessions and often invited priests to hold religious services in their homes; when entering the premises of other merchants they crossed themselves and kissed each other three times.[27] But Pavel Chekhov was extraordinarily pious even by the standards of Russian merchants, who were known for their particular devotion to the rituals of the Orthodox church, obsessive attendance at services, and their observance of all fasts. Orthodox services tend to be long, but Pavel Chekhov would have been happy for them to be still longer: even the priests complained when he was a choirmaster, because he liked to proceed at such a slow pace, drawing everything out. Chekhov's brother Alexander recalled that their father never missed a service, and ensured that his children did not either. One of the reasons why Pavel was such a poor businessman was probably the excessive amount of time he dedicated to the church. As a major port with several churches, Taganrog had its own Cathedral Church of the Assumption, a spacious building with a single large dome, built in 1829 in the middle of the town's main square. It was here that Pavel Chekhov led the choir for several years, and it was here that his third son, Anton, was baptized, with both godparents from local merchant families.[28]

Where Pavel Egorovich was unusual was in his interest in education and culture, neither of which were traditionally respected in merchant households. His writer son used to apologize to his correspondents for seeming continually to be thinking about money, and blamed it on the circumstances of his upbringing. Every aspect of life in Taganrog revolved around money, and he lamented the fact that he had been forced to grow up in an environment in which it had played such a large role. His father would lament that he only ever made losses in his trade, a complaint Chekhov may have had in the back of his mind when he later wrote the darkly humorous 'Rothschild's Violin'. In this story a curmudgeonly coffin maker, so mortified by his losses, concludes that he will only ever make a profit when he dies, and no longer needs to feed himself or pay taxes:

Таганрогъ.   Соборъ

Uspensky Cathedral, Taganrog, where Chekhov was christened

As he walked home, he realized that being dead would bring only profit: he would not need to eat or drink, pay tax, or offend people, and since people get to lie in their graves for not just one, but for hundreds and thousands of years, then you would make a huge profit if you added it all up. From life you just made a loss, but from death you made a profit. This was, of course, a reasonable way of looking at things, but it was annoying and painful to come to terms with: why was the world set up in such a strange way so that life, which a human being only gets once, brings no profit?[29]

Chekhov's father was not a successful merchant, but all the same he was considerably more enlightened than the majority of his class. It is true that he initially sent Anton and Nikolai to the Greek school in Taganrog, believing he would be setting them up for lucrative careers if they could speak the language: the most prosperous businessmen in Taganrog were all Greek, after all, and success was measured by the numbers of clerks one was able to employ. Pavel Chekhov was held in great respect for sending all five of his sons to the Taganrog *gymnasium*. He, of course, had received only a rudimentary education growing up as a serf, learning to read and write at the age of eight at the village school. Although he did not write much or have all that much to say, he attached great importance to the ability to write beautifully (even his shopping lists were penned in an ornate calligraphic style), which again seems to betray an excessive attachment to form. As a boy, Pavel had also been taught by the village priest to read music and to play the violin (which he held on his chest rather than under his chin, in the folk music style). He took an active interest in politics and local affairs and liked reading French boulevard novels, but it was newspapers he enjoyed the most. Each issue would be read from beginning to end, before being carefully tied up with string and then stored at the end of the year. Pavel Egorovich subscribed to the first Taganrog newspaper when it appeared in the 1860s, and made his sons read it out aloud. Although it mostly contained news of interest to merchants, the paper also carried a few stories from the national and foreign press, as well as local news.

In 1874, the Chekhovs finally moved into their own house on Elizavetinskaya Street, not far from where Anton was born. Pavel Egorovich was swindled by the contractor who built it, and ended up sinking all his capital into the house's construction. The modest one-storey dwelling was neither well built nor particularly attractive. Matters worsened when the new shop he had opened near the railway station failed to prosper: his business had started to go downhill when the railway network was extended to Rostov and not Taganrog. The grain traders who had brought their deliveries by horse and cart now switched to using trains. The bay had by this time become so shallow that maritime trade was also no longer viable, and by the time the railway line *was* extended to Taganrog, it was too late to save Pavel Egorovich's business. Less than two years later, he had to abscond in order to avoid being thrown into the debtors' prison. Alexander and Nikolai were students in Moscow by this time, and Pavel's nephew Mikhail was also in Moscow, working for a haberdashery company run by a wealthy merchant called Gavrilov. So Moscow was the obvious destination for Pavel Egorovich to run to. He made a careful list of the clothes and linen he was to take with him to Moscow:

1 pair of black trousers
1 pair to wear
1 knitted coat

1 top hat
1 straw hat
1 warm coat
1 pair of boots
1 pair of galoshes
1 pillow with a case
10 pairs of socks
5 shirts
4 shirt-fronts
4 handkerchiefs
2 towels
3 sheets[30]

He was joined soon after by his wife and their two youngest children, but it was agreed that Anton and Ivan should complete their education in Taganrog. They were therefore left behind, boarding initially with the house's new owner Gavriil Selivanov. Chekhov tutored Selivanov's nephew Pyotr Kravtsov, and was later invited to spend time out in the steppe with his family. When Chekhov returned to Taganrog as an adult, it was essentially a dead town, its quiet, deserted streets exuding an atmosphere of sadness and neglect. To one of his contemporaries, visiting Taganrog felt like walking through a quiet cemetery.[31]

Although Chekhov's merchant background receded in importance as he entered the ranks of Russia's burgeoning professional class, first by acquiring a degree in medicine, then literary celebrity, it remained an essential part of his make-up. It is telling that when he became a student at Moscow University in 1879, he registered with the police as a *meshchanin*. At the beginning of his second year, however, he registered himself as being of merchant background.[32] The plays of Alexander Ostrovsky had reinforced a set of negative stereotypes which had characterized merchants as dishonest, uneducated and narrow-minded people prone to gluttony and cruelty. Chekhov was to play a major role in helping to change their public perception. The young merchant hero of his story 'Three Years' is in many ways a transitional figure – educated but not yet completely liberated. By the time Chekhov came to write *The Cherry Orchard* a decade later, the suffocatingly closed world which we see in plays like *The Storm* (best known via Janáček's opera *Katya Kabanova*) had finally opened up. Chief beneficiaries of Russia's industrialization, merchants became the new elite – cosmopolitan, educated, and extremely wealthy. Konstantin Stanislavsky, co-founder of the Moscow Art Theatre, the company which championed Chekhov's innovative plays, was an example of the new breed of cultured merchant industrialists from Moscow who had a serious interest in art and a lot of money to invest. Chekhov thought Stanislavsky would be the ideal person to play the hard-working merchant Lopakhin in *The Cherry Orchard*, who is portrayed at least as sympathetically as the hapless gentry whose cherry orchard he purchases. But it was precisely because of his own merchant origins that Stanislavsky did not want the part, but that of the nobleman Gaev. Since commercial enterprise had never enjoyed a good reputation in Russia, Stanislavsky wished to play down how he had come by his money. Like many nouveau riche merchants at the turn of the century, he hoped to do that by buying a country estate and adopting the old-world lifestyle of the nobility, a class by then in its death throes. Even Chekhov fulfilled a dream of becoming a landowner when he bought his miniature estate at Melikhovo, but was characteristically ironic when referring to the pleasures of being lord of the manor.

III

The Don Steppe

... but if the traveller in spring or autumn steps off the platfom of any small station and listens in the morning or evening to the calls of birds and the hum of insects, filling the whole steppe with life, he will perhaps understand why to the dweller on the steppe there is no dreariness in its apparent monotony.

Murray's Handbook for Travellers to Russia, 1875

In April 1887, just before he wrote his first story for a serious literary journal, Chekhov took the train back to Taganrog in order to spend several weeks travelling round the steppe. He had not been home in six years, and needed to see southern Russia again, he said, in order not to 'dry out'; he wanted to resurrect in his memory things that had already grown dim so that his writing might be more vivid.[33] So he started taking detailed travel notes to store up as a creative reserve for future stories, and sent them as letters to his family. On the last leg of his two-day train journey from Moscow, a few hours before reaching his destination, his mood suddenly soared: 'The weather is glorious, there is a smell of the steppe and the sound of birds singing. I can see old friends – kites flying over the steppe . . . The kurgans, the water towers, the buildings – it's all familiar and unforgettable . . .'[34]

After staying for a while in Taganrog, where he caught up with relatives and old friends, he set off travelling once more and was again intoxicated by 'bare steppe, kurgans, kites, larks, blue horizon . . .'.[35] He had to spend one night during his travels at a remote station, waiting for his connection, and managed to find a second-class carriage to sleep in that was parked in a siding. Stepping out in the small hours to relieve himself, he was awestruck by the beauty of the nocturnal steppe landscape and described it in a letter to his family: '. . . outside it was utter magic: the moon, the vast steppe with its kurgans and wilderness; deathly silence, the railway carriages and rails standing out sharply in the shadows – it seemed like the world had become extinct . . . It was a scene I won't forget in a million years.'[36]

The old Russian word *steppe*, meaning 'lowland', has no equivalent in other languages, but the word combination used by the Japanese, 'ocean of land', conveys well the fundamental features of the vast treeless plain that extends all the way from the Danube in the west, through Central Asia to Mongolia and China.[37] A halfway house between forest and desert, the steppe, with its temperate climate, was the perfect natural environment for the pastoral way of life of the Scythian horsemen. They were among the first inhabitants of the land of southern Russia and the Ukraine to benefit from its fertile 'black earth' soil which, when uncultivated, produces a profusion of wild flowers, herbs and grasses, some of them more than six feet tall. The Scythians lived in the saddle (inspiring the Greeks to create the mythical half-man, half-horse beast they called a centaur), and when their kings died, their horses were buried along with them, laid out in concentric rings. *Kurgans*, the vast burial mounds raised over their tattooed bodies, have for centuries been an intrinsic and indeed fundamental part of the steppe landscape of southern Russia, and a key ingredient of one of Chekhov's most important sources of lyrical inspiration. Henry

Seymour, a rugged young British traveller who came to these parts in the early 1850s, had mixed feelings about the attractions of a landscape in which kurgans were one of the few characteristic features:

> For a short period, in April and May, the Steppes present a beautiful appearance. The brilliant green of the rising crops of corn, and the fresh grass, intermingled with flowers of the most lively colours, are pleasing to the eye, and give a charm to the monotony of the scenery. A hot scorching sun, however, soon withers the grass, which assumes a brownish hue, and clouds of dust increase the dreariness and parched appearance of the Steppes. During the winter the ground is covered with snow, which at times lies several feet deep. Unimpeded by mountains, forests, or rising ground, the winds from the north-east, passing over many hundred miles of frozen ground, blow with restless violence, and often uninterruptedly for several weeks.[38]

Yet these boundless plains of waving grasses, streams and gullies were an endless source of fascination for Chekhov, and might partly account for his lifelong restlessness: *skuchno* – I'm bored – was a frequent refrain in his letters. 'It's a fantastic region,' he declared in a letter at the end of the 1890s. 'I love the Don steppe and used to feel at home in it as if it was my own house; I knew every little ravine.'[39] Despite having visited exotic places like Ceylon, and stayed in cities like Venice, Rome and Paris, Chekhov never lost his enthralment with the steppe. In the summer of 1894, he began dreaming about travelling through the steppe again, and sleeping under the stars at least for a few days. 'I used to live in the steppe for months at a time, I loved the steppe, and now it seems quite enchanting in my memory,' he wrote nostalgically five years later.[40]

Chekhov's enchantment had begun with the wondrous tales about the steppe told to him by his nanny Agafya Kumskaya, who was kept on by his parents until his youngest brother was eleven. Agafya Alexandrovna had spent most of her life as a serf on an estate in the middle of the steppe north of Taganrog, and told the Chekhov children legends that had been passed down to her about the battles of local heroes against the Tatars and Turks in ages past, and about all kinds of treasures and magic hats hidden in the kurgans.[41] Like most people at that time, she had no idea of the ornate burial customs of the Scythians, so memorably described by Herodotus, or the riches of their artistic treasures. The kurgans had begun to be excavated only in the late eighteenth century, after the southern territories finally became part of the Russian Empire. Knowledge of the Scythians themselves was still relatively scant even in learned circles. But the local people in the steppe had nevertheless always known there was treasure of some sort in the kurgans: they had been looted repeatedly over the centuries for the exquisite gold jewellery buried in them. Agafya Alexandrovna's heroes dated from a much later period than the Scythians, their exploits mythologized by generations of peasant families in order to explain the existence of the mysterious mounds in the landscape around them, not to mention the strange names some of them had, such as Saur-Mogila – 'Saur's Grave'. Many popular legends had been spun about this particular kurgan, which had acted as a kind of frontier between the Russians and the Turks and Tatars in the mediaeval period; Saur appears in them either as an evil Turkish khan or a Cossack hero.

The atmosphere of the stories that entranced Chekhov as a small boy is reflected in 'Fortune', the first story he wrote after returning from his travels in the south in 1887. As he explained in a letter, it was about 'the steppe: the plain, night-time, a pale dawn in the east, a flock of sheep, and three human figures talking about treasure'.[42] Panteley, a passing ranger who has stopped to get a light for his pipe, starts telling two shepherds, watching their sheep one summer night by the highway, about the buried treasure supposed to be hidden in the kurgans:

Stroking his long whiskers, which were covered with dew, he climbed heavily on to his horse and narrowed his eyes as he gazed into the distance, looking as if he had forgotten to say something or had somehow not finished what he had to say. Nothing stirred in the blueish distance, where the last visible hill merged with the mist; the kurgans which towered here and there above the horizon and the endless steppe, looked severe and lifeless; in their mute immobility one could sense past centuries and complete indifference to human beings; another thousand years would go by, millions of people would die and they would still be standing there, as they did now, neither sorry for those who had died, nor interested in the living, and not one soul would know why they stood there and what secrets of the steppe they contained.[43]

'Fortune' is set in the district north of Taganrog, and Chekhov not only mentions Saur's Grave by name, but also refers to the mixed population of the steppe, which included German colonists, religious sectarians called *Molokans* ('milk drinkers'), Tatars, Kalmyks, Jews and Armenians:

> The sun had not yet risen, but distant Saur's Grave, with its pointed top which looked like a cloud, and all the other kurgans were already visible. If you climbed to the top of Saur's Grave, you could look out and see a plain that was as flat and boundless as the sky, manor houses and estates, German and Molokan farms, villages; a far-sighted Kalmyk would even be able to see the town and railway trains. Only from up here was it possible to see that there was another life in the world beyond the silent steppe and ancient kurgans, a life which was not concerned with buried treasure and the thoughts of sheep.[44]

Chekhov was not given to false boasting, nor to praise of his own work in general, but he proclaimed 'Fortune' to be the best story he had written at that time,[45] and it was to remain one of his favourite pieces of prose. It certainly scored an immediate success with his readers: his brother in St Petersburg told him that issues of the newspaper which published it were still being read in the city's cafés a week later and getting very worn; this was highly unusual, he pointed out, because cafés usually changed their papers daily.[46]

The very first travelling Chekhov had done as a boy was into the steppe, and it had been a major event: his family went on a trip together only once while he was growing up, and even then his father had stayed behind to look after the shop. One only has to look at an old map of Russia to realize how sparsely populated the southern regions were in the nineteenth century. The steppe began right where the town ended, just beyond the cemetery, and Chekhov clearly longed for the chance to go off on adventures when he went there in the summer to go hunting for tarantulas with his friends. The opportunity finally came when he was twelve years old, and he was allowed to visit his grandparents with his eldest brother Alexander. Egor Mikhailovich and Efrosinya Emelyanova lived on Count Platov's estate, about forty miles north of Taganrog. It was a journey of two days by cart (there was no railway), which seemed a huge distance, and as a consequence they barely saw their grandchildren when they were growing up. The Chekhov family had no summer dacha to go to back then, and finances never permitted them to take a holiday. Not surprisingly, Chekhov was wildly excited at the thought of going on a journey – so much so that he could barely sleep the night before departure. His father had idealized the steppe landscape in which his parents lived to such an extent that the impressionable young Chekhov boys thought they were visiting an earthly paradise.

On the hot July day of their departure they were up soon after five, and after being taken by their father to the front room to bow to the ground three times and say prayers in front of the icon they were ready to leave. Ten minutes after kissing the hands of their mother and father, Alexander and Anton were out of the confined space of the town and in the wide open expanses of the steppe, among butterflies, kites and larks. But disappointment came even before they reached their destination: the two men driving the cart back to the Platov estate fell asleep and the horse meandered off the route, causing the boys a lot of unease, particularly when it grew dark. The estate village, when they arrived, was quite pretty with its white church, straw-roofed huts, poppies and sunflowers, but it was not exactly the idyll they had been led to expect. And their grandparents were not particularly friendly. It was threshing time and Chekhov was soon bored with the job he was given of sitting by the windmill for days on end writing down endless measures of grain. But he was not bored with travelling. The following year his mother took him and his brothers and sister (in a cart drawn by oxen) back to the deserted manor house by the river that he and Alexander had stayed in the previous summer, and they once again roamed past the dovecotes and through its neglected gardens and orchards.[47]

Chekhov's first real adventures came when he was in his last years at school, by which time the rest of his family was in Moscow. He spent those summers in Taganrog, staying with friends who had a farm out in the wilds and a lifestyle which was the direct opposite of the suffocating atmosphere of religious piety and filial obedience that had characterized his own home. He went back there in 1887 when he was down from Moscow, and his letters home vividly convey its attractions. The little straw-roofed house was situated in what he called the 'Switzerland of the Don region', which is the chain of hills you come to when travelling north from Taganrog, about sixty miles inland. Chekhov described it as 'hills, little gullies, little woods, little rivers and steppe, steppe, steppe . . .'[48] With none of the hills higher than about 500 metres, it was not, to be honest, exactly like the Swiss Alps, which, of course, Chekhov had never seen (nor ever would), but it was certainly picturesque. The earthen-floored house was not much like a chocolate box Swiss chalet either. Inside, the walls were covered with rifles, pistols, sabres and whips, he wrote, and each morning he was woken by the sounds of a gun being fired through a window at chickens and geese and the yelping of disobedient dogs being punished. There were no ashtrays, lavatories or other mod cons, for miles around, and Chekhov explained that in order to respond to the call of nature it was necessary to go down into the gully and choose a bush, first making sure there was no viper or other such creature underneath it. And to do that it was necessary to run the gauntlet of the huge number of vicious dogs the family owned. 'I have to walk in convoy otherwise there will be one less writer in Russia,' he quipped.[49] He did not get much sleep as there were dogs outside howling all night, and the setter under the hard wooden divan on which he slept liked to bark in reply.

A favourite occupation was shooting at bustards, the largest game bird in Europe, a native of the steppe. Maybe it is because Chekhov's friends shot so many of them that the great bustard, *Otis tarda*, is now a globally threatened species. They were a sitting target really: these turkey-like birds are not that good at flying, particularly in poor weather, and are prone to collide with overhead cables due to their lack of manoeuvrability when airborne. Chekhov's hosts engaged in an unending cycle of slaughter: they shot sparrows, swallows, magpies and crows so they could not eat the bees, they killed the bees so they did not ruin the fruit trees, and they cut down the trees so they did not drain the soil. It was not exactly refined living. The goose soup he was fed at lunch time reminded Chekhov of bathwater left behind by tubby marketwomen, and the after-dinner coffee looked and tasted as though it was made of roasted dung. Nevertheless he had a glorious time. When he was not making bonfires and picnicking outdoors, going shooting, talking about politics, or being chased by rabid dogs, he obviously enjoyed being left to his own devices. And it was healthy living. Chekhov claimed you could cure yourself of fifteen consumptions and twenty-two rheumatisms by staying in the depths of the steppe at his friends' house.

After a repressive childhood in which he was cooped up either at school, in a church or in his father's shop for long periods at a time, it was not surprising that the teenage Chekhov felt an overwhelming sense of liberation in this sort of environment when he came to spend his summers on the steppe. Nor is it surprising that he came to associate the steppe's boundless open spaces with freedom. Pyotr, the son of the retired officer who owned the farm where Chekhov stayed (and who had been tutored by Chekhov back in Taganrog), wore the red-striped uniform of a Don Cossack regiment, like his father had, and it is tempting to think that some of the full-blooded Cossack ways rubbed off on their guest. The Cossacks were descended from peasants who had run away in the late Middle Ages in order to escape enslavement as serfs, and had settled in the Ukrainian and southern Russian steppe after an initially nomadic existence on horse-back like their Scythian forebears. By the nineteenth century, they had developed a distinct ethnic identity of their own through intermarrying with the local Tatar population. They retained a fierce independence, while at the same time remaining loyal to Russia. Riding a horse and shooting a gun were second nature to these macho defenders of Russia's southern frontier. This is not an image we associate with the bespectacled Chekhov of later years, certainly, and it is interesting that he spent two days staying at a nearby monastery after leaving his gun-toting friends in 1887. Having tasted a little of the Cossack way of life, however, he surely admired their down-to-earth, uninhibited ways, which were so different from those he had grown up with.

It is worth remembering that Chekhov was not always short of breath and racked by coughing. He loved the outdoors (what person would choose to spend several months travelling overland to Siberia?) and freedom became increasingly important to him, both personally and artistically. His ideal as a writer was 'to be a free artist and nothing more'. 'My holiest of holies is the human body, health, intelligence, talent, inspiration, love and absolute freedom, freedom from violence and lies, in whatever form,' he wrote famously in a letter in October 1888.[50] It must have been unbearably painful for him to find the sphere of his activities become increasingly restricted with the onset of his illness. Chekhov also seems to have associated the wide open spaces of the steppe with love. During a conversation about love at first sight with a close friend, he confided a memory of a hot summer's day during his late teens when he was standing by a well looking at his reflection, out in the middle of the steppe somewhere. A girl of about fifteen came to fetch water, and he was so captivated by her that he could not stop himself from kissing her, after which they both stood for a long time looking silently into the well: he did not want to go, and she had completely forgotten about the water. This first experience of love at first sight may have something to do with the way in which the natural world, and the steppe in particular, is poeticized in Chekhov's work as a sacred place.[51]

By the time he was ready to go home after his travels in the steppe in the spring of 1887, Chekhov felt that he had filled himself up with enough poetry to last five years. Now it was time to start distilling the experiences of his childhood, refracting them through the impressions of his recent visit in the hope of inspiring in his readers an appreciation for the beauties of the landscape he had grown up in. Spurred on by the success of 'Fortune', he now started planning a much longer story about the steppe. After seven years of publishing short, largely ephemeral pieces in comic journals and newspapers, it was time to write something more substantial for submission to a serious literary journal. Aware that whatever he produced would be closely scrutinized by the entire Russian literary establishment, it is not surprising that it took him six months to pluck up the courage to start writing. Numerous writers and critics had noticed his potential and urged him to start taking his literary activities seriously; equally, there were many others who did not really know how to deal with his apparently plotless prose and wistful style, resented his success and lowly beginnings, and were primed to find fault. Chekhov had, moreover, chosen a highly unusual subject. In the wake of the great realist novels, with their penetrating psychological analysis and big philosophical ideas, it was hardly fashionable at that time to focus on the natural world, and no Russian writer apart from Gogol had ever thought to champion the steppe, let alone see poetry in it. Deciding to tell the story of the journey of a nine-year-old boy being taken across the steppe in late summer to start at a school in another town was also a courageous decision. The lonely Egorushka, who understands neither where he is going nor why, and is unhappy at having to leave his mother, is hardly a conventional literary hero, and the story has no plot as such.

Chekhov might not have been able to smell the hay when he started

'The Steppe', as he put it, but it is a testament to the strength of his inspiration that he felt as if he were still in the middle of the steppe on a hot summer's day when he had taken command of his material.[52] 'For my debut in a literary journal I have chosen the steppe, which people have not written about for a long time,' he wrote to an older writer colleague, when he was hard at work:

> I describe the plain, the lilac horizon, sheep farmers, Jews, priests, night-time storms, coaching inns, steppe birds etc. . . . Maybe it will open people's eyes and show them what riches, what realms of beauty lie still untapped and how much room to breathe Russian artists have. If my story manages to remind my colleagues about the steppe, which they have forgotten about, if just one of the themes I have sketched out in my insignificant and dry way gives a poet somewhere pause for thought I will be happy.[53]

Chekhov addresses the unsung beauty of the steppe right in the middle of the story. The sun has gone down on the second day of the journey, and Egorushka has dozed off to sleep in the dilapidated old carriage he is travelling in with his two chaperones, his uncle Ivan, a merchant, and Father Khristofor, both of whom are making the journey across the steppe to sell wool. While Egorushka sleeps, the narrator emerges from the shadows, to reveal himself as a person who has a highly emotional relationship to the landscape the young boy is travelling through:

> You travel on for an hour or two more . . . You come across a silent old grandfather kurgan or an ancient stone figure, placed there goodness knows when or by whom, a night bird flies noiselessly over the earth, and slowly into your mind come the steppe legends, the stories of people you have met, the tales told by your nanny from the steppe, and everything you have managed to grasp with your soul and see with your own eyes. And then you begin to feel triumphant beauty, youth, strength, and a passionate thirst for life in the chirring of insects, suspicious figures and kurgans, in the deep sky, in the moonlight, the flight of the night birds, in everything you see and hear; your soul responds to this beautiful and severe native landscape, and you wish you could be flying over the steppe with the night bird too. Yet you sense tension and sadness in this triumphant beauty and surfeit of happiness, as if the steppe is aware that

it is lonely, that its riches and its inspiration, superfluous and uncelebrated, will be pointlessly wasted on the world, and through the joyous humming you can hear its mournful, hopeless cry: a singer, a singer![54]

Chekhov may have retained ambivalent feelings about Taganrog, whose thin patina of European culture concealed an Asiatic town of unpaved streets and squalor, but his love for the steppe remained unbounded throughout his life as a key source of poetic inspiration. A frequent criticism levelled at him was that he never made it clear where he stood on issues and that he remained coolly impartial in his writing. He wore his heart on his sleeve as far as the steppe was concerned, however, as the passage above shows. It was he who alone answered the steppe's call for a singer. Almost a decade later, as a convalescing consumptive in faraway Nice, he wrote two more stories set in the steppe. 'If I didn't have the bacillus, I would settle in Taganrog for two or three years,' he wrote nostalgically to his Taganrog correspondent Pavel Iordanov soon after finishing them. Remembering all his experiences on the steppe as a young man made him feel sad, he told Iordanov; he was sorry that there were no writers in Taganrog 'and that this valuable and beloved material is not needed by anyone'.[55]

The beauty of the steppe landscape for Chekhov was always tinged with melancholy, and he was well aware that many Russians found its boundless expanses oppressive. Responding in February 1888 to a story Dmitry Grigorovich was thinking of writing about a young man committing suicide, Chekhov argued that, while in the West people perished because they suffocated from a lack of space, in Russia it was because there was an excess of it. The struggle between man and nature in Russia was unique:

On the one hand there is physical weakness, nervousness, early sexual maturity, a passionate thirst for life and for truth, dreams of work as wide-ranging as the steppe, restless analysis, poverty of knowledge alongside rich flights of thought, while on the other hand there is the boundless plain, the severe climate, a grey, severe populace with a difficult, cold history, the Tatar yoke, the bureaucracy, poverty, ignorance, damp cities, Slavic apathy and so on . . .[56]

The last reference Chekhov made to the steppe in his writing was an indirect but highly personal one. During a particularly long pause in the middle of *The Cherry Orchard*, his last work, we hear the mysterious sound of a breaking string. The sound is distant, 'as if it had come from the sky', and is described as 'dying away, sad'. The play's romantic dreamers typically refuse to believe the practical-minded Lopakhin's rational explanation that 'a bucket must have broken loose in the mines somewhere far away'. The hopeless Gaev thinks it's a heron, the eternal student Trofimov thinks it's an owl, and whatever it is, it gives Ranevskaya the creeps.[57] Chekhov had first heard this sound when visiting a coal mine as a teenager, according to his sister. Apart from picturesque gullies and ravines, the 'Switzerland' of the Don region was famous for its mines, which produced over half of Russia's coal. Chekhov told his family that there were mines near to the farm he stayed on in the spring of 1887, and he first introduced the sound of the breaking string into 'Fortune', the story written immediately following his return home:

> A noise pierced the quiet air and echoed across the steppe. Something far off banged threateningly, hit against rock and carried across the steppe with an echoing 'Takh! Takh! Takh! Takh!' When the sound died away, the old man looked questioningly at the impassive Panteley, who was standing not moving a muscle.
>
> 'That was a bucket breaking loose in the mines,' said the young man.[58]

Recalling that line in *The Cherry Orchard*, completed less than a year before he died, was Chekhov's subtle and discreet way of alluding to his own life, while also paying homage to the austere landscape which had inspired his first major work of literature and some of his finest, most poetic writing. No wonder the stage directions indicate that the sound is distant, 'as if it had come from the sky', and 'dying away, sad'.

Chapter 3

MOSCOW

I

Nomads in the City

As soon as I finish school, I shall fly to Moscow on wings, I like it very much!

Letter to Mikhail Chekhov, 4 November 1877

It was often a shock for the denizens of St Petersburg to leave behind its stately architecture and rectilinear avenues and arrive in Moscow. After the calm order of a geometrically planned city with elegantly proportioned buildings and streets of enormous width came chaos – a mass of cobble-stoned, meandering roads on which crowded together a haphazard collection of stuccoed mansions, onion-domed churches, and tiny wooden houses with iron roofs, in a riot of red, green, yellow, white and gold. Chekhov was probably also shocked by Moscow's irregularity when he made his first visit in 1877 at the age of seventeen: Taganrog, after all, a town of the same vintage as St Petersburg, was also designed according to a grid system. Because of the large number of wooden houses, usually with cows grazing in their grassy backyards, Moscow still had the feel of a country town in the late 1870s, and people from St Petersburg liked to look down on Russia's patriarchal second city as a 'big village'. Some of the capital's more snobbish residents did their best to avoid having to visit Moscow altogether, preferring to mingle with soldiers and uniformed government officials on the streets of Petersburg rather than merchants and *muzhiks* in bast shoes in Moscow. Chekhov, on the other hand, came from the completely opposite direction. He had barely been anywhere apart from the steppe, and Moscow seemed mesmerizing. To Muscovites, he would have seemed very provincial, his diction immediately betraying his origins. The Chekhovs all spoke with a distinct southern intonation and Anton was to retain the soft 'g' for the rest of his life, pronouncing Taganrog as 'Takhanrokh', as the locals still do.[1]

Chekhov's family had been in Moscow since the previous year, when Pavel Egorovich's failed business had forced them to leave Taganrog. Anton's two older brothers were then already students there: Alexander studying mathematics and science at the university, Nikolai studying painting at Moscow's main art school. Perhaps in rebellion at their repressive, harsh childhood, they were both leading dissolute lives. His brother Ivan, who had remained at school in Taganrog with him, was dispatched to Moscow to start teacher training in June 1877, leaving Anton the sole family member remaining in Taganrog. He arrived in Moscow for the first time that Easter, laden down with family possessions that his father had asked him to bring:

> Mamasha wants you to try and make sure you bring the brass coffee pot and the two brass bowls . . . and bring the mirror, because we don't have one, all we can do is look at the moon. You won't be able to bring the icon case, I don't suppose, because it weighs nearly forty pounds, so don't bring that, and the glass would break anyway, but don't spend money on having it sent . . . Bring the icon of St Nicholas, the book with the Regulations for Communion, the big Bible (Mamasha is asking for it), the padlocks, if they are there, pen-knives and Kolya's school coat . . . 1 pound of olives, 1 pound of halva, 1 pound of ship's biscuits . . .[2]

Chekhov had come to Moscow on a one-way ticket, and family finances at that stage were so parlous that it took a while to raise the money to buy his return fare to Taganrog. This resulted in him turning up with a spurious sick note to explain his absence at the beginning of the new school term. He had enjoyed his visit to Moscow, having been taken to the theatre and shown round the Kremlin and all the other main tourist attractions by his brothers. But much as he had a good time, Chekhov was clearly very shaken by his mother's frailty. 'Please be so kind as to continue offering comfort and support to my mother, who is physically and mentally in a very poor state,' he wrote to his cousin soon after his return. 'She regards you not just as a nephew, but as something much more. My mother's character is highly susceptible to the strong and positive influence which comes from moral support of any kind from a third party. Well, that is a pretty silly request, isn't it? But it is one you will understand, especially as I speak of "moral", that is to say spiritual, support. To us, nothing in this malicious world is more dear than our mother, and therefore you would exceedingly oblige your humble servant by taking care of his half-dead mother.'[3] The effusive language of this letter (one of the very earliest to have survived) is typical of Chekhov's early epistolary style, and is matched by a suitably extravagant calligraphy full of flourishes and curls. Both the style and the calligraphy were to be drastically pared down as he grew older.

Another of the few surviving early letters Chekhov wrote at this time shows the seventeen-year-old's charming naivety. 'Not long ago I went to the Taganrog theatre and compared it with your Moscow theatres,' he wrote to Mikhail that November. 'There is a big difference! And there is a big difference between Moscow and Taganrog.'[4] Meanwhile, Chekhov continued to receive desperate letters from his out-of-work father. Even though he was only just about managing to keep his head above water himself by working as a tutor, he was expected to send money to his family in Moscow. 'We don't have a kopeck, please send us at least three roubles,' wrote Pavel Egorovich in one letter; 'we've nothing to pawn. I am dying of grief . . . even if you have to borrow, send us money, or sell something . . . all hope is on you.'[5] It was a terrible burden for a teenager to have to assume responsibility for the welfare of his parents. But Pavel Egorovich also made it clear how much he and his wife appreciated their son's help:

> Where there is money, there is honour, respect, love, friendship and all good things, but where there is none – oh, that makes things tough! The people around you become quite different . . . Antosha! Remember this when you grow older, be a benefactor to all who ask your help, never turn your back on the poor. Your parents are an example. How we now appreciate every donation, every gift, sent from God through good people.[6]

The very fact that these early letters have been preserved, surviving endless moves in the 1870s and 1880s says a great deal about how much Chekhov took his father's letters to heart.

Chekhov moved permanently to Moscow two years later, a year after his Aunt Fenichka had moved north to join the family. Passing his final exams at the *gymnasium* made him eligible to become a student at Moscow University, and in September 1879 he was admitted to the medical faculty. His destitute parents had been counting on his arrival, sending him regular letters in which they reminded him of the importance of keeping on the straight and narrow and working hard until he graduated. 'When you finish your university course and are given a job, you can do what you like,' wrote Pavel Egorovich on 1 January 1879, 'but it is bad and harmful for young people to go out on the town all night without sleep and then sleep until one o'clock the next day; that means studying is wasted, etc. It is not a rare occurrence in Moscow, but an actual fact, Antosha!'[7] This was precisely the lifestyle favoured by Alexander and Nikolai, and Anton was increasingly looked upon as the family's salvation. 'Beloved son Antosha,' wrote his mother a month later, 'we are in great need now . . . If you could come as soon as you can.'[8] 'I've had an awful time waiting for letters from you,' she wrote in June; 'I miss you very much.' Occasionally Misha chipped in to let his elder brother know about his latest exam results or the aquarium he had set up (only the goldfish were too expensive, he lamented), but most of the letters from Moscow exhorted Chekhov to trust and obey his Papasha and Mamasha, his true friends, rather than follow his own instincts, and to follow the true light of religion. And then, when his final exams were over, Chekhov was instructed to sell their remaining possessions, as even a few kopecks made a difference to their meagre income. They had been forced to sell his mother's silver spoons, much to Evgenia Yakovlevna's dismay, and at one point were crammed into one room, with two of the boys having to sleep in a cubbyhole under the stairs. Pavel Egorovich would not have parted with the family icons, but the only other decorations were their cheap pictures of London, Venice and Paris – cities which they could only dream of visiting.[9]

Chekhov's family had moved twelve times since migrating to Moscow. He joined them in a dank basement flat owned by the Church of St Nicholas-on-Grachevka, in an insalubrious part of the city near the red light district. Grachevka Street was notorious for its hardened criminals. Bolshoi Golovin Lane, where the family moved to next, was

Trubnaya Square, Moscow

full of brothels. Nearby was Trubnaya Square, or Truba as it was commonly known, named after the pipe (the *truba*) in the white city wall through which the little Neglinnaya River trickled. Trubnaya Square was famous for its Sunday pet market, and every spring on the Feast of the Annunciation, hundreds of goldfinches, chaffinches and siskins would be set free. This was in keeping with a tradition whereby all respectable Russians considered it their duty to let at least one bird free on Annunciation Day. Chekhov was to live in this area for the next six years, and one of his most memorable early works was a vignette about the Trubnaya Square market. Nikolai Leikin, the editor to whom he submitted it for publication in the new Petersburg journal *Fragments*, thought it had too much of a Moscow flavour and promptly rejected it. 'In Moscow on Truba' appeared in November 1883 in the Moscow-based *The Alarm Clock* instead.[10] After *Fragments*, *The Alarm Clock* was the most popular comic journal in Russia, and was certainly more established, having been founded in 1866. Some of Chekhov's earliest Moscow memories found their way into this brief but vivid piece, which clearly made him homesick for the steppe and his bird-catching days in warm Taganrog. Even at this early stage, Chekhov was beginning to develop a distinctive style:

Hundreds of sheepskins, winter coats, fur caps and top hats swarm like lobsters in a pot. You can hear the many-voiced singing of birds, which reminds you of spring. If the sun shines or if there are no clouds in the sky, the singing and the smell of hay makes you day-dream and carries your thoughts far, far away. A row of carts extends at one end of the square. On the carts you will not find hay, cabbages or beans, but goldfinches, siskins, demoiselle cranes, larks, black and grey thrushes, blue-tits and bullfinches. They are all jumping about in clumsy home-made cages, looking with envy at the free sparrows and warbling. The goldfinches will go for five kopecks, the siskins cost more, and the other birds have a completely unfixed price.

'How much is the lark?'

Even the man selling them does not know how much his lark is. He scratches the back of his head and says whatever figure comes into his head – either a rouble or three kopecks, depending on who is buying. There are expensive birds too. On a soiled little pole sits a faded old thrush with a scrawny tail. He is respectable, pompous and motionless, like a retired general. He gave in to his captivity ages ago and has been looking at the deep blue sky with indifference for a long time now. He is probably considered a sensible bird because of his indifference. You cannot sell him for less than forty kopecks. Thronging round the birds are schoolboys, workmen, young people in fashionable coats, enthusiasts in unbelievably threadbare hats and trousers so shabby they look as if they have been eaten by mice.[11]

As well as birds, there were hares, rabbits, hedgehogs, guinea-pigs and ferrets on sale, and then there were fish:

The fish section is the most interesting. There are about ten muzhiks sitting in a row. In front of each of them there is a bucket and in these buckets is a small inferno. In the green, murky water teem little carps, burbots, minnows, snails, frogs and molluscs. Large water beetles with broken legs dart about on the surface, clambering over the carps and hopping over the frogs. The frogs climb over the beetles, the molluscs climb over the frogs. As a more expensive fish, the dark green tench have an advantage: they are kept in a special jar where they cannot exactly swim about, but they have a bit more room to breathe . . .

'The carp is a great fish! A carp, your excellency, will never die! You

can keep him for a year in a bucket, and he'll still be alive! I caught these
fish a week ago now. I caught them in Perervo, sir, and walked back with
them all the way. The carp are two kopecks each, the burbots three, and
the minnows are ten for ten, all alive and kicking! You can have them for
five. And how about some worms?'

The vendor reaches into the bucket and pulls out with his dirty, stubby
fingers a soft little minnow or a baby carp no longer than your nail. Near
the buckets are spread out lengths of fishing line, hooks and traps, and
pond worms reflect a fiery crimson in the sunshine.[12]

Chekhov was a passionate fisherman, and Trubnaya Square was
where he would sometimes direct his brother Ivan to buy tackle for
summer fishing at the dacha. It was also where he came to buy fish to
put in his pond when his family moved out of Moscow to Melikhovo
in 1892. As a scruffy student standing in the market and logging
impressions into his memory for his story, he can hardly have imagined
that one day he would have his own pond to fish in. Trubnaya Square
was also, of course, where his brother Misha bought the fish for the
family aquarium. Many years later, Chekhov sat down to write his story
'In the Cart'. As she is travelling home by cart to the village where she
is a teacher, his character Marya suddenly has a flash of recollection:
'And with amazing clarity, for the first time in all these thirteen years,
she was able to vividly remember her mother and father, her brother,
the apartment in Moscow, the aquarium with the little fish and
everything else down to the smallest detail; suddenly she heard the
sound of the piano and her father's voice.' Chekhov was clearly
remembering the hard early years in Moscow, and also thinking
nostalgically of his Moscow youth when he wrote this story in 1897,
having been sent to Nice in the vain hope of curing his tuberculosis.

Living conditions were spartan and very cramped in the flat on
Grachevka: there were nine people living in four rooms, three of whom
were lodgers taken in by the Chekhovs in order to make ends meet.
The situation had eased a little, as Pavel Egorovich was at least earning
a regular salary. After long months of unemployment, he had been
forced to swallow his pride and take a job as an accounts clerk for a
merchant on the other side of town who had a haberdashery firm, and
he was to live chiefly on his employer's premises for the next few years.
Two of his nephews already had jobs at Gavrilov's warehouse: Mikhail,

the son of his eldest brother, and Aunt Fenichka's only son, Alexei, who had started work at the age of thirteen.[13] Pavel Egorovich's meagre income did not go far, and Alexander and Nikolai were reneging on their duty to help. As soon as Chekhov received the first instalment of his student grant, therefore, it was pounced on. A few weeks later the family moved again, the grant from the Taganrog City Council (one of twenty awarded that year) enabling them to take up residence in a superior first-floor flat.

Chekhov had already stepped into his absent father's shoes by this time: Alexander was living in student lodgings on his own, and Nikolai was unreliable. Both brothers had problems with alcoholism, but in their sober moments they enjoyed some success contributing to the comic journals that were published in Moscow and Petersburg. Such publications were to become increasingly popular with the burgeoning literate population of Moscow's lower classes. As soon as he had settled into his student routine, Chekhov followed his brothers' example, and started sending off stories to various editorial offices in the hope of supplementing the family income. It is possible Chekhov had at least one publication already behind him. His Russian biographer Mikhail Gromov provides compelling evidence for ascribing *The Dragonfly*'s inclusion of some humorous verse and a comic dialogue between two young men called Sasha and Kolya (the names of the eldest Chekhov brothers) in November 1878 to Anton Pavlovich.[14] That piece, like almost everything else Chekhov wrote for the next five years, was published under a pseudonym. If Gromov's supposition is correct, we need to revise our dating of the beginning of Chekhov's literary career by over two years.

Editors responded to submissions in 'post boxes' on their back pages, and Chekhov was probably crestfallen to see the first piece he submitted after moving to Moscow rejected by *The Alarm Clock* in November 1879. Two weeks after sending in his next story to the Petersburg weekly *The Dragonfly*, however, he received the good news that his story was 'not bad at all' and would be published. In his follow-up letter, the editor offered Chekhov a rate of five kopecks a line. That would mean quite a few minnows if he was interested in buying fish, but not much else. The story was published two months later, in March 1880, along with another piece submitted at the same time. To make any money, writers had to be prolific, and they often adopted an array of pseudonyms to disguise the fact that there was only one author hiding behind them. Chekhov, in addition, had his future reputation as a doctor to think about, and he was to publish under a variety of different names in his first years as a writer. While his brother Nikolai signed his drawings with his own name, he himself usually opted for 'Antosha Chekhonte', a nickname given him back in Taganrog.

In the autumn of 1880, the Chekhovs upped sticks and moved again, to a first-floor flat in a brick building on nearby Golovin Lane, three houses in from Sretenka Street; it would remain their home for the next five years. Pavel Egorovich was still being chased for debts incurred back in Taganrog, and on one occasion he was threatened with arrest,[15] but the family had slowly begun to return to normality. For the first time since moving to Moscow they could manage without lodgers, and could take on a serving girl, Anna, to help with cleaning and cooking. Ivan soon moved out of Moscow to nearby Voskresensk to take up his first teaching job; the youngest Chekhovs, Masha and Misha, were completing their schooling and going on to college, Nikolai seemed set to do well as a painter, and Anton began to work harder than ever as more of his stories were accepted for publication. Over the years the family acquired a second servant, a dog (a whippet called Korbo), a cat (Fyodor

Sretenka Street, Moscow

Timofeyich), and a piano, and the new friends they made in Moscow were invited round for meals. Although the scale of the entertainment was modest (no dancing, no cards), guests later remembered evenings spent at Golovin Lane as being particularly convivial. The Chekhovs were nostalgic for southern cooking in Moscow, and so the dishes Evgenia Yakovlevna served were a reminder of the life they had left. Supper almost invariably included the famous Taganrog potato salad with olives and spring onions, and it is telling that the family immediately started growing aubergines, tomatoes and peppers in greenhouses as soon as they acquired their own garden at Melikhovo a decade later.

Chekhov particularly took to Moscow. In May 1881, as he neared the end of his second year as a medical student, a school friend in Kharkov received an ecstatic letter from him. 'Come to Moscow!!!' Chekhov wrote. 'I really love Moscow. No one who gets used to it can ever leave. I am always going to be a Muscovite. Come and work as a writer. You can't do that in Kharkov, but it pays 150 roubles a year in Moscow – that's what I get at any rate.'[16] It was later in 1881 that a new journal called *The Spectator* was founded. Chekhov and his older brothers had soon virtually taken it over, and *The Spectator* editorial offices became more like their own private club. Chekhov published eleven pieces in *The Spectator* before it began to fizzle out; insufficient financial backing meant it was unable to compete with other publications at that stage. The general style and quality of these pieces can be gauged from a frivolous little story he published in one of its last numbers that December under the title 'This and That':

A lovely frosty afternoon. The sun sparkles in every snowflake. Not a cloud or a gust of wind.

A couple are sitting on a bench on the boulevard.

'I love you!' he whispers.

Pink cupids play on her pretty cheeks.

'I love you!' he continues . . . 'As soon as I saw you, I realized what I was living for, and what the goal of my existence was! It is life with you or complete non-existence! My dear! Marya Ivanovna! Is it yes or no? Marya! Marya Ivanovna . . . I love you . . . Manechka . . . Answer me or I will die! Yes or no?'

She lifts her large eyes up to him. She wants to tell him 'yes'. She opens her little mouth wide.

'Aagh!' she shrieks.

Racing across his snow-white collar are two big bedbugs, trying to outpace each other . . . Oh, what horror!![17]

In 1883 the proprietor of *The Spectator* could afford to start the journal up again, but again it only survived for a few months. However, Chekhov was its main contributor during its second incarnation. By this time its former secretary, Chekhov's eldest brother Alexander, had left Moscow. He initially moved back down to Taganrog with his common-law wife Anna Ivanovna on what would be just one of the many stops on his peripatetic career, and in November 1882 Chekhov sent him an update on family affairs:

> Nikolka [Nikolai] has gone to Voskresensk with Maria, it's Misha's name-day, Father is sleeping, Mother is praying, Auntie's thinking about herbs, Anna is washing dishes and is about to bring down the chamber-pot, I am writing and wondering how many times tonight my whole body will start twitching for daring to try to be a writer. I'm getting on with my medical studies . . . There's an operation every day. Tell Anna Ivanovna that the old paper-boy who sold the *Spectator* has died in hospital from prostate cancer. We're just carrying on quietly as usual, reading, writing, hanging around in the evenings, drinking the odd glass of vodka, listening to music and singing, et cetera . . .[18]

Chekhov was certainly kept busy by his medical studies during the day, while the need to earn money meant that much of his spare time was spent sitting at his desk scribbling diverse stories and sketches, without any guarantee that they would be published. In the autumn of 1881 he had started writing the occasional review and proved to be an incisive critic. Unlike swooning audiences everywhere else in Europe, he was not very impressed with the doyenne of the French stage Sarah Bernhardt ('la grande Sarah') who came to Russia on tour with the Comédie Française. Her Adrienne Lecouvreur (in Scribe and Legouvé's play) was moving, Chekhov argued, but too mannered and narcissistic to bring the emotional Russian audience to tears. A Russian production of *Hamlet* at the first private theatre in Moscow in 1882 met with greater approval from Chekhov the critic.

As well as going to the theatre, Chekhov also enjoyed hearing music.

He went to see Glinka's *A Life for the Tsar* at the Bolshoi with his sister
in his first winter in Moscow, and in November 1881 got to know the
Spanish virtuoso violinist and composer Pablo Sarasate during his
Russian tour (having perhaps already met him when he had played in
Taganrog). A few weeks later Sarasate sent Chekhov his photograph
from Rome, writing to him in Italian: 'To my dear friend Doctor
Antonio Chekhonte, Pablo Sarasate. Rome, Piazza Borghese . . . With
love.'[19] Maybe it was Sarasate who inspired the parodic story 'The
Sinner from Toledo', which Chekhov published in *The Spectator* that
December under the heading 'translated from the Spanish'. Chekhov
was good at cod-Latin, but he did not know a word of Spanish, and he
never went anywhere near Spain.

Much of the music Chekhov heard was at home. In June 1882 he
and Nikolai went to the national exhibition of art and industry that was
held in Moscow and were particularly struck by a demonstration given
in the piano section. The performer was Pyotr Shostakovsky, a Moscow
musician who founded the Russian Philharmonic Society and
conducted his own orchestra. Shostakovsky dazzled the Chekhov
brothers with his performance of a rhapsody by his teacher Liszt, and
Nikolai was so taken with it that he started to play it several times a day.
Some times he played to Shostakovsky himself, who became a family
friend. Nikolai had inherited his father's musical gifts and taught
himself the violin as well the piano. To judge from his repertoire (apart
from Liszt, he was very fond of the Chopin nocturnes), he was
extremely competent.

Chekhov was particularly close at this time to his brother Nikolai.
Before his sad descent into alcoholism and his subsequent fatal illness,
Nikolai had everything to look forward to. His prodigious artistic
talents promised success as a serious painter, and were also recognized
by regular commissions from journals like *The Alarm Clock*. His friends
were to become some of the most important figures in the Russian art
scene. Two of them also became friends of Anton. First of all there was
the painter Levitan, with whom Chekhov shared an almost identical
approach to landscape, the prime source of lyrical inspiration to both
of them. The painting of the River Istra in summer time which Levitan
gave Chekhov in 1885 was to follow him wherever he moved, the
canvas finally settling along with its owner in Yalta. The course of
Chekhov's friendship with Levitan was not always smooth, but there

Chekhov and his brother, Nikolai, February 1882

were few people to whom he was closer. The loss of his letters to
Levitan leaves a huge hole in his correspondence. In 1891, in a letter
to his sister, Chekhov was thrilled to report Levitan's first major success
after seeing his canvas 'Quiet Monastery' exhibited in St Petersburg. It
is this same painting (with a few details changed) which Yulia Lapteva
is moved by in 'Three Years', Chekhov's masterly 1895 story of
Moscow merchant life:

> Yulia stopped in front of a small landscape and looked at it
> dispassionately. In the foreground there was a little river, a timber bridge
> over it, a path on the other side disappearing into dark grass, then some
> woods on the right hand side and a bonfire near it: no doubt people were
> watching over the horses pasturing for the night. In the distance an
> evening sunset burned.
>
> Yulia imagined going over the bridge herself, then along the path,
> further and further, with everything quiet all around, corncrakes calling
> sleepily and the fire flickering in the distance. And for some reason it
> suddenly seemed to her that she had seen those clouds which stretched

out over the red part of the sky, the forest and the field long ago and many times over; she felt completely alone, and it made her want to go walking down that path further and further and further; and the reflection of something eternal and unearthly hovered around the place where the evening sun was setting.[20]

Another of Nikolai's friends was the architect Franz (Fyodor) Shekhtel, who would go on to create Moscow's most fabulous Art Nouveau buildings in the early 1900s. Among these was the extraordinary house he designed for the merchant millionaire Stepan Ryabushinsky, where Chekhov's friend Maxim Gorky was later virtually imprisoned by Stalin in the 1930s. Shekhtel remained more Nikolai's friend, but his connection with Chekhov was long-lasting. In 1895 Shekhtel designed the little house in the garden at Melikhovo where Chekhov wrote *The Seagull*, and in 1902 he received a commission to convert the old theatre on Kamergersky Lane as a permanent home for the Moscow Art Theatre. After Chekhov's death he designed the new library building in Taganrog, which was named after the donor of a large part of its collection.

Nikolai never lived to fulfil his artistic promise, but before he went into terminal decline, he illustrated many of his younger brother's early stories, and some evocative photographs of them taken in the early 1880s commemorate their collaboration. The brothers are captured posing in a well-appointed room with heavy Victorian furniture, long drapes and lighted candles, both neatly turned out in jackets and ties. The bespectacled Nikolai is seated at a small table looking at the large sheet of paper he is holding in one hand, with a paintbrush in the other. His box of paints sits open on the table, while a portfolio imprinted with his initials stands propped up against the table legs in the foreground. A slightly dreamy looking Chekhov is standing with his legs crossed, leaning up against a bureau, looking down at his brother's picture. One of Nikolai's sketchbooks contains drawings of the famous statue of Pushkin that was unveiled in Moscow with much fanfare in June 1880. The drawings on the sketchbook's yellow, white and blue leaves were studies for illustrations that were to appear in journals like *The Alarm Clock* and *The Spectator*, and commemorated an event which was regarded as one of national importance. This was, after all, the first statue of Pushkin to be erected in Russia, and it had been paid for by public subscription. Turgenev came all the way from Paris, and Dostoevsky from St Petersburg in order to give speeches to mark the occasion, and Chekhov was no doubt with his brother at least some of the time while he was capturing the proceedings on paper. He was as much a devotee of Pushkin as any other educated Russian, and Uncle Mitrofan in Taganrog started crying because he was so moved by what his nephew Anton wrote about the great poet in a letter at that time.[21]

In addition to their creative collaboration, Anton and Nikolai spent much of their free time together, and sometimes their respective worlds of medicine and art collided. In January 1882, Nikolai drew a cartoon for *The Alarm Clock* depicting drunken professors and students celebrating St Tatiana's Day (the figure standing in the foreground, glass in hand, is perhaps his brother). It was on 12 January 1755 that the Empress Elizabeth had signed the edict consenting to the foundation of Moscow University, and St Tatiana's Day had marked the beginning of the student vacation ever since. The debauched scenes which took place annually at the Hermitage restaurant (shown in Nikolai's picture) were legendary. As soon as he became a student himself, Chekhov joined in with gusto, and later instituted an annual St Tatiana's Day dinner for his writer friends in St Petersburg. In anticipation of unruly behaviour on St Tatiana's Day, the proprietors of the Hermitage would replace the restaurant's silk furnishings with wooden tables and stools, take up the carpets and throw sawdust on the floor. 'Tatiana' happens to rhyme with the Russian word for drunk (*piana*) and policemen would be enjoined to remember *dien Tatiany, studienty piany* and not rush to arrest the inebriated students as they staggered home in the small hours.

The Hermitage was located on Trubnaya Square, where the pet market was held, and was one of Moscow's famous restaurants. It had been founded by a Russian merchant and a French chef in the 1860s and was renowned for its superb cuisine, fine wines (some of which were reputed to have come from the cellars of Louis XVI) and smartly dressed waiters, who wore shirts of Dutch linen tied with silk belts. It was a favourite haunt for the Moscow intelligentsia, some of whom had breakfast, lunch and dinner there, doing business from their regular tables. Tchaikovsky celebrated his disastrous wedding here in 1877, and it was at the Hermitage that Dostoevsky and Turgenev were both fêted with celebratory dinners. This was where Chekhov liked to come with his friends, and it was on one of these occasions in 1897 that he suffered the severe lung haemorrhage which led to the official diagnosis of tuberculosis. Chekhov could never have imagined such a scenario in the early 1880s when he was joining in rowdy choruses of 'Gaudeamus igitur'.

Chekhov liked to drink like any other student, but rarely to excess. The reputation for industry and self-control which was such a distinct feature of his adult personality was forged early on. In 1882 he began writing for *Fragments*, which represented a step up the ladder from the low-grade Moscow journals he had been writing for until then. By 1883, he was earning from his writing not just the 150 roubles a year he had earlier boasted about, but about 100 roubles a month. This was about three times as much as his student stipend and three times as much as his father's salary. But that did not mean writing was always easy, as a letter sent to his editor Nikolai Leikin in August 1883 makes clear. Most Muscovites escaped the city heat and headed for their dacha in the summer months, but Chekhov was still working:

I am writing in the most awful conditions. In front of me is a pile of non-literary work battering mercilessly at my conscience, a visiting relative's baby is howling in the next room and in the room the other side my father is reading aloud to my mother from [Leskov's story] *The Sealed Angel* . . . Someone has started up the music box, so I have to listen to [Offenbach's] *La Belle Hélène* . . . I'd like to do a bunk to the dacha, but it's one o'clock in the morning . . . It's hard to imagine a more awful situation for someone who wants to be a writer. My bed is being slept in by the relation who has come to stay; he keeps on coming up to me and engaging me in conversation about medical subjects. 'My daughter's probably got colic; that must be why she's crying all the time.' I have the great misfortune to be a doctor, and there seems to be no single individual who does not think it incumbent on him or her to talk to me about medicine. And if they get tired of discussing medicine, they start off on literature . . .[22]

It says something about how Chekhov's attitude to writing was beginning to change at this time that he excluded everything he wrote before 1883 from the edition of his collected works that he put together at the end of his life. In these early years he was still producing hundreds of stories, but he later disowned most of them. Such was the

fate meted out to 'Drama at a Shooting Party', which was published
serially in a Moscow newspaper over the course of many months,
beginning in November 1884. Chekhov was later so embarrassed by the
steamy love scenes and melodramatic plot twists of this murder mystery
that he pretended he had never written it. It certainly comes as a
surprise to discover that this master of elegant, chiselled prose ever
wrote a novel, let alone a gripping page-turner. It is an immature work
stylistically, written in the hard-up early years for money which proved
difficult to extract: the newspaper owner tried to fob Chekhov off with
offers of theatre tickets and new pairs of trousers.[23] As many Chekhov
critics agree, though, it is under-rated. In 1884, Chekhov also brought
out his first book at his own expense, in a print-run of just over a
thousand copies. *Tales of Melpomene*, named ironically after the muse
of tragedy, contained six of 'A. Chekhonte's' best stories to date, all on
theatrical themes.

The Chekhovs had acquired a reputation among their Moscow
friends for their warm hospitality, but conditions in the small flat on
Sretenka were cramped. Apart from the pleasure of making a small
profit when *Tales of Melpomene* sold out, Chekhov had also begun to

*The Church of St John the Warrior, Moscow, opposite which
the Chekhovs lived in 1885*

make more money from publishing some of his stories in *The Petersburg Newspaper*, one of the capital's biggest daily broadsheets. This was a definite step up from the comic weeklies, and he decided they could afford to move. So, in the autumn of 1885, a year after Chekhov qualified as a doctor, they relocated to the area south of the river known as the Zamoskvorechie, near to where Pavel Egorovich worked. It was the stronghold of Moscow's merchants. The first flat proved to be so damp that after a few weeks it was exchanged for a much larger flat on the same street, Yakimanka (whose strange-sounding name came from the Church of Saints Joachim and Anna which stood in the area). The Chekhovs' flat was on the ground floor of an old house with columns that stood opposite the baroque Church of St John the Warrior. It was the largest property they had rented in Moscow and Chekhov was able to have his own study with a fireplace. Various musician friends started coming to take part in the Tuesday night soirées that were revived here, some of them paying court to Chekhov's sister Masha at the same time. Chekhov, meanwhile, had begun to acquire literary admirers. One friend who came round one evening when Chekhov had severe stomach ache later recounted an ingenious method that a local chemist had devised for acquiring his autograph. Ivan Babakin, the young village boy Chekhov had taken under his wing at their summer dacha, was dispatched to procure some castor oil capsules from the chemist. When Chekhov opened the box to find two enormous pills, he had laughed. After writing 'I am not a horse' on the box in large letters, he sent Ivan back to the chemist.[24] Thus had the chemist acquired his autograph.

After a while, the flat on Yakimanka proved to have its problems too. The upstairs tenant hired his premises out for wedding receptions, funeral wakes and dinners, and it proved to be very noisy. Another move loomed. Rather than pay rent all summer, the family decided to give up the flat when they moved out of town to their dacha the following spring. Earlier that year, Chekhov had started contributing stories to the Petersburg-based *New Times*, Russia's most popular and influential daily newspaper, and the fee he earned gave him unprecedented buying power. After seven years of moving from flat to flat, in the autumn of 1886, he was able to rent a whole house for the first time. It would be the family's first proper home in Moscow and they would stay there for the next four years. Just before they moved,

Chekhov published his first short story under his own name and shortly afterwards received an unsolicited fan letter from Dmitry Grigorovich, a well-known Petersburg figure. Grigorovich thought it was time Chekhov started taking his writing seriously:

> I'm convinced that you are destined to write several superb, truly artistic works. You will be committing a grave sin if you do not justify these expectations. But for that what is necessary is respect for talent, which is such a rare gift after all. Give up writing for deadlines. I do not know what your income is, but if it is small, it would be better if you starved, like we starved in our day, and stored up your thoughts for work that is well conceived and thought through, written in happy hours of inner concentration rather than in one sitting . . .[25]

Grigorovich's words fell on fertile ground. Deep down Chekhov knew that the stories he was now writing were of artistic worth, but he needed validation from someone in the literary establishment in Petersburg, because no one in his milieu took him seriously. Chekhov immediately wrote Grigorovich a long, effusive letter in reply:

> Your letter, my dear, beloved bearer of good tidings, struck me like a bolt of lightning. I almost burst into tears and felt very moved, and now feel as if it has left a deep mark in my soul . . . People close to me have always been scornful of my writing, and do not cease to give me friendly advice not to give up a proper profession for the pen-pushing. I have hundreds of acquaintances in Moscow, including a few dozen who write, and I cannot remember a single one of them who has read me or saw me as an artist . . .[26]

The writers at the weekly literary club he attended in Moscow, he explained, would simply laugh in his face if he went and read Grigorovich's letter out to them. No, he had never spent more than a day writing a story, but with his medical practice (which Grigorovich had, of course, no idea about), he never had more than a couple of hours of leisure time late at night to devote to writing. And then, of course, he did not have the energy to work seriously on anything. All hope, he concluded, was therefore on the future. Chekhov's conservative Uncle Mitrofan did not really approve of earning one's living as a writer, so it was not without some pride that his nephew sent a letter to him in Taganrog to tell him what had happened, employing some forgivable epistolary licence by slightly conflating Grigorovich's first two letters:

> There is a major writer in Russia, Dmitry Grigorovich, whose portrait you will find in your copy of *Modern Figures*. Not long ago, quite out of the blue, and not being acquainted with him, I received a sizeable letter from him. Grigorovich is such a respected and popular personality that you can imagine how pleasantly surprised I was! Here are some passages from his letter: 'You have *real* talent, a talent which places you far above the writers of the new generation . . . I am over sixty-five, but I have preserved so much love for literature, I follow its progress with such keen interest, and am always so glad to encounter something lively and gifted that, as you can see, I could not restrain myself from extending both my arms to you . . . When you are next in Petersburg, I hope to see you and embrace you, as I now embrace you in absentia.[27]

Emboldened by Grigorovich's letter, Chekhov now began giving similar avuncular advice to his older brother Alexander, who also had pretensions to a literary career, noting with a bit of a swagger that he was now the writer to watch.[28] *Motley Tales*, his second short story collection, published in May 1886, certainly attracted a lot of attention.

Another brother who now received avuncular advice that March was the wayward Nikolai, whose dissolute lifestyle prompted Chekhov to write him an extraordinary letter – extraordinary both because it was very long (the two brothers saw each other on a regular basis, after all), and because of what it said. Chekhov's exhortations to Nikolai actually tell us a great deal about his own sense of moral purpose: civilized people respect human beings as individuals, he admonished Nikolai, enumerating a further seven precepts which clearly followed a plan he had worked out for himself. They have compassion for other people, the list continued, they respect other people's property, they do not tell lies even in the most trivial matters, they do not denigrate themselves in order to provoke the sympathy of others, they are not vain, they value their talent, if they have it, and work at developing their aesthetic sensibility, and they are fastidious in their habits. Bearing in mind the singleness of purpose which was to characterize Chekhov's attitude towards his writing (the nonchalance he affected was a highly effective smokescreen), it is particularly interesting to note the way he embellished his comments to Nikolai about dedication to one's craft. Civilized people take pride in their talent, he thundered on, sacrificing for it peace of mind, women, wine, and all the bustle and vanity of the world. Chekhov took his own lessons to heart. And in concluding his letter to Nikolai by telling him to 'work unceasingly, day and night, read constantly, study, exercise will-power', stressing that every hour was precious, there was probably more than Grigorovich's wake-up call at work.

Nikolai had tuberculosis. His reaction to having been given this death sentence was to give up. For the last eighteen months, Chekhov had known that he too had contracted this fatal disease, and now fell victim to ominous coughing fits each spring and autumn as the seasons changed. In November 1884 he had completed his first commission for *The Petersburg Newspaper*: fifteen pieces of daily reportage from a high-profile Moscow fraud trial. Although Chekhov himself had suggested the assignment, he had not anticipated how gruelling it would be to sit in court day after day and then rush home and write 'like one possessed' in order to meet his deadlines. The exhaustion took its toll on his fragile health. Chekhov's main Petersburg editor had for some time been trying to persuade his young protégé to make the journey to the capital, where his work was being published to increasing acclaim. After the trial finished, Chekhov was forced to confide in him that he had been spitting blood. It was not tubercular, he emphasized to another correspondent,[29] but of course it was. He was unable even to get on with his writing properly, let alone board a train.[30] As a doctor, he knew exactly what he was dealing with.

Chekhov's reaction to contracting tuberculosis was the opposite of that of his brother. An early awareness of living on borrowed time spurred him on to industry, not sloth. The letter from Grigorovich helped him to start valuing his artistic gift: if he did not completely sacrifice for it peace of mind, women, wine, and all the bustle and vanity of the world, he nevertheless came close. And this new dedication to his art was not accompanied by the ruthlessness and egocentricity often associated with creative genius, but again by their opposites. Looking ahead to the next eighteen years of his life, Chekhov's activities outside his writing – his work as a doctor, the solicitude with which he cared for his parents, his work to reform the inhumanity of Russia's penal system, his contribution to famine relief and to the prevention of cholera, his construction of schools and planting of trees, and his campaign to build a sanatorium for tuberculosis sufferers – all speak of a highly developed ethical philosophy which was perhaps partly the legacy of his Christian upbringing. Chekhov may have rejected the dogma of the Church in adulthood, but under the influence of people like Father Vasily in Taganrog even his artistic activities were guided by the same, highly discreet, humanitarian goals.

II

Dr Chekhov's Casebook

Moscow was the city where Chekhov began his literary career, and where he made his stage debut as a dramatist. Moscow was also the city where he studied and practised medicine. Chekhov's medical practice may not have given him very much in monetary terms (in fact, hardly anything at all), but the experience of treating patients was to prove invaluable for his creative work, not only in terms of subject matter but technique. As he said in a typically pithy autobiographical note he compiled for a Moscow University almanac published in 1900:

> I do not doubt that my medical activities have had a powerful influence on my work as a writer; they have significantly expanded my field of observation, enriched my knowledge, and only people who are doctors themselves will be able to appreciate the true value of all this; medicine has also been a guiding influence, and I have probably avoided making many mistakes as a result of my close relationship with it. My acquaintance with the natural sciences and the scientific approach has always kept me on my toes, and I have tried, wherever possible, to deal with scientific facts; where that has not been possible I have tried not to write at all. I should point out in this connection that the conditions of creative work do not always allow complete agreement with scientific

facts; you cannot depict a death from poisoning on stage as it happens in real life. But you must be able to sense there is an agreement with scientific facts even when you have to resort to convention, that is to say, the reader or the spectator must realize that it is only convention, but that the author writes from a position of knowledge.[31]

Only immediately after graduating did Chekhov ever seek a full-time position as a doctor. Once he started becoming successful as a writer, medicine receded into the background, but it remained a constant presence in his life, and never lost its importance for him. He was friendly with numerous doctors throughout his life, depicted scores of them in his stories and plays, did his best to support the cause of public health, and helped a medical journal when it was threatened with closure.

His choice of medicine as a career had been rather arbitrary to begin with, as he confessed in his autobiographical note, but it was not one he regretted. The most important thing was for him to acquire a university education which could open up avenues, both professional and social, that would otherwise have been closed to him as a lower-class meshchanin. In other words, a university degree, to which his *gymnasium* education gave him access, was Chekhov's passport to freedom. He toyed for a while with the idea of studying medicine in Zürich, and then considered the German university town of Dorpat (modern day Tartu in Estonia), which was part of the Russian Empire. As a boy in Taganrog he had been treated by a German doctor from Dorpat;[32] it was also where Dr Nikolai Pirogov, Russia's greatest nineteenth-century medical scientist, had taught for many years. But Moscow University was the natural choice, and it turned out to be a good one. If Moscow was becoming a dynamic and powerful city in the closing years of the nineteenth century, thanks to the forces of capitalism, medicine was also undergoing a profound transformation in Russia, and some of its most brilliant figures were linked to Moscow University. The 1880s when Chekhov was a student, were a time when its medical school particularly flourished.

When Chekhov graduated with his doctor's certificate in 1884, after five years of rigorous training, he was entering a highly respectable profession. This had not always been so. The practice of medicine, like so much else, was very backward in Russia and only began to enjoy a degree of prestige after the great reforms of the 1860s. Until the beginning of the eighteenth century, indeed, the doctors were all foreign. It was in Moscow that Peter the Great set up the first training institution for Russian doctors; eventually there were five others: the Medical-Surgical Academy in Petersburg, and the medical faculties of Dorpat, Vilna (present-day Vilnius – another city with a largely foreign population), Kharkov and Kazan. But the status of Russian doctors remained very low compared to that of their foreign colleagues, and their activities were strictly controlled by the state via the Table of Ranks. Status was made visible through the different uniforms for differing medical posts.

The medical profession offered commoners the possibility of social betterment: acquiring a degree brought with it some desirable privileges, such as exemption from the demeaning poll tax and the hated military service. But it was rare for doctors to rise above the lowest position in the Table of Ranks, and the profession therefore attracted few members of the gentry. State remuneration in addition was extremely modest. Since most medical personnel did not even make it on to the bottom rung of the Table of Ranks, and therefore lacked any kind of official recognition (the regime wished to protect the privileges of the noble class), even having completed the five-year degree, their position in society was significantly lower than lawyers, civil servants and army personnel. In the 1860s doctors were still being lumped together with piano tuners and typesetters when it came to classifying professions, and it was almost axiomatic that doctors came from poor backgrounds. All these factors together conspired to produce a recruitment crisis, and it was partly to solve it that a law was passed in 1876 which enabled the country's medical faculties to provide student scholarships.

Chekhov was the beneficiary of a scholarship from Taganrog, and he was one of the first generation of Russian doctors who did not have to become lowly government functionaries, their status and income determined by a controlling state. First of all the reforms of the 1860s led to the establishment of *zemstvo* medicine: a free national health care service administered by the new units of elective local government established all over Russia. Medical provision in rural areas was primitive, to say the least, with one doctor to tens of thousands of patients, so the influx of doctors and the building of clinics and hospitals funded by the zemstvo was a major step forward. From its position of backwardness, Russia suddenly vaulted itself into a position where it had taken the lead: no other European country had yet developed an equivalent of public zemstvo medicine. The Swiss-born F. F. Erisman, who founded hygiene science in Russia, was a leading figure in the movement for community medicine. He settled in Russia in 1875, four years before Chekhov matriculated, and that same year began the publication of long articles on public health in the leading journal *Notes of the Fatherland*. In 1882 he became Professor of Hygiene at Moscow University, and so was one of Chekhov's teachers. Another major advance in Russian medicine came when doctors started to professionalize their activities and develop autonomy. The Pirogov Society, formed in 1881 when Chekhov was in his second year as a medical student, was named after the surgeon and educator who had just died. It was a national organization that committed itself to continuing Pirogov's quest to improve standards in public health and advance medical education. The first Congress, held in St Petersburg in 1885, attracted 573 delegates, only 44 of whom worked as zemstvo doctors, with twice as many working for hospitals and universities. The 1902 Congress, by contrast, the Society's eighth (which featured a special matinee performance of *Uncle Vanya*) attracted 1,994 delegates, 412 of whom worked for the zemstvo, with approximately 300 employed in either private practice, hospitals or universities.

When Chekhov later moved out of Moscow to his country estate at Melikhovo, he became an active supporter of the zemstvo medicine programme being developed in the Moscow province, which earned a reputation for being a model of its kind. And he played his part in helping to erase the huge chasm that existed between the educated population and the people by treating peasants himself. In her book on nineteenth-century Russian medicine, Nancy Mandelker-Frieden provides a graphic example of this divide:

> A zemstvo physician who worked in Samara province for many years restrained the peasants from falling on their knees and addressing him as 'Your Honour' or 'Your Excellency' or 'Your Majesty' and later recalled how 'painful it was to see the debasement of the human personality. It was necessary to wean the population from these slave-like habits and explain that a physician was not a lord but a person who also served and worked.'[33]

Earlier in the century, physicians had to hover around doorways not daring to sit down, and were often treated little better than serfs; the zemstvo doctor at end of the nineteenth century was an often idealized figure, admired for his commitment to the noble cause of working for the people. Russian medicine had come a long way.

There was a total of around 13,000 doctors practising in Russia when Chekhov entered his first year of medical school, and about 16,000 when he graduated along with 200 other young men. Russian physicians were severely tested by the famine of 1891–92 and the cholera epidemics of 1892–93, which revealed that Russia's medical provision was still very backward when compared with that of other European countries. As usual, the Tsarist administration impeded progress through its complicated bureaucratic apparatus and restrictive practices. In the face of the obstacles it put up, many Russian doctors succumbed to apathy and despair: Dr Ragin in Chekhov's searing story 'Ward No. 6' is one such figure. Chekhov himself took an active role in both the famine relief effort and the campaign to fight the cholera epidemics. His conscientiousness as a doctor had been inculcated at an early age, and he had received consistently high marks in his exams which he had to pass at the end of every year at medical school. Medicine was not a subject for slackers.

When Chekhov matriculated, Russia's oldest university had four faculties (medicine, law, history and physics), several thousand students, a hundred or so teaching staff, and a uniform: dark green jacket with gold buttons, and a blue-lined fur cap.[34] Chekhov spent his first two years as a medical student attending lectures in the two main buildings, situated opposite the Kremlin. Dissections began in his second year, along with studies in physiology, embryology and pathology. In 1882 Chekhov began the practical side of his training in the university's clinics on nearby Rozhdestvenka Street. This was where he attended anatomy classes, and observed post-mortems. The following year he had to travel up to the top of Petrovka Street to the Novoekaterinskaya – or New Catherine Hospital – to acquire skills in surgery. The Novoekaterinskaya, founded in 1775, was Moscow's oldest and largest hospital, with 852 beds. From 1833 it had been housed in an elegant yellow classical building with the longest portico in the city and twelve Ionic columns. Before it was turned into a hospital it had been the Gagarin Mansion, and formerly the aristocratic English Club, where Pierre Bezukhov challenges

The New Catherine Hospital in Moscow

the dastardly Dolokhov to a duel in *War and Peace*. After the Revolution it became Municipal Clinical Hospital No. 24. In 1883 Chekhov was a student of the distinguished Professor Alexei Ostroumov at the Novoekaterinskaya; in 1897 he became Ostroumov's patient when he was taken, after his haemorrhage at the Hermitage restaurant, to the university clinics in their new location near the Novodevichy Convent, near to where Tolstoy lived.

It was in 1884, the year that he graduated, that Chekhov first developed the symptoms of the tuberculosis which would later kill him. He was one of those doctors who choose not to admit to illness, however, hoping that a healthy mental attitude would be the best kind of preventative medicine. In the case of tuberculosis this only worked up to a point. Rumours of Chekhov's frail health had been rife for a while, but still people were shocked to discover how ill he was in 1897. After this date, Chekhov put into practice the lessons he had learned from Marcus Aurelius and suffered his illness stoically, making light of its unpleasant symptoms right until the very end.

Most of Chekhov's practical medical work took place in the late 1880s, immediately after he qualified. He acquired valuable experience at the zemstvo hospital near Voskresensk where his family spent their summer in 1884, and also spent two weeks working as a locum in nearby Zvenigorod. In June he wrote a revealing letter to Nikolai Leikin about a post-mortem that he conducted that summer out in the countryside:

> The body was dressed in a red shirt and new trousers, covered by a sheet, and on top of the sheet was a towel with an icon. We asked the policeman if he could get us some water; there was a pond with plenty of water in it near by, but nobody would let us have a bucket for fear of our making it unclean. One peasant from this village, which is called Manekhino, devised a cunning plan: they would steal a bucket from neighbouring Trukhino, because no one could care less about a bucket belonging to somebody else . . . When and where and how they were going to steal it was not clear, but they were terribly pleased with their stratagem and there were smiles all round . . . The actual post-mortem revealed twenty broken ribs, a swollen lung and a strong smell of alcohol from the stomach. Death had resulted from foul play in the shape of strangulation. The drunk man's chest had been crushed by something heavy, probably a well-built peasant's knee. There were a number of abrasions on the body caused by attempts at resuscitation. Apparently the Manekhino peasants, when they found the body, rocked and pummelled it so enthusiastically for two hours that the murderer's future defence lawyer will have every right to ask an expert witness if the ribs had not been broken as a result of these attentions . . . Somehow however I don't think these questions will ever be asked. There will be no counsel for the defence, nor indeed any accused either . . .[35]

Chekhov applied for a position in the children's hospital in the area in 1884, but he ended up practising as a part-time private physician in Moscow. Since most of his patients were friends and colleagues, or else people who were extremely poor, he never made any money. Indeed, he almost made a loss after having to pay for cabs. And on one occasion he spent four hours just getting to one of his patients. Then, in April 1889, when his state of mind was like the cold spring weather ('mud, cold, rain'), Chekhov had to start visiting his own brother twice a day.[36] Nikolai had stopped drinking, but his 'artistic' way of life had finally caught up with him. A few months later on a hot summer's day, surrounded by his family at their dacha retreat in the Ukraine, he would die of tuberculosis.

Until 1888 or so Chekhov toyed with the idea of abandoning literature for medicine, and this is when he wrote letters about medicine being his wife and literature his mistress (in one signing himself 'Antony and Meditsina', thus making medicine, a feminine noun in Russian, into a person). He was still writing hundreds of stories at this point, but he was also seeing hundreds of patients, some of whom he received between the hours of twelve and three, and some of whom he visited at home. But Dr Chekhov really never stood a chance against Antosha Chekhonte, the best-selling author. Once he started writing for literary journals the numbers dropped – to the benefit of his writing, but to the detriment of his medical career. Even as a doctor, he had been attracted to the literary side of medicine, planning a doctoral dissertation first on the topic of sexual authority, and then on the history of medicine in Russia. His medical background was of inestimable value, of course, when he came to write about the penal colony on the Siberian island of Sakhalin, after his painstaking research into the living conditions of its inhabitants. And at the end of his life his medical training impelled him to do something for the numerous terminally ill people who migrated south to Yalta in the futile hope of finding a cure without any way of supporting themselves. Most people would agree that Chekhov paid the debt to science that he clearly felt he owed.

III

The Expanding Chest of Drawers

> Tatyana (with her Russian soul,
> herself not knowing why)
> loved the Russian winter
> with its cold beauty:
> hoar-frost in the sun on an icy day,
> sledges, and the pink glow
> Of snow in a late dawn.[37]

The semi-detached house that the Chekhovs moved into in the autumn of 1886 was situated on Moscow's Garden Ring Road, a very wide and rather quiet street which ran round the northern edge of the city and was lined with trees (like the inner boulevard parallel with it). Chekhov never lived in the most elegant part of Moscow, the 'white city' district located immediately west of the Kremlin, but the area where his new home was located was thoroughly respectable. Because of its unusual box-like shape, with four protruding front windows on two floors – somewhat untypical for Moscow – Chekhov referred to the new house as a chest of drawers, and he liked to quip about the liberal colour of its masonry (i.e. red, like the carpet on the stairs and the velvet-covered banister). There were trees surrounding the house and hedges growing behind its iron railings in the front garden.

Much had happened in Chekhov's life by the time he signed the lease for the Chest of Drawers in 1886. As a qualified doctor and an increasingly successful writer, he was now indisputably the chief breadwinner in the family, and he would continue to provide for his parents and his sister until the end of his life (Pavel Egorovich contributed a little from his warehouse job, where he still had his main lodgings, but when he retired four years later, at the age of sixty-five, he became totally dependent on his son). During the three and a half extraordinarily productive years that Chekhov lived in the house on Sadovaya-Kudrinskaya, he became nationally famous as a writer and playwright, and was acclaimed as a major star in Russia's literary firmament before he was thirty years old.

The relatively opulent surroundings in which the family now lived reflected Chekhov's changing fortunes. The new house was certainly the most well-appointed accommodation they had ever occupied; they had eight rooms at their disposal. Apart from Chekhov's book-lined study on the ground floor, there were rooms for the rest of the family and its retainers, and a spacious sitting room upstairs where Nikolai could play his favourite Chopin nocturnes on the rented piano. The various musician friends the family had acquired continued to take part in convivial soirées each week, and the Chest of Drawers now also began to attract figures from Moscow's literary and theatrical world. Tchaikovsky was one of the more illustrious visitors. He was another person who wrote Chekhov an unsolicited fan letter, having been bowled over by the musicality of his stories and their human warmth, and the admiration was mutual. On one occasion he came to pay a call, and the cigarettes he left behind were smoked by some of Chekhov's less illustrious visitors.

Increasing numbers of young ladies also paid calls to the house. Chekhov's sister Masha took a job teaching at a girls' *gymnasium*, and often brought home attractive female friends who would be eyed up by her brothers. This was particularly the case with Masha's colleague Lidia Mizinova, who first visited the house in 1889. While she waited shyly downstairs in the hall on her first visit, she came to the conclusion that Masha had lots of brothers, not realizing that Anton and Misha were going up and down the stairs repeatedly in order to look at the beautiful girl their sister had become friends with. Chekhov was no stranger to female company. He was tall and handsome and attracted strings of admirers throughout his life, but his flirtations rarely developed into serious relationships.

With the opening up of the archives in the last years of the Soviet regime, it has become possible to study previously censored passages of Chekhov's correspondence which confirm that he was by no means celibate before he fell in love with Olga Knipper at the end of his life. That much is suggested by various early stories in his output, such as one he wrote in 1888 (usually translated as 'An Attack of Nerves') about a student's violent reaction to visiting a brothel for the first time in Moscow's red-light district, near to where the Chekhov family had first made their home in the city. By the end of the twentieth century, Chekhov critics had largely removed the halo that Stalinist morality had rather effectively placed over his head in the 1930s, and shown a much earthier side to his personality. But revelations of encounters with prostitutes cannot disguise the fact that Chekhov mostly resisted the overtures of the women who became infatuated with him. He liked to keep his cards close to his chest where romantic feelings were concerned, and he liked to maintain self-control. In his memoirs, the director Vladimir Nemirovich-Danchenko recalls just one occasion when Chekhov dropped his guard and revealed that one married woman he had been pursuing had turned out to be a virgin – and even then he did not say whether their relationship was ever consummated.[38]

Misogyny is one way of explaining the reserve Chekhov maintained in his relationships with women, whose sexuality he appears to have seen as a threat to his creativity (misogyny is certainly present in his writing). The strong ethical code he developed is another. There was a brief, secret engagement with a young Russian-Jewish girl in early 1886, but no other serious involvement – although he came close on a number of occasions to yielding. Indeed, until he met Olga Knipper much later in his life and started exchanging letters with her, Chekhov's romantic life remained something of a mystery, at least where his feelings were concerned.

There were about six other women with whom he had relationships of varying intensity, and their much more demonstrative natures are clear from the letters they wrote to him. Of these, the first and most important of them was Lidia Mizinova. So adept was the writer at keeping his feelings hidden that his family, and most of his friends, were under the illusion that it was he who was more infatuated with her. Only after his death did it emerge that it had been the other way around. The beautiful Lidia, or Lika, as she was known, had ash-blonde hair and grey eyes (was she an inspiration for the grey-eyed Anna in 'The Lady with the Little Dog'?), and she was smart and funny. Chekhov was immediately attracted to her. As they became acquainted shortly before he set out on his epic trip to Siberia, it was some while before their relationship was able to develop, but Lika's name crops up several times in the letters he sent home. 'Tell Lika not to leave such large margins on her letters,' he wrote on one occasion to his family, slightly piqued that she had not written to him at all.[39]

It was perhaps fortunate that Chekhov had started his literary career working for low-grade comic journals, since the 1880s were generally a very bleak time for Russian belles-lettres, and this was one of the reasons why he felt compelled to seek a complete change of scene in 1890 and go to the other end of the world. The sweeping changes brought about in national life by the great reforms of the 1860s had initially given the intelligentsia hope that further democratization would follow. When these hopes were not fulfilled, its more radical members decided to take matters into their own hands and resort to violence. Tsar Alexander II was assassinated in March 1881. How Chekhov reacted to this event we do not know; he was not a political animal. But it was he who would later most vividly convey what it was like to live under a Tsar determined to preserve the status quo at all costs. Stories such as 'Ward No. 6' and 'The Man in a Case' stand as eloquent, albeit indirect, condemnations of Alexander III's reactionary policies. And dealing with censors was an unpleasant fact of life that even contributors to comic journals had to contend with. Russian intellectual and literary life was crippled by increased surveillance and various other restrictive measures during the 1880s. Working for comic journals did not attract so much attention from the authorities, but despondency settled on Russia's educated population like a cloud of fine dust, permeating everything, and affecting even as positive-thinking a person as Chekhov. With stories called 'Sorrow' and 'Misery', and his next two collections called *In the Twilight* and *Gloomy People*, it was not all that surprising that his readers began to label him as a pessimistic writer.

There was indeed a great deal to be depressed about in late nineteenth-century Russia, and all stemmed from the iniquities of the country's reactionary and autocratic method of government. The shortcomings of the Romanov regime were later highlighted by the tragedy which occurred on the day of Nicholas II's official coronation in the Kremlin in May 1896. Thousands of people had converged on Moscow to catch a glimpse of the Tsar, and the imperial family graciously decided to issue half a million token gifts to mark the occasion, plus some special prizes. Provision for their distribution was woefully inadequate, however, and in the stampede which followed about 2,000 patriotic Russian subjects were crushed to death. The brutality and indifference shown by the authorities following this tragic event was deeply shocking to Chekhov.

Against the atmosphere of hopelessness induced by the repressive regime, Moscow was nonetheless booming. The abolition of serfdom and the introduction of self-government in the early 1860s had changed the city's fortunes for ever. Moscow had seen an increase in population of only 60,000 in the thirty-four years between 1830 and 1864, but in the subsequent seven years its population grew by 238,000. If there were 602,000 people living in Moscow in 1871, there were 754,000 by 1882. Of this number, 555,000 (which includes the eight Chekhovs) were not born in the city.[40] Moscow had always been the economic centre of Russia, and this status was reinforced by the belated building of a national railway network. All the main railway lines converged on Moscow. Changes to the way the city was governed brought about a shift in power from the hands of the nobility to the people who engaged in trade – the merchants. Chekhov had thus moved to Moscow at one of the most dynamic periods of its history. The city had been a backwater for most of the nineteenth century, but the forces of capitalism were now taking over from the life of the old-world country estate, which had been financed by the serfs. Moscow's old merchant families shed their patriarchal image and became railway tycoons and factory magnates, investing their new wealth in hospitals, museums and theatres. The city's appearance began to change towards the end of the nineteenth century, but it was not until the 1890s that the building of wooden houses was banned for the first time.

In the 1880s the Moscow that Chekhov inhabited still felt like a big village to people from St Petersburg. After the great fire of 1812, the goal had been to rebuild Moscow as quickly as possible, and this had resulted in the sharp contrasts of the old and new city. A few streets away from modern department stores lit by electricity were Asian-style bazaars with vendors selling pies; elegant, colonnaded classical mansions stood next to minuscule wooden houses painted yellow; alongside modern municipal buildings were mediaeval churches with cupolas covered in gold stars, and bustling European boulevards led to winding lanes that seemed not to have changed for centuries. This irregularity was reflected in the diversity of the population thronging Moscow's streets: men and women smartly dressed in the latest European fashions jostled with long-haired, bearded priests in tall black hats; merchant wives in coloured headscarves and strings of pearls and peasants in shabby sheepskins mingled with an assortment of Tatars, Georgians and Armenians, who came from the further reaches of the empire to trade.

Moscow would always seem both more deeply Russian and more Oriental than St Petersburg, and it was precisely these qualities that made Chekhov so attached to the city. He loved its undulating tree-lined streets, the buzz of its restaurants and theatres, and he loved the fact that there was a church on almost every street corner. Most of all he loved the sound of the bells rung in the 450 belfries all over the city, particularly during winter when there was snow on the ground. No other city in the world could match it. When the first snow fell each winter, Chekhov was always reminded of Pushkin's magical lines from the beginning of chapter five in *Eugene Onegin*. Indeed, sitting at his desk one morning in early November 1889, he wrote in a letter that on seeing snow for the first time he felt the same thrill as Pushkin's Tatyana, and regretted that his Petersburg correspondent was not there to see it with him.[41] In a more-or-less word for word translation, the verse which Chekhov refers to reads:

> . . .Waking in the early morning,
> Tatyana looked outside and saw
> white courtyards, flowerbeds,
> roofs and fences,
> light patterns on the windowpanes,
> the trees all clothed in wintry silver,
> cheerful magpies,
> and a dazzling winter carpet
> softly covering the hills.
> All around was brilliant white.

By the time of that snowy November morning, Chekhov had been living in the Chest of Drawers for three years. He had worked prodigiously hard during that time, and described his regime as that of a government functionary. Typically, he would write from nine to lunchtime, receive patients between twelve and three, then pick up his pen again from evening tea until bedtime – but often those hours were extended, and not just because Chekhov particularly liked to work by candlelight. So housebound did he become on occasion that his mother and his aunt took to referring to him as an old grandfather.[42] In September 1888, he declared to one friend that he had barely been out of the house for ten days, and his fingers were sore from writing.[43] In the past twelve months he had not only written 'The Steppe', his first story for a literary journal (a work of novella length), as well as various other pieces of fiction, but a full-length play called *Ivanov*, and a one-act farce.

It was with *Ivanov* that Chekhov made his extremely noisy stage debut in November 1887. Everything about his literary career had been iconoclastic so far, beginning with the unassuming way it had started. If 'The Steppe' challenged prevailing notions about prose fiction, *Ivanov* was a play which seemed to turn every stage convention on its head. There was so much that was theatrical about Russian culture that it took a very long time for actors and audiences to acclimatize to the innovations of Chekhovian drama. Theatre was at the heart of the Russian Orthodox religion, and it was the elaborate rituals of its services – its icon processions, incense-burning, bell-ringing, the lighting of candles, the opening and closing of doors and endless genuflections – to which Chekhov's father was particularly attached. And this is precisely what Chekhov rebelled against in his last four plays. The source of his heresy may perhaps be found in the pomp and splendour he had to endure as a child when he and his brothers were forced by their father to sing in church choirs in Taganrog. Chekhovian theatricality, with its unvoiced emotions, silences, and muted climaxes is the antithesis of the drama enacted annually during the Orthodox Church's magnificent long Easter services, in which the clergy in ornate vestments process outside and around the church, carrying the Cross, the Gospel and icons, followed by the congregration. But as with his religious faith, so with the theatre. Chekhov rejected the externals and the dogma, but retained the essence. In their seamless flow, their symbolism, their stylization and their rhythms, Chekhov's plays in fact emulate the synthetic aesthetic structure of the Russian Orthodox liturgy, in which everything is interconnected and subordinate to a common goal. If there is something of the Wagnerian 'endless melody' in Chekhov's plays, which requires them to be performed almost like orchestral scores (and 'conducted' by a director), it is a quality shared by the Russian liturgy, which was explicitly likened to a 'music drama' by the great twentieth-century theologian Father Pavel Florensky. In their unconventional movement towards catharsis, Chekhov's plays, like his stories, can also be termed 'religious'. Chekhov was as much concerned with the question of how one should live as were Dostoevsky and Tolstoy, after all; he just found a more economic way of posing it.

It certainly took a while for Chekhov to distil his raw material into the concentrated form of his last plays. His earliest writing for the stage, like some of his early prose, was melodramatic, emotional and very prolix: the four long acts of his earliest play, *Platonov*, written in the early 1880s, are full of histrionics. *Ivanov*, his next full-length play, and the first to be staged, is a kind of halfway house. But it was already unconventional, and followed his stories in packing an unexpected punch at the end. As he wrote to his brother Alexander in October 1887:

Contemporary dramatists fill their plays exclusively with angels, scoundrels and jesters – but you just try and find those sorts of people anywhere in Russia! You might possibly find some, but they won't be as extreme as dramatists require. I wanted to do something original: I

haven't produced a single scoundrel or a single angel (although I couldn't
resist jesters), I have not condemned anybody, I have not vindicated
anybody . . .[44]

Ivanov was written to commission, for Russia's first proper
independent theatre. It opened in Moscow after Alexander III
succumbed to the inevitable and abolished the Imperial Theatres
monopoly on 24 March 1882. Before that date, privately run
commercial theatres were simply banned in St Petersburg and Moscow.
The Tsarist government aimed to control every aspect of Russian life,
from the production and consumption of vodka to the plays and operas
staged in its two main cities, perceiving almost that the very idea of a
theatre run by its subjects was politically subversive. The Imperial
Theatres Directorate was like any other government ministry, full of
bureaucrats and pen-pushers pursuing a highly conservative
programme. Actors also became state employees. If serfdom had held
back Russian society from entering the modern world, the ossified
routines of the Imperial Theatres prevented Russian drama from
becoming a vibrant art form. Censorship was not abolished along with
the monopoly, of course, but it was a start. Fyodor Korsh, a trained
lawyer, had a theatre up and running in central Moscow just six months
later. That brought the number of drama theatres in Moscow to a grand
total of two (a third theatre, which established itself in the 1880s,
devoted itself to vaudeville and cheap spectacle). Along with the
Bolshoi (grand) Theatre, Moscow's home for opera and ballet, the
Imperial Theatres continued to run the Maly (little) Theatre next door,
where classical Russian drama remained the staple fare. The Maly
staged about 180 performances each season: now it had to contend
with a competitor. Korsh had his work cut out, since most of the
700,000-strong population in Moscow had not yet acquired the habit
of going to the theatre. The Imperial Theatres never had to worry about
shortfalls in their budget, but Korsh had to make a profit in order to
survive.

Because theatre was still such an elitist pursuit in the 1880s, Korsh
almost bankrupted himself in the early years, despite the fact that he
had no permanent troupe on the payroll. But in 1885 he took over a
splendid new theatre, built in the pseudo-Russian style, and began to
hold his own. His next shrewd move was to commission the 27-year-old

Chekhov to write a play. This did not come about because of Korsh's artistic judgement, which was not particularly refined, but because he wanted humorous plays in his repertoire. At this point Chekhov still enjoyed a reputation as a comic writer, and when he started criticizing Korsh's latest flimsy production, he was challenged to do better. The budding playright's enthusiasm for the project can be gauged from the fact that he wrote it in ten days flat at the end of September 1887, having hung a notice on his door saying 'very busy'. On 9 October the Petersburg newspaper *New Times* reported that Chekhov had written a four-act comedy; on 2 November the play was submitted to the censor, and on 19 November it was performed in public after only four rehearsals.

Because there were only two theatres producing serious drama in Moscow, a first night was a major event. Every member of the small world which made up the literary and theatrical intelligentsia in Moscow wanted to see Chekhov's play, particularly when they discovered that Vladimir Davydov, Russia's most distinguished actor, was going to play the lead. The three performances of *Ivanov* did not deliver what the audiences were expecting (a lightweight comedy) and they caused a furore. Here was a play which seemed to be subverting conventions at the same time as it was

The Korsh Theatre, Moscow, where Ivanov *premiered in 1887*

pandering to them. Even friends like Levitan and Shekhtel were confounded, and Chekhov's sister almost fell into a faint. One cantankerous writer reported to Nikolai Leikin in Petersburg that he could not understand why such 'terrible rubbish' was called a comedy, since the main character was a complete scoundrel, and, furthermore, the author seemed to sympathize with him: how outrageous![45] Russian actors and Russian audiences were not used to ambiguity in their theatrical productions. Decades of conventional stagings at the Imperial Theatres had led to a situation where roles, costumes and sets were all clear-cut and very predictable. It was fine when Chekhov then went on to write the one-act farces that were to prove huge money-spinners for him (his next play for the Korsh Theatre was *The Bear*, which became a runaway success from its first performance on 26 October 1888), but the Russian public needed to be initiated before it could appreciate the audacious novelty of Chekhovian drama. Against this background, the innovations introduced later by the Moscow Art Theatre seem all the more remarkable.

The year 1888 had been an *annus mirabilis* for Chekhov. A few months after his official literary debut with 'The Steppe' that March, the second edition of his third short story collection appeared, having been published the previous summer: in October *In the Twilight* went on to be awarded the Pushkin Prize by the Academy of Sciences. His popularity as a playwright was also left in no doubt when *The Bear* was given its Moscow premiere that same month. Chekhov seemed unstoppable. When a revised version of *Ivanov* was staged with great success by the Imperial Theatres in St Petersburg a few months later, it seemed that 1889 was also going to be a good year. In truth, everything had begun to unravel for Chekhov, much as it did for the central character in his most important work of fiction that year, a work misleadingly entitled in English translation 'A Boring Story'. The word *skuchno* does indeed imply boredom, but it also variously implies sadness, desolation, gloom, despondency, yearning . . . all of which Chekhov experienced in 1889 as his brother Nikolai grew seriously ill and then died. Chekhov had started a new full-length drama entitled *The Wood Demon*, and bravely managed to complete it at the end of the year. After it had been rejected by the Imperial Theatres, it was finally staged at the very end of December by a small commercial theatre in Moscow, but it was massacred in the press. Chekhov was deeply stung, and five years would pass before he sat down to write another play. Only after he had written *The Seagull* did he start work on revising *The Wood Demon*: the result was *Uncle Vanya*.

The vicissitudes of 1889 plunged Chekhov into a deep malaise that ultimately galvanized him into taking some drastic action. By conceiving the idea of travelling across Siberia to study the penal colony on the remote island of Sakhalin, he would at once satisfy his thirst for adventure and fulfil his vision of carrying out work that would be of some practical benefit to humanity. A few months after the fiasco of *The Wood Demon*, the weeks before his departure were full of activity as he carried out research and made preparations for the journey. He was thus already mentally elsewhere when he read a derogatory reference to him in *Russian Thought* just before he left. *Russian Thought* was the only serious literary journal in Moscow, and enjoyed a reputation as a bastion of liberalism. It could also be very dogmatic and self-righteous, however, and took exception to Chekhov's lack of overt ideological commitment in his writing. Such petty-minded carping was precisely what had plunged Chekhov into gloom in the first place, and made him want to escape. Incensed, he fired off a furious letter to its publisher. It was one of the most powerful letters he ever wrote in his life, its length alone speaking volumes about how closely he took to heart such aspersions on his character:

On page 147 in the book review section of the March edition of *Russian Thought*, I came across the following phrase: 'As recently as yesterday, even the High Priests of unprincipled writing such as Messrs Yasinsky and Chekhov, whose names . . .' etc., etc. I appreciate that it is not usually done to respond to criticism, but this is not criticism, it is libel, pure and simple. I might have been inclined to pass over even libel, but since I shall be leaving Russia in a few days' time, perhaps never to return, I could not leave this calumny unanswered.

I have never been an unprincipled writer, nor – what amounts to the same thing – a scoundrel.

It is true that my entire literary career has consisted of an unbroken series of mistakes, sometimes grievous ones, but the explanation for this lies in the limitations of my talent and has nothing whatsoever to do with whether I am a good or a bad person. I have never blackmailed anyone, nor have I ever libelled or denounced anyone. I have eschewed flattery,

lies and insults. In short, while there are many of my stories and leading
articles I should be happy to throw out as worthless, I am not now
ashamed of a single line. I must assume that by 'unprincipled' you are
referring to the sad fact that I, an educated man whose work is often seen
in print, have done nothing for those I love; my activities have left no
trace on, for example, the zemstvo, the new law courts, the freedom of
the press, freedom in general, and so on. If such is indeed the case, then
I can only say that *Russian Thought* ought to regard me as a comrade in
arms rather than the butt of its accusations, since in these respects it has
done no more than I have. And that is the fault of neither of us.

Even when judged objectively as a writer, I do not deserve to be
accused publicly of lack of principle. Hitherto I have led a sheltered life
within four walls; you and I meet one another no more than once every
two years or so, and I have never in my life come across Mr Machtet.
You may judge from this how seldom I leave my house; I studiously avoid
literary soirées, parties, conferences and so on. I have never visited any
editorial office uninvited, and have taken pains to ensure that my friends
should see me more as a doctor than as a writer. In short, I have always
conducted myself with discretion in writing circles, and my present letter
is the first piece of immodesty I have ever perpetrated in ten years of
writing activity. I am on excellent terms with my colleagues; I have never
presumed to sit in judgement either on them or on the magazines and
newspapers for which they write, since I do not consider myself
competent to do so. Moreover, I believe that in the present subservient
position of the press, any word uttered against a journal or a writer can
be seen not only as an unkind and insensitive attack but as actually
criminal. Up till now, the only magazines and newspapers to which I
decline to contribute have been those whose manifestly inferior quality
is obvious to all, but when I have been obliged to choose between one
publication or another, my custom has been to favour those who most
needed my services for material or other reasons. This is the reason I
have always worked for the *Northern Herald* rather than for your paper
or for the *Herald of Europe*, and it is also why I have earned no more
than half what I could have had I taken a different view of my
obligations.

The accusation you have levelled at me is nothing short of libellous.
There is no point in asking you to retract it, since it has already been
exposed in all its malign force and cannot now be simply chopped out

with an axe. Neither can I excuse it as a careless or irresponsible lapse, because I am quite aware that your editorial office consists of unimpeachably decent and civilized people who, I trust, do not simply write and read articles but take responsibility for every word in them. The only recourse I have is to ensure you are not left in ignorance of the error, and at the same time to ask you to believe in the genuinely heavy heart with which I am writing this letter. It is self-evident that your attack on me makes it impossible to contemplate even conventional social intercourse between us, still less any professional relations.

A. Chekhov[46]

Thus ended the second period of Chekhov's Moscow life.

Chapter 4

SUMMERS AT THE DACHA

I

New Jerusalem

With the countryside all around looking so meek and pensive, Ivan
Ivanych and Burkin were filled with love for the landscape in this
subdued weather, and both were thinking how magnificent and
beautiful their country was.

'Gooseberries'

At the beginning of May, the weather in Moscow can suddenly change.
Fur coats have to be hurriedly exchanged for short-sleeved shirts and
people start coming out on the streets again, blinking in the bright
sunshine. Central Russia's continental climate means that the transition
from winter to spring can be extremely abrupt. As soon as it becomes
warm, Muscovites start longing to go to their dachas. On cue, Russian
newspapers begin publishing advice columns on gardening matters, and
the main arteries into Moscow become clogged on Sunday evenings
with big jeeps creating new lanes on the hard shoulders in order to
circumnavigate the tailbacks, terrorizing into submission the uninsured
little Soviet-made cars with their trays of eggs on the back ledge. During
the six months of the 'dacha season' all the big Russian cities empty at
weekends, and virtually shut down for the whole of July and August as
everyone heads for the country to escape the sultry heat of the
metropolis. Since most dachas still have no central heating, the dacha
season is brought to a natural end with the first snowfalls.

The rhythms of Russian life have not changed much since Chekhov's
lifetime. He too was an enthusiastic 'dachnik', and no study of his life
and work can really be complete without an appreciation of the role
played by the summers he spent with his family at dachas in the Russian

and Ukrainian countryside; references to dachas and dachniks fill his stories and plays from beginning to end, and the wistful green landscapes he looked out on from his dacha (he always placed his desk in front of a window) inspired some of his finest writing.

Deeply enshrined in the Russian psyche, the concept of the dacha is a phenomenon that really has no equal in any other culture. In *The Cherry Orchard*, the nouveau riche businessman Lopakhin implores the old-world landowner Madame Ranevskaya that she should forgo the pleasures of fragrant white blossom every spring and let out her land as dacha plots so that she can pay off the debts that threaten to engulf her. 'Dachas and dachniks – forgive me but that's so vulgar,' Ranevskaya replies, encapsulating the Russian nobility's traditional feelings of contempt for middle-class aspirations to country living. Exactly a hundred years later, the last mohicans of the intelligentsia (the modern-day equivalent of the pre-revolutionary aristocracy) are similarly scornful of the pretensions of today's nouveau riche Russian who prefers to call his dacha a *kottedzh* (cottage), even though it will probably be a vast marble-clad gothic pile protected by security fences and leather-jacketed heavies at the gate. *The Cherry Orchard* is set in early twentieth-century Russia, but it is also entirely prophetic of early twenty-first-century Russia. Ranevskaya's beloved cherry orchard is unequivocally beautiful but it no longer fulfils any useful function; the artistic and intellectual heritage of the intelligentsia is similarly a thing of great beauty, but one that no longer seems to be needed by anybody in the fast new commercial world of contemporary Russia where the businessman is king. This is just one of the many ways in which Chekhov's work proves its timelessness.

The Russian country cottage has certainly undergone a significant evolution since its beginnings as a simple gift of land bestowed by the state (the word 'dacha' comes from the verb 'to give').[1] Anxious to consolidate St Petersburg as a conurbation, Peter the Great forced his nobles to build second houses on the plots of land he gave them just outside the city. Throughout the eighteenth century the dacha was thus the preserve of Russia's social elite – a fashionable villa used for socializing in the summer months, and quite distinct from one's city mansion or hereditary manorial estate deep in the Russian heartlands. As the urban populations of St Petersburg and Moscow grew, however, Russian subjects of all backgrounds began to yearn for pastoral holiday retreats, and the nineteenth century saw a proliferation of residences of all shapes and sizes outside the city, often in purpose-built dacha colonies (which are still popular today). With the belated expansion of Russia's railways at the end of the nineteenth century, it became possible to venture further afield, and the burgeoning middle class began to ape the fabled lifestyle of Russian aristocratic landowners (such as Chekhov's Ranevskaya) whose fortunes were then going into terminal decline. Chekhov was part of this burgeoning middle class, as he himself was only too well aware. It was while mingling with well-to-do dachniks in the Moscow countryside during his final years as a medical student that he first successfully effected the transition from meshchanin to *intelligent*.

If the southern Russian steppe takes pride of place in the hierarchy of Chekhov's sources of lyrical inspiration, the countryside around Moscow comes a close second. It is well known that he pined for Russia during his long years of exile in the Crimea, where he was surrounded by sea and mountains and lush sub-tropical vegetation: the walls of his Yalta home are pointedly lined with pictures of homely plains, green meadows and quiet rivers, most of them painted by his sister Maria or his friend the landscape painter Isaak Levitan. In a prominent position in the alcove in Chekhov's study, above the sofa he used to recline on when friends came to visit, is Levitan's canvas of a tranquil river winding through meadows with a forest in the distance. 'The River Istra' was painted in 1885, and undoubtedly served as the source of many nostalgic memories of the happy times Chekhov had spent with Levitan that summer when they were both staying at dachas nearby. When Levitan learned during his visit in December 1899 that Chekhov missed the gently undulating landscape of Central Russia, he immediately got out his palette and painted a nocturnal scene of haystacks in a field on a piece of card, which was then fitted into the recess in the fireplace across from his friend's desk.

As a young man, Chekhov spent many summers near the banks of the Istra, a tributary of the Moscow River. In 1880, when he was in his second year as a medical student, his brother Ivan obtained a job as the teacher at the village school in Voskresensk, a small town about thirty-five miles west of Moscow.[2] Tsurikov, the wealthy factory owner who was the school's governor, generously provided Ivan with spacious living quarters, which meant that the impoverished Chekhov family suddenly had a dacha to go to in the summer months. According to Misha, the youngest member of the family, it was 'earthly paradise' after the cramped and squalid accommodation they had in Moscow.[3] Chekhov came for visits in the early 1880s, and made useful contacts in the local medical fraternity, who gave him some useful work experience before he graduated, but he was initially kept busy during the summer vacation by writing for Moscow journals, which provided his family with some badly needed income. It was only in 1884, the year that he graduated, that Chekhov started coming to Voskresensk for several months at a time. He went fishing for hours in the mornings and cut a dash in his black cape and broad-brimmed hat in the evenings during leisurely walks with other local doctors, the friendly officers of a battalion stationed nearby, and other interesting representatives of the Moscow intelligentsia on vacation.[4]

Just as the identikit nineteenth-century Russian country estate always contained certain key ingredients – a classical-style house with columns and a mezzanine, an annexe (always known by the German word *Flügel*), a path lined with linden trees, a landscaped 'English' park and a lake – there were also certain requirements for the ideal dacha. Apart from beautiful scenery, dachniks like Chekhov sought forests to hunt for mushrooms, and a river or a pond in which to fish and contemplate nature. Voskresensk provided ample opportunity for Chekhov to indulge these enthusiasms. It also boasted a magnificent monastery, located high on the banks of the Istra. He went there often, and particularly revelled in what he called the 'velvety' sound of its bells, which carried for miles across the fields.[5]

The New Jerusalem Monastery was founded in the mid-seventeenth century by the controversial Patriarch of Moscow, Nikon, whose liturgical reforms were to lead to the far-reaching schism of the Russian church. To save Russian pilgrims the bother of having to travel all the way to Palestine, Nikon created an exact replica of the Church of the Holy Sepulchre in Jerusalem in the monastery's cavernous Cathedral of the Resurrection, the *Voskresenskii sobor*, but it burned down in 1726. The cathedral that Chekhov visited was the Baroque replacement, designed by Rastrelli and built in the 1750s with funds provided by a munificent ancestor of Ivan Chekhov's employer Tsurikov.[6] 'I'm residing in New Jerusalem and visiting the monks,' Chekhov wrote to his publisher and main correspondent Nikolai Leikin in May 1883.[7] The following summer he went back to visit the monks and spent over two months in Voskresensk. He clearly found attending the ornate Easter

The New Jerusalem Monastery, Moscow region

services the monastery held on Sundays an inspiring experience. 'I am living in New Jerusalem now', he wrote to Leikin in June 1884; 'and I'm living with aplomb because I can feel my doctor's licence in my pocket. The countryside around here is gorgeous. Open spaces and a complete absence of dachniks. Mushrooms, fishing and the local infirmary. The monastery is poetic. I've been thinking of subjects for "sweet sounds" while standing through Vespers in the shadows of the galleries and arches. I've got lots of ideas but I am really not in the right frame of mind to write . . .'[8] A year later Chekhov was still inspired:

I have put traps in the river and keep taking them out of the water because I am so impatient . . . I don't have words to describe the landscape around here. If you are in Moscow in the summer and come to New Jerusalem on a pilgrimage, I can promise you something the likes of which you have never seen anywhere else . . . The landscape is luxurious! I could pick it up and eat it . . .[9]

The inspiration was to bear fruit some years later in stories like 'The Princess' (written in 1889), in which Chekhov unleashed the full force of his satire against the genteel but self-serving lady visitors who liked to pay frequent summer visits to monasteries such as New Jerusalem, mistakenly thinking they were welcome guests.

There was another monastery nearby that Chekhov also liked to visit: the much older Savvin-Storozhevsky Monastery, founded at the end of the fourteenth century on the bank of the Moscow River in Zvenigorod. In the summer of 1883, Chekhov and some of his brothers joined a group of young doctors and walked the fifteen miles or so there from Voskresensk in a day, thus reversing the direction of the famous icon procession held annually each summer. The following July, just after graduating, Chekhov spent a couple of weeks working as a locum for the local doctor in Zvenigorod. He lived in the doctor's house. 'Half the day is taken up with seeing patients (30 to 40 people a day),' he wrote to Leikin, 'and I spend the rest of the time resting or getting dreadfully bored sitting by the window looking out at the gloomy sky which for three days now has been pouring down horrible endless rain . . . In front of my window there is a hill with pine trees; to the right is the police chief's house, further to the right there is a rotten little town which was once a place of some importance . . . On the left I can see a run-down rampart wall, then a little wood and St Savva peering out of it.'[10] In the evening he often visited the local medical assistant, whose daughter later recalled him sloping off into the garden to sit with a book under a lime tree that in 1954 acquired a memorial plaque.[11]

In 1885, the Chekhov family spent their first summer at a proper dacha – rented from the charming Kiselyov family whose estate lay on the banks of the Istra, just up the road from New Jerusalem. Ivan had been given a lift home in Alexei Kiselyov's troika after a winter party and the Chekhovs had become friends with him and his wife, Maria. Early the following May the Chekhov family took up residence in an annexe on the Kiselyovs' estate at Babkino. Chekhov led the advance party with his mother and sister. 'I've rented a dacha already furnished, with vegetables, milk etc.,' Chekhov wrote dreamily to Leikin just before he left, filling his letter with rows of pensive dots, and going on to describe the scene that Levitan would paint later that summer:

> ... the estate is very beautiful, it stands on a steep bank ... The river is down below, full of fish, beyond the river is an enormous forest and there is also a forest on the other side of the river ... There are greenhouses near the dacha, flowerbeds and the like ... I love being in the countryside in the beginning of May ... It's fun to watch the leaves coming out, and hear the nightingales begin to sing ... There is no one living anywhere near the estate and so we will be quite alone ... [12]

A few days later, at six in the morning, he was sitting in front of the large square window of his room at Babkino, at the sewing machine table he used as a makeshift desk, writing a letter to his brother Misha who was still stuck in Moscow. As well as telling him about the dreadful journey from the station (there was no train to Voskresensk at that point – the journey to Babkino entailed taking a train a few stops along the main line to St Petersburg and then travelling along bumpy roads by cart before finally crossing the river), and about running into Levitan, who had come to stay at a dacha on the other side of the Istra, he gave his brother a detailed account of the state of the fishing in the area. Like Misha,

Zvenigorod, near Moscow

Chekhov took his fishing seriously. He had not had much luck with a rod so far, he explained; all he had caught apart from some ruff and gudgeon was a chub. As members of the minnow family, these fish are small anyway, but this particular specimen had been so small, Chekhov said, that it was really only ready to start going to school, rather than the frying pan. He had enjoyed better luck with the special tackle designed for catching perch, and with his fish traps. Quite how seriously Chekhov took his fishing can be gauged from the fact that he had been up at three-thirty that morning to inspect the traps he had set up the day before with Vanya Babakin, a local boy who went to the school where his brother taught, and who had been doing odd jobs for the Chekhov family during the summer months for the last couple of years:

> As for my traps! It turned out they were easy to bring. They didn't get squashed in the luggage and they got tied to the back of the cart . . . One is in the river now. It's already caught a roach and an absolutely huge perch. The perch is so enormous that Kiselyov is going to come and have lunch with us today. The other trap was in the pond to begin with, but it did not catch anything there. Now it's behind the pond in the feeder stream otherwise it will be put in a stretch of the river; yesterday it caught a perch and earlier this morning Babakin and I pulled *twenty-nine* carp out of it. What do you think about that? Today we are going to have fish soup, baked fish and fish in aspic . . . So bring two or three traps with you. You can get them in the fish shops by the Moskvoretsky Bridge. I paid 30 kopecks for mine, but you should be able to pay between 20 and 25. Take them home in a cab, of course.[13]

It is not surprising that Chekhov found it hard to write the satirical pieces on Moscow life his editor Leikin was clamouring for during the summer months, and he was glad to be given a temporary reprieve. 'Writing articles when you can go fishing and loaf about is awfully hard,' he wrote to Leikin in July 1885, 'and the fishing really is splendid. The river is right in front of my window – 20 feet away . . . You can fish with whatever is to hand – rods, traps, pike tackle . . . This morning I pulled out a pike from one trap which was as big as Albov's story [about fish], which to be honest is as heavy and indigestible as beluga soup. Not far from me there is a deep (16 foot) pool with an absolutely huge number of fish in it . . .'[14] Leikin was a keen fisherman too; in May 1883, he had given Chekhov a copy of his book *Carps and Pikes*, which had just been published in St Petersburg.[15] Chekhov used to say that he liked fishing because it was an occupation that did not get in anyone's way and did not require him to think. He was also very good at it, and could tell just by looking at a river what kind of fish it would contain. One young companion, who fished for perch with him from early morning until late evening in the summer of 1902, remarked that Chekhov's catch was always bigger than his, even though they sat next to each other.[16]

It was, of course, no coincidence that when Chekhov did start writing stories while at his dacha in the summer of 1885, many of them had a connection with fishing. Sitting for hours on the river bank,

ЩУКА
Esox lucius L.
(pike)

НАЛИМ
Lota lota Z.
(burbot)

ГОЛАВЛЬ
Leuciscus cephalus L.
(chub)

ЛИНЬ
Tinca tinca L.
(tench)

КАРАСЬ
Carassius carassius L.
(crucian carp)

ОКУНЬ
Perca fluvitilis L.
(perch)

Illustrations of the fish Chekhov used to catch,
from Sabaneev's Fishes of Russia

sometimes in the company of Vanya or his brothers, and sometimes in the company of Levitan, who painted while he fished, he certainly had plenty of time to think up new stories. Back in August 1883 he had published a story called 'The Daughter of Albion', which famously depicts a coarse landowner fishing with the English governess while his wife and children have gone out for the day:

> Gryabov, a large fat man with a very big head, was sitting cross-legged like a Turk on the sand, fishing. His hat was sitting on the back of his head and his tie was askew. Next to him stood a tall thin Englishwoman with bulging goggle eyes and a large birdlike nose, which looked more like a hook than a nose. She was dressed in a white muslin dress, through which scrawny yellow shoulders protruded. A gold watch hung from a gold chain round her waist. She was also fishing. Both were as still as the river on which their floats bobbed.[17]

When another landowner comes down to the river to find Gryabov, he is amazed by the latter's rude treatment of the supercilious governess, who appears not to speak a word of Russian. He is further shocked when Gryabov strips naked in front of the governess in order to go and detach his fishing hook, which has caught on a rock at the bottom of the river. Apparently, there actually was a red-haired English girl, called Miss Matthews, who went fishing at Babkino, having accompanied her employers on a visit to the estate; Misha Chekhov thought this story had all the hallmarks of the locality.[18]

In July 1885, when Chekhov took to spending days on end fishing, he thought up a story, called 'The Burbot', in which two increasingly cross carpenters who are building a bathing hut by the river try vainly to catch a burbot which has hidden among the roots of a willow. There were apparently a couple of carpenters building a bathing hut in Babkino too.[19] Then there was the famous comic story 'The Malefactor' (July 1885), about a slow-witted peasant who fails to see why it might be dangerous to remove the odd screw from railway sleepers to use as sinkers for his fishing rod, and cannot understand why he has been arrested.[20]

Taking pity on unfortunate dacha dwellers sitting interminably with a line and a worm at the end of their fishing rods, Chekhov also composed a 'dense treatise' on fishing in June 1885, explaining to his readers that it had been assembled in numbered paragraphs to make it seem more serious and scholarly:

> 1. You can fish in oceans, seas, lakes, rivers, ponds, and around Moscow also in puddles and ditches.
>
> *Note*: You can catch the biggest fish at a fishmonger's.
>
> 2. You must fish away from populated places, otherwise you risk catching a young lady *dachnik* out bathing by her foot or hearing the phrase: 'Do you have a licence to fish here? Or were you looking for a bruising?'
>
> 3. Before casting your rod, you must put a bait on the hook – whatever suits the kind of fish . . . Actually you can fish without bait because you're not going to catch anything anyway.
>
> *Note:* Pretty young lady dachniks sitting on the bank with a rod in order to attract husbands-to-be can fish without bait. Those who aren't pretty must use bait: one or two hundred thousand or something like that . . .

Chekhov also provided his readers with thumbnail portraits of the eleven most common types of fish to be found in the environs of Moscow. These included pike ('Eats everything in sight: fish, crayfish, frogs, ducks, children . . .'), perch ('The males are entrepreneurs but the females give concerts'), carp ('Sits in slime half-asleep, waiting to be eaten by a pike') and tench ('Lazy, slobbering, inert fish in a dark green uniform, who will be awarded a pension for its years of service').[21] Chekhov's characterizations correspond remarkably well with Leonid Sabaneev's classic *Fishes of Russia: The Life and Fishing of Freshwater Fish*, whose revised second edition was published in Moscow in two volumes in 1882. An unparalleled work of Russian ichthyology yet to be superseded, it is still regularly republished, and Chekhov undoubtedly acquired much of his knowledge of freshwater fishing from having pored over Sabaneev's lively and highly personal biographies of each species, complete with delicate line drawings of not only the fish, but also the different kinds of tackle to use in catching them. A few extracts from Sabaneev's voluminous chapter on the pike, the *shchuka*, will probably suffice to convey the flavour of this unique work:

> Pikes can undoubtedly live for several hundred years. When they were cleaning the Tsaritsyno ponds near Moscow at the end of the last century

a 2-metre long pike was found with a gold ring which had the inscription 'introduced by Tsar Boris Fyodorovich [Godunov]' . . . As well as fish, the pike does not spare any living creature, and there is no limit to its greed: during the so-called feeding frenzies, when it is most hungry, the pike attacks large birds like geese which it, of course, cannot get the better of, and also fish of the same size. Vavilov has recorded that a pike once caught a goose by its leg and would not unclench its jaw even when it had been pulled on to the bank . . . I personally have often watched an enormous number of these predators catching large and small sandpipers . . . At first I could not understand what to attribute the mournful squeaks and sudden disappearance of the birds to, but then realized it was pikes up to their tricks . . .[22]

Sabaneev's vivid evocations of the lives of fish probably further stimulated Chekhov's imagination as he sat on the bank of the Istra on those hot summer days: fish imagery even permeates the stories not about fishing. In June 1885, for example, he wrote a story with a character called Nastasya Lvovna who is 'a plump young blonde with a protruding lower jaw and bulging eyes, exactly like a young pike'.[23]

To Leonid Sabaneev belongs the honour of being the first person to publish something by Chekhov under the writer's own name. In the summer of 1883 Chekhov had written a story, set in Voskresensk, about a peasant who narrowly escapes punishment from a local landowner for shooting a starling on his land – and, moreover, doing so before St Peter's Day (29 June) when shooting was still legally forbidden.[24] 'He Understood', which was actually finished on St Peter's Day,[25] was too long to be published in the comic journals which were still Chekhov's regular outlets at this time, so he submitted it to the monthly journal *Nature and Hunting*, which Sabaneev edited. Having published a wide array of scholarly articles on topics such as the fauna of the Central Urals and the birds of the Moscow region, Sabaneev had begun publishing *Nature* at his own expense in 1873, and then joined forces with the *Journal of the Imperial Hunting Society* in 1878. The combined journal was still run on a shoestring, however, so Chekhov had to agree to waive his honorarium when Sabaneev wrote back an enthusiastic letter of acceptance in October 1883.[26]

As two people with an unusually deep concern for the natural environment, Chekhov and Sabaneev ought to have had much to talk about when they met at the end of 1883. In 1876, with a view to protecting Russia's fauna and maintaining an ecological equilibrium, Sabaneev had conducted the first-ever national survey of hunting. He ascertained that the increase in the population of predatory animals posed a serious threat to the game traditionally hunted in Russia, a problem exacerbated by the overall decline in hunting with hounds across the country. Sabaneev had earlier written about the culling of predatory animals, particularly wolves,[27] out of concern for protecting the traditional livelihoods of peasants in rural areas. But he certainly did not advocate the barbaric methods employed in Moscow in January 1882, when packs of graceful borzois (traditional Russian wolfhounds) were loosed on wolves released from boxes in front of an audience of cheering spectators in the city's horse-racing arena. Chekhov was there, reporting on the event for a Moscow journal. He was horrified by what he saw:

> The wolf falls, taking with it to the grave a poor opinion of human beings . . . It's no joke, man has brought shame on himself by this quasi-hunt! . . . It's one thing hunting in the steppe, in the forest, where human bloodthirstiness can easily be excused by the possibility of an equal battle, where the wolf can defend itself and run . . .[28]

Chekhov was not by any means an implacable opponent of hunting – 'St Peter's Day', a comic skit about an unruly shooting party, which was the twelfth story he published (in June 1881),[29] was 'dedicated with pleasure to gentlemen hunters who are either bad at shooting or cannot shoot'.[30] All the same, he himself was never as keen on shooting as his friend Levitan. It would be some time before he fully formulated his own environmental philosophy (he had, after all, just turned twenty-two), but his outspoken condemnation of the wolf-baiting certainly contributed to the outcry that led to it never again being exhibited to a public audience.[31]

Chekhov was clearly rather in awe of the Sabaneev family. Apart from Leonid Sabaneev, with his encyclopaedic knowledge of the natural world (he was apparently able to distinguish individual birds among the hundreds singing in a forest),[32] there was his elder brother Alexander, Professor of Chemistry at Moscow University, who was currently teaching Chekhov at medical school. There were five other brothers working in different spheres, and in the summer of 1884 Chekhov published a short article about them all.[33] In an eerie parallel to the future course of Chekhov's life, Sabaneev was treated for advanced tuberculosis in the summer of 1897 by the famous Prof. Ostroumov, the same doctor who had treated Chekhov just a few months earlier when he had started haemorrhaging from the lungs. Like Chekhov, Sabaneev was sent against his inclination to Yalta, where he died at the age of fifty-four in March 1898 – six months before Chekhov moved to the Crimea himself. He was buried in the cemetery in Autka, the Tatar village on the outskirts of Yalta where Chekhov was to build his house.[34] Chekhov has left no record of visiting Sabaneev's grave, but he kept, and brought with him all the way to Yalta, the issue of *Nature and Hunting* in which his story had appeared back in December 1883.[35]

During his summers at Babkino, when he was not fishing Chekhov went out shooting with Levitan – he reported to Leikin in the middle of July 1885 that his family had just consumed sixteen grouse and duck shot by Levitan.[36] He also played croquet, treated patients from the nearby villages, and went for walks to think up ideas for the stories he worked on every morning and afternoon. His favourite walks took him to the woods to hunt for mushrooms and past the lonely little church which held only one service a year. Across the river in Babkino, its ghostly bell could be heard tolling at night when the watchman who lived in the adjacent lodge struck the hour. The church inspired two suitably atmospheric stories: 'The Witch' (1886), about the deacon of a remote church who believes his unhappy wife conjures up snowstorms and bad weather in order to lure male travellers to take refuge in their house,[37] and 'An Evil Business' (1887), in which a similarly remote church is burgled at night while the watchman's attention is distracted.[38]

The Chekhovs so enjoyed staying at Babkino in 1885 that they rented their dacha from the Kiselyovs for the following two years as well. It was a good arrangement; they paid a modest sum for the annexe in the grounds, but were free to enjoy the estate's amenities – the landscaped park, the river, and the stimulating society of their new friends, who subscribed to all the literary journals.[39] After eight o'clock supper, the Chekhovs would usually walk over to the main house to spend convivial evenings with the Kiselyovs and their summer guests, who included the retired tenor Mikhail Vladislavlev who, back in 1863, had performed Siegfried's forging song in Moscow in front of Wagner, and was still capable of hitting a top D. A permanent summer guest was Alexei Kiselyov's father-in-law, the former Moscow Imperial Theatres

Director Vladimir Begichev, a talented and cultured man now in his late fifties who had co-written the scenario for Tchaikovsky's ballet *Swan Lake*. While he played patience, his daughter Maria, Vladislavlev, and other guests would sing or play the piano. It seems Chekhov learned a lot about music while he was staying at Babkino, and was regaled with stories about the celebrated musicians, including Tchaikovsky, who were family friends.

The months spent in the Moscow countryside were fundamental to Chekhov's creativity in the middle of the 1880s, inspiring an increasing number of poetic stories in among the more frivolous pieces that were hastily scribbled to pay the rent and satisfy the demands of a reading public clamouring for cheap laughs. On 6 May 1885, the day Chekhov set off with his family to stay at Babkino, his first story for a national newspaper was published.[40] He was still signing his work 'Chekhonte', but writing for *The Petersburg Newspaper*, with its higher circulation and greater prestige, gave him the confidence not only to start taking his writing more seriously, but also to write serious stories. Among the most lyrical pieces of prose written under the direct impact of the forests and the fields was a story called 'The Huntsman', set on a hot July day at the beginning of the shooting season:

A sweltering, muggy midday. Not a cloud in the sky . . . The scorched grass looks dejected and hopeless: even if there were to be rain, it is too late for it to turn green now . . . The forest stands motionless and silent, as if the tops of the trees are looking somewhere or waiting for something.

A tall, narrow-shouldered man of about forty, wearing a red shirt, high boots and patched trousers handed down from his boss, is sauntering with a lazy swagger along the edge of the clearing. Now he is sauntering down the road. On the right is a mass of greenery, and on the left a gold ocean of ripened rye stretches as far as the eye can see. He is red-faced and sweating. A white cap with a straight jockey's peak, obviously a charitable gift from some gentleman, sits rakishly on his handsome head of fair hair. There is a game-bag swung across his shoulder in which there is a squashed black grouse. The man is holding a cocked double-barrelled gun in his hands and looking through narrowed eyes at his scraggy old dog which has run on ahead and is sniffing around in the bushes. Everything alive has hidden from the heat . . .[41]

It was this story that prompted the venerable Dmitry Grigorovich to write his famous fan letter to Chekhov on 25 March 1886:

About a year ago I happened to read a story by you in the *Petersburg Newspaper*; I don't remember what it was called now; I just remember that I was struck by qualities of particular originality, but mainly by the remarkable authenticity and truth in the depiction of the characters and the descriptions of nature. Since then I have read everything signed by *Chekhonte*.[42]

Chekhov claimed that he never spent longer than a day writing his stories, and revealed that 'The Huntsman' was written down by the river.[43]

It was very hot at the end of May 1886 when Chekhov came back with his family to the dacha at Babkino for the second time. Desperate for rain, the peasants had even started walking round the fields with icons.[44] Although he had his hands full with sick villagers seeking his care, and then both his unruly elder brothers to keep an eye on when they came to stay, the heat made Chekhov feel listless. Finally the weather changed, the Istra burst its banks after weeks of incessant rain, and the year's harvest was ruined. It seemed to Chekhov as if the whole summer was ruined too.[45] He felt rather the same way the following summer, when his family returned for a third stay at Babkino. Bad weather made Chekhov miserable, and the letters he sent in 1887 conveyed his low spirits:

The weather here at the dacha is foul. Endless rain and dampness. The landscape looks so foul I can't bear to look at it. I envy you if it's dry, warm and quiet where you are. I've got a cold, the members of my family all have colds and bronchitis, the cab drivers charge a fortune, I'm not catching any fish . . . there is no one to drink with and I can't drink anyway . . . time to shoot myself really!

Some boys have just brought me a pair of woodpeckers and asked twenty kopecks for them; I gave them five and let the birds go. They obviously got a taste for it though and brought me another pair. I took the birds and slapped them round the ears. There's an example for you of my amusements at the dacha.[46]

It was clearly time for the family to look further afield for their summer retreat; Chekhov was growing restless.

II

Luka

Venice is incredibly reminiscent of Luka.
Letter to N. Lintvaryova, Genoa, 1 October 1894

Soon after 'The Steppe' was published in March 1888, the family started wondering where they should spend the summer. After his travels to the steppe the previous spring, Chekhov wanted to go south again: to the region around the Svyatogorsk Monastery or to the leafy area on the sea outside Taganrog where there were dachas to rent. He needed fresh inspiration now, and did not want to return to Babkino.[47] He had also begun to cough a great deal, which made a dacha in the south an even more attractive proposition. Through the recommendation of a friend, Chekhov eventually settled, sight unseen, on a dacha near the town of Sumy in the eastern part of the Ukraine (since he was the one paying, he had the right of veto). The dacha was once again a *Flügel* on the estate of an impoverished gentry family called Lintvaryov, but in a considerably worse state of repair than Babkino. Misha was commissioned to make a detour on his journey to Taganrog at the end of April to inspect the property. After the carefully tended flowerbeds of Babkino, Misha was dismayed to find a garden that looked more like an abandoned wood, complete with the graves of the owners' ancestors, not to mention an enormous puddle in the middle of the central courtyard in which there were ducks and pigs splashing about. And the liberal-minded Lintvaryovs took a dim view, according to Misha, of his student uniform with its shiny buttons, which to them proclaimed conservative tendencies.[48] Chekhov was not put off, however, and he left on 4 May with his sister and mother on the train from Moscow. He would be away from home for the next four months.

Chekhov took to the new dacha straightaway and wrote to his brother in a state of exultation:

Ivan! We've arrived. *The dacha is splendid*. Misha lied. The location is poetic, the annexe is spacious and clean, the furniture is comfortable, and there is lots of it. The rooms are bright and attractive and the landlords seem very nice.

The lake is huge, about a kilometre long. From the look of it, there is a ton of fish in it.

Tell Papa that we look forward to seeing him, and that it will be quiet for him here. Babkino can't hold a candle to this dacha. The noise at night alone is enough to drive you wild! Everything smells glorious, the garden is completely ancient, the Ukrainians are very amusing, and the courtyard is spick and span. There is not even a trace of a puddle.

It's incredibly hot. I don't have the energy to go around in a starched shirt.

Greetings to everyone; hope you are well. Travelling to Sumy is boring and very tiring. Bring a bottle of vodka with you. The vodka here stinks of the WC.

I'll keep Papa here for 3 weeks. That will be pretty good!

Yours, A. Chekhov

The river is wider than the Moscow river. There are lots of boats and islands. Details to follow tomorrow or the day after tomorrow.[49]

The dacha may have been convenient, as Chekhov wrote in his follow-up letter, but it did not have any conveniences, and he wondered what it would be like beetling into the bushes when the weather was not so warm and dry.[50] But having one's posterior bitten all over by mosquitoes[51] was a small price to pay for being able to sit by an open window and hear nightingales, cuckoos and hoopoes singing in the garden, and horses whinnying as villagers rode past on their way to the river to fish.

The river was a major attraction. The Lintvaryovs' estate was situated on the steep southern bank of the River Psyol, a beautiful deep tributary of the mighty Dnieper, fringed with oaks and willows. The opposite bank was gently sloping, and dotted with white cottages and gardens. The previous year Chekhov had watched an icon procession by boat on the feast of St Nikolai during his visit to the Svyatogorsk Monastery; in 1888 on 'Spring Nikola', as it was popularly referred to ('Winter Nikola' being celebrated in December), he enjoyed watching villagers travelling down the river in boats, playing violins. Every day, he went by boat to the watermill to fish, and he decided that rowing was extremely good exercise.[52] The locals were also passionate fishermen and Chekhov reported to his brother Ivan that he had got to know many of them, was learning all their secrets, and had already caught a pike and a perch. He had brought with him a rod and floats, but he asked Ivan to bring from Moscow an assortment of hooks of various sizes necessary for catching cat-fish, plus a selection of novels and lives of saints to give away to the lads who dug worms for him.[53] He went fishing all night with the local fishing enthusiasts on the eve of Trinity Sunday (the feast celebrated fifty days after Easter, which traditionally marks the transition from spring to summer in the Russian calendar). 'But what is most important,' Chekhov wrote revealingly in another early letter that summer, 'is that it is so spacious here that I feel I have received for my hundred roubles the right to live in a space which has no visible end to it.'

Despite, or because of, his adventures in the steppe the previous spring, Chekhov's deep-seated need to experience a sense of physical freedom had become, if anything, more intense. He was also utterly intoxicated by the beauty of his surroundings, the sounds, the sights and smells of which became a rich reservoir of memories to draw on in the coming years for the stories and plays he would write. The way of life in Sumy seemed to fit the sort of cliché long ago rejected by editors, and included:

> . . . nightingales that sing day and night, the sound of dogs barking far
> away, old, overgrown gardens, very poetic, sad estates, totally run-down,
> in which live the souls of beautiful women, not to mention old servants,
> former serfs with one foot in the grave, and young girls thirsting for the
> most clichéd kind of romance; not far from me there is even the trite
> cliché of a watermill (with 16 wheels), with a miller and his daughter
> who always sits at the window obviously waiting for something. Every
> single thing I see and hear seems familiar to me from ancient lore and
> fairy tales.[54]

The Chekhovs joined a well-established community when they arrived at Luka, as the Lintvaryovs' estate was called, and Ivan was sent a diagram showing who lived where; this even included the little cottage that was home to Panas, one of the young boys who dug for worms. The Chekhovs' annexe was a building with a porch and columns, facing on to a little garden with an olive tree in it. Next door to them was another holidaymaker, and the kitchen where the Polish cook Anna (wife of the local postman) prepared meals for the family: lunch was served at one, tea at four and dinner at ten, although Chekhov liked to eat earlier – he disliked going to bed on a full stomach, and was proud to report that he was not drinking vodka at all. Further along was the house rented by Grigory Artemenko, who had a job at the local factory and an ability to reel in huge cat-fish every night. The widowed Alexandra Lintvaryova, mistress of the estate, lived with her three grown-up daughters and younger son in the unpretentious white manor house surrounded by trees, and the eldest son, Pavel, lived in a separate annexe with his pregnant wife (Chekhov helped with the birth of their baby son in early July).[55] The garden was full of tulips and lilac when the Chekhovs arrived, and the white acacia was just about to come into blossom.

Chekhov warmed to the Lintvaryovs, who represented the more earnest, public-spirited side of the Russian educated classes. As at Babkino, he and his siblings tended to spend their evenings sitting in the antique chairs in the main house's drawing room, listening to music and talking about literature. From the descriptions he gave in his letters that summer, the matriarch Alexandra Vasilievna seems like a benevolent and more sprightly version of Uncle Vanya's mother in the play. 'The old mother is a very kind, podgy woman who has had her share of suffering,' he wrote. 'She reads Schopenhauer and goes to church for the akathist;[56] she dutifully studies every issue of the *Herald of Europe* and the *Northern Herald* and knows writers I haven't even dreamt about.'[57] Her two eldest daughters, both about Chekhov's age, were doctors. Zinaida, the eldest, was blind from a brain tumour and also epileptic. She was a fiercely stoic woman, revered as a saint by the local peasants (Chekhov wrote an obituary of her when she died at the age of thirty-four three years later). The stories from Chekhov's new collection, *In the Twilight*, were read aloud to her, and her laughter and quiet equanimity in the face of death made him feel strange that people had so little consciousness of their own mortality. The second daughter, Elena, who was twenty-nine, was a kind and intelligent woman who sent the family asparagus every day and confessed to Chekhov that – shades of Anna Sergeyevna in 'The Lady with the Little Dog' – she had never been happy and never would be. She was too plain to attract suitors, Chekhov wrote in a letter, and yet she clearly longed to have a family. In the evenings, when there was music in the drawing room, she could be seen walking frenziedly up and down the tree-lined avenue in the garden like a caged animal. Chekhov spent some time receiving patients with her, and found that he was rather more optimistic than she was in his prognoses, and certainly less inclined to become so emotionally involved with each case.

Long-haired Natalya, the third daughter, had a strong bony body which reminded Chekhov of a bream. Muscular and suntanned, with an extraordinarily loud laugh, she was a teacher who ran a school in the grounds of the estate at her own expense, and – shades of the elder sister Lida in 'The House with a Mezzanine' – defiantly taught Krylov's fables in Ukrainian translation, which was against the law.[58] She was also rather plain, according to Chekhov, and somewhat sentimental, despite having read Karl Marx. Georgi, the 23-year-old son, was a fine pianist with a fixation on Tchaikovsky and an admiration for Tolstoy's anarchic ideas about how to live; Pavel, his older brother, had been expelled from university for subversive activities.[59]

The Lintvaryovs had lots of guests over the summer, and the Chekhovs did too. Towards the end of May the venerable writer Pleshcheyev arrived off the Petersburg train at one o'clock in the morning and stayed for three weeks, idolized by the Lintvaryovs as if he was a wonder-working icon.[60] He had everyone gripped with his stories of being sentenced to death, only to be reprieved by the Tsar just before he was about to be hanged along with Dostoevsky back in 1849. Then Chekhov's younger brother Misha arrived from his travels in the Crimea, followed by the recently widowed eldest brother, Alexander, and the populist writer Barantsevich, who left his trousers behind when he departed: Chekhov wrote to ask him which museum they should be donated to. (Pleshcheyev, meanwhile, left his shirt behind, which meant, according to Russian superstition, that he would return.)[61] Several other friends turned up to stay, as did the two remaining brothers, Ivan and Nikolai at the beginning of June. And at the end of the month, Chekhov's father was given two weeks' leave from his job in Moscow to come for a holiday.

Chekhov himself went visiting too. He decided that he liked the Ukraine so much he wanted to buy a *khutor*, a farmstead, somewhere deep in the countryside. So, on 13 June, the day after he caught six crucian carp, he set out with the Lintvaryovs in a huge antique Gogolian sprung carriage with four hired horses, to Sorochintsy. They were going to stay with the Smagins, relatives of the Lintvaryovs who were going to help him find a property. He travelled about 250 miles in ten days, and came back thinking he was going to give up writing. Claiming he was fed up with literature (he had not yet written anything that summer), his new idea was to settle down in a village on the banks of the River Psyol and devote himself to medicine, spending his winters in St Petersburg. Apart from the beauties of the landscape, Chekhov was impressed by the standard of living of the Ukrainian peasants (traditionally much higher than in Russia), whom he characterized as 'intelligent, religious, musical, sober, decent, jolly and well-fed'.[62] But it was really the landscape which sent him into ecstasies. 'Everything I saw and heard was so fascinating and new that I hope you won't mind if I don't describe the journey in this letter,' he corresponded afterwards, limiting himself to mentioning quiet nights fragrant with the smell of freshly cut hay, the sound of distant violins, and rivers and lakes glistening in the dusk.[63] One letter he began about his trip had to be torn up after three pages, as he had too many impressions, and felt he had been unable to convey even a twentieth of what he wanted to say.[64] To Pleshcheyev he mentioned gorgeous landscapes and vistas which had made his heart stop, and which could only be adequately depicted in novels or short stories, languorous sad sunsets, and the wonderful music played at the weddings he had come upon on his journey. The Smagins' estate, with its marvellous poplars, where Chekhov stayed for five days, was equally atmospheric:

The Smagins' estate is huge and spacious, but old, neglected and lifeless, like last year's spider's web. The house has subsided, the doors don't shut, the tiles on the stove are pushing each other out and forming corners, young cherry and plum saplings are growing up through the gaps in the floorboards. A nightingale had made a nest in between the window and shutters in the room in which I slept, and while I was there naked little nightingales which looked like undressed Jewish children hatched from the eggs.[65] Well-fed storks live in the threshing barn. And there is an old man living in the apiary who is reminiscent of Tsar Gorokh and Cleopatra.

Everything was decrepit, but incredibly poetic, sad and beautiful . . .[66]

Chekhov came back to Luka brimming with ideas for what he was going to do when he was rich. Sheltering inside one day during a fierce storm (the boats were all full of water), he dreamt up a scheme to set up what he called a 'climatic station' for Petersburg writers. The idea was that under the influence of all the open space and their meetings with delightful Ukrainians, they would come to see that the focus of their literary endeavours was totally misguided, and give up, as he planned to do.[67]

Restless as always, Chekhov took off again from Luka in July to go on a trip to the Crimea, which he was visiting for the first time. He had been invited to stay with his new friend, the Petersburg newspaper magnate Alexei Suvorin. After ten days of ceaseless conversation with Suvorin at his palatial dacha on the sea in Feodosia, Chekhov went off on an adventure with his son Alexei Jr, who was two years older than he. They first took a steamship down the Black Sea coast to Sukhumi in Abkhazia, where they stayed in the New Athos Monastery. Chekhov bought his mother an icon and made friends with the local bishop, who was travelling through his diocese on horseback. As if he had not had enough stimulating experiences that summer, he was now smitten by the exotic scenery of the Caucasian peaks, and reeled off lists of unfamiliar sights to his correspondents back home in Russia: eucalyptuses, tea bushes, cypresses, cedars, palms, donkeys, swans, buffaloes, blue-grey cranes, and 'most importantly, mountains, mountains and more mountains . . .' Since the highest peaks Chekhov had seen previously were the hills north of Taganrog (the 'Don Switzerland'), it is understandable that he was impressed. It felt to him that a thousand subjects for stories were peering out of every bush and shadow, and from the sky and the sea, and he cursed himself for not being able to draw.

From Sukhumi, the travellers continued their journey by boat to Batumi, and then travelled inland to Tbilisi and Baku along the Georgian Military Highway, which Chekhov felt was 'poetry, not a road, an amazing, fantastic story'.[68] They intended to cross the Caspian Sea and go to Persia via Bukhara and Samarkand, but their epic journey was abruptly curtailed by news of the death of Suvorin Jr's brother from diphtheria. Having guiltily bypassed the grieving family in Feodosia, and now keen to get home, Chekhov did not feel quite in the mood to visit his relatives in Taganrog when his train stopped there: it was 6 August, the Day of the Transfiguration, and he knew his relatives would be in St Mitrofan's Church, whose cupola he could see from the station.[69] Within days Chekhov was back in the Ukraine, but already dreaming of going to Constantinople and Mount Athos the following year.

Ensconced again at the Lintvaryovs' tumbledown estate, he found it hard to imagine he had really seen dolphins, waterfalls, mountain crevasses, and trees entangled with creepers that were like veils in the tropical heat . . . It was the middle of August and in the Ukraine peasants were bringing the grain to be threshed; an endless string of squeaking carts seemed to pass the Chekhovs' dacha on the way to the barn.[70] Looking out through the window at the mass of green foliage sparkling in the late summer sunshine, Chekhov began to grow dejected at the thought of the 'prose of Moscow life' to which he would shortly have to return, with its cold weather, bad plays and 'Russian thoughts'. He made another trip to the Poltava region to try to buy a khutor, but could not agree a price with the owner. Seeing all the grain being threshed made him remember the long summer days of his boyhood that he had to spend by the threshing machine noting down weights, while staying with his grandfather out in the steppe: the slow carts, the clouds of dust, the sweaty faces and low wolf-like noise produced by the machine were etched in his memory as clearly as 'Our Father', he said.[71]

After the ecstasies of the first summer spent at Luka, Chekhov was keen to return the following year. This time he rented two separate annexes for his family, in order to have more space for guests. At first everything was as before. Chekhov had written very little in the summer of 1888, but now he found he was able to write every day, and the Lintvaryovs seemed even more charming than the previous year. It was soon incredibly hot, which meant having to go swimming at least twice a day, and sleeping with all the windows open. 'I can't believe my eyes,' Chekhov wrote in early May:

> . . . Not long ago it was snowy and cold and now I am sitting by an open window listening to nightingales, hoopoes, orioles and other such creatures shouting unceasingly in the garden. The Psyol is magnificently gentle, the colours of the sky and the horizon are warm. The apples and cherries are in blossom. There are geese walking around with their young. In a word, spring has arrived in full force.[72]

But the restless Chekhov constantly needed new experiences, and he confessed as much to a friend, adding that his brother's constant coughing in the room next door was not helping his rather flat mood. He wished he were not a doctor and so aware of what was going on.

The thirty-year-old artist Nikolai was indeed now very sick with tuberculosis, and the hours Chekhov spent crayfishing were dominated by gloomy thoughts of his brother's imminent death. They had brought Nikolai down from Moscow in a first-class compartment, and were waiting on him hand and foot. For the first month he had been able to go outside, but now he was mostly confined indoors and unable to breathe easily lying down. He dreamed of getting well and being able to paint again. On 4 June, Chekhov wrote with a heavy heart to his doctor colleague Nikolai Obolonsky about his condition.[73] Guests helped – Chekhov confessed that he felt he was in a tiny boat in the middle of the ocean when he was alone. His friend Suvorin came down from Petersburg to visit in early May, and he and Chekhov did a lot of fishing. But the strain was beginning to take its toll, and Chekhov was relieved when his brother Alexander also arrived from Petersburg to take over some of the duties of caring for Nikolai. Chekhov needed a break, and on 16 June he set out with his brother Ivan, his guest Pavel Svobodin, and the Lintvaryovs on a visit to the Smagins' estate. As luck would have it, Nikolai died early the following morning, and a telegram brought everyone back home on an excruciating journey involving an eight-hour wait at a remote railway station until two in the morning. For want of anything better to do, Chekhov set off to look round the town, and had sat freezing on a park bench where he overheard actors rehearsing a melodrama behind a wall.

Chekhov was overcome with guilt, and felt that the dreadful weather on the journey had been his punishment for abandoning Nikolai:

Wet and cold, we arrived at the Smagins at night, got into cold beds and went to sleep to the sound of cold rain. In the morning there was the same revolting Vologda weather; I'll never forget the muddy road, the grey sky or the tears on the trees for my whole life – it will be impossible to forget because the next morning a man came from Mirgorod with a wet telegram: 'Kolya has died.'[74]

With the exception of the early loss of the infant Evgenia, the Chekhovs had not really experienced death in the family and were completely grief-stricken to see Nikolai in a coffin; Anton was the only one not to cry, Alexander wrote bitterly to their father in Moscow.[75] Nikolai was buried in the tranquil village cemetery, which smelled of creeping velvetgrass and was full of birds singing their hearts out, Chekhov told one of his brother's friends by letter, with his grave marked by a cross you could see from a long way off. The funeral proceeded according to the local custom, with the family carrying the open coffin on their shoulders, accompanied by banners and the tolling of the church bells. A memorial service was conducted on the ninth day, as was traditional in the Orthodox Church. The detail of the extremely long letter Misha sent to Pavel Egorovich in Moscow two days after Nikolai's death speaks eloquently of how shaken the family were:

Soon they started ringing the bell for the deceased in the church on someone's instruction, the priest came with his assistant, they served a service for the dead, during which many tears were shed; then the services for the dead started to be held every day, twice, at 11 in the morning and 7 in the evening. The deceased lay surrounded by flowers with an incredibly peaceful, but very emaciated, expression on his face. The first day was dreadful for us. Towards evening the assistant came and started to read psalms, and three old women who had agreed to sit with the body all night. I made Mama go and lie down; she wanted to stay up and keep watch over Kolya all night came too. We sent Masha, who was worn out with crying, to stay the night in the big house with the Lintvaryovs. It was an awful night. The next morning the crying started again, and everyone sobbed during the service for the dead in the morning; our family, other people too, our landlords and the peasants. At midday a coffin with white brocade was brought from town and we put Kolya into it only during the evening service, on Mama's insistence. The coffin was covered with a veil and surrounded with wreaths and flowers. Psalms were read all the following night again, and you could hear the muffled conversations of the old ladies sitting by the coffin. When we started to take Kolya to the church the next morning, mother and Masha were sobbing so much it was terrible to look at them. Masha and the Lintvaryov ladies took out the coffin lid, but the coffin was carried by six of us: Antosha, Vanya, Sasha, me, Ivanenko and Egor Mikhailovich Lintvaryov. We said prayers at every corner. The service was very formal, with the church completely lit up; everyone there held candles. During the service a cross was taken out to the cemetery, and at home all the rooms were cleaned and swept and the furniture was taken outside. We took the coffin out of the church the same way. We carried it still open and only closed it by the grave itself. We said prayers at every corner and the priest read the Gospel. A lot of people followed the coffin. Icons were carried with the coffin, like in Taganrog, as if it was a church procession. Everyone sobbed at the cemetery when we had to say goodbye, mother was grieving and could not bring herself to part with the body. The coffin was lowered into the grave, it was covered over, a cross was put up and Kolya was buried. The wake was very modest: all the locals who had taken part in the funeral were given a pie, a handkerchief and a glass of vodka, and the clergy and the Lintvaryovs had lunch and tea with us. After lunch Mama and I went to the cemetery again, Mama mourned and cried, and then we came back.[76]

After taking his family off to another town for a few days to give them a change of scene, Chekhov felt desperate to escape to somewhere far away, and on 2 July he got on a train, intending to join Suvorin in the Tyrol. But in the end he was in such low spirits he only got as far as Odessa, where it was so hot he spent half his money on ice cream.[77] After a change of plan, he spent several weeks leading a pointlessly sybaritic life in Yalta, feeling guilty that he had abandoned his grieving, scared family. Soon, he found he was regretting having so many acquaintances, and rarely had the chance to be alone. He told his sister he missed Luka, and spent hours by the shore listening to crashing waves and rolling pebbles, the sounds of which reminded him of the laughter of people on the estate. He returned finally to Sumy in the middle of August for the last few weeks of the summer. It was a grim end to a grim summer, as one of his last letters testifies:

Nikolai's last days, his suffering and his funeral had the most depressing impact on me and on our whole family. I felt so awful inside that the summer, the dacha and the Psyol all became loathsome. The only diversion was letters from kind people who hastened to offer their sympathy having found out about Nikolai's death in the papers. Letters don't amount to much, of course, but when you read them, you don't feel lonely, and loneliness is the most rotten and tedious feeling.[78]

III

Aleksin

I'm leaving for Aleksin today to listen to the nightingales.
Letter to A. Urusov, 3 May 1891

Nikolai's death was one of the factors which played a role in Chekhov's decision to undertake his eight-month journey to Siberia the following year, so it was not until 1891 that the time came round for the family to rent a summer dacha again. In March Chekhov travelled to Western Europe for the first time; the day after his return to Moscow, the family left for the dacha that Misha had managed to find for them at the last minute – anything rather than stay in steamy Moscow all summer. It was located in Aleksin, a small town on the River Oka, a hundred or so miles south of Moscow, but the little wooden house at the edge of a birch wood was not as heavenly as the previous dachas had been. It was quiet, there was a good view of the Oka and the railway bridge stretching over it, but there were only four rather cramped rooms, it was six minutes' walk to the river, the walk back was uphill, and there were too many other dachniks in the vicinity for Chekhov's liking. After his amazing trip through Italy and France, dacha life seemed a bit flat, and he felt as though he had been taken prisoner and put in a fortress.[79]

Chekhov was keen to get a lot of writing done that summer. He allocated Mondays, Tuesdays and Wednesdays to his book about the penal colony on Sakhalin; Thursdays, Fridays and Saturdays were devoted to the mythical novel that he had been working on over the years (which would never actually materialize), and he reserved Sundays for dashing off 'little stories'. It was a bit of a squash with all his family there, including his father who had now finally retired from his job. There was also the mongoose he had brought back from the tropics, which was fond of pulling corks out of bottles and smashing china. Fortunately, Chekhov did not have to endure the sensation of feeling like a crayfish sitting in a sieve with lots of other crayfish for very long.[80] When Levitan and their mutual friend Lika Mizinova travelled down from Moscow by boat for a visit, they met a neighbouring landowner with the glorious name of Evgeni Bylim-Kolosovsky. Within two days he had sent round two troikas to bring the Chekhovs over to his estate for tea, and not long after that the family had vacated the dacha and moved into the cavernous upper floor of his house. Chekhov liked it so much he was prepared to pay almost twice as many roubles in rent.

Like so many other country estates, Bogimovo was run down and neglected, and therefore almost inevitably poetic in Chekhov's eyes. Catherine the Great had apparently stayed in the enormous mansion while she was on her way to meet up with Potemkin on her grand tour. The main house boasted an enormous columned ballroom on the first floor, with a musicians' gallery, a grand piano and a billiard room. The rooms were so large that they echoed. Chekhov loved it. 'It's delightful, it really is!' he exclaimed in a letter on 18 May. 'The rooms are as big as the ones in the Hall of the Nobility, and the park is glorious, with paths such as I have never seen, a river, a pond, a church for my old folk and absolutely every convenience. The lilac and apple trees are in blossom. It's bliss in a word!'[81] Sitting at the pond by the abandoned mill, fishing for carp or perch, he was able to forget all his sorrows.

Chekhov installed himself in the ballroom with the columns and enormous windows, sleeping on an old divan that could have seated twelve people. He rose with the lark, making himself coffee sometimes as early as four in the morning, and then settled down to write on the window sill, from where he could look out on to the park.[82] Five years later, he would draw particularly on his experiences living at Bogimovo in 1891 when he came to write 'The House with the Mezzanine', one of the most lyrical of his stories. The narrator is a landscape painter, renting accommodation for the summer from a landowner reminiscent of Bylim-Kolosovsky:

> He lived in the grounds, in one of the annexes, while I was in the old mansion, in a vast ballroom with columns, which had no furniture except the large divan I used to sleep on, and a table at which I played patience. Its old pneumatic stoves always used to moan, even when the weather was calm, but during thunderstorms the entire house would start shaking, as if it was about to break into pieces. It was quite frightening, especially at night, when all ten of the large windows would suddenly be lit up by lightning.

The description of a walk the narrator takes one evening seems to sum up what Chekhov perennially found so magical about the lost world of the Russian country estate:

> I spent hours on end looking out through my windows at the sky and the birds and at the avenues in the park; I read everything that arrived by post, and I slept. And every now and then I would leave the house and go wandering off somewhere until late in the evening.
>
> Once when I was returning home, I happened to stray into an estate I had never come across before. The sun was already beginning to disappear, and evening shadows stretched along the flowering rye. Two rows of old and very tall fir trees closely planted together stood like solid walls, forming a dark, beautiful avenue. I climbed over the fence without any difficulty and set off down this avenue, slipping on the needles which lay on the ground several inches thick. It was quiet and dark, except high up at the tops of some of the trees, where there was a glimmer of bright golden light, which made rainbows in the spiders' webs. The scent from the needles was so strong it was almost overpowering. Then I turned down the long linden avenue. Here too there were signs of neglect and old age; last year's fallen leaves rustled sadly under my feet, and shadows hid in the twilight between the trees. To my right in an old orchard there was an oriole singing, reluctantly and feebly; it was probably old too. But at this point the lindens came to an end; I walked past a white house with a veranda and a mezzanine, and before me suddenly unfolded a vista of the house's front courtyard, a large pond with a bathing hut and a cluster of green willows, a village on the other side, and a tall narrow bell tower, at the top of which there was a cross, burning in the reflection of the setting sun. For a second I was bewitched by the sense that all this was something familiar and cherished – as though I had seen this exact vista at some point in my childhood.[83]

As with the previous dachas, there was some interesting company at Bogimovo. A picnic organized so that all the dachniks could get to know each other led to a riotous ride in a *tarantas* at three in the morning, during which the horses bolted, toppling the carriage; Chekhov landed on his nose.[84] (A tarantas was a four-wheel carriage pulled by three horses that could travel at 8 miles an hour. It had a folding hood but no springs or seats, and travellers simply reclined on its floor on straw or cushions.) Among the dachniks at Bogimovo, Chekhov particularly enjoyed talking to a zoologist with whom he had nightly debates about evolution and degeneration – debates which find their echo in the arguments of his character von Koren in the story 'The Duel', which he was currently working on. Friends came for brief visits, and Chekhov did his best to lure Lika Mizinova, to whom he had begun to grow increasingly attached:

> We have a marvellous garden, shady paths, secluded nooks, a river, a mill, a boat, moonlit nights, nightingales, turkeys ... There are some very clever frogs in the river and in the pond. We often go for walks, and I usually close my eyes and crook my right arm, imagining you are walking beside me.[85]

If Lika had hoped to arouse Chekhov's jealousy by consorting with his friend Levitan earlier in the summer, she had been successful, but Chekhov remained in high spirits. Writing to his sister who had gone to stay with the Lintvaryovs in July, he urged her to return as soon as possible, because the household had fallen into disarray. 'As before we very rarely have quarrels,' he wrote to her in his typically deadpan style; 'only at lunch and at dinner.'[86] When Masha returned, she went back to her painting, while their father talked endlessly about bishops, Ivan fished and their mother fussed about.[87]

Soon came St Elijah's Day on 20 July, the last Orthodox feast of the summer, traditionally marking the beginning of the harvest and the turn towards autumn. 'A cold wind started blowing after Elijah,' Chekhov wrote in a letter a few days later. 'It smells of autumn. But I love the Russian autumn. There is something unusually sad, inviting and beautiful about it. I'd like to fly away somewhere with the cranes. Back in my childhood I used to catch singing birds in the autumn and sell them at the market. What joy! Better than selling books.'[88] It is not difficult to recall here the numerous stories Chekhov wrote in which he attached particular smells to the seasons, and the discussion about migrating cranes in *Three Sisters*, which Masha associates with having a meaning in one's life: 'I feel that man should have a faith or be trying to find one, otherwise his life just doesn't make sense,' she says in Act 2. 'Think of living without knowing why cranes fly, why children are born or why there are stars in the sky. Either you know what you're living for, or else the whole thing's a waste of time and means less than nothing.'

By the end of August, it had become draughty in the enormous ballroom and Chekhov started longing for carpets, fireplaces and learned discussions. Within a few days he would return to rented accommodation in Moscow for the last time.

Chapter 5

ST PETERSBURG

I

Fragments of Fame

A young man dreams of dedicating himself to literature, writes constantly to his father about it, finally gives up his job, goes to Petersburg and dedicates himself to literature – he becomes a censor.

Notebook No. 1

Thank you for the invitation to Petersburg. I would love to come and visit you, but . . . all I have in my pocket are conductors' and policemen's whistles . . . !

Letter to N. Leikin, 11 August 1884

Chekhov spent three days visiting St Petersburg during the last six years of his life, when he was based in Yalta. He had always been more closely tied to Moscow, and if the association was made indelible by repeated expressions of nostalgia in letters sent from his Crimean exile, it was set in stone with the plaintive refrain of 'To Moscow!' in his play *Three Sisters*, whose main characters gave voice to his own yearnings. Olga Knipper, who played the first-ever Masha, a role specially created for her, simply assumed that Chekhov did not care for St Petersburg. Immediately after the premiere of *Three Sisters* in January 1901, the Moscow Art Theatre went on tour to St Petersburg for the first time, taking their Chekhov productions with them. When Olga was not on stage or attending parties, she enjoyed going for walks along the embankment of the frozen Neva River, wrapped up in furs. She liked the physical appearance of St Petersburg, she wrote to Chekhov in Yalta, particularly its wide pavements and the European lustre that everything in the city seemed to possess, but she did not think that he shared her

*Nikolaevsky Station, Moscow, where Chekhov boarded
trains for St Petersburg*

enthusiasms.[1] 'You write that I don't like Petersburg. Who told you
that?' Chekhov wrote back. 'I do love Petersburg, I have a distinct
weakness for the place. And I have so many memories bound up with
the city!'[2] Those memories stretched back fifteen years, to the start of
his literary career, and telling Olga in that same letter that he had just
been reading about the assassination attempt on Pobedonostsev
probably triggered the earliest of them.

   There were distinct reasons why the assassination attempt on the
Procurator of the Holy Synod and chief adviser to Alexander III
might have made Chekhov think back to the first visit he made to St
Petersburg in 1885, shortly before his twenty-sixth birthday. He had
arrived back in Moscow just before Christmas that year, full of
excitement and bursting to tell his family about the new
acquaintances he had made during his two-week stay in the capital.
And he was still reeling from the unexpectedly warm reception he
had received there as a talented new writer. Chekhov's pious father,
however, who had never been to St Petersburg, was more interested
in hearing about the Senate and the Holy Synod. These government
departments were located in two mammoth buildings and were
connected by an arch. They looked out over the most famous

monument in the city, the statue of the Bronze Horseman, down by the Neva. Chekhov's father was angry that his son had not paid a visit.[3] But Pobedonostsev (his name in Russian comes from the word for 'victor') was the last person Chekhov would have wanted to call on, not least because he had just experienced the first real shock of having his work censored, following a 'pogrom' on the journal to which he contributed.[4] Far less impressed by authority figures than his conservative father, Chekhov studiously avoided the world of Russian officialdom throughout his life.

Konstantin Pobedonostsev wielded great power over Russian cultural life at the end of the nineteenth century. No one fitted the description of the 'Tsar's Eye' (the nickname given to those holding the post of Procurator) better than he did. A staunch defender of autocracy and an implacable opponent of reform, the bespectacled and sour-looking Pobedonostsev determined the course of Russia's domestic policy under Alexander III, and was thus largely responsible for the atmosphere of gloom and paranoia which Chekhov evokes to such chilling and satirical effect in his mature stories. (One literary critic later claimed that Pobedonostsev was the first Russian bureaucrat to develop a complete theory of stagnation.) The repressive measures he advocated after the assassination of Alexander II were so unpopular in educated circles that they won him the additional nickname of 'The Grand Inquisitor'. (Dostoevsky, who had consulted him on the writing of *The Brothers Karamazov*, was one of this dour man's few close friends.) As the lay head of the Russian Orthodox Church – a civil appointment made by the Tsar – Pobedonostsev had licence to intervene in questions of censorship as well as in matters of national education and religious freedom, and his edicts cast a pall over Russian literary life. The stagnant short-story years of the 1880s and 1890s provide a striking contrast to the preceding decades under Alexander II, a dynamic era of enormous, soul-searching novels and public debate. Morale was undermined when Dostoevsky and Turgenev died in quick succession in the early 1880s, and Tolstoy placed his fiction writing second to the preaching of moral ideas. It was further eroded when Russia's most distinguished literary journal, *Notes of the Fatherland* (or *National Annals*), was closed down because of its allegiance to 'dangerous' (i.e. Populist) political ideas. The journal had been a mouthpiece of liberal thought for forty-five years.

It was not the best time to be a writer. But this was precisely when Chekhov appeared on the scene. Pobedonostsev's tenure as Procurator of the Holy Synod, in fact, spanned the entire length of Chekhov's writing career, beginning in 1880 (the year the young medical student made his literary debut), and ending with his resignation in 1905, the year after Chekhov's death. Pobedonostsev came to see *Uncle Vanya* at the Moscow Art Theatre in 1899,[5] but was not known to have been one of the playwright's admirers. Like all Russian writers, Chekhov had to endure the humiliation of submitting every work he wrote to the censor, and then complying with whatever demands it made for excisions and alterations. This had as deleterious effect on his sense of self-worth as an artist as on all his other colleagues in the Russian literary fraternity. The assassination attempt on Pobedonostsev in 1901 took place just weeks after the Procurator had finally succeeded in engineering the excommunication of Tolstoy from the Russian Orthodox Church, after years of trying to silence his voice of moral protest. It was an event greeted with widespread derision by the intelligentsia, since it only served to increase the authority of the 73-year-old writer, who had anyway not changed his hostile stance towards the Church for over two decades. The standing of the fatally compromised Church, by contrast, sank even lower.

St Petersburg may have been the seat of government in Russia, a city teeming with soldiers and uniformed officials, but it was also the country's literary capital, and no provincial writer with aspirations could afford to ignore it for long. Chekhov's entire literary career in fact was entwined with St Petersburg, beginning with the very first two pieces he published in 1880 in the comic journal *The Dragonfly*. With the second of these, 'What Do You Come Across Most Often in Novels, Short Stories Etc.?', Chekhov showed that he was a sophisticated reader, and had got the measure of the techniques of successful literary construction. Although he later borrowed from the canon when it suited him, his ironic compendium of typical characters and devices also indicates his intention not to follow the clichéd path himself. What you most often came across in novels, short stories etc., then, according to Chekhov was:

A count, a countess bearing traces of her former beauty, a neighbour who is a baron, a liberal-minded writer, an impoverished nobleman, a foreign musician, obtuse servants, nannies, governesses, a German manager, a squire, an heir from America. People who are ugly, but likeable and attractive. A hero who saves the heroine from a horse which has bolted, strong-spirited, and capable of showing the power of his fists at any given opportunity.

Unscalable heights, impenetrable, unembraceable, incomprehensible distant spots on the horizon, in other words – nature!!!

Fair-haired friends and red-haired enemies.

A rich uncle, liberal or conservative, depending on the circumstances. His admonitions are not as useful to the hero as his death.

An auntie in Tambov.

A doctor with a concerned expression, giving hope that the situation is critical; will often have a stick with a knob on the end and a bald head. And where there is a doctor, there will be rheumatism caused from righteous labour, migraine, inflammation of the brain, care of wounded duellers and the inevitable advice to take the waters.

An aged servant who worked for the old masters, ready to go anywhere for them, even throw himself into the fire. A great wit.

A dog who can do everything but talk, a parrot and a nightingale.

A dacha outside Moscow and a mortgaged property in the south.

Electricity, in most instances connected for no earthly reason.

A briefcase of Russian leather, Chinese porcelain, an English saddle, a revolver which does not misfire, a medal in a buttonhole, pineapples, champagne, truffles and oysters.

Chance eavesdropping as the cause of great revelations.

An innumerable number of interjections and attempts to use appropriate technical vocabulary.

Subtle hints at rather sticky circumstances.

The frequent absence of an ending.

Seven mortal sins in the beginning and a wedding at the end.

An ending.[6]

No, the weekly *Dragonfly* was not quite in the same league as the monthly literary journals, those bastions of high seriousness and good taste read by the high-minded intelligentsia, but it was very popular. When the editor inexplicably stopped accepting his submissions a few months later, Chekhov was forced to find an outlet with the two main comic journals in Moscow, *The Spectator* and *The Alarm Clock*.

His big break had come in October 1882, when Nikolai Leikin, the chief contributor and newly appointed editor of the new 'weekly illustrated journal' *Fragments* (the word 'oskolki' could also be translated as 'splinters'), took the train down from St Petersburg to come on a talent-scouting mission in Moscow.

Leikin was best known as the leading feuilletonist for *The Petersburg Newspaper*, one of the new independent dailies that had sprung up as a result of the Great Reforms in the late 1860s. It had an impressive circulation of about 20,000 readers, and Leikin entertained them with light-hearted stories about diverse aspects of merchant life in the capital until his death in 1906.[7] He was an extraordinarily prolific writer: in addition to the thousands of articles he churned out over the course of his career, he produced some seventy books of stories and sketches, which – unlike those of his protégé – now all sit gathering dust on library shelves. He liked what Chekhov was writing, and published his first piece in *Fragments* a month later. A couple of the stories Chekhov thought up for Leikin are short enough to be quoted in toto, and convey well the spirit of his typical submissions in the early days. In January 1883, for example, *Fragments* published 'Thoughts of a Reader of Newspapers and Journals', signed by 'The man without a spleen', which was full of corny puns derived from the names of Russian publications:

> Don't read the *Ufa Province News*: you won't find any information about Ufa province in it.
>
> The Russian press has many sources of light at its disposal. It has the Komarovo *Light*, *The Rainbow*, *Light and Shade*, *The Ray*, *The Little Light*, *Dawn* et caet. So why is it still so dark then?
>
> It has *The Observer*, *The Invalid* and *Siberia*.
>
> The press has *Entertainment* and *Little Toy*, but it does not follow that it has much fun . . .
>
> It has *The Voice* and its own *Echo* . . . Yes?
>
> Whatever is ephemeral cannot boast about its *Century* . . .
>
> *Rus* has little in common with *Moscow*.
>
> *Russian Thought* is sent . . . in a strong envelope.
>
> Then there is *Health* and *The Doctor*, but meanwhile, how many graves there are![8]

The following month 'The man without a spleen' submitted 'A Lawyer's Novel (A Statement)', following a model that was popular at the time in the weekly comic journals:

> In eighteen hundred and seventy-seven, on the tenth of February, in the city of St Petersburg, Moscow district, 2nd quarter, in the house of the merchant of the second guild Zhivotov, on Ligovsky Street, I, the undersigned, met the daughter of a titular counsellor, Maria Alexeyevna Barabanova, 18 years of age, of the Russian Orthodox faith, literate. Having met the said Miss Barabanova, I experienced feelings of attraction to her. Since on the basis of article 994 of the Legal Code, unlawful cohabitation is punishable not only by repentance in church but also by legal costs, through the provision of the relevant statute (see the case of the merchant Solodovnikov, Appeal department decision, 1881), I asked for her hand and her heart. I married, but did not live long with her. I fell out of love with her. Having signed over all her dowry to my name, I began to frequent inns, eldorados, gardens of delights, and carried on frequenting them for five years. And since, on the basis of statute 54 of vol. 10 of Civil Legal Proceedings, five years of separation without contact provides grounds for divorce, then I have the honour of humbly requesting Your Excellency to petition for divorce from my wife.[9]

Chekhov, or rather Antosha Chekhonte, soon became a regular, and increasingly popular contributor to *Fragments*. In addition to the short stories and parodies, Leikin commissioned him to start sending in satirical 'Fragments of Moscow Life', under a new pseudonym to protect his identity. After they had exchanged friendly letters for a while, Leikin then suggested that he visit St Petersburg. In June 1884 Chekhov particularly wanted to be in the capital to promote his first short story collection, *Tales of Melpomene* (i.e., sell some of the copies he had paid for up front), and attract some critical attention. Coming to Petersburg was his 'most cherished dream', he averred in a letter to Leikin in May 1884, but since he had to pay 200 roubles to finance the book's publication, on top of supporting his family, paying the rent on the summer dacha, and covering his sister's university fees and so on, he simply did not have the extra hundred roubles he would need to make the trip.[10] He was, after all, only making a few kopecks a line for his stories – rather less than the 9,000-rouble retainer paid to Leikin as the star journalist on the *The Petersburg Newspaper*.[11] In the event, Chekhov need not have worried about being left with remainders: *Tales of Melpomene* sold out within a year and made a profit, but it received only two small mentions in the St Petersburg press. Leikin issued another invitation to Petersburg later that summer, which Chekhov was again forced to decline, once more lamenting the fact that he had neither enough money, nor a nice aunt who could hand out long-term loans.[12] Plans for a trip that winter also came to naught after Chekhov fell ill and began spitting blood.

In the summer of 1885 the need for Chekhov to start making his presence felt in literary circles in the capital became more pressing. People in the writing world wanted to meet Antosha Chekhonte in the flesh! By now, his work was appearing almost exclusively in Petersburg publications, and his continuing failure to visit the capital the following autumn started to become a joke. Petersburg really was not China, Leikin reasoned; it really was time he made the acquaintance of Sergei Khudekov, the editor of *The Petersburg Newspaper*. 'I myself know it's not China,' Chekhov replied in October 1885; 'and as you know, I've been feeling the need to make this trip for a long time now, but what am I to do? Thanks to the fact that I live in a large family, I never have a spare ten roubles in my hands, and the trip will cost a minimum of 50 roubles even if I do it as cheaply as possible. Where am I going to get the money from? I wouldn't know how to extract it from my family, and don't even consider that as a possibility anyway.'[13]

In the end, it was the wealthy Leikin who made the journey possible by taking Chekhov back with him after his next trip to Moscow, paying for his first-class rail fare and putting him up for two weeks at his own expense. Even allowing for his understandable wish to embellish a few details, it is clear from the letter Chekhov wrote to his Uncle Mitrofan back in Taganrog the following spring quite how important his first trip to 'Piter' had been:

> After you left us, just before Christmas, a St Petersburg editor came to Moscow and took me back to St Petersburg with him. He took me first class on the express, which must have cost him a fair bit. I was given such a warm reception there that for the next two months my head was still spinning from all the praise. I had a magnificent apartment to stay in, a

pair of horses, fabulous food, free tickets to all the theatres. I have never in my life lived in such luxury as I did in Piter. As well as lavishing praise on me and offering me the utmost degree of hospitality, I was presented with 300 roubles and sent home again first class . . . It turns out I am much better known in St Petersburg than I am in Moscow.[14]

Nevsky Prospekt, St Petersburg

Arriving in St Petersburg for the first time in 1885 was certainly a thrilling experience for Chekhov. As one British aristocrat put it earlier in the century, such was the monumental scale of the streets and buildings that carriages were reduced to nutshells and people to insects.[15] The dignity and grandeur of granite-clad St Petersburg was everywhere apparent. Having heard people in Moscow constantly complaining about St Petersburg, Chekhov could not help but be awed as he stepped off the overnight train and encountered wide avenues filled with speeding troikas gliding noiselessly over the snow, spacious squares, enormous classical buildings painted in bright colours, imperial ministries, opulent mansions, embassies, and foreign-looking domed cathedrals. Just off Nevsky Prospekt, right in the middle of town, was Nikolaevskaya Street, where the editorial office of *Fragments* was originally located, and it was one of Chekhov's first ports of call. A few doors down was the unusual Old Believer Church of St Nicholas the Miracle Worker, which Leikin showed him.[16] He was also taken to the Hay Market, the setting for much of *Crime and Punishment*, and to the Field of Mars to see Leifert's famous puppet show. And on Nevsky Prospekt itself, near the Fontanka River, was Palkin, one of the city's top restaurants. Chekhov was taken to dine among the aspidistras of its ornate high-ceilinged dining room by his new Petersburg acquaintances; he had never been anywhere so smart.

Palkin was something of an institution in St Petersburg, renowned for its traditional Russian cuisine, and popular with Dostoevsky (who lived nearby) and other local luminaries. Several branches had opened since Anisim Palkin founded his first inn in 1785, but the one on the corner of Nevsky Prospekt and Vladimirsky Avenue was the most famous. When it opened in 1875, its vast premises, in one of the busiest parts of the city, featured a marble staircase leading to the first floor complete with fountain, a winter garden of tropical plants, a pool stuffed with sterlet (small sturgeon), a concert hall, and numerous private dining rooms, all richly furnished. On Sundays in the 1890s, you could even dine to the accompaniment of music from the Preobrazhensky Life Guards band. On Sundays in the 1990s, you could come and play roulette. It is perhaps typical of the unpredictability of Russian business practices that when entrepreneurs decided to open 'an elite casino club' on the site of the former restaurant (which had functioned as a cinema in Soviet times), they decided to resurrect Palkin too. Its cuisine may have made it a fixture for the Russian beau monde,[17] but it is unlikely many budding young writers can afford its prices these days.

Chekhov was given a royal reception by Leikin in 1885, but their professional relationship was actually becoming quite fraught. Leikin was a journalist first and foremost, and he wanted material that fitted the template of his journal: stories had to be short and funny, and cranked out without too much deliberation. Chekhov was never going to be a writer in Leikin's mould. He was an elegist as much as a comic, with a poetic temperament, and he found it increasingly difficult to write to order. He found the Moscow reportage particularly irksome. And it was hard having to be funny all the time. And who knows how much impact suddenly starting to cough blood had on Chekhov's frame of mind in 1884? With his limited horizons,

Leikin, meanwhile, was simply unable to appreciate Chekhov's more ambitious, serious stories, which he found inferior. He wanted stories which provided entertainment. To be fair, *Fragments* was a comic journal. Leikin became increasingly proprietorial when Chekhov began to branch out (which publishing in *The Petersburg Newspaper* allowed him to do). He then naturally felt somewhat threatened by Chekhov's resulting success in literary circles. But Chekhov never ceased to be grateful to Leikin for helping him at such a seminal point in his career. Despite the cloak-and-dagger operations, which he suspected were going on behind his back in order to keep him in the *Fragments* stable, he was highly appreciative of Leikin's generous hospitality. Like Chekhov, Leikin had been born into a merchant family, with a father who had gone bankrupt. He had done very well for himself through journalism, and in addition to buying a palatial estate out of town that had belonged to Count Stroganov,[18] he had a comfortable apartment on the Petrograd side of St Petersburg, near the Peter and Paul Fortress. Chekhov got on best with Leikin when it came to talking about dogs and fishing, which they were both keen on: Leikin had two vociferous dogs, and he later presented Chekhov with two pairs of puppies.

One of Chekhov's tasks during his visit to Petersburg was to discuss with Leikin the arrangements for his new short story collection: the publisher of *Fragments* had agreed to publish seventy of Chekhonte's most successful stories, under the title *Motley Tales*. Another task was to call on the editorial offices of *New Times* and *The Petersburg Newspaper* (where he was received like the 'Shah of Persia'), and meet other people in the St Petersburg literary world. The warmth of his reception made him embarrassed that he had not taken his writing more seriously, he wrote afterwards to his brother Alexander; it was difficult getting used to the fact that people were reading his work.[19] But the knowledge that he was being read by the literary community in St Petersburg had an immediate effect on his writing. 'Heartache', published in *The Petersburg Newspaper* a month after his return, is a prime example of a finely crafted early story on a serious theme which would never have passed muster with Leikin. Rarely, for a work by Chekhov, it is actually set in St Petersburg (but more probably inspired by Moscow), and its mixture of sadness and humour was to become his trademark. A grief-stricken cab driver attempts, on a snowy winter night, to talk about the death of his son to his fares, but no one wants to listen and he ends up talking to his horse. Chekhov's ability to set a scene was already masterly. Writing to order for Leikin had honed an inbuilt talent for concision to which he now began to add emotional depth:

> Evening twilight. Large flakes of wet snow are circling lazily around the streetlamps, only just lit, and settling in a soft, thin layer on roofs, the backs of horses, shoulders and hats. Iona Potapov the cabbie is all white, like a ghost. He is as hunched up as a living person can be, and is sitting on the box without moving. Even if an entire snowdrift fell on him, he probably would not consider it worth shaking the snow off himself . . . His old mare is also white and motionless. Standing there stock still, with her angular frame and legs straight as sticks, she looks like one of those one-kopeck gingerbread horses close up. She is probably deep in thought. Having been torn away from the plough, from familiar grey scenes, and thrown into this maelstrom of monstrous lights, with its relentless din and people rushing about, it would be impossible not to think . . .[20]

It was precisely stories like 'Heartache' which had the readers of The Petersburg Newspaper turning eagerly to page three whenever they appeared.

II

Messengers from the North

> Who could have ever imagined that such a genius would emerge from the latrine?
>
> *Letter to Mikhail Chekhov*, 25 April 1886

> I've just been walking down Nevsky. Everything is full of amazing *joie de vivre*, and when you look at the pink faces, the uniforms, the carriages and the ladies' bonnets, it feels like there is no sorrow in the world.
>
> *Letter to Mitrofan Chekhov*, 13 March 1891

Wheels were set in motion after Chekhov returned home from St Petersburg at the end of his first visit in December 1885. Within a matter of weeks, Alexei Suvorin, the proprietor of Russia's biggest newspaper, had sent an envoy to talk to Chekhov about writing for *New Times*. It was tricky, the envoy explained, because Chekhov had now been to St Petersburg, and, according to his intelligence, had now promised to write for *The Petersburg Newspaper* twice a week (previously it had only been once a week – on Mondays, the only day of the week that Leikin did not file). Leikin had apparently also offered Chekhov a 600-rouble annual retainer as long as he stopped writing for *The Alarm Clock*, which was the main Moscow rival to *Fragments*. The envoy reckoned that negotiation would have been much easier a few weeks earlier, before he had got on that train.[21] But he ended up walking in through an open door. Chekhov was thrilled to be asked to write for *New Times*.

Like Leikin, Suvorin was much older than Chekhov, twenty-six years older to be precise (and with a son two years older than Chekhov). Suvorin was also a writer, whose voluminous legacy, like Leikin's, has similarly been consigned to oblivion. But he was considerably more interesting. As with so many of the people who came to prominence in Russian life in the last decades of the nineteenth century, Suvorin was a self-made man. His father had been a peasant conscript, promoted to captain for his valour in 1812, and his mother was the daughter of a priest. After spending several years as a school teacher in the provinces, during which time he started contributing to comic journals and the national press, he was invited to begin a full-time journalistic career in Moscow, working for a daily newspaper and also writing for all the most prestigious journals. A few years later he moved to St Petersburg, and while Chekhov was growing up in Taganrog, Suvorin slowly built up his empire. Finally, in 1876, he became the owner of the bankrupt *New Times*, a daily which had been founded in 1862. Suvorin turned it around, and for the next few decades it was the most important newspaper in Russia, with a circulation of up to 70,000 in its heyday. Back in the 1860s Suvorin had been a liberal: a novel he published was considered so inflammatory it was pulped by state order, and he was arrested for publishing an article on the radical critic Chernyshevsky. A decade later his politics had changed, and *New Times* under his ownership developed an increasingly unsavoury reputation for its support of the regime: it is indicative that when Suvorin died in 1912, Nicholas II sent a wreath to his funeral.[22] As well as owning the press which printed the newspaper, Suvorin also eventually acquired his own publishing house (which pioneered cheap pocket editions), bookshops across the country in all the major cities and at railway stations, a historical journal and a theatre.

Just over a month after reaching an agreement to write for *New Times*, Chekhov submitted his first story, signing it, as usual, with his Antosha Chekhonte pseudonym. When the readers of *New Times* opened their copies of the Saturday supplement edition on 15 February 1886, however, it was Chekhov's real name that they saw printed on the page. Although Chekhov had nurtured hopes of keeping his real name for all the medical articles he was planning to publish (and never did because he became too famous as a writer), he had acquiesced to Suvorin, who was adamant that the pseudonym now be dropped. There was all the difference in the world in having Suvorin as an editor, as the first letter Chekhov wrote to him makes clear:

Dear Alexei Sergeevich,

I received your letter. Thank you for the flattering remarks about my work and for publishing my story so quickly. You can judge for yourself how refreshing and even inspiring for my writing it has been to have the kind of attention from such an experienced and talented person as yourself . . .

I share your opinion about the ending of my story and thank you for your useful suggestions. I've been writing for six years, but you are the first person who has bothered to provide suggestions and the reasons for them.

The A. Chekhonte pseudonym probably is strange and a bit recherché. But it was thought up in the misty dawn of my youth, I have grown used to it, and so I don't notice its strangeness . . .[23]

'The Requiem', Chekhov's first story for *New Times* was a pearl: Andrey Andreyich, a simple-minded but devout rural shopkeeper has stayed behind in church in order to ask the priest to serve a requiem in memory of his beloved daughter Maria, recently deceased. During the service, he had sent up a petition to the altar, and now cannot understand why Father Grigory should berate him for appealing 'for eternal rest for God's servant, the whore Maria'. It turns out that Maria had, in fact, become a famous actress, who was even written about in the newspapers, but Father Grigory in vain tries to persuade her father that there is nothing inherently sinful in working in the theatre, that it is not his place to condemn, and quite inappropriate to use such indecent words. As Father Grigory intones the words of the service in the deserted church, Andrey Andreyich cannot quite bring himself to forgive his daughter for prostituting herself to the stage, and the story ends with her troubled soul finding release elsewhere:

> A stream of bluish smoke rises from the censer and hangs in the broad, slanting ray of sunlight which crosses the dark and lifeless emptiness of the church. It seems that the soul of the deceased girl is floating alongside the smoke in that ray of sunlight. Twisting like a child's curls, the thin streams of smoke rise up towards the window as if dispelling all the despair and sadness that poor soul contained.[24]

Leikin would have never let Chekhov get away with this sort of prose. But it was precisely this sort of prose, and the powerful evocation of the night-time storm in 'The Witch', his second story for *New Times*, which made Dmitry Grigorovich finally dip his pen in ink in St Petersburg a month later and exhort the 26-year-old Chekhov to take his writing more seriously. He had spent months trying to persuade Suvorin to overcome his prejudices and read the stories Chekhov was publishing in *The Petersburg Newspaper*, and he had finally been vindicated.

Meanwhile, the pages of *Motley Tales*, Chekhov's second short story collection, were being prepared for printing at the typographers in Petersburg. It was time for him to make his second visit to the capital. He was again beset with financial difficulties, and was again coughing blood – now a regular occurrence, particularly in spring when the snows began to melt. On 25 April 1886, however, he returned to spend another two weeks in St Petersburg. On this occasion, he travelled at his own expense, and took a room in a boarding house near the railway station on Pushkin Street, just off Nevsky Prospekt. After arriving off the overnight train and having a wash – he told his brother Misha in a letter written at the end of his first day – he put on his new trousers, his new coat and his pointed shoes, and set off on a triumphant tour of the city's editorial offices. It was a fifteen-kopeck cab drive, down Nevsky to Troitsky Lane, where the *Fragments* editorial team had relocated and which was still Chekhov's first port of call. The pianist Anton Rubinstein, whom, according to some of his friends, Chekhov resembled, would move into an apartment further down the street the following year, and the street now bears his name – Chekhov had been very amused when his brother Alexander named his new-born son Anton in February 1886, quipping in a letter: 'What boldness! You might just as well have called him Shakespeare! After all, there are only two Antons in the world: me and Rubinstein.'[25]

Chekhov received an enthusiastic welcome at the *Fragments* office, which he used as his mailing address during his stay. The journal's proprietor was not at his desk when he went round to the press next door, so he set off to visit his new friend Ivan Bilibin, who took him for a boat trip on the river and then for lunch at Dominique, a popular restaurant with a billiard room, on Nevsky Prospekt opposite the Kazan Cathedral. But that was not all, he wrote jubilantly to Misha. Next came a visit to *The Petersburg Newspaper*, and finally an audience with Suvorin himself.[26] It made all the difference that Chekhov was no longer being paraded as Leikin's 'discovery'. He and Suvorin immediately saw eye to eye on this occasion, and the relationship they struck up during his visit two years later would, over the years, develop

Suvorin's bookshop, Nevsky Prospekt, St Petersburg

into what would be for both of them the most important and the closest friendship of their entire lives. *Motley Tales* was the first and last collection Chekhov published with *Fragments*. In 1887, *New Times* became Chekhov's main publisher, issuing nine separate editions of collections and individual stories at a thousand copies each. The first collection, *In The Twilight*, was reprinted twelve times; when it was re-issued in 1891, there were a further eleven reprintings.[27]

The obvious question of why Chekhov, a man who loathed despotism in all its forms, and whose whole life may be regarded as an implicit – indeed, sometimes explicit – criticism of the Russian government's venal and unjust policies, should have entered into such a longstanding and fruitful relationship with Suvorin and his newspaper is a difficult one to answer. Both were complex individuals, from different generations, with completely different personalities and widely differing incomes. What they had in common was a passion for writing, a high degree of intelligence, a peasant background, Voronezh province (where Suvorin and Chekhov's father grew up) and a large helping of the Orthodox Church. At the beginning, Chekhov needed the money that Suvorin was offering – it was far more than he was getting anywhere else. He later confessed that when he first started writing for *New Times*, he felt as if he was in California.[28] And despite his self-effacing manner, Chekhov was ambitious: whatever its politics, *New Times* was considerably more prestigious as a place to publish than *The Petersburg Newspaper*. And it provided him with a greater creative freedom than he had enjoyed elsewhere: the stories he published in *The Petersburg Newspaper* and the comic journals were noticeably more straightforward. Suvorin's high expectations and keen interest also stimulated Chekhov to produce the best work he could for him, and from *New Times* it was a much smaller step to the prestigious literary journals than from *The Petersburg Newspaper*. But he also felt uneasy about contributing to a publication that was held in derision by the liberal intelligentsia, and immediately began to worry that he would be barred from publishing in literary journals as a result.[29]

Eventually Chekhov found it impossible to reconcile the newspaper's reactionary orientation with his friendship with its proprietor, and the virulently anti-semitic stance it adopted over the Dreyfus case in 1897 caused a rift in their (already cooling) relations that never really healed. But for a good ten years the two men enjoyed each other's company. They travelled twice to Western Europe together, and met regularly in Petersburg, Moscow, and at Suvorin's luxurious seaside dacha in Feodosia in the Crimea (such a landmark you could buy a postcard with a picture of it). In between their meetings, they corresponded: Chekhov wrote Suvorin 337 letters between 1886 and 1903. He probably received as many in exchange, although none have survived to tell the other side of the story: Suvorin destroyed them all soon after Chekhov's death. (He went specially to Yalta to collect them, giving up his letters from Chekhov in exchange.) Suvorin was the recipient of Chekhov's best letters, the sounding board for his most serious ideas about literature, the theatre, human psychology, Russia. Initially Chekhov may have been rather naive about the implications of publishing with *New Times*, but he and Suvorin found each other such stimulating company that he could soon no more dispense with the publisher than he could turn his back on the man. There was no one he found as thought-provoking, no one who seemed so well read. As for Suvorin, whose incisive personality can be gauged from the letters to writers who did not predecease him, it was Chekhov's personality which most enchanted him. There was perhaps no other person he loved more outside his own family.

Although he occasionally took a room in a hotel such as the fashionable Angleterre on St Isaac's Square, after 1888 Chekhov usually stayed with Suvorin and his family in their vast apartment on Ertelev Lane, a street renamed Chekhov Street in his honour in 1923. In a fashionable area, right in the heart of the city not far from the Fontanka River, the Suvorin family residence was conveniently close to the printing press, a few minutes' walk down the same street, and the main Suvorin bookshop on Nevsky Prospekt itself. Around the corner were the editorial offices of *New Times*, on Malaya Italianskaya – a street so called because of the Italian garden whose perimeter it bordered (it was renamed Zhukovsky Street in 1902). For Chekhov there were pluses and minuses to being a house guest. On the plus side were two luxuriously appointed rooms which came with a grand piano, a fireplace, a handsome desk, and Vasily the valet (who was better dressed than Chekhov, and bemused him by going about on tiptoe trying to anticipate his desires). There was also Suvorin's magnificent library of literary and religious works, and portraits on the walls of his favourite writers: Shakespeare, Pushkin, Turgenev and Tolstoy.[30] Having to sustain long conversations with Suvorin's wife and dine *en famille*, despite the presence of their three dogs, was definitely on the side of the minuses. The Suvorin children thought Chekhov was a genius because he had written a story about a dog who goes off to perform in a circus (*Kashtanka*), and stared at him continuously throughout dinner, expecting him to say something very clever. What most cramped Chekhov's style, though, was that he had to behave himself: he could hardly roll up drunk at the Suvorins', let alone in female company.[31]

When he managed to escape after his first long day spent at Ertelev Lane in March 1888 (his hosts did not retire until three in the morning), and could step out into the snowy streets, he headed round the corner to the editorial offices of *The Northern Messenger*, which had become Petersburg's leading literary journal. The previous month it had published 'The Steppe', his longest story to date, and his first major work, thereby reassuring him that his association with *New Times* had not barred his route to literary respectability. *The Northern Messenger* had arisen in 1885 to take the place of *National Annals*, which had been shut down by the government the previous year, and Chekhov developed a very warm relationship with Alexei Pleshcheyev, his editor there. Publishing a story in one of the so-called 'thick' (literally 'fat') monthly journals was still of huge symbolic significance to any aspiring Russian writer who wished to be taken seriously. There were four main titles in the 1880s, three of them based in St Petersburg, but the prestige was no longer what it was (or later would be in the Soviet period). As a member of the parvenu younger generation who had only recently joined the ranks of the intelligentsia, Chekhov attached far less importance to literary journals than did his crustier older contemporaries. As he wrote to the poet Polonsky just before 'The Steppe' was published:

Isn't it the same whether a nightingale sings in a big tree or a bush? The requirement that talented people should only publish in thick journals is small-minded, smacks of servility and is harmful like all prejudices. This prejudice is stupid and ridiculous. There was a point to it when the publications were headed by people with clearly defined outlooks, such as Belinsky, Herzen and so on, who not only paid a fee, but drew people to them, taught and educated them, but now when we have some very grey kind of people with stiff collars running these publications, allegiance to thick journals won't stand up to criticism, and the difference between a thick journal and a cheap newspaper is only quantitive, that is to say, from the point of view of an artist, it is not worthy of respect or attention. There is one convenient aspect to writing for a thick journal, though: a long piece won't get chopped up and is printed whole. When I write a long story, I will send it to a thick journal, and the small ones I will publish wherever the wind and my will want to take them.[32]

This is exactly what Chekhov did. Over the course of his career, he deftly tailored each piece according to the publication in which he placed it, continuing to write in a wide range of styles for a variety of different audiences.[33]

With the publication of 'The Steppe' in *The Northern Messenger* in February 1888, Chekhov became a star in Russia's literary world. The seal of approval from a fat journal meant a great deal to him, despite his professions of nonchalance: witness the unusually long period of writer's block he suffered before sitting down to write the story. And his star began to burn even more brightly when he was awarded the Imperial Academy of Science's Pushkin Prize for Literature that year. Writing to his brother Alexander who had been talking to Suvorin, Chekhov was incredulous to hear the news as early as the previous October that he might be awarded the prize, thinking that his colleague Korolenko was more deserving; he also reckoned his association with *New Times* was sufficient to rule him out of the contest.[34] But Suvorin had a hand in the affair and was rightly confident about the outcome. The price of all the fame, of course, was criticism. After his first forays to the capital, Chekhov began making regular visits to Petersburg during the winter months, and the adulation he now received was both bemusing and intoxicating. His collection, *Motley Tales*, had made him famous. He was the most fashionable writer in Petersburg, he boasted to his uncle in January 1887 following his most recent visit; his stories were read out at soirées, people pointed him out to each other wherever he went, everyone wanted to make his acquaintance, and critics were writing about his work.[35]

The first few reviews of his stories were a major event, not only for Chekhov but his whole family, particularly when they praised him to the skies. With the publication of *Motley Tales* in May 1886, however, began a rising tide of critical opinion in the capital's press which was less favourable. Chekhov had to learn to deal with a particular phalanx of Petersburg critics who were confounded by the absence of any kind of ideological freight in his work, and were offended by the unorthodox trajectory of his literary career. In a country where the word 'writer' had often been synonymous with the word 'martyr', there was something almost indecent to the older generation about the rise of a young Turk via the pages of cheap comic journals, particularly when he was clearly not prepared to pay obeisance to the usual shibboleths and put his literary talent to the service of fighting moral causes. *Motley Tales* was the first collection by Chekhov to receive serious attention in the national press. It was also reviewed in the serious literary journals, and the anonymous critic for *The Northern Messenger* spared no punches. Alexander Skabichevsky (for it was he, a former associate of *National Annals*) characterized Chekhov as a clown, who would wither away in complete oblivion under a fence like a squeezed lemon. His book, meanwhile, represented the 'tragic spectacle of a young talent committing suicide'.[36] Chekhov was so wounded by this review that he could never quite forget it, but the Populist critics like Skabichevsky became so predictable in their attacks on his work for its apparent lack of ideals, that the only sane response was to laugh.

Critics were also disconcerted by Chekhov's reluctance to align himself with any particular group. The formation of factions and opposing splinter groups, and the ensuing passionate debate over differing principles, has always been a characteristic phenomenon in Russian society – not only in the literary sphere, but across the board. You could almost say it was an inbuilt part of national cultural identity. Engagement was expected *a priori*. But Chekhov refused to play the game; in fact he confounded everybody, as he did in almost every area of his life. The compassionate, liberal-minded young writer aligned himself (if he aligned himself with anyone at all) not with a group, but with one person – a right-wing newspaper tycoon twice his age. He loathed *partiinost*, the idea of being a member of a group or a party ('partiinost', which also means 'party spirit', later became a byword in Communist vocabulary), as he made abundantly clear, and perhaps just a touch tactlessly, to the literary editor of *The Northern Messenger* in January 1888:

Our fat journals are all dominated by dull groups and cliques. It's
suffocating! I don't like the fat journals because of that, and it does not
make me want to write for them. Being a member of a group, especially
if it's arid and lacking in talent, is incompatible with freedom and the
grand scale.[37]

This was the nomadic, southern Chekhov speaking, the Chekhov who
had spent the previous summer roaming the steppe. He did not want
to be pinned down.

Notwithstanding the occasional friction caused by inhospitable
reviews, Chekhov loved going to St Petersburg. His visits to the capital
meant leaving his duties and responsibilities behind in Moscow, and
travelling to a sophisticated and cosmopolitan city where he was wined
and dined and could devote his time completely to literary business. It
was like going on holiday. 'Piter is magnificent,' he wrote to his family
from the capital in December 1887; 'I feel like I'm in seventh heaven.
The streets, the cabbies, the food – everything is excellent, and there are
so many clever and decent people, you can just take your pick.'[38]
Sometimes there were outings to the Mariinsky to hear the occasional
opera or concert, and there were also visits to the latest exhibitions and
to artists' studios, and frequent trips to the theatre. In March 1891
Chekhov and Suvorin went to see the great Italian actress Eleonora
Duse perform in *Antony and Cleopatra* at the Maly Theatre on the
Fontanka during her Russian tour. This was the new independent
theatre which Suvorin would take over in 1895 ('Maly' – small – was
a misnomer; it had over a thousand seats). The fact that Chekhov wrote
so few letters during his Petersburg visits says a lot about the frenetic
social life he led there; it also means we actually know comparatively
little about what he actually got up to.

While Chekhov looked forward particularly to spending time with
Suvorin during his visits to Petersburg, he also enjoyed his meetings
with the numerous friends he made in the city. He initiated annual
dinners for writers at the Maly Yaroslavets on Bolshaya Morskaya Street
(another restaurant which specialized in Russian cuisine), but after the
rowdy nightlife of Moscow dining establishments, the more sedate
socializing that Petersburg writers generally engaged in at home in their
drawing rooms provided an agreeable change. And from the end of
1886, he even had family in the city: his elder brother Alexander had

moved to the capital with his family and taken up employment with Suvorin as a journalist on *New Times*. Alexander was able to write and tell Anton what was going on the city, particularly with regard to his brother's affairs (as in June 1887, when he let him know that his story 'Fortune' was still being read in cafés along Nevsky Prospekt a week after publication).[39] He was also able to carry out useful errands for his brother from time to time. In return, Chekhov provided occasional medical care, on one occasion jumping on the first train to Petersburg when there was a typhoid scare.[40]

Suvorin assumed that Chekhov himself would soon move to Petersburg, where most writers indeed naturally gravitated. During his first meeting with Alexander in January 1887, he baldly declared that Moscow was no place for a 'thinking person'.[41] Chekhov also toyed for a long time with the thought of moving to Petersburg,[42] but it was more an escapist fantasy than anything else. As someone with incipient tuberculosis, the city's notoriously damp climate meant he could never seriously contemplate moving north. Also, he was a dutiful son, and felt an obligation to look after his impoverished parents, so he had to content himself with short trips of a few weeks' duration. Although his longest visit, in 1893, lasted a month, Petersburg never occupied the place in his affections that Moscow did. His ambivalent feelings about the city, which stemmed partially from becoming the subject of incessant gossip, became more pronounced after the disastrous production of his play *The Seagull* in 1896. St Petersburg may have been the centre of Russian intellectual life, but there was a coldness to it which Chekhov did not like.

III

Chekhov and the Imperial Theatres

As you go along Nevsky, you glance towards the Haymarket: clouds the colour of smoke, the setting sun a crimson globe – Dante's hell!

Notebook No. 1

New forms of life follow always new forms in literature (the precursors), and that is why they will always be so abhorrent to the conservative human spirit.

Notebook No. 1

In January 1889, a revised version of Chekhov's play *Ivanov* was given its Petersburg premiere, following its first performance in Moscow just over a year earlier. The Moscow production had taken place at the privately owned theatre run by Fyodor Korsh. In Petersburg, *Ivanov* was staged at the state-run Alexandrinsky, still at that time the most important drama theatre in Russia. For most of the nineteenth century, the Russian government maintained successful control of theatrical life in Petersburg and Moscow, banning private companies from performing during the main season. In Petersburg, the Alexandrinsky and the Mikhailovsky were the state-owned venues for spoken drama. After the state monopoly was lifted in 1882, impresarios were quick off the mark in the more entrepreneurial Moscow, the merchant capital (Korsh opened his theatre the same year), but it took over a decade for private theatres to establish themselves properly in the more staid capital.

In the meantime, the 'Alexandrinsky', the elegant classical theatre built by Rossi in 1832 and named after the wife of Nicholas I, remained the most important stage in the capital for drama. Since the theatre was government-run, there was no problem with funding: it had plenty of money to hire the best technicians, the best producers and the best

The Imperial Alexandrinsky Theatre, St Petersburg, where
The Seagull *premiered in 1896*

actors if it so desired (another reason why it took a while before private companies were in a position to compete). But the government's tastes in art were as reactionary as its tastes in politics, so neither the repertoire, nor the manner in which plays were produced offered much in the way of artistic excitement. And like any other government department, the Directorate of the Imperial Theatres was run by bureaucrats, who ensured that the path from the initial submission of a new play to opening night was as complicated as possible. Fortunately for Chekhov, he had his friend Suvorin on hand to conduct all the negotiations with the Imperial Theatres on his behalf for the staging of *Ivanov* at the Alexandrinsky. Suvorin knew all the right people and was familiar with procedures at the theatre. Standing in the middle of the city in its own square, just off Nevsky Prospekt, the enormous yellow building could seat nearly 2,000 people, so the production of new plays was not entered into lightly. But having your play staged at the Alexandrinsky was hardly a casual undertaking for authors either.

Chekhov travelled up from Moscow a couple of weeks before the first night of *Ivanov* in order to attend rehearsals. The wrangles he had with the actor playing the lead did not inspire confidence: Vladimir Davydov had played Ivanov in the original Moscow production, but the part had now changed and he did not understand it. There were other casting problems, which caused the date of the premiere to be delayed by a few days. Despite Chekhov's misapprehensions, however, *Ivanov* proved to be a huge success, and the author was given a standing ovation after the third act. The enthusiastic reviews which appeared in *New Times* and *The Petersburg Newspaper* only enhanced Chekhov's already high standing in the eyes of the Petersburg public. Suvorin's wife wrote to Chekhov that in seven years of going to the Alexandrinsky, she had never been so moved. She was one of many friends and admirers who wrote to him in similarly ecstatic terms.[43] At some point during this visit, Chekhov had his photograph taken at Shapiro's studio on Nevsky Prospekt. A few months later his brother Alexander wrote to tell him that Shapiro had put the portrait in his window and that it was attracting a lot of attention from passers-by. On one occasion Alexander eavesdropped on the conversation of a group of young ladies as they stood there with their faces pressed to the glass, and reported to his brother that they had detected passion in his eyes, and had even admired his tie. He was most disgruntled, however, that none of them had talked about his brother's soul or his intelligence.[44]

Hot on the heels of *Ivanov* came Chekhov's one-act farce *The Bear*. It created a furore when it was premiered at the Alexandrinsky on 7 February 1889. The female lead, Elena Popova ('a comely widow landowner with dimples in her cheeks'), was played by the great Maria Savina, and when Chekhov fulminated against Petersburg theatre in 1901, he made an exception for her, as well as a partial exception for Davydov. *The Bear* had become a favourite with the amateur dramatics fraternity all over Russia after its first performance in Moscow the previous October. Even before the Petersburg premiere, Chekhov was proudly able to inform his friends that it had been enthusiastically staged by the Imperial Ministers of Finance and Foreign Affairs in their home-spun productions.[45] And then there was Chekhov's other perennially popular one-act farce *The Proposal*, which was premiered in St Petersburg on 12 April at a small chamber theatre, and then staged at the Alexandrinsky on 12 September. That summer even royalty had dabbled with Chekhov. On 10 August, the Alexandrinsky actor Pavel Svobodin wrote to tell Chekhov that he had just acted in *The Proposal* before the Tsar. The command performance had taken place in the little wooden theatre located in Krasnoe Selo, just outside the city, where the troops were stationed during the summer months. The theatre employed members of the imperial troupes to perform comedies, operettas and ballets for members of court and other highly placed officials while they were at their dachas. Svobodin reported to Chekhov that the imperial family and their retinue had much enjoyed the show, with Alexander III laughing particularly loudly. Indeed, he said, the cast had received two curtain calls, which was unheard of in that stuffy, protocol-infested theatre. The Tsar's Eye may have been disapproving, but the Tsar himself not only read Chekhov, but was a fan, it turned out, when the actors were presented to him afterwards.[46] Chekhov was very amused. 'I am awaiting the order of St Stanislav and appointment to the State Council,' he wrote to a friend.[47] That was unlikely, however, as the Tsar did not really know who he was. Alexander III saw *The Bear* many times, and invariably went to congratulate Svobodin on his performance in the title role, telling him how much he had laughed. He would also invariably ask who the author was. 'The author of

Ivanov,' Svobodin would reply. 'Ah, Ivanov!' the Tsar would exclaim, 'jolly good!'[48]

Chekhov had made a name for himself in St Petersburg literary circles as a prose writer, and now he had conquered the imperial stage as well. He seemed to be everywhere. So it was hardly surprising that in November Leikin decided to feature the man of the moment, his former contributor, on the cover of *Fragments*. The full-page spread showed Chekhov in a cart poised at a crossroads in the middle of the steppe: which road was he going to take – the dramatic road or the story road?[49] As we know, he took both those roads, and simultaneously, to judge from a comment in his famous letter to Suvorin of 21 November 1895 about *The Seagull*. 'Well, I've already finished the play,' he wrote. 'I began it *forte* and ended it *pianissimo* against all the rules of dramatic art. It's come out as a story.' But then Chekhov would not be the first Russian writer to rebel against what was expected of traditional genres.

It was agreed that *The Seagull* would be submitted directly to the Alexandrinsky's repertoire committee after it was approved by the censor. Chekhov was quite apprehensive, and not only because he felt less comfortable writing plays than short stories. On the first night of a new play, he was always terrified of how the audience would react. It was like stepping in front of a bear, he said once, except that an audience was more frightening.[50] There were also, in the case of the Imperial Theatres, all the bureaucratic hurdles to contend with. Chekhov had firmly established his reputation at the Alexandrinsky in 1889 with the productions of *Ivanov* and his two vaudevilles, but the theatre's committee had rejected his new play *The Wood Demon* when it was presented to them that October, and it would be several years before he picked up the manuscript again and transformed it into *Uncle Vanya*. By that time, Svobodin, the actor who had become Chekhov's close friend and the driving force behind the composition of *The Wood Demon*, was no longer around: he had died of tuberculosis after collapsing on stage in 1892. Chekhov had even more cause to be nervous about how *The Seagull* would be received, as it was far more ambitious in exploring new territory than any other play he had written. From the point of view of conventional drama, it was nothing short of revolutionary.

After *The Seagull* had been typed out, the manuscript was sent off to the Central Administration for Matters Relating to the Press, to be scrutinized by a government censor. That was in March. In May it turned out that the censor objected to, among other things, the indifference with which Treplev regarded his mother's relationship with her lover. The censors had become so crazy, joked the friend who was kindly overseeing the play's progress through the censorship committee, that there were rumours that literature was soon simply going to be abolished.[51] Chekhov finally received his manuscript back in July, and duly sent it on to St Petersburg after making the required changes.[52] Then came the Theatrical-Literary Committee at the Alexandrinsky, which had reservations about the play's unpleasant Ibsenesque qualities and apparent lack of logical structure, but nevertheless approved it for inclusion in the theatre's repertoire on 14 September.

The more forward-thinking actors in the company, many of whom had been involved in the production of *Ivanov* seven years earlier, were excited at the prospect of a new Chekhov play. But then came another problem. The renowned comic actress Elizaveta Levkeyeva decided she wanted the play to be performed on her benefit night on 17 October, when the twenty-fifth anniversary of her acting career with the Imperial Theatres would be celebrated. While first-rank actors at the Alexandrinsky were allotted annual benefit nights, those of the second tier, like Levkeyeva, had to wait patiently for anniversaries, and then often chose works for performance which might not even include a role for them, if there was a greater likelihood of there being a full house.[53] This was the reasoning behind Levkeyeva's choice; she also remembered the warm reception *Ivanov* had received – but she had yet to see the script of *The Seagull*. Chekhov joked that the plump forty-seven-year-old was going to take the role of Nina, the slender seventeen-year-old, but, of course, there was no appropriate part for her in the play.[54] She was a talented actress, but one who remained her naturally comic self in whatever role she played, liable to provoke chuckles the minute she appeared on stage. Chekhov was therefore understandably alarmed at the suggestion that Levkeyeva should play Shamrayev's wife, since that would lead the audience to expect something funny, and they would certainly be disappointed.[55]

Just nine days were allocated for rehearsals, and when the bewildered cast first read through the play on 8 October, they immediately realized that its complexity and novelty demanded a far longer preparation time.

Chekhov was despondent when he arrived from Moscow and came along to the fourth rehearsal. Half the cast still had not learned their lines, some were not bothering to show up at all, and he was tempted to call the production off.[56] And then, less than a week before the premiere, Maria Savina decided that she really could not play Nina. Vera Komissarzhevkaya, her replacement, was an inspired choice: she was not only ten years younger than Savina, but she intuitively understood what the play was about – unlike many of her colleagues. Chekhov was impressed with her performance in rehearsals, and began to feel more optimistic: her acting had been so moving one day that the people sitting in the stalls had actually started crying, bowing their heads in embarrassment.[57]

But the play was doomed. A theatre which was run by the Russian government was never going to be a showcase for avant-garde theatre, let alone a revolutionary work like *The Seagull* which undermined its very foundations. Its productions were classical, like the theatre itself – highly predictable, conventional and unadventurous, redeemed only by the quality of some of the works staged and the acting of its company. Chekhov's play, however, was a work which, as he put it, did 'dreadful violence to stage conventions', beginning with the fact that it contained a great many conversations about literature (and what place did *they* have in the theatre?), but hardly any action. It was subtitled 'A Comedy', but where were the jokes? Everything was ambiguous, and there was neither an obvious hero or heroine, nor a familiar plot line ending in a satisfying denouement. Furthermore, the characters were ordinary people! When Chekhov wrote that he had begun his play *forte* and finished it *pianissimo* 'against every rule of dramatic art', he was acutely conscious of how subversive it was. Conventional late nineteenth-century European drama fell into a set number of categories, such as vaudeville, melodrama, classical tragedy and comedy, and *The Seagull* seemed to fit into none of them and all of them. It had far more in common with the unfamiliar, modern drama of Ibsen, Strindberg and Maeterlinck, who also discarded theatrical effects in favour of symbols and the creation of a particular mood.

The people who made up the typical Alexandrinsky audience, particularly those who packed the huge theatre on 17 October 1896, had little to no appreciation of the innovations in Chekhov's new play. The bank clerks, shop owners, officers and middle-ranking civil servants who had bought tickets were expecting to see something light-hearted. They were happy to pay over the odds in return for being entertained by Elizaveta Levkeyeva, one of their favourite actresses. And they were not disappointed by the comedy in which she starred, which was the second item on the double bill. But they were not prepared for the sophisticated, nuanced drama of irony and parody which preceded it. They had laughed uproariously at Chekhov's hilarious little vaudevilles when they had been performed at the Alexandrinsky, but what was this? Following a dismal dress rehearsal, the cast lost whatever confidence they had gained during rehearsals, and then completely lost their nerve when the audience started tittering – which they did almost as soon as the curtain was raised on an inept-looking second-hand set. By the time Komissarzhevkaya began reciting Nina's famous monologue in the first act, the titters had turned to outright guffaws. The actors were heckled throughout the play.

Chekhov's diary entry for 17 October recorded laconically: 'My *Seagull* was performed at the Alexandrinsky theatre. It was not a success.'[58] He fled the theatre halfway through the performance and went wandering through the freezing cold Petersburg streets until the early hours. At noon the next day he decided he would prefer to climb aboard the slow train back to Moscow and face a twenty-two hour journey rather than stay a minute longer in the capital. Sitting among the shopkeepers and Chekhov's bewildered friends and supporters at the Alexandrinsky had been journalists from all the major newspapers. Many of them were longing to cut him down to size and had been sharpening their knives. 'Probably no other play in the whole history of poor Levkeyeva's employment with the theatre has experienced such a breathtaking failure or been such an overwhelming fiasco,' wrote one critic. Another described the hissing as being so venomous it was as if a million bees and wasps had filled the auditorium. No matter that the subsequent performances were well received, and that provincial theatres were soon clamouring to stage the play. Attempting to defend Chekhov in the review he wrote for his own newspaper, Suvorin deplored the relish with which the critics had described the previous night's catastrophe.[59] Leikin decided it was time for another Chekhov front-page special. On the cover of *Fragments* for 26 October 1896, Chekhov was depicted sitting astride a seagull flying over a marsh, being shot at by huntsman-critics.[60]

A month after the premiere of *The Seagull*, Chekhov received a letter from Nemirovich-Danchenko, who spoke of his growing antipathy towards St Petersburg 'with its newspapers, actors, celebrities of the moment, and banal attempts at literature and public life'.[61] In his reply, Chekhov said that he understood what he meant. Despite his recent ordeal, however, he still felt there were many good things about St Petersburg, if only Nevsky Prospekt on a sunny day or Vera Komissarzhevkaya, whom he now regarded as a very fine actress.[62] All the same, it was with little enthusiasm that he agreed to go back to the capital the following March to sit for a portrait that had been commissioned for the Tretyakov Gallery. In the event, just before his planned departure his lungs seriously haemorrhaged, keeping him in Moscow, so the artist came to him instead. Chekhov went on his last proper visit to St Petersburg that July, staying as usual with Suvorin, with whom he discussed love, death and friendship.[63] Three days after he arrived, Suvorin left for Paris, having failed to persuade his friend to accompany him. Before Chekhov left the following day, he took a ferry down the Neva to visit Leikin's estate.[64]

Olga Knipper, who was later to become very important to Chekhov, could not entirely be blamed for thinking that he did not like Petersburg when she later challenged him about it in 1901. By the time she became acquainted with him in 1898, he had essentially stopped visiting the city. This was not solely due to his illness, nor to the deterioration in his relations with Suvorin which took place at around this time, although both were factors. Chekhov confessed to Olga in 1901 that it was the theatre in St Petersburg that he did not like or respect, not the city itself, adding the revealing comment 'I reject it completely.' It had felt as if he himself had failed, not just his play, when *The Seagull* had been performed at the Alexandrinsky. His surprisingly vehement language reveals feelings that were clearly still very raw. Chekhov did make two more very brief visits to St Petersburg, but neither was undertaken with enthusiasm and both were concerned exclusively with the publication deal that he had drawn up with a new publisher. In 1899 he left on the same day that he had arrived, and in 1903 he stayed only one night.

Chapter 6

SIBERIA AND THE WEST

I

Sakhalin

I do not like it when an educated exile stands by the window and looks silently at the roof of the neighbouring house. What is he thinking about? I do not like it when he talks to me about trivial matters, while at the same time looking at me with an expression that seems to say: 'You are going home, but I am not.' I do not like it, because I feel unbearably sorry for him.

From Siberia, 18 May 1890

If a purse is almost indispensable in Regent Street, a revolver is absolutely so on Sakhalin.

Charles Hawes, *In the Uttermost East*, 1903

On 21 April 1890, Chekhov set out on what would prove to be a momentous journey across Siberia. Travelling for almost three months, partly by rail, partly by rickety horse-drawn *tarantas*, and partly by boats of varying sizes, via Kazan, Ekaterinburg, Omsk, Tomsk and Blagoveshchensk, his destination was one of the Russian Empire's most remote eastern points: the island of Sakhalin. In the early hours of 14 October, after ninety-five gruelling days spent making a study of the penal colony on the island, which lies just north of Japan, he set off on his journey back home, this time travelling by sea. The route navigated by his Russian steamship took in Vladivostok, Hong Kong, Singapore, Colombo, Port Said and Constantinople (cholera in Japan had prevented the *Petersburg* docking in Nagasaki) and lasted almost two months. Shortly after Chekhov embarked on his voyage, Grand Duke Nikolai Alexandrovich, the future Tsar Nicholas II, also set off on a journey halfway round the world to the Far East, and the two travellers crossed paths in the Suez Canal.[1] Chekhov was glad to see land after eleven boring days at sea but, to judge from the silence in his correspondence, he could muster no enthusiasm for the pageantry marking the first official stop on the tsarevich's Grand Tour – hardly surprising, bearing in mind his recent intimate acquaintance with one of the more putrid efflorescences of the Romanov regime. As for Nicholas, his letters reveal that he was far more interested in pyramids and belly dancers than in making the acquaintance of the young writer who had spent three months probing the underbelly of Russian life.[2]

On 5 December, Chekhov finally disembarked in Odessa, and boarded a train for Moscow. The fleet of imperial vessels bearing the future Tsar, meanwhile, continued on its journey to India, Ceylon, Singapore, Siam, China, and finally Japan. There had been tension in Russia's relationship with Japan in recent decades over competing claims to Sakhalin, and the fact that diplomatic feathers were only slightly ruffled when the tsarevich was attacked by a Japanese policeman with a sword indicates the level of official cordiality that had been reached by 1890. Once safely back on Russian territory, Nicholas proceeded to return home to St Petersburg overland, and his route, via Blagoveshchensk, Omsk and Tomsk, retraced the path that Chekhov had taken twelve months earlier. The crown prince was the first member of the Romanov family to cross the entire Siberian continent. Alexander III envisaged an important role for his son in bringing Siberia 'closer to the rest of the Empire'. In Vladivostok Nicholas launched the construction of the eastern part of the famous railway that would soon link up the Asian and European halves of the enormous country he would unexpectedly rule just three years later. It is significant that the tsarevich's Grand Tour took him to Asia rather than to the more traditional capitals of old Europe. Siberia was Russia's Wild West; it was the continent of the future, and, apart from the mild irritation of a very un-Californian climate, it had everything to offer. The Trans-Siberian Railway was built with the aim of exploiting all those untapped resources in Asia, and opened in 1900 to great fanfare.

The interest in Siberia which Chekhov and Nicholas shared was, of course, inspired by completely different preoccupations. For the young Nicholas, Siberia was a reflection of Russia's imperial grandeur – and perhaps just a stepping stone to further expansion in the Far East. Some have speculated that his Grand Tour may have instilled in him an ambition of one day adding both China and Japan to his colonial portfolio. For Chekhov, Siberia was a place of adventure and of horror. If its endless empty spaces provided him with the opportunity to escape a stifling and humdrum metropolitan literary world and find fresh air and liberation, its penal colonies enabled him to perform a humanitarian service by acting as eye-witness and so justify his travels to such exotic parts.

As a literary celebrity, Chekhov's journey to Sakhalin had attracted a fair amount of attention in the Russian press. *New Times* had first announced his plans as 'sensational news' back in January 1890,[3] but it is unlikely they were viewed as such by the 24-year-old tsarevich (six years younger than Chekhov). As someone with more than a vested interest in preserving the status quo, Nicholas was never going to be enthusiastic about the idea of a Russian subject wanting to write about the 'unfortunates' (as they were euphemistically referred to) who had been condemned to hard labour and exile in Siberia. His tour, naturally, also received significant attention in the national press, and later became the subject of a luxuriously produced three-volume book, *Travels in the East of Nicholas II*, which Chekhov bought at special request for the Taganrog library, but with a reluctance that was not only due to its exorbitant price.[4] The last volume, which appeared in 1897, of course made no mention of Chekhov's outspoken book about the convicts of Sakhalin which had appeared two years earlier, although the enforced colonization of Siberia by exiles had all along been part of the official strategy to develop the Asian territories. Ironically, the route taken by his Imperial Highness's frigate, the *Memory of Azov*, was very similar to the one plied by the steamers of the Voluntary Fleet, which ferried thousands of convicts to Sakhalin from Odessa each year. Chekhov's yellow-funnelled boat, the *Petersburg*, had been launched as the *Thuringia* in the Scottish shipyards of Greenock in 1870, having been built to make the crossing between Hamburg and New York. It was adapted for the conveyance of convicts in 1889, and, like others in the fleet, made the journey from Odessa to Vladivostok twice a year in the summer months, before navigation north of Vladivostok was closed by ice. Before Chekhov embarked in 1890, the vessel had just discharged its final cargo of sixty-eight men and women destined for a life of exile on Sakhalin.

Chekhov's interest in Siberia and the Far East should certainly be seen in the context of Russia's intense preoccupation with Asia in the latter part of the nineteenth century – but not confused with it, despite his reverence for Nikolai Przhevalsky, the explorer and military officer who championed Russian imperialist expansion in Asia so aggressively. It is hard to square Chekhov's somewhat schoolboyish enthusiasm for a man of jingoistic, and sometimes downright racist, views with the humanitarian impulses which inspired the book he was to write about the convicts and indigenous tribes of Sakhalin, but Przhevalsky was a major inspiration. Chekhov undertook his journey to Siberia at a crossroads in his life. He had with ease become the leading writer of his generation, but that was a contributing factor to the deep sense of dissatisfaction and restlessness he felt in 1889: with the exception of the shining beacon of Tolstoy, there was no one else to compete with or look up to on the literary scene. Chekhov needed to be stimulated, but in the rather dull years of Russian literature under Alexander III, no other writer of his stature emerged, and he clearly found this dispiriting. As he was to put it famously in a letter a few years later, 'nothing being written today contains any alcohol' – it was all lemonade. He was willing to concede that in science and technology the age may have been one of greatness, but for people like us, he continued, '. . . it's a stodgy, sour, dull sort of time':

> We definitely lack that 'je ne sais quoi', and so when the skirts of our
> muse are lifted up nothing is to be seen there but an empty space . . . We
> have neither immediate nor distant goals, our souls are empty. We have
> no politics, we don't believe in revolution, we have no God, we're not
> afraid of ghosts, and personally I don't even fear blindness or death. A
> man who desires nothing, hopes for nothing and fears nothing cannot be
> an artist.[5]

Chekhov could not but be affected by the despondency which descended like a cloud on the Russian intelligentsia when censorship tightened and attempts were made to undo the 'damage' of the 1860s reforms. 'I have grown indifferent to reviews, to conversations about literature, to gossip, to success and failure, to earning big fees,' he wrote to Suvorin in May 1889; 'in a word I have become the fool of fools. It's as though my soul has gone into hibernation. The only explanation I can find for it is that my personal life has also gone into hibernation. I'm not frustrated or worn out or depressed, I've simply become somehow less interesting. I need someone to put a bomb under me.'[6]

Chekhov's malaise in 1889 was also attributable to the fact that his brother Nikolai was dying from the disease which he knew would also kill him sooner or later. He clearly wanted to go on an adventure and do something extraordinary with his life before it was too late. Apart from his commitment to literature and medicine, his own frail health and his family obligations prevented him from travelling the world and becoming a full-time explorer like Przhevalsky, but he was unwilling to capitulate completely to a sedentary life. And as a man with a deeply ingrained sense of moral duty, he also wanted to do something worthwhile. The obituary he wrote of Przhevalsky in 1888 makes it clear why this was important to him:

> Such people have had a huge educational impact, quite apart from their services to scholarship and the state. One Przhevalsky or one Stanley is worth a dozen educational institutions and a hundred good books. Their ideas and their noble ambition, which has the national and scholarly honour at its heart, their stubborn, invincible striving towards a certain goal, no matter what privations, dangers and temptations for personal happiness are entailed, the wealth of their learning and industry, their acclimatization to heat, hunger, homesickness, wasting fevers, their fanatical faith in Christian civilization and in science make them ascetics in the eyes of the populace, personifying the highest moral strength.

Chekhov's obituary of Przhevalsky is an extraordinary document, defining with crystal clarity the strong ethical values of a writer often condemned as unprincipled by his contemporaries. The personalities of people like Przhevalsky, Chekhov maintains, were like 'living documents', showing society that there still existed people of asceticism and faith besides all those 'conducting arguments about optimism and pessimism, writing banal stories, unnecessary projects and cheap dissertations out of boredom', and besides the 'sceptics, mystics, psychopaths, Jesuits, philosophers, liberals and conservatives' (in other words, all his contemporaries). Przhevalsky's last great spiritual feat, Chekhov notes, was to suppress his homesickness and ask to be buried in Central Asia, where he had conducted his fieldwork.[7]

Chekhov gets so caught up in hero worship that what he does not do in his obituary is discuss Przhevalsky's achievements, namely the collection he assembled of extensive geographical, ethnographical and meteorological data about huge areas of Inner Asia, large numbers of invaluable zoological specimens, and the discovery of the wild camel, and the horse which now is known by his name. Przhevalsky undertook four main expeditions in the 1870s and 1880s. First, he travelled across Siberia to Mongolia and China, then south-east over the Tien Shan mountains, then towards Lhasa and finally into the Gobi Desert. He found the emptiness of the Gobi Desert particularly entrancing, and vowed that he would not exchange it for all the gold in the world.[8] The books he wrote about his travels won him national fame back in Russia as an intrepid hero, and an adoring audience of swooning females to whose attentions he was, as a homosexual, completely immune. Before he departed on his last expedition with renewed hopes of reaching Lhasa, the Asian 'Rome', Przhevalsky was promoted to Major-General and given an audience with the Tsar. Alexander III's then teenage son, Nicholas, meanwhile, had been receiving thrilling dispatches from Przhevalsky about his skirmishes with the natives which, bearing in mind their political slant, can have only fanned the flames of his passion for the Orient. Przhevalsky assured the heir apparent that the peoples of Asia longed to become subjects of the Tsar, whose name, he wrote elsewhere, appeared in the eyes of the Asiatic masses 'in a halo of mystic light'. As an unashamed apologist for Russian chauvinism, Przhevalsky's attitude to these peoples was one of complete contempt.

It is easier to understand Chekhov's uncritical admiration for this Russian Livingstone, heralded as the most famous traveller in Asia since Marco Polo, when one remembers the torpidity and stagnation of Russian intellectual life under Alexander III: Przhevalsky's energy was simply electrifying.[9] Chekhov would have surely travelled more in his lifetime if he had been able to, and if he had not felt such a deep sense of duty towards his needy family. No writer seems to lament being bored more often; certainly no Russian writer shared his wanderlust. In his letters, he speaks of wanting to travel to countries as diverse as Sweden and Egypt, and advised one young writer that the best thing he could possibly do at his age was travel. The reference in his obituary of Przhevalsky to ten-year-old schoolboys wanting to run away to accomplish heroic feats in America or Africa suggests that his longing for adventure was very deep-rooted; back in 1887 his story 'Boys' had actually depicted a foiled attempt of two school friends to run away to America:

> ... they both opened up an atlas and started studying a map in it: 'First we go to Perm,' said Chechevitsyn quietly ... 'then Tyumen ... then Tomsk ... then ... then ... to Kamchatka ... and from there the Samoyeds can take you by boat through the Bering Straits ... And then you are in America ... There are lots of furry animals there.'[10]

When he set out for Sakhalin, following this very route, Chekhov was still dreaming of returning via America, a dream which he was unfortunately forced to abandon. One of his favourite books as a teenager was a travel book: Goncharov's *The Frigate Pallada*, an account of the Russian seafaring diplomatic mission to Japan led by Admiral Putyatin in 1852. This is where Chekhov would have first read about Sakhalin.

We should also approach Chekhov's journey to Sakhalin in the spirit of Fridtjof Nansen's quest for scientific knowledge and adventure. A few months before Chekhov set off for Sakhalin, Nansen arrived back in Norway from his first epic voyage across Greenland's ice cap, having first completed a doctorate in zoology. Chekhov may not have completed the doctorate he planned himself, but his book about Sakhalin and its prison colony was conceived with one vaguely in mind, and certainly written to repay what he felt was his debt to medicine. Nansen wrote a book about Eskimos, having spent a winter living among them during his Greenland exploration; Chekhov's book (this being Tsarist Russia) was about convicts, but also about Sakhalin's aboriginal population. In 1913, Nansen was himself to write a book about Siberia, having travelled extensively through it.[11] His career provides an ironic contrast to that of Przhevalsky: he would win the Nobel Peace Prize in 1922 for his international relief work, having organized the introduction of special passports to help the thousands stranded after the collapse of the great European empires in the 1920s. Chekhov was inspired by similar humanitarian goals, and might very well have been a contender for the Nobel Peace Prize had it been founded during his lifetime. Before he set out on his journey, he wrote an impassioned letter to Suvorin about why it was so important to think about Sakhalin:

You say, for instance, that nobody needs Sakhalin or finds it of the slightest interest. Can this really be so? Only a society that does not deport thousands of people to it at a cost of millions could find Sakhalin entirely devoid of usefulness or interest. Sakhalin is the only place, except for Australia in times gone by, and Cayenne, where one can study a place that has been colonized by convicts. All of Europe is interested in it, so how can it be that we are not? A mere twenty-five or thirty years ago our own Russian people performed amazing feats exploring Sakhalin, enough to make one glorify the human spirit, but we don't care about any of this, we don't know anything about these people, we just sit inside our own four walls complaining that God made a mess when he created mankind. Sakhalin is a place of unbearable suffering, on a level of which no other creature but man is capable of causing, whether he be free or in chains. People who have worked there or in that region have faced terrifying problems and responsibilities which they continue to work towards resolving. I regret that I am not sentimental, otherwise I would say that we ought to make pilgrimages to places like Sakhalin as the Turks go to Mecca, and sailors and penal experts ought to examine Sakhalin the way soldiers examine Sevastopol. It is quite clear from the books I have been reading and am still reading that we have let *millions* of people rot in jail, and let them rot to no purpose, treating them with an indifference which is little short of barbaric. We have forced people to drag themselves in chains across tens of thousands of miles in freezing conditions, infected them with syphilis, debauched them, vastly increased the criminal population, and heaped the blame for the whole thing on red-nosed prison supervisors. All of Europe now knows that the blame lies not with the supervisors, but with all of us, but we still think it is none of our business, we're not interested. The much-vaunted sixties did *nothing whatsoever* for sick people or for prisoners, and thus violated the principal commandment of Christian civilization. These days we do at least try to do something for the sick, but for prisoners we do nothing at all; the way our prisons are run holds absolutely no interest for our judiciary. No, I assure you, Sakhalin is necessary and interesting, and my only regret is that it is I who am going there and not somebody more experienced in the field and more able to generate interest in society at large. Personally, my reasons for going are trivial.[12]

Of course, Chekhov's reasons for going to Sakhalin were far from trivial, even if they did include his desire for a big adventure. The research he carried out before departing showed that.[13] Feeling he needed to acquire expertise, not only in Sakhalin's geology, but in its botany, zoology, meteorology and ethnography, he pored over every book about the island he could lay his hands on, starting with the memoirs of Admiral Voin Rimsky-Korsakov, elder brother of the composer and first commander of the Siberian fleet. He studied maps, memoirs and dry tomes about the Russian penal code. His sister and his new friend Lika Mizinova made notes for him in Moscow's main research library. He wrote letters and had meetings with government officials, and even got hold of a samizdat copy of the American journalist George Kennan's newly published and celebrated book *Siberia and the Exile System*, which was officially forbidden in Russia owing to its frankly critical stance. He started writing about Sakhalin's history even before he left. The preparatory work Chekhov undoubtedly most enjoyed was reading the books by explorers like Krusenstern and La Pérouse, who had completed heroic round-the-world voyages. The Russian translation of Darwin's account of his voyage on the *Beagle* was also very useful.[14]

Chekhov's decision to undertake the journey and complete a census of the prison population on the island came as a shock to his family and friends. He had been to the Crimea and to the Caucasus on summer holidays, but that was not the same as setting out on a journey to the other end of the Russian Empire under inhospitable conditions. (The consensus is that the trip proved extremely detrimental to his health, his protestations to the contrary notwithstanding.) It took him almost as long to get to Sakhalin as the time he spent on the island, but he relished the opportunity of seeing more of the world, and, in particular, more of the vast country he lived in.

After a short train ride to Yaroslavl there was a boat trip down the Volga on the *Alexander Nevsky*, with 'water meadows, sun-drenched monasteries, white churches, an incredible sense of space; lovely places to sit and fish wherever you look'. He saw the church that his friend Levitan had immortalized in his most famous canvas, 'Eternal Rest', and tugs pulling along strings of barges, which reminded him of a young man being pursued by his wife, mother-in-law, sister-in-law and grandmother. The scenery started to become bleaker on the wilder

Kama River. The weather was bad, and to Chekhov it seemed that the people in the towns he was passing through did nothing but make clouds, wet fences, mud and boredom. There were ice floes on the river still, and none of the birch trees had come into leaf; aesthetics had basically gone to the devil, as he put it in a letter home. At Perm Chekhov transferred to a train carriage, which took him to Ekaterinburg in the Urals, where he sat with his right foot in Europe and his left in Asia. He was coming to the despondent conclusion that all towns in Russia looked the same with their unpaved streets, log houses with carved window frames, high fences, white-walled churches, and bazaars.[15] Then came Tyumen, headquarters of the state exile administration, and the gateway to the vast Siberian continent, large enough to contain the entire territory of the United States without its boundaries being touched. At this point, Chekhov transferred to horse-drawn transport, and started the first of the travel pieces he sent back for publication in *New Times*. Travelling in May brought to mind the nightingales which would be singing in the lush Ukrainian landscapes where he had spent the previous spring, while the bare trees, cold and ice that surrounded him made him think about the sweet-scented acacia and lilac which would be blossoming in Taganrog. Initially he must have had doubts: his body ached from

Ekaterinburg

travelling along such bumpy, uneven surfaces, he was spitting blood, and the tea tasted and smelled as if it was an infusion of sage and cockroach. He was overcome by the huge numbers of ducks, wild geese, sandpipers and swans flying overhead, but the melancholy song of cranes interrupting the silence made him sad. Before too long, Chekhov was also encountering dozens of shackled convicts marching along in convoy, accompanied by soldiers with rifles. They were hardly a mood enhancer.

More than half a million convicts walked along the Great Siberian road to their places of exile during the nineteenth century. Exiling criminals to Siberia was a practice which had commenced in the first half of the seventeenth century, soon after Russia had conquered this vast territory. It became a convenient way for the government to rid itself of troublesome subjects, once it had subjected them to its standard punishments of impaling on stakes, amputation of body parts, branding with irons and so on. But exile gradually came to replace execution and mutilation as it dawned on successive tsars that criminals could perform a useful function in populating its newly acquired territories. The demand for cheap labour after the discovery of minerals in these parts only made this kind of punishment more appealing, and so the list of crimes for which one could be exiled grew longer and longer. Eventually, they included everything from murder, theft and desertion to fortune telling, snuff-taking and vagrancy. Under Catherine the Great, landowners were given unlimited powers to hand over disobedient serfs for exile to Siberia, and even village communities could expel the most troublesome of their members. Until the exile administration was set up in the early nineteenth century, convicts marched eastwards into what George Kennan called a 'chaos of disorder, in which accident and caprice played almost equally important parts'.[16] Chekhov had vowed not to follow in the footsteps of the American journalist who had exposed the Russian government's inhumane practices so mercilessly, but he did not shrink from writing about the exiles he came across during his journey.

In mid-May, the traveller arrived in Tomsk, where he bought his own tarantas to travel in, and some chocolate from sheer boredom. He spent a week recuperating at Tomsk. He was exhausted, having travelled non-stop through the night several times, and the wind and rain had made the skin on his face erupt like fish scales. It was not until he reached the mighty Yenisei River that he began to feel truly inspired by the landscape. If the Volga was a self-effacing beauty, whose sadness would turn all your hopes into Russian pessimism, he wrote in the ninth and last of his travelogues, the fast, strong currents of the Yenisey had quite the opposite effect. The mountains on its far bank, moreover, reminded him of the smoky, dreamy peaks of the Caucasus, and he mentally cursed Levitan for not having accompanied him. Chekhov was intoxicated by his first Siberian spring as he travelled through a forest of firs, pines, larches and birches that seemed to have no end: here was the magnificent *taiga*, which he had heard so much about. Birch trees had darker leaves in Siberia, he noticed, and were not as 'sentimental' as in Russia. Spring had indeed arrived, and for the first time Chekhov's spirits began to soar as his body began to warm up in the sunshine. It was not true that the taiga was silent and had no smell, he discovered: the air was thick with the scent of sun-drenched pine resin; he was surrounded by birdsong and the incessant buzzing of insects. And the sides of the road he travelled were covered with pink, yellow and pale-blue flowers that were a feast for the eye.[17]

As well as his travel pieces, Chekhov wrote some exuberant and

Krasnoyarsk and the Yenisey River

very lengthy letters back home to his family and friends. Signing himself *Homo Sachaliensis*, he sent one letter to his family from Krasnoyarsk in May 1890, in which he happened to mention that Yukhantsev and Rykov were resident there.[18] Both men had been convicted of bribery and embezzlement in high profile cases in the late 1870s and early 1880s (in Yukhantsev's case to the tune of two million roubles) and had been the butt of incessant jokes in the comic journals to which Chekhov contributed. In mentioning their names, he would have certainly been thinking about the court reportage he filed from Moscow to *The Petersburg Newspaper* about the Rykov case in 1884, and perhaps also, with a wry smile, he was remembering some of the spoof items in an irreverent 'Bibliography' he had published back in January 1883:

> The following new books have been published and are on sale:
>
> *On the abolition of tax payable on bamboo sticks imported from China*. Brochure. Price 40 kopecks.
>
> *Guidebook to Siberia and its surrounding areas*. With a map and a portrait of Mr Yukhantsev. Part 1: The best restaurants. Part 2: Tailors, coach-builders, salons de coiffure. Part 3: Addresses of 'those ladies'. Part 4: Index of rich young spinsters. Part 5: Excerpts from Yukhantsev's notebook (anecdotes, vignettes, dedications).
>
> *Is there any money in Russia and where is it?* By Rykov. Price 1 rouble.[19]

As they read his letter from Krasnoyarsk, Chekhov's family may well have pondered the extraordinary changes that had taken place in their lives since they had burst out laughing when this piece appeared seven years earlier.

On 5 June, Chekhov wrote to Nikolai Leikin from Irkutsk that coping with freezing weather, biting winds, interminable waits for ferries across flooded rivers, impassable mud and day-long delays while his tarantas was mended, had been awful. He had suffered from sleeplessness, hunger and fear (there had been one frightening collision with five mail carriages coming the other way at great speed one night) and he had dust permanently in his nose, but he regretted nothing:

The city of Irkutsk

All the same I am happy and I thank God for giving me the opportunity and the strength to embark on this journey. I have seen and experienced a lot, and everything is exceptionally interesting and new for me, not as a writer, but simply as a human being. The Yenisey, the taiga, the stations, the drivers, the landscape, the wildfowl, the physical torments caused by discomforts on the road, the enjoyment from getting some rest – all this together is so good I don't have the words to describe it. Just being day and night in the fresh air for over a month is interesting and healthy; for a whole month I have seen the sun rise and go down every day.[20]

By the time Chekhov reached Irkutsk, he was so filthy that the brown suds which poured off him when he went to the bathhouse made him feel as if he was a horse. Irkutsk was the best town he had yet seen in Siberia, and he spent a week recuperating there, and enjoying its amenities, which included a theatre, a museum, good hotels, wooden pavements and municipal gardens.

After Irkutsk, where he sold his tarantas, came a short journey along the Angara River to the steep, tree-covered shoreline of Lake Baikal, which the locals referred to as a sea. Chekhov had heard that you could see almost as far as a mile down in some of the lake's deepest places, and he told his family that he had seen rocks and mountains drowning in its delicate turquoise waters that had made his skin come out in goosebumps. The picturesque scenery and its warm and gentle colours again made Chekhov long for Levitan to be there enjoying it with him. Siberian poetry began with the mirror-smooth waters of Lake Baikal, he wrote to a friend; it was just prose up until then. Seeing bears, sables and wild goats was also pretty thrilling. After the trip across Baikal, which he described as wondrous and utterly unforgettable, came the last leg of the journey by horse-drawn transport. The drivers were now Buryat rather than Russian, and their horses very wild. The weather was by this time very warm, and Chekhov felt he was in paradise; the scenery of the Transbaikal seemed to contain all his favourite landscapes:

> I found in one place everything I have ever dreamed of: the Caucasus, the Psyol valley, the area round Zvenigorod, the Don. In the afternoon you can be rolling along in the Caucasus, by nightfall you are in the Don steppe, next morning you wake from a doze and find yourself in Poltava – and all within six hundred and sixty miles.[21]

At Sretensk, Chekhov boarded the steamer *Yermak* (named after the Cossack who had begun Russia's conquest of Siberia in the late sixteenth century), and travelled further east along the Shilka and Amur rivers. The first-class cabin felt luxurious and rather strange after all that time travelling by road, spending cramped nights in the tarantas together with two travelling companions making the same journey. He missed the jingling of the harness bells, but it was a joy to be able to stretch out his legs fully. Progress was initially slow along the shallow waters of the Shilka River, and at one point came to a complete halt when the boat ran aground, necessitating lengthy repairs to its hull. Chekhov had intended to continue with his travel pieces, but the engine of the *Yermak* shuddered so badly that writing was simply out of the question. All he could do was eat, sleep, talk, and gaze through his binoculars at the immense numbers of wild birds and the luxuriant and wild foliage they were passing through. He had fallen totally in love with the Amur. 'It is quite beyond my powers to describe the beauties of the banks of the Amur,' he wrote to Suvorin:

... I can but throw up my hands and confess my inadequacy. Well, how to describe them? Imagine the Suram Pass in the Caucasus moulded into the form of a river bank, and that gives you some idea of the Amur. Crags, cliffs, forests, thousands of ducks, herons and all kinds of fowl with viciously long bills, and wilderness all around. To our left the Russian shore, to our right the Chinese. If I want I can look into Russia, or into China, just as I like. China is as wild and deserted as Russia: you sometimes see villages and sentry huts, but not very often. My brains have addled and turned to powder, and no wonder, Your Excellency! I've sailed more than six hundred miles down the Amur, and before that there was Baikal and Transbaikal . . . I have truly seen such riches and experienced such rapture that death holds no more terrors for me.[22]

On board the *Yermak*, Chekhov reported to his family, the talk was all about the gold which had been discovered in the region. Every peasant seemed to be prospecting for gold, he discovered, and nouveau riche Russian gold-dealers were drinking champagne like water, he noticed. The conversation flowed as freely: when in Siberia, with no one to make arrests, and nowhere further to be exiled, people could be as liberal as they liked and say exactly what they thought. So different were the mores out in Asia that Chekhov felt as if he were somewhere

An Amur River steamer similar to the one Chekhov travelled on

like Texas or Patagonia; everything was utterly foreign. The disregard for conventional European values led to Orthodox priests in the Far East wearing white silk cassocks and openly engaging in gold smuggling (not to mention disregarding the fasts), men handing over women for cash while at the same time treating them with utmost chivalry, and also shooting vagrants without any compunction – all accompanied by a total absence of interest in Russian culture. The writer Chekhov? Who was he? The locals barely knew who Pushkin was.

On 26 June, after a week of swimming in the warm waters of the Amur and dining with gold smugglers (one of whom tried to press an enormous wad of cash on him for treating his pregnant wife), Chekhov reached Blagoveshchensk, the main administrative town in the region. The newfound wealth brought by the discovery of gold nearby had increased the town's population rapidly since its foundation in 1856, and along with the smart new brick buildings traditionally to be found in boomtowns were amenities like brothels. If Blagoveshchensk itself did not make much impression on Chekhov, his experience with a Japanese prostitute certainly did, to judge from the graphic account he gave Suvorin (which prudish Soviet censors swiftly excised from editions of his correspondence). In Blagoveshchensk, Chekhov transferred from the *Yermak* to the *Muravyov-Amursky*, a passenger boat named after the charismatic Governor General of Eastern Siberia who had spearheaded Russia's colonialist expansion into China. It was Muravyov whose far-sighted vision had led to the acquisition of the Amur territory in the 1850s, and the consequent annexation of Sakhalin. With his eye on the lucrative tea trade with China, Muravyov knew Russia had to find a waterway to the Pacific or lose out to the British. A major breakthrough was the belated discovery in 1849 that Sakhalin was an island, which meant that Siberia was connected both to the Sea of Japan and the Pacific through the Amur.[23]

Chekhov had begun to see increasing numbers of Chinese from Irkutsk onwards (they reminded him of the old monks his brother Nikolai used to paint), and on the *Muravyov* he shared a cabin with an opium-smoking Chinaman who inscribed the margin of one of his letters with some beautiful hieroglyphics which read 'I'm going to Nikolaevsk. Hello.' Chekhov was rewarded for having been bitten continuously by gadflies on the *Yermak* by now seeing meteors flying round his cabin – fireflies which were just like electric sparks. After following the path of the Amur south to Khabarovsk, the *Muravyov* then turned north, arriving in Nikolaevsk on 5 July. It was at this point that his letters home stopped, and his book began.

The Island of Sakhalin has a reputation for being a rather dry and impersonal book, with a style dictated by the need for its central message of human injustice to be delivered with the utmost efficiency. This does not hold true of its opening chapters, however, which describe the final leg of his journey and the history of the discovery of the island in conversational and sometimes intimate tones. Nikolaevsk, which stands where the mouth of the Amur delta meets the narrow Tatar Strait separating Sakhalin from the mainland, was the location for Russia's first fortress in these parts, and was named patriotically after Tsar Nicholas I. It had seen a fair amount of international traffic during the pioneer years earlier in the century, but the little town was not well-equipped to receive visitors now: there was no hotel, and Chekhov felt that the unframed windows of its hundreds of abandoned houses were staring at him like the eye-sockets of a skull. He was forced to spend the next two nights sleeping on the *Muravyov*, and when it weighed anchor again, he was for a time left completely stranded. Just as the sun was going down, and he was succumbing to a certain amount of panic, a local Gilyak agreed to row him out to the *Baikal*, the steamer which would carry him on to Alexandrovsk, the main port of Sakhalin. After the rhythmic combination of long and short sentences in Chekhov's short stories, with their clusters of adjectives, and sentences trailing off into dots, the sober clarity and tautness of the prose in *The Island of Sakhalin* is indeed marked, but occasionally gives way to a lyricism more reminiscent of his fiction:

> On the right-hand shore there was a forest burning; the wall of green was throwing up crimson flames; clouds of smoke fused into a long, black, motionless strip which hung over the forest . . . It was a huge fire, but there was silence and calm all around because it was no one's concern that forests were perishing. Clearly the green riches here belong only to God.[24]

As the *Baikal* chugged slowly south, Chekhov began believing he was at the end of the world, and that there was nowhere further to sail to. Into his soul rushed the sensations he felt Odysseus must have experienced when, dimly expecting to encounter extraordinary creatures, he had sailed into unknown waters – the waters that one day Chekhov would gaze out to when he was growing up. Accompanied by a pair of whales blowing fountains of spray into the air, in warm clear weather, on 11 July the *Baikal* reached the coast of Sakhalin, whose taiga was also on fire. Whatever poetic frame of mind Chekhov had been in earlier was now replaced by anxiety and foreboding:

> Through the smoke and darkness spreading over the sea, I could not see the jetty or any buildings and could only make out the dim lights of the post, two of which were red. The awful picture which was crudely cut out of the darkness, the silhouettes of mountains, the smoke, the flames and the sparks from the fire seemed quite fantastic.[25]

It seemed to Chekhov that he had already arrived in hell. The next twenty chapters of his book, clearly not written in such leisurely circumstances as the first three, take the reader on a tour of Sakhalin's main settlements, and describe with unflinching detail the lives of the hard-labour convicts, exiles and officials, as well as those of the island's aboriginal peoples. Chekhov's arrival coincided with an official visit by the Governor General of the Amur region, Baron Andrei Korf. Exile was not imposed for life, he assured Chekhov during their meeting, the hard labour assigned to the convicts was not excessively onerous, and there were neither sentries nor chains. Chekhov took pains to assure the reader that the very opposite was the case, and exposed prostitution, starvation and brutal corporal punishment in flat contradiction of the baron's Panglossian optimism. The Governor General's visit was accompanied by speeches, dinners, music and fireworks, but Chekhov found it all depressing. No amount of Bengal flares could turn the river in Alexandrovsk from a cook's daughter into a society lady, as he put it, and the cannon which blew up when it was fired seemed somehow symbolic. There might have been a party atmosphere at the Governor's residence, but elsewhere the mood was sombre:

> Nevertheless, it was miserable on the streets, despite such merrymaking. There were no songs or accordions or a single person getting drunk; people were wandering about like shadows, and were

as silent as shadows. Hard labour is still hard labour even when it is illuminated by Bengal flares, and music only inspires a deathly longing when it is heard from afar by a person who will never return to his homeland.[26]

By the time Chekhov made his historic visit, Sakhalin was the largest and most notorious penal settlement in Siberia, but it had not always been a penal colony, and it had not always been Russian. The sterlet-shaped island, twice the size of Greece, had first been explored by the Japanese, who found it was already inhabited by aboriginal peoples, principally Gilyaks and Ainu. Russians had started pushing eastwards into Asia from the sixteenth century onwards, lured both by the riches to be obtained in the fur trade and the possibility of escaping bondage to Ivan the Terrible. When the government began seriously expanding its eastern frontiers in the nineteenth century, Sakhalin naturally loomed into view due to its strategic importance in relation to Japan and China. In May 1805, the naval officer who captained the first Russian circumnavigation of the world suggested that it be taken for the empire, and confidently asserted that two cutters with sixteen guns and sixty men would be sufficient to sink the entire Japanese fleet.[27] It was not until the late 1840s, however, that the first Russian flag was raised on Sakhalin, with the first settlements following in 1853. After a flurry of diplomatic visits, Japanese resistance to the notion that Sakhalin belonged to Russia was finally overcome. In 1875 Japan agreed to exchange Sakhalin for the Kurile Islands. Six years later Russia founded a penal colony on the island, intending to use convict labour to excavate its rich coal deposits. Its population was then just a couple of thousand. By 1904, the population of Sakhalin had swelled to over 40,000. About a quarter of this figure were convicts serving terms of hard labour in the island's six prisons, with about a thousand exiles arriving each year on vessels of the Volunteer Fleet. The latter had been founded by voluntary public subscription in 1878 as a buttress against the Turkish navy and to protect Russia's Asian coastlines, but was largely subsidized by the government. The original three steamers which participated in the Russo–Turkish War had been joined by eleven other ships, some of which were converted so that they could be used to transport convicts to Sakhalin and other penal institutions, as well as freight to Vladivostok.

The famous Sakhalin convict Sofya Blyuvshtein

It took Chekhov a while to accustom his ear to waking to the sounds of clanking chains as convicts marched past his lodgings each morning. When he asked why even cockerels wore shackles, he received the reply that everything was chained up on Sakhalin. The work that he carried out on the island was in its own way a kind of hard labour. In order to get to speak to the inhabitants, he hit upon the ruse of conducting a census. His aim was to interview every single member of the island's population, filling in a questionnaire for each of them which he could later use as material for his book. He was clearly rather taken with this kind of statistical calibration, and he would later assist in the national census that was conducted in 1897, but his interest can be dated much earlier. One wonders whether, as he trudged round Sakhalin's settlements, he ever recalled the irreverent 'Supplementary Questions for the Personal Details Form of the Statistical Census suggested by Antosha Chekhonte' that he had published right at the beginning of his writing career in 1881:

16. Are you a *clever* or a *stupid* person?
17. Are you an *honest* person? A *swindler*? A *robber*? A *rogue*? A *lawyer*?

18. Which columnist is most to your liking? *Suvorin*? *'Letter'*? *'Amicus'*? *Lukin*? or *Yuly Shreyer*?

19. Are you a *Joseph* or a *Caligula*? A *Susannah* or a *Nana*?

20. Is your wife *blonde*? *brunette*? *black-haired*? or *a redhead*?

21. Does your wife *beat* you or *not*? Do you *beat* her or *not*?

22. What did you weigh when you were ten years old?

23. Do you consume hot beverages? *Yes* or *no*?

24. What did you think about on the night of the census?

25. Have you *seen* Sarah Bernhardt? or *not*?[28]

Chekhov worked flat out for the ninety-five days he spent on Sakhalin, rising at 5 a.m. every morning and walking, mostly alone, from hut to hut where he listened to heart-rending stories of human misery from people who had nothing to live for:

> It was a quiet, starry night. A night watchman was tapping, and a stream was gurgling nearby. I spent a long time standing there, staring at the sky and at the huts, and it seemed a miracle to me that I was six and a half thousand miles from home, in some place called Palevo, at the end of the world, where they did not even remember the days of the week, nor had any need to, since it was absolutely the same whether it was Wednesday or Thursday.[29]

With corruption rife among the guards and officials, what possible hope was there for redemption? Because of the climate and because peasants could never return to Russia at the end of their sentences, Sakhalin had no chance of ever becoming a vibrant colony like Australia. The aboriginal population had shrunk drastically since the Russian occupation. It was no wonder that so many Sakhalin exiles, driven by an overwhelming longing for freedom, attempted to escape, even though they knew the chances of success were slim. The vitality of a colony, Chekhov pointedly remarked, did not depend on prohibitions and orders, but on conditions guaranteeing a life that was peaceful and well-provided for. There was nothing remotely resembling any kind of civilized society when he visited Sakhalin in 1890, as far as he could see. And how could there be when sentries were even posted to stand guard outside churches while convicts prayed, and when the government's idea of Russifying the natives was

Gilyak storehouses for dried fish, Sakhalin

to hand out guns and badges? Sakhalin's inhospitable climate rendered most of it unfit for cultivation: its east coast was frozen for half the year, and much of its territory was impassable. Ships only called between June and October, and sometimes even the telegraph cable was cut off during the winter months. Chekhov was hard-pressed to find beauty on Sakhalin, but was clearly thinking of Levitan when suggesting that landscape artists might find inspiration in the yellow sunflowers, green rye and pink, red and crimson poppies of the Arkov valley.[30]

By the time Chekhov had finished his work on Sakhalin, 8,719 of the cards he had printed on the island had been filled out. He had clearly had some assistance with the task in one settlement; 584 of the 1,368 cards show the handwriting of someone else – a person who filled out 222 cards on his own. This person was a Buryat priest who Chekhov became friendly with on Sakhalin, and who not only accompanied him on some of his travels round the island, but travelled back to Russia with him on the *Petersburg* and lived for a while with his family in

Moscow. As native Siberians, Buryats were traditionally Shamanists, but Father Irakly had converted to Christianity after being the sole person in his village to survive a flood. He had then become a missionary, after taking holy orders in a monastery in the Transbaikal region where he came from. Almost the only Orthodox monk without a beard and moustache, he had served as a priest for eight years when Chekhov arrived on Sakhalin, and it was he who helped him make contact with some of the political prisoners there. Chekhov had been expressly forbidden from talking to this section of the island's populace, and Father Irakly's assistance came at a considerable risk to himself.[31]

It was with a huge sense of relief that Chekhov was finally able to leave Sakhalin. Empty of its convict cargo, the *Petersburg* started rolling heavily after they left Hong Kong, but there were compensations. The hell of Sakhalin was mirrored by the paradise of Ceylon, where Chekhov had the opportunity to spend some blissful moonlit hours in the company of a bronze-skinned woman in a coconut plantation, and to acquire what he thought were two mongooses (one later proved to be a vicious palm civet).

A year later, back home in Russia, he worked through the trunkful of notes he had brought back with him from Siberia and finished the first eight chapters of his book. He went on to complete it over the following two years. By this time he had patched up his differences with the editors of the journal who had slandered him as 'unprincipled' on the eve of his departure, and *The Island of Sakhalin* initially appeared in serial form in *Russian Thought*. He had saved the most harrowing chapters until last, and his account of a flogging was, not surprisingly, initially forbidden by the censor. *The Island of Sakhalin* was first published as a book in 1895, and was soon creating waves in official circles and inspiring several other people to write books about the Siberian exile system. One idealistic young lady from St Petersburg was so deeply affected by Chekhov's book that she even moved to Sakhalin so that she could dedicate herself to alleviating the lot of its benighted population.[32] At one point in his book, Chekhov describes a modest white house on the shoreline which turned into a lighthouse at night, its lamp shining brightly as if the red eye of hard labour was itself looking out at the world. His book also acted like a lighthouse, drawing attention to one of the worst aspects of the Tsarist regime. In the seventh of the travel pieces he published while travelling out to

Sakhalin, he exhorted his readers to take a look at the literature on prisons and exile: 'Two or three little articles, two or three authors, and goodness me, it's as if prisons, exile did not exist in Russia! Our thinking intelligentsia has been saying for 20–30 years now that criminals are a product of society, but how indifferent it is to that product!'[33]

Chekhov returned home in 1890 with his faith in Russia badly dented. In the first letter he wrote after returning home (addressed, of course, to Suvorin), he lamented how little justice and humility there was in Russia, and how poorly patriotism was understood. Having caught a glimpse of some of the British Empire's colonies, and heard Russian complaints about exploitation of the natives, Chekhov concluded that at least the British brought transport, sanitation, museums and Christianity with them, whereas the Russians indulged purely in exploitation:

> A drunken, debauched wreck of a man may love his wife and children, but what good is his love? The newspapers all tell us how much we love our great Motherland, but what is our way of expressing this love? In place of knowledge there is limitless impudence and arrogance, in place of work there is idleness and bestiality; there is no justice and the idea of honour goes no further than 'pride in one's uniform' – a uniform which is most usually to be found decorating the docks in our courts. What we must do is work, and let everything else go to the devil. Above all we must be just, and everything else will follow.[34]

In 1904, the truth of Chekhov's words was demonstrated when the steamroller of Russian imperialism was finally brought to an abrupt and humiliating halt by the Russo–Japanese War. Hostilities broke out a few months before his death. Establishing a naval base on the Pacific and occupying Manchuria in 1900 had been an encouraging prelude to Russia's ambition to conquer Asia: such was the empire's false sense of superiority when it acquired a twenty-five-year lease from China to expand into its north-eastern provinces, that the foreign minister declared that one flag and one sentry was all that was required to secure Port Arthur: Russian prestige would do the rest.[35] But Japan was no longer prepared to tolerate Russia's expansionist aims. Having enjoyed spending time with the Japanese Consul to Sakhalin back in 1890,

Chekhov was one of the few people in Russia who did not still see Japan through a 'yellow fog of ignorance' – as a quaint place where people whiled away their time with geishas, elaborate tea ceremonies and flower arranging.[36] He read news of the war's progress avidly, and with great concern. The way in which the Orient had taken hold of his imagination can be seen from the fact that he expressed a serious intention to travel to the front and work as a doctor that summer, even though by that time he barely had the strength to go for a walk, let alone carry out medical duties. The alarming news about the war's progress troubled him greatly during his last days, and no doubt partly lay behind his delirious mutterings about a sailor just before he died.[37]

Sakhalin was the only Russian territory that Japan invaded during the war, and it temporarily acquired the southern half of the island under the terms of the peace treaty drawn up in September 1905. In the chaos before the penal colony was finally shut down the following year, over 30,000 Russian inhabitants managed to escape.[38]

Chekhov attempted very little creative work in the year that he travelled to Sakhalin, but his story 'Gusev', which was begun just before the last leg of his fifty-two-day sea journey back to Odessa, and finished in Colombo, bore the stamp of his recent experiences, and stands out as one of his most unusual and artistically ambitious pieces of fiction. The story is set in the sick-bay of a ship similar to the *Petersburg*, and at the beginning of a similar voyage: through the Sea of Japan to Hong Kong and on to Singapore. The patients in the sick-bay – a sailor, three privates and an impoverished clergyman – have all served in the Far East and are now returning to Russia. The anger the cleric Pavel Ivanych expresses towards the Russian authorities, who have washed their hands of consumptive peasant soldiers by loading them on to ships of the Voluntary Fleet, undoubtedly echoed Chekhov's own feelings. Over 400 discharged Russian servicemen had come on board the *Petersburg* at Vladivostok, and two had died and been thrown overboard by the time the ship reached Singapore. Partly acting on Chekhov's advice, five sick bulls were slaughtered and thrown overboard as well.[39] Three out of the five patients in the sick-bay die during the course of 'Gusev', which has more sentences trailing off into rows of impressionistic dots than any other story he wrote, echoing the delirious state of its central character. The peasant soldier Gusev is, in fact, so delirious when Pavel Ivanych dies that he does not even notice his body being removed from the sick-bay. Within a matter of days he too is dead, and his body is being sewn up in sailcloth to be thrown into the deep to be eaten by a shark. Chekhov finished this story in Colombo, and its fantastic ending seems inspired by that exotic locale:

> Then another dark body appears. It is a shark. It glides underneath Gusev grandly and nonchalantly, as if not noticing him, and Gusev lands on its back; then it turns belly up, basks in the warm, clear water and lazily opens its jaws, showing two rows of teeth. The pilot fish are thrilled; they stop and look to see what is going to happen next. The shark teases the body a little, then nonchalantly places its mouth underneath it, carefully grazes it with its teeth and the sailcloth is ripped along the whole length of the body from head to toe; one of the weights falls out and frightens the pilots by striking the shark on its side before descending quickly to the seabed.
>
> But meanwhile up above, clouds are clustering together over where the sun is rising; one cloud is like a triumphal arch, another like a lion and a third like scissors . . . A broad green strip of light emerges from behind the clouds and stretches out to the middle of the sky; a little later a violet one joins it, then a gold one, and a pink one . . . The sky turns a delicate lilac colour. The ocean frowns at first as it looks at this magnificent, mesmerizing sky, but then itself takes on those tender, radiant, passionate colours which are difficult to describe in human terms.[40]

II

Europe

I'm in Venice. Put me in a madhouse.
                              Letter to Maria Kiselyova, 25 March 1891

Abbazia and the Adriatic are wonderful, but Luka and the Psyol are better.
                              Letter to Natalya Lintvaryova, 21 September 1894

After travelling as far east as he could almost possibly go, where else could Chekhov visit next but Western Europe? He had done privation; now it was time for decadence. It was a relatively quick turnaround. He arrived back in Moscow in early December 1890. After the open spaces of Siberia, he felt very cramped resuming his city life in the small flat that his family had rented while he was away, and he was soon itching to travel again. By March he was on his way to St Petersburg to meet up with Suvorin and catch the express train to Vienna. And it was not just any old train – Suvorin's sybaritic tastes dictated that they travel in style, and so their carriage boasted comfortable beds, carpets, mirrors and enormous windows. A far cry from the tarantas of the previous year. Chekhov travelled to Western Europe on five occasions in his life. There were two visits undertaken with Suvorin in 1891 and 1894, both whistlestop tours of the great cities, and then there were two much longer sojourns he spent on the French Riviera for health reasons. He had longed to take off from the south of France and visit Africa, but by this time he was tragically unfit for the rugged adventures that had been the stuff of his boyhood dreams. The last time Chekhov travelled to Western Europe was to die.

The itinerary for the 1891 tour took in Vienna, Venice, Bologna, Florence, Rome, Naples, Nice, Paris and Berlin, and was completed in six weeks. Chekhov's reaction to arriving for the first time in the Austrian capital was one of naive amazement and delight. 'If only you could know how magnificent Vienna is!' he wrote excitedly to his family back in Moscow:

. . . there is no comparison with any other city I've ever seen in my life. The streets are wide and immaculately paved, there are masses of boulevards and squares, all the houses have six or seven storeys, and as for the shops – well, they are not shops so much as an utterly stupefying dream come true! The ties alone in the windows run into billions! And what amazing things they have in bronze, china, leather! The churches are enormous, but their size caresses rather than oppresses the eye because they seem to have been spun from lace. St Stephen's Cathedral and the Votiv-Kirche are particularly beautiful, more like cakes than buildings. The parliament building, the Town Hall, the University, all are magnificent; yesterday I understood for the first time that architecture is truly an art form. And in Vienna this art form is not scattered about randomly as it is with us, but extends in terraces for miles on end . . .[41]

Two days later, however, Chekhov was in Venice, and he already had to revise his opinion that Vienna was the *ne plus ultra*:

I must say that for sheer enchantment, brilliance and *joie de vivre* I have never in all my life seen a more wonderful city than Venice. Where you expect to find streets and lanes there are canals, instead of cabs there are gondolas, the architecture is staggeringly beautiful and every little corner has its historical or artistic interest. You drift along in a gondola seeing the palaces of the Doges, Desdemona's house, the homes of famous painters, churches . . . And inside these churches are sculptures and paintings such as one sees only in dreams. In a word, enchantment . . . It's quite easy for a poor, benighted Russian to lose his wits in this world of beauty, riches and freedom. You simply want to stay here for ever, and when you stand in a church and listen to the organ being played it's enough to make you become Catholic straight away.[42]

But then it started raining, and Chekhov's spirits immediately plummeted. 'It's raining as hard as you can imagine, and Venezia the *bella* has ceased to be particularly *bella*,' he lamented to his family; 'there's a feeling of melancholy wafting from the water, and it makes one long to flee to somewhere where the sun is shining.' A week into the tour and the travellers were in Florence. Chekhov was enjoying himself, but he was not really in his element, and he soon tired of visiting museums. 'I saw the Venus dei Medici and thought that were she to be dressed in the sort of clothes people wear nowadays she would look most unattractive, especially around the waist,' he said in his next letter home, signing himself Antonio. The skies continued to be overcast and, for Chekhov, Italy without the sun was like a face behind a mask. The glories of Renaissance art somehow failed to make their mark. 'I've seen everything I was supposed to and dragged myself to everywhere I was told go to,' he confided to a friend; 'if someone gave me something to smell, I smelled it. Now I am drained of all feeling except exhaustion and a longing for cabbage soup with buckwheat kasha. Venice put me under her spell and turned my head, but the moment I left, Baedeker and bad weather took over.'

Either Chekhov's Siberian experience had spoiled him for the pleasures of cultural tourism in the old world, or he was by nature unsuited for such pursuits. Either way, the tour did not prove to be as enjoyable as he had expected. Once the initial novelty of being in the great cities of European civilization had worn off, he quickly got bored, and it is telling that by the time the party reached Rome, all Chekhov wanted to do was get out of town and lie on the grass somewhere. This is not to impute any philistinism to him: he found Italy an enchanting country, and was mystified that Levitan had not taken to it. 'If I were an artist with no ties and plenty of money I would spend the winters here,' he wrote; 'after all, it's not simply that the natural surroundings and the warmth of Italy are beautiful in themselves, but Italy is the only country where art reigns over all, and simply to be aware of this is very stimulating.' Part of the problem was simply the opulence of being part of Suvorin's entourage: 'We stayed in the best hotel in Venice, like doges, and here in Rome we're living like cardinals, because our hotel is the former palace of Cardinal Conti, now the Hotel Minerva: two huge drawing rooms, chandeliers, carpets, fireplaces and all kinds of useless clutter, costing us 40 francs a day.' This was again a far cry from the accommodation in Siberia which had been at best spartan, and maybe he felt he somehow had to do penance. There was an exhilarating horse-ride from Pompeii to the bottom of Vesuvius, and then an excruciating ascent by foot:

> Dragging oneself up Vesuvius is sheer torture: ash, mounds of lava, molten rock that has congealed in waves, clumps of vegetation and all kinds of rubbish. One step forward, half a step back, the soles of your feet are sore, your chest aches . . . On you plod, but the summit is as far away as ever. Give up and turn back? No, I would be too ashamed, and besides I would expose myself to ridicule. I started the ascent at two-thirty, and got to the top at six. The crater is several score metres across; I stood on its rim and looked down into it as if into a cup. The ground all round about is covered in a deposit of sulphur that gives off clouds of vapour. Evil-smelling white smoke belches forth from the crater itself, molten rock and sparks fly everywhere, and Satan lies snoring beneath the smoke. There is a huge cacophony of sounds: waves breaking against the shore, the heavens thundering, rails clattering, boards crashing down. It is terrifying, and yet one is gripped by a desire to leap straight down into the monster's mouth. I now believe in hell.[43]

Chekhov visited another kind of hell when they moved on to Nice and stayed in a smart hotel on the seafront. At least the air smelt nice there, he noted, and it was warm and green. But not in the roulette halls of nearby Monte Carlo, where Chekhov tasted the thrills and dangers of gambling, and managed not to succumb to them, unlike so many of his compatriots. In this Chekhov was indeed unusual. Pushkin gambled away his poetry, Tolstoy gambled away his house and Dostoevsky gambled away everything he had, but Chekhov was able to walk away, glad nevertheless to have tried his luck a little. He was certainly not immune to fine living, but the 'roulette-style luxury' of the French Corniche reminded him of a luxurious WC. 'There is something hanging in the air which you feel offends your sense of decency,' he wrote to his family; it was something which 'vulgarizes nature, the sound of the sea, and the moon'.[44]

Having been almost continuously on the road for the previous twelve months, Chekhov felt slightly jaded by the time he arrived on the Côte d'Azur. After the privations of travelling in Siberia the previous summer in the most austere conditions possible, it was something of a shock now to stay in luxury hotels and dine in smart restaurants in the manner to which Suvorin was accustomed. With the memory of the prison colony he had visited on Sakhalin clearly still in his mind, Chekhov was slightly nauseated by the amount of time people abroad seemed to spend eating and sleeping, and also by the richness of French cuisine, where every morsel seemed to be garnished with artichokes, truffles and nightingales' tongues. Writing home to his family, he concluded that it was much better in Siberia in that respect, since one generally never had any lunch or dinner there, or got any sleep, and he confessed that he had actually felt much better for it.

His squeamishness may also have been attributable to the fact that he was writing during the last week of Russian Orthodox Lent, knowing that devout believers such as his parents would have begun a final strict fast, in addition to the earlier relinquishing of meat, eggs, dairy products and alcohol. At midnight on Great Saturday would begin the joyful celebration of Easter – the biggest festival of the Russian year – accompanied by special Easter foods to break the fast, the exchange of painted eggs, family celebrations and the jubilant ringing of bells. Even for lapsed believers like Chekhov, Easter spent away from home was significant enough to him to be worthy of comment, and his

15 April letter to his family is headed 'the Monday of Passion Week'. On Palm Sunday, the day before, he had gone to the Russian church in Nice, and wrote to tell his family, knowing they would be interested, that as well as the usual lighted candles, the congregation had held proper palm leaves rather than the sprays of pussy willow used in Russia as a substitute. He also told his family that there were women singing in the choir, rather than young boys, which made the singing slightly 'operatic', but that they had given a magnificent rendition of a simple 'Our Father' and a Bortnyansky setting of the much-loved hymn 'The Assembly of the Angels'. Seeing people place foreign coins on the plate during the collection and hearing the church servitors speaking French was also a novelty.

Being able to go to an Orthodox church outside Russia was not to be taken for granted for most of the nineteenth century: the pious Gogol had nowhere to go during the winter he spent in Nice in 1844. Building an Anglican or a Lutheran church in Catholic countries was one thing (the English church in Nice was built in 1822), but the Vatican was clearly not keen for there to be places of worship built by the church it had been in feud with since the mid-eleventh century. The Church of Saints Nicholas and Alexandra in the Rue de Longchamps in Nice, which dates from the late 1850s, is in fact the oldest Russian Orthodox church outside Russia. It was built at the instigation of Tsar Nicholas I's widow, the Dowager Empress Alexandra Fyodorovna, who had spent the winter in Nice in 1856, the year after her husband died.[45] Construction began while the city (Nizza as it was then called, the name still used by Russians) was still in the domain of the Italian Counts of Savoy, and the Roman Catholic authorities would not allow either a belfry or a cemetery to be attached to the church.[46] They also insisted that the building should look like a private residence, which explains why Chekhov had to go upstairs to the first floor to enter the church proper. The challenges posed by the restrictions, and communication problems between the architect in Russia who designed the church (believing it would be bigger) and the French architect who actually built it, resulted in the single large room being dwarfed by the ornately carved iconostasis made out of oak which was brought all the way from St Petersburg, along with a sixteenth-century icon of the Vladimir Mother of God personally donated by the Dowager Empress. The only concession apparently won by the Russians was the construction above the nave of a sky-blue cupola, the symbol of heaven one traditionally finds in Orthodox churches. The Church of Saints Nicholas and Alexandra was consecrated in January 1860 – the month in which Chekhov was born.

Chekhov's last stop in Europe in 1891 was Paris, where he marvelled at how tall the Eiffel Tower was, saw some naked women at the Folies Bergères (or some similar establishment), got tangled up in political demonstrations, and felt a rush of homesickness when forced to celebrate Easter at the Russian Embassy church. It was the first Easter he had spent abroad. Although he jocularly referred to the West as Sodom and Gomorrah when he returned to Russia, Chekhov certainly enjoyed himself. He was not one of those Russians stricken with intense homesickness the minute he stepped on foreign soil. All the same, and notwithstanding his broken pince-nez left behind in Russia, without which he was short-sighted and undoubtedly missed a lot, he did not find French painters as good as Russian ones, certainly not in the genre of landscape painting. Levitan had the edge, as far as he was concerned.[47]

He next visited Western Europe in the autumn of 1894, again with Suvorin. They were abroad for about a month and their hastily put-together itinerary this time included Abbazia, Trieste, Milan and Genoa, along with some of the cities they had visited before: Vienna, Venice, Nice, Paris and Berlin. From the few, sparse letters he sent back home from this trip it is clear that Chekhov did not become any more enamoured of Western Europe the second time around. He enjoyed the beer, and saw some Italian actors perform in a stage version of *Crime and Punishment* which brought him to the depressing conclusion that Russian acting by comparison did not even have lemonade in it, let alone any alcohol. But he seems to have most enjoyed visiting a crematorium in Milan and following the labyrinth of quiet paths in Genoa's Cimitero di Staglieno. Situated on a hillside planted with cedars and cypresses outside the city, the cemetery's ornate tombs and marble sculptures were justly celebrated, and Chekhov was as amazed as other visitors to find not only lifesize statues of the deceased, but also of their distraught widows, mothers-in-law and children.[48] Perhaps he had developed a fondness for such places, having spent time while he was growing up wandering through Taganrog's leafy cemetery, older even than the Genoa cemetery, and similarly full of marble tombs and

statues erected by the town's wealthy Greek and Italian merchants.
Suvorin may have been bemused to travel with a companion who
preferred the outdoors to the priceless relics of ancient civilizations; he
commented that what Chekhov had been most interested in during
their trips abroad was cemeteries and circuses.[49]

Chapter 7

MELIKHOVO

I

A Place in the Country

Conversation on another planet about the earth in a thousand years time: do you remember that white tree? . . . (a silver birch).

Notebook No. 1

Whatever sort of roses I plant, they all turn out to be white.

Comment to Maria Chekhova

It was snowing on the February day in 1903 when Chekhov wrote to tell Stanislavsky about his vision for the first act of *The Cherry Orchard*, his play about the death of old Russia. 'Blossoming cherry trees can be seen through the windows, an entire garden of white,' he wrote from Yalta, 'and the ladies will be in white dresses.'[1] Perhaps he was thinking back to his first February in Yalta four years earlier when the temperate Crimean climate had brought the cherry trees there into early blossom. But it is more probable that he was thinking nostalgically about the cherry orchard he had left behind at his estate in Melikhovo in 1898. 'I was sorry you weren't here when the garden was all white with blossom and there were nightingales singing,' he wrote to Suvorin during his first spring there in 1892.[2] Chekhov was told there were cherry trees in the garden at Melikhovo when he moved in, but at first he had to take this on trust because it was not until the snows melted that he could actually discover where they were. Despite the fact that his orchard started producing so many cherries in July that his family did not know what to do with them, planting more trees was one of Chekhov's first priorities. By the time the snow fell again that autumn,

Chekhov's house and garden at Melikhovo

he had planted sixty more cherry trees, of the renowned Vladimir variety whose fruit is deep red in colour, large and sweet.

As he sat at his desk in Yalta conjuring up the clouds of white blossom that would fill the play which would be his last completed literary work, Chekhov may have been thinking back particularly to the summer of 1897. The cherry trees at Melikhovo produced an abundance of fruit that year. 'I am going away soon, so I am doing nothing at the moment but wandering round the garden eating cherries,' he wrote to Nikolai Leikin; 'I pick twenty at a time and stuff them all into my mouth at once. They taste better like that.'[3] Or maybe he was thinking of the hot July days of the following summer at Melikhovo, when his father made sixteen and a half pounds of cherry jam. (And this was despite Pavel Egorovich recording in his Melikhovo diary a few days earlier that the sparrows had pecked all the cherries from the trees.)[4] Notwithstanding the change in his lifestyle necessitated by the onset of tuberculosis, the unexpected death of Pavel Egorovich a few months later brought one of the happiest periods of Chekhov's life to an abrupt end. The estate was sold in 1899 to a timber merchant who proceeded to chop down the cherry trees. He could not help thinking back wistfully to his orchard in Melikhovo, where the cherries blossomed each successive spring.

Chekhov loved cherry blossom simply because it was beautiful, but he also associated it with his childhood and southern upbringing. In 'The Steppe', his first story for a literary journal, we see cherry trees through the eyes of nine-year-old Egorushka. The carriage the boy is travelling in has just set off from his southern home town one early July morning at the beginning of the long journey across the steppe, and is passing the cemetery:

> Looking like white blobs from far off, white crosses and gravestones peered out happily from behind the wall, nestled among the green leaves of cherry trees. Egorushka remembered that when the cherry trees blossomed, these white blobs merged with the white cherry blossom to become a white sea; and when they ripened, the white gravestones and crosses were spattered with crimson dots like blood . . .[5]

The leafy Taganrog cemetery also stood on the edge of town, and Chekhov knew it well. It might have been one of the many places where he came to pick cherries as a boy. As he stood eating cherries underneath his very own trees for the first time in July 1892 in Melikhovo, Chekhov experienced a long-forgotten frisson. 'It feels strange that no one is chasing me away,' he wrote to Suvorin; 'I used to get my ears boxed every day for picking fruit when I was a child.'[6] Rather more chilling, in the light of what the cherry orchard comes to symbolize in his play, is the connection made in this passage from 'The Steppe' between the white blossom of a tree and the maturing of its red fruit (which ought to represent life forces) with blood, death and sterility. In the play, the cherry orchard comes to stand for a whole social system which has many beautiful qualities, but is fundamentally superannuated. On a much more private level, since Chekhov would not have forgotten the haunting image he created fifteen years earlier in 'The Steppe', the orchard stands for life itself, and his own life in particular.

Cherry orchards may have been subliminally linked with death in Chekhov's mind from an early age, but they were also inextricably linked for him with the mystique of the Russian country estate – the *usadba* – which had traditionally been one of the bedrocks of the country's feudal ways. The fortunes of Russian landowners were already in decline when Chekhov was growing up; it was a natural consequence of the Emancipation of the Serfs, which took place when he was one year old. As a young boy he had heard the mother of a school friend talk about the huge cherry orchards she used to have on her Ukrainian estates before she became impoverished, like so many other members of the gentry. From his vantage point in dusty, cramped Taganrog, a country estate must have seemed like an Arcadian paradise, a fairytale world of endless space and beauty, which was all the more entrancing since it was so far from his own life; also, it was beginning to disappear. When he was able to escape from Taganrog and travel into the steppe, Chekhov finally saw acres of white cherry blossom for himself. It was an image which was implanted more vividly in his creative imagination when he travelled back south to the steppe in the spring of 1887 to visit his friends the Kravtsovs, and was overwhelmed by the beauty of the flowering orchards on their estate.[7] It made him long all the more to have an estate of his own.

Chekhov was not interested in having an estate in order to be lord of the manor and have a retinue of staff; it was the idea of shady paths, cool stretches of water and blossoming trees which captivated him. This becomes clear when one reads his early thriller *Drama at a Shooting Party*, in which there are several lyrical passages mixed in with the parody and racy dialogue, and phrases ending poetically with his signature . . . They are, significantly, exclusively concerned with evoking the manorial estate where the action takes place: 'I remember the Count's garden with its luxurious cool orangeries and the shade of its narrow neglected paths . . . Those paths, protected from the sun by an arch of interlaced green boughs of old lime trees, know me well . . .'[8] When Chekhov's narrator describes the beauty of a white-blossoming cherry orchard on the far side of the lake, and its once sumptuous grounds, one has the distinct impression the author is expressing his own feelings: that this estate is located in the southern Russia of Chekhov's childhood we know from the reference to a kurgan. A few months after the last instalment of *Drama at a Shooting Party* appeared, Chekhov wrote to Leikin to congratulate him on buying Count Stroganov's old estate outside St Petersburg. 'I love everything that goes under the word estate in Russia,' he commented revealingly; 'that word has still not lost its poetic colouring.'[9] Chekhov was not a sentimental man, and there was no higher word in his lexicon than 'poetic'. It invariably implied an elegiac kind of beauty. His reaction upon setting eyes on Leikin's new property a few months later is also revealing, however. The former merchant's son was revelling in being able to reside in luxury, but his nouveau riche lifestyle repelled Chekhov, who retained modest tastes to the end of his days. Melikhovo, indeed, was the very opposite of Leikin's opulent palace.

Melikhovo lay some forty-five miles south of Moscow, about fifteen miles from the town of Serpukhov, and six miles from the nearest railway station of Lopasnya, which was on the main line (Lopasnya was also the name of the local river). The purchase of the estate had been an impulsive move: Chekhov bought it, sight unseen, in the dead of winter. Inspired by his summers at Luka and his trips into the outlying countryside, he had initially set his heart on somewhere in the Ukraine. When these plans did not work out, he became somewhat reckless. He had been desperate to move out of Moscow ever since his return from Siberia at the end of 1890. After the magical summer spent at the run-down estate at Bogimovo, his desire for space only intensified. He found everything to do with business and money boring, and he was often swindled by the more unscrupulous people he dealt with because of it, so his younger brother Misha was brought in to negotiate on his behalf when the Melikhovo estate came up for sale. Chekhov visited the property only when the deeds had been signed, on a snowy day in late February 1892. With an eye to getting out his fishing rod at the earliest opportunity, he brought down with him from Moscow twenty small tench in a jar, which he had purchased in a fish shop in the city. They were immediately deposited in the pond, and thus became the estate's first new residents, a week before the Chekhovs themselves moved in; carp followed shortly afterwards.[10] Tench were certainly a good choice for the pond. From experience (and perhaps study of Sabaneev's *Fishes of Russia*), Chekhov would have known that they grew quickly, could be fished in spring, were easy to catch, and were generally rather lazy ('phlegmatic' was Sabaneev's choice description). Tench liked to live in still waters, preferably deep down in the slime.

For those brought up on a diet of Tolstoy and Turgenev, the words 'Russian country estate' will conjure up visions of majestic classical mansions, grand staircases and colonnaded ballrooms with exquisite marquetry floors, belvederes and enfilades, elegant empire furniture, orangeries, pavilions and parks. But there were estates and estates, and Melikhovo was at the other end of the scale. There were no belvederes, and there were certainly no orangeries, as Chekhov commented sadly to Suvorin after he taken his first tour of inspection of the estate. With less than a dozen low-ceilinged rooms, the main house was actually smaller than many of the residences built for the stewards of some of the more imposing aristocratic properties. Its only columns had been installed by the previous owner to support the roof on the veranda, whose quaint, vaguely oriental design led the locals to think he must be a Tatar. The house did not even have a mezzanine (the half-floor which was a staple of even modest country houses), let alone a bathroom. What it did have was a tin roof and a profusion of *klopy* and *tarakany*: bedbugs and cockroaches. The previous owner, an artist of dubious taste who painted sets for a theatre in Moscow, had clearly lived in some style with his wife and mistress, their filthy children and some malodorous cats. For his 13,000 roubles Chekhov did get a lot of land, however – some 570 acres – about half of which was covered with spindly young birch trees. There was a ramshackle barn, a hen house, a cattle shed, and various other wooden outbuildings with thatched roofs. There was a well, an orchard and vegetable garden, a couple of ponds, and a wooden fence which went all the way round the perimeter of the estate from its red entrance gates. Most importantly there was a *lipovaya alleya* – a lime tree path – that quintessential ingredient of the Russian country estate. For Chekhov it was the very best thing about Melikhovo.

Along with the buildings, Chekhov inherited an out-of-tune grand piano, some carts and various farming implements, plus a variety of rather clapped-out animals, namely three horses, a cow, ten old hens, four geese and two shaggy dogs, Sharik and Arapka. This line-up was to change, with the canine contingent soon augmented by Byeloloby (Whitebrow), who gave his name to a children's story about a dog which Chekhov was to write at Melikhovo. But none of the Chekhovs had all that much of an interest in animal husbandry. In 1894 a family friend compiled an inventory of Melikhovo's sleighs, carriages, carts, ploughs and livestock, listing the horses with accompanying thumbnail biographical sketches, thus:

> *Kirghiz*: 8 years old. For going to meet the express train 100 times and throwing his owner just as many times, he gets the top prize.
> *Malchik* [Boy]: 5 years old. A horse who likes to perform; dances elegantly in harness.

Anna Petrovna: 98 years old. Too old to be fertile, but we live in hope.
Bites coachmen.
Kazachka [Cossack girl]: 10 years old. Hates having a bit in her mouth.
Kubar [topsy-turvy]: 7 years old. Docile and patient.[11]

It was Kubar who was Chekhov's favourite, and the horse he would ask
to be sent to the station to meet him when he arrived by train from
Moscow. Apart from playing the piano in the evenings, this inventory
was perhaps the most valuable service performed by Alexander
Ivanenko, who in the early years was Melikhovo's resident
prizhivalshchik – another indispensable feature of the Russian country
estate. The prizhivalshchik (fem. prizhivalka), a relative or family friend
who had no income and was given free board and lodging on a
longterm basis, was as familiar a figure in Russian households as the old
nanny and the ageing retainer. Constantly aware that they were there
on sufferance, such people tended to be excessively ingratiating, as
unobtrusive as possible and usually very dull. The comic character of
the impoverished landowner Telegin in Chekhov's *Uncle Vanya* is a
classic example of a prizhivalshchik (the play, which is subtitled 'Scenes
from Country Life', was completed at Melikhovo). Telegin is so much
part of the furniture that the voluptuous Yelena has not even bothered
to learn his name, which provokes him to remind her who he is: 'I
live with you now, ma'am, on this estate ... I have lunch with you
everyday, if you would care to notice.'[12] Although Ivanenko was
rather younger and far more interesting, he was another of life's
unfortunates, and Chekhov clearly had elements of his personality
in mind when was creating the character of the hapless bungler
Yepikhodov in *The Cherry Orchard*. He was a talented musician and
had won a place to study piano at the Moscow Conservatoire. When
he arrived late in his first year due to illness, however, he was forced
instead to take up the flute: all the pianos had already been committed
to other students.

As was common, Melikhovo was also the name of the village in
which the estate was situated. Melikhovo was a relatively common
name for a Russian village, and was derived from 'melissa', the Greek
word for bee. Not surprisingly, the area around Chekhov's estate was
renowned for its apiaries. The beekeeping brothers at the nearby
monastery even won medals for their honey in the 1860s, and Chekhov

himself nurtured hopes of installing hives when he moved into his estate. 'How I would like to have an apiary!' he wrote to Suvorin after just a few weeks in his new home. 'I have an excellent place for one. There's room for 200 hives. And it would be so interesting.'[13] He had many dreams when he first moved in; like his plan to build an orangery and keep 2,000 hens,[14] this one was not fulfilled.

Chekhov was proud finally to become a landowner himself – it was the fulfilment of his long-cherished dream – but his attitude to his new status was always ironic, not least because of the large mortgage he had taken on to buy Melikhovo. And there is more than a dash of self-referential irony in 'Gooseberries', his satirical portrait of a minor official who scrimps and saves in order to acquire a country estate. The story was one of the last pieces of prose Chekhov wrote at Melikhovo. It was completed in the summer of 1898 before he left for Yalta, and portrays a self-satisfied man so bent on pursuing his dream of cultivating gooseberries that he fails to notice they are completely sour. Tolstoy had written a story claiming that a person only needed six feet of earth. Chekhov countered provocatively that actually people needed the whole globe:

People say that a person only needs six feet of earth. But in fact it's a corpse that needs six feet of earth, not a person. And people also say these days that it's a good thing when members of our intelligentsia feel drawn to the land and want to live on country estates. But those country houses with their plots of land are nothing other than those six feet of earth. Leaving city life and all its struggles and stresses; leaving all that in order to lock oneself away in the country – that's no life, that's being selfish and lazy; it's a kind of monasticism, but monasticism without any sacrifice. People don't need six feet of earth, or even a house in the country, but the whole globe, the whole of nature in its entirety, so they can have the space to express all the capacities and particularities of their free spirit.[15]

Of the neighbouring landowners, Chekhov became most friendly with Prince Sergei Shakhovskoi, who in 1894 made Chekhov the godfather of his daughter Natalya. Shakhovskoi's much grander seigneurial residence, a mile down the road at Vaskino, fitted rather more closely the traditional image of the Russian country estate. The

main house was wooden, but built in the classical style with a long
enfilade of rooms with shuttered windows and columns, and a couple
of libraries whose bound volumes Chekhov enjoyed poring over. The
house was flanked by the obligatory annexes and a carriage house, these
built in brick, and was located in the middle of an eighteenth-century
landscaped park which came complete with its own church. Its lands
were three times the size of Melikhovo.

Shakhovskoi came from a family with a distinguished lineage. His
grandfather had been a Decembrist – one of the liberal-minded nobles
who had tried unsuccessfully to stage a coup in December 1825 in
order to introduce a democratic form of government – but these were
hard times for Russian aristocrats. In the spirit of the times, Shakhovskoi
worked conscientiously for the zemstvo, Russia's first form of local
government, but this did not help him pay off his debts. By the spring
of 1894, he had become so hard up he had to sell his ancestral home. In
an echo of *The Cherry Orchard*, Vladimir Semenkovich, the engineer
who bought Vaskino, started letting out parts of his new property in the
summer to dachniks.[16] The way of life of the Russian nobility had truly
begun to crumble. When he had sold Melikhovo and was living in Yalta,
Chekhov once asked Semenkovich if he had a spare dacha for some of
his friends. He had sometimes gone over to Vaskino to visit his new
neighbours, with whom his relations were cordial, but often it was
because he wanted to hear Mrs Semenkovich play the piano. She was a
distinguished graduate of the St Petersburg Conservatoire, and a noted
interpreter of Beethoven sonatas.[17]

II

Paterfamilias

Papasha groaned all night. When I asked him why he had been
groaning, he replied: 'I saw Beelzebub.'
                                    Letter to Alexander Chekhov, 30 December 1894

Frost 12°. Full Moon. O. P. Kundasova and the Girl were taken to the
station. Evening frost 16°. We ate fish soup.
                                    Pavel Chekhov, diary entry, 30 December 1894

There were many attractions to buying Melikhovo for Chekhov. It meant no more rent to pay on apartments in Moscow, and no more worries about finding a summer dacha: the estate could be lived in all year round. The cost of living became cheaper. Melikhovo immediately became a beloved holiday destination for Chekhov's brothers, all of whom had regular nine-to-five jobs and lived in town. Then there were assorted aunts, in-laws and cousins who came to stay as well. Although there was not a huge amount of space left in the house after his parents and his sister had taken over rooms, Chekhov now had somewhere quiet to work. He could at last escape from the literary limelight and start discreetly doing some good works. He also at long last had a garden to cultivate and the space to plant trees. The flatness of the landscape around Melikhovo would not have been to everyone's liking, but it suited Chekhov's unpretentious tastes. He found it inspiring, in fact, and was particularly entranced by the areas where there were trees. 'It's wonderful in the forest,' he wrote to Suvorin in May 1892. 'Landowners are very stupid to live in parks and orchards, and not in the forest. In the forest you can feel the presence of divinity.'[18] Ever the dutiful son, Chekhov could now provide his parents with a permanent home where they could live to the end of their days in security and comfort.

Chekhov had always lived with his mother in Moscow, but his father became a member of the household again now that he had finally retired from his live-in job at Gavrilov's warehouse. Melikhovo was the first property which anyone in the family had owned since the house Pavel Egorovich had built in Taganrog almost two decades earlier. Chekhov's father had to accept that he was not the authority figure at Melikhovo, which was not always easy. The rest of the family lived in Melikhovo on a part-time basis. Masha rented a flat in Moscow to live in during the school year, but came down every weekend and every holiday. With her organizational skills, quiet industry and unquestioning devotion to her brother, she immediately became an indispensable presence. Before he got married in 1896 (the wedding took place in the church at Vaskino), Misha spent long periods at Melikhovo working as the estate manager, sometimes setting off before dawn to work in the fields in the summer months. Ivan got married in the little wooden church in Melikhovo in 1893, and frequently came down from Moscow to help out during the school vacations, working in the vegetable garden, for example, or churning butter.[19] Alexander made several visits from St Petersburg, often with his two young sons who, on one occasion, he left with his younger brother without even the provision of a change of clothes.

The first task which faced the Chekhovs when they moved into Melikhovo in March 1892 was to make the house habitable. The previous residents had left it in a squalid state, and rooms had to be cleaned and painted, floors repaired, and the kitchen relocated to the building next door, which had previously been used as servants' quarters. Chekhov took over the sunniest room in the house for his study; this had previously served as the artist's studio. Its three large windows looked out over the garden – apple blossom in early spring, and roses later on in the summer. Within the first few weeks he had hung Levitan's painting of the River Istra on his wall (a souvenir of happy days at Babkino), and the photograph of him posing with Suvorin, Svobodin and Davydov in St Petersburg. Outside, the garden was tidied up, superfluous fences taken down, nesting boxes attached to tree trunks for starlings (a reminder of life in Taganrog), and work started in the greenhouses in preparation for the cultivation of cucumbers, radishes and other summer vegetables. Carpenters, joiners and stove-builders had to be taken on, as well as farm hands and people to work in the house. It was not easy, and Chekhov readily acknowledged his lack of experience in rural management. As he said to one friend, all he knew was that the earth was black,[20] and the family was frequently taken advantage of in the early days by wily peasants. One of their horses was surreptitiously changed overnight for an old nag.

But slowly life settled into a rhythm. Once they became used to their new surroundings, the family began giving nicknames to the constituent parts of their kingdom, calling one of the ponds the 'aquarium' because of its diminutive size. They also augmented their menagerie with a pair of purebred silver-grey Romanov sheep (noted for their exceptional fertility), a fine pig, a bull, doves, and several more cows. True Russians, the Chekhovs also soon sniffed out where on their estate to find mushrooms, which were consumed with great relish at the dinner table. Except on the occasions when Chekhov's father harangued his wife or chuntered on interminably about imperial decorations, mealtimes at Melikhovo were usually convivial. Chekhov had bought a bell which was fixed to a post in the garden, and at noon every day it was rung twelve times to call the family in to lunch. The sound of the bell could be heard several miles away, and it became the custom for everyone in the district to stop work and sit down to lunch at noon.[21] Chekhov would sit at one end of the table in the dining room at Melikhovo, so he could quietly slip away and retreat to his study when he wanted. His father was given the place of honour at the other end of the table, where he would drink from his own special carafe. It looked as if it contained a herbal concoction, but it was actually vodka. Sometimes the family dined on fish that had been caught in their own pond.

Each member of the family assumed responsibility for a particular task. Misha managed the work in the fields, where rye and oats were planted, and Masha took over the cultivation of vegetables for the family dinner table. When exotic summer produce such as melons, corn, aubergines, artichokes and asparagus started to appear, the family took to jokingly referring to the vegetable garden as 'the south of France' and the name stuck. Many of the local peasants had never even seen tomatoes before; for the Chekhovs it was a nostalgic nod to their southern roots. Evgenia Yakovlevna took charge of daily meals, along with the devoted family cook Maryusha (shortly to retire), and she supervised the pickling of cucumbers and cabbage and the drying of apples in preparation for the winter months.

Chekhov's father, meanwhile, took on the job of clearing paths in the garden, but he was otherwise rather useless until the jam-making season came around. He had considerably mellowed now that he was in his seventies, but was still not always the easiest person to live with, as a letter from Chekhov to Alexander soon after they moved in shows:

> Papasha is philosophizing as usual, asking questions like: why is there snow lying here? Or: why are there trees over there, but none here? He spends his whole time reading the newspapers, and then tells Mamasha that a society has been founded in Petersburg to fight the classification [a confusion with 'falsification'] of milk. Like everyone from Taganrog, he is incapable of any work besides the lighting of candles in church. He is very strict with the peasants.[22]

Pavel Egorovich was indebted to his son for his material wellbeing, but sometimes behaved as if he were the master of Melikhovo. Following the long years of humiliating poverty, he liked the new feeling of social superiority that came with living on an estate and having staff. Occasionally he exploited it, and Chekhov then quickly lost his patience, on one occasion berating his father for turning away peasants who had come to receive medical treatment. It turned out they had upset the neatly raked (but pointless) pattern Chekhov senior had made in the gravel outside the house for want of anything better to do.[23] And Chekhov drew the line when his father decided to hold an open-air service in the garden at Melikhovo, and arranged for the icons to be brought over specially.[24] On their first Easter at Melikhovo, Chekhov was happy to hire a priest from the monastery to come and conduct vespers in the village church, where services were normally only held two or three times a month. And he became an enthusiastic member of the choir along with his family and their guests, which impressed the local peasants in the congregation; they had never been to an Easter service sung so beautifully in their church. Later Chekhov had a belfry built, and he erected crosses on the church's cupolas. They could be seen several miles away, particularly when they reflected the light of the setting sun – an image Chekhov had long been fond of conjuring up in his stories. He did not mind the priest coming to sprinkle holy water in the house, or pour it into the ponds and the well, nor did he object to the occasional icon procession coming through the estate. And he was happy for the local priest and his sexton to be regular guests at lunch, but holding church services in the garden was just a little bit *de trop*.

With churches in all the local villages and a sixteenth-century monastery nearby (where there were four different churches to choose from), there were many places for Pavel Egorovich to go to take communion, and he was happy at last to be able to give spiritual matters his undivided attention. The family liked to rise early in the country, so bedtime was usually at ten o'clock, which shocked visitors from the city. After lamps were extinguished, the house would fall silent except for the sound of Pavel Egorovich softly chanting his prayers before the large icon in his incense-filled room.

When Chekhov's father was not reading the Bible or playing his violin, he was likely to be sitting at his desk, writing one of his pompous letters or another diary entry in his ornate, sloping script. The diary, published in its entirety for the first time in 1995, is a magnificent chronicle of the Melikhovo years, albeit seen from a very particular angle. Thus we find out what the temperature was in the early morning and at noon, which church Pavel Egorovich went to on a certain day, when he went to the monastery on foot, and how much he paid when he stayed the night there one time when he was fasting (one rouble). We find out on which hot summer days he went for a dip in the pond (also when Sharik the dog went swimming), when and where a new sleigh was bought, and when Roman, the retired soldier who was employed as the family's main workman, was too drunk to fetch the post. We learn when Pavel Egorovich sent letters to his son Misha in Uglich, and when an errant cow strayed into the garden and ate the Chekhovs' cabbages. We are told exactly how many peasant men, peasant women and peasant children came to pay the traditional visit on Easter Sunday, following the celebratory fireworks and cannon fire, when nightingales sang in the garden, when it snowed, when Ivanenko talked too much, and when Ivanenko spent too long beating himself with birch twigs in the bath-house. Pavel Egorovich's barely suppressed irritation is also apparent in his entry for 12 February 1898, in which he records how many pancakes everyone ate on Shrove Tuesday. He was clearly not fond of Masha's friend Maria Drozdova, and it is hard to believe that Chekhov did not recall this particular diary entry when he created Ferapont's immortal line in *Three Sisters* about the merchant who died from eating forty pancakes (or was it fifty?):

12. Morning −18°. Everyone ate blini. Midday −10°. Drozdova ate 10 blini, Kolya [Alexander's son] 6, Masha 4. There is no water in the wells. The bull was brought in. Evening: −15°.[25]

But Pavel Egorovich's diary tells us next to nothing about the inner lives of the inhabitants of Melikhovo – how bad weather made Anton Pavlovich feel as flabby as overcooked macaroni and unable to write, for example, or how the sensation of ageing made him feel as if there was a jug of sour milk in his heart.[26] On the terrible day of 19 October 1896, when Chekhov returned home to Melikhovo, in a state of utter despair after the disastrous premiere of *The Seagull*, his father recorded simply:

Morning: fog, +3°. Roman prepared the window frames for the kitchen.
The twigs were chopped. Noon: +5°. Antosha, Masha and [Lidia]
Mizinova arrived from Petersburg. The things left behind in the train
were returned to Lopasnya untouched. Evening: +2°.[27]

Pavel Egorovich never wrote very much in his diary – a few lines at
most – although he did become slightly more expansive as the years
went by. On Easter Monday, 14 April 1897, a few days after Chekhov
returned home from Moscow after two weeks lying flat on his back in
Dr Ostroumov's clinic recovering from the massive haemorrhage he
had suffered, his father was moved to write:

> Morning: –1°. Eastern wind. Went to mass at Vaskino at 6.30 but missed
> it. Noon in the sun: +15°. Everything was delicious at lunch today, there
> were lots of conversations. Antosha liked the roast beef. Ants appeared
> in the house and on my desk.[28]

With a father like this, it would seem obvious where Chekhov got
his sense of humour from: irony is present in almost everything he ever
wrote. But irony was completely foreign to Pavel Egorovich. He may
not have even initially realized he was being made fun of when his
children started filling in the occasional blank days in the large
accounts books he used for his diary. It started in March 1893. Pavel
Egorovich had not always been meticulous about noting something
down every day; a few gaps had crept in here and there. First of all
Masha contributed a few earnest sentences such as 'Snow and rain.
The pond is filling up.' This inspired her brother to join in as well,
noting less seriously on 15 March: 'The ram is jumping. Maryushka is
happy.' And then, when Pavel Egorovich left for Moscow two days
later, Chekhov really got into his stride with a masterly rendition of his
father's style:

> 17. P. E. Chekhov left for Moscow. +2° during the day. The oats were
> delivered.
> 18. –1°. It is snowing. Thank goodness, everyone has left and just M-me
> Chekhov and I remain.
> 19. –5°. Masha and Mizinova arrived. A clear day. The lentils and
> buckwheat were delivered.

20. –5°. A clear day. The greenhouses are ready. Mamasha dreamed of a goat on a [chamber?] pot.

21. +5°. Semashko arrived. We had roast udder.

22. +6° We heard a lark. A crane flew over in the evening. Semashko left.

23. +3° Mamasha dreamed of a goose in a *kamilavka* [the cylindrical black hat worn by Orthodox priests]. This is a good sign. Mashka has a stomach upset. We slaughtered the pig.

24. We made sausages.

25. –2° A bright morning.[29]

Pavel Egorovich took much greater care to write something every day after that. In fact, when Chekhov next had the opportunity to act as ghost-writer for his father, he was completely conscientious: whatever feelings of mirth he had for the absurdity of some of the diary entries now mingled with affection and respect for the enterprise. Thus in the middle of the diary page for October 1895, Pavel Egorovich's curling calligraphic script is suddenly replaced by the refined but spare lettering of his son's distinctive small hand:

10. Morning: –3°; the garden and the fields are white with frost. The flowers have been caught by the frost. A clear day. Weather: +15°. We planted tulips. We dug over the vegetable garden.

11. Overcast. Weather: +6. Levitan left.

12. Morning: +5°. There was no frost during the night. Firewood is being brought from the forest. It was warm and clear all day. The roses were covered with straw.

On 13 October, after Chekhov had started filling in the entry for the day: ('During the night and in the morning: +8°. Overcast. Weather: +11°'), his father arrived home to complete it: 'P.E. returned from Moscow at 1.30pm.'[30]

The source of Chekhov's glorious sense of the absurd becomes easier to understand in the light of Pavel Egorovich's chronicle of their lives. Perhaps his father's literary style, a naive mixture of the high and the low, even influenced the surreal mixture of ideas for stories, snippets of overheard conversation and quirky observations to be found in his notebooks. While sometimes serious, the lapidary phrases Chekhov jotted down are often extremely funny, their brevity providing an ironic counterpoint to his father's terse sentences:

> The opinion of a professor: it's not Shakespeare who is important, but the notes to his works

> A dachshund was walking down the street and was ashamed that it had crooked legs

> He married, furnished a house, bought a writing desk, got everything in order, but found he had nothing to write

> The girl spoke enthusiastically about her aunt: she is very beautiful, as beautiful as our dog!

> I was happy only once in my life – under an umbrella

> A Play: The Bean of Life[31]

Perhaps Chekhov's masterful economy of expression was even influenced by Pavel Egorovich's concise literary style, which was undoubtedly honed much earlier during the Taganrog years – some of his father's bald sentences vividly evoke the atmosphere at Melikhovo.

Chekhov never really became close to his father, who continued to exasperate him in all sorts of ways, and he could never forgive him for the lashings he had received as a child. Yet there is something touching in Chekhov's careful preservation of the plodding letters his father had sent him when he was out in Siberia – letters which accompanied him all the way back to Moscow – that is not just explained by a fastidious nature. At Melikhovo father and son managed to live harmoniously for six years in close proximity. As time went by, and Pavel Egorovich continued to mellow, he and his diary imperceptibly became an indispensable fixture of Melikhovo life. Chekhov was certainly grateful for all the digging that the old man had started to do in the garden. In September 1898, less than a month before his father's death, Chekhov had written to him from Yalta with instructions regarding the new apple trees, larches and poplars he had ordered, and a request that his roses be covered with leaves before the first frost.[32] It did not occur to him that he would not be spending the following summer at Melikhovo, so news of Pavel Egorovich's sudden death came as a great shock. Chekhov was probably taken aback by how much he had taken his father's presence in Melikhovo for granted. 'I don't think life at Melikhovo will be the same after father's death,' he wrote to Masha as soon as he heard the news; 'it is as if the flow of Melikhovo life stopped when his diary stopped.'[33] Pavel Egorovich had been particularly fond of peonies, sometimes going so far as to note in his diary when the red Moscow peonies came into flower, when the white ones were in bloom, and when there were four peonies blooming at once.[34] In memory of his father, Chekhov had some of them dug up and shipped to Yalta, where he planted them in his new garden.

The flowers in the garden were definitely Chekhov's province, along with the trees. The hundreds of bulbs planted in autumn produced tulips, narcissi, hyacinths and irises in the spring, to be joined by carnations, lilies and roses, sweet-scented jasmine, lupins, violets, stocks, fritillaries, tobacco plants, and a host of other carefully chosen shrubs and plants. As well as the trees in the orchard, many other new trees were planted, including firs and pines from seed.[35] This was Chekhov's first garden, so he made a few false starts here and there, as he readily admitted. He also had the occasional spot of bad luck (his newly planted apple tree saplings were eaten by hares in the first spring, for example),[36] but his flowers soon began to bloom in profusion, and by 1895 he was writing to his friends to boast of their glorious scent, especially in the evenings.[37] He was particularly proud of his roses, and lady dachniks staying next door at Vaskino were thrilled to be presented with hand-picked bouquets when they came to visit. To their great disappointment, though, the petals would sometimes start falling off on the way home: Chekhov slyly only picked roses in full bloom from stems that needed pruning anyway.[38] The garden inevitably found its way into Chekhov's writing. Apart from the famous blossoming cherry trees, there is a reference to fragrant heliotrope in *The Seagull*, worked on at Melikhovo in the summer of 1895, and to sweet-smelling mignonette and oleander in 'The House with the Mezzanine', completed the following year. The story 'The Black Monk', meanwhile, written in 1893, has as its setting a garden run by a famous horticulturalist:

Kovrin had never seen such amazing roses, lilies and camellias like the ones Pesotsky had, or such tulips in every imaginable colour, from snow-white to jet black; in fact he had never seen such an incredible profusion of flowers anywhere else. Spring had only just begun and the most opulent blooms were still hiding away in hothouses, but what was blossoming along the paths and in the flower beds was enough to make you feel that you were in a kingdom of delicate colours as you wandered about the garden, especially in the early morning when dew drops sparkled on every petal.[39]

Chekhov had two 'assistants', a pair of black and tan dachshunds, and they would accompany him faithfully on his daily horticultural inspections. Bromide and Quinine were a gift from Leikin. They were born sometime in the spring of 1892, and Chekhov wrote excitedly to Leikin after moving into Melikhovo in order to expedite their arrival.[40] It was actually a whole year before they made the journey by train from St Petersburg. The puppies immediately started causing chaos once they stepped over the threshold, as Chekhov reported to Leikin on 16 April 1893:

> The dachshunds finally arrived yesterday. They got very cold and hungry and tired coming from the station, and were fantastically happy to get here. They raced around all the rooms jumping up affectionately on everyone and barking at the servants. Once they had been fed they felt completely at home. During the night they dug up the soil from the window boxes, complete with the seeds which had been sown in them, and distributed the galoshes from the front porch to all the rooms. In the morning, when I was walking them in the garden, they caused panic in the breasts of our yard dogs, who had never in all their lives seen such monstrous creatures . . . Everybody has fallen for the dachshunds; they now constitute the main topic of conversation. Huge thanks to you.[41]

It was Masha who thought up the names Bromide and Quinine, while her brother supplied the patronymics, viz. *Brom Isayevich* and *Khina Markovna*. The dogs slept in Chekhov's study. Quinine's legs were so short that her stomach seemed almost to drag along the ground when she walked, but she would come up to Chekhov every evening, put her front paws on his lap and gaze at him adoringly. The love was mutual. Brom was equally affectionate.

With other dogs around, it was only a matter of time before puppies started appearing. Sharik and Arapka, the farm dogs, had produced Muir and Mirrielees, named after Moscow's most famous department store. Brom promptly fell in love with Mlle Mirrielees when she came on heat (as Chekhov reported to various friends), while Quinine fell for another yard dog later in the year and produced her first pups in February 1894. Then, the following January, they fell incestuously in love with each other, and Saltpetre (*Selitra*), the survivor of a litter of two (and the spitting image of Brom, apparently) continued the dynasty.[42] Leikin sent Chekhov a photograph of Brom and Quinine's father that spring to show his children; both dogs apparently sniffed it for a long time, but felt nothing and ran off.[43] Chekhov had intended giving Saltpetre to Count Orlov-Davydov, a local landowner, but in the end she became the playmate of the six Semenkovich children at Vaskino.[44] Confusingly, Chekhov's brother Alexander in St Petersburg acquired a dachshund puppy which he also called Saltpetre in July 1896. She looked just like Quinine, he said. He had hoped his brother would give him one of Brom and Quinine's offspring, and his wife was particularly disgruntled when this failed to happen.[45] Chekhov reported to Masha in June 1897 that 'Isayich and Markovna' were once again 'engulfed in passion',[46] but it is not clear that any further pure dachshund pups were born. Chekhov had written to Alexander that February to tell him that Quinine was now giving birth three times a year to puppies which were a strange mixture of crocodile and mongrel.[47]

Chekhov sent regular bulletins to Leikin about Brom and Quinine, writing to him in April 1897, for example, to tell him that they were getting fat on their idle life, but were very happy. After mentioning in this letter that the family's loyal guard dog Sharik had died, Leikin generously offered Chekhov another pair of puppies – laikas, known for their strength and endurance. Unlike the dachshunds, these Siberian huskies, bred for hunting in the taiga (their name comes from the verb 'to bark'), would be perfect as guard dogs. Sharik had been mauled by Zalivai, a hunting dog given to the Chekhovs, and was the only canine member of the household ever to merit an obituary in Pavel Egorovich's diary ('He was a good and faithful watch dog').[48] It had not been a good spring: the ferocious Zalivai had also attacked Brom,[49] another of

Quinine's puppies died on the same day that a cat was shot,[50] and then came the news that there were rabid dogs in the area.[51] Leikin cheered Chekhov up when he offered him the laika puppies: Nansen and Laika arrived on 3 August, four days before Quinine had her next litter of puppies. 'They already feel at home, are playing, and whimpering from the heat and from fleas,' Chekhov wrote to Leikin the next day. 'I am in debt to you for the dogs. They are a very, very nice present, and I do not know how to thank you. I keep going to have a look at them. My sister too.' Wildly jealous, Brom and Quinine did their best to growl and be fierce.[52]

The naming of Nansen provides us with some intriguing insights into Chekhov's character. He was named after Fridtjof Nansen, who just the previous autumn had returned from his second epic expedition. Nansen had set off from Norway with his crew in the summer of 1893, travelling east along the coast of Siberia and then north until their specially designed ship, the *Fram*, became ice-bound. He was hoping to prove that a ship frozen in the seas off the coast of eastern Siberia would be carried by the current towards the North Pole and then south towards Spitzbergen (as indeed it was). After a year and a half of slow progress, Nansen's restless spirit got the better of him, and he and a companion set off with huskies, sledges and kayaks for the North Pole. When poor conditions forced them to retreat, at a latitude of eighty-six degrees and fourteen minutes, they had come closer to the Pole than anyone in history. Nansen returned home to a hero's welcome in Norway in 1896. Chekhov would have followed the reporting of the expedition in the Russian press with a keen interest. He had been entranced by the idea of the North ever since his trip to Siberia, and had begun expressing a desire in his letters to journey to Scandinavia.

III

The *Muzhiks*

Living in the country is inconvenient, the intolerable *rasputitsa* has begun, but something is going on in nature which is so amazing and moving that it makes up for all the inconveniences of life with its poetry and novelty. Every day brings a surprise better than the one before. The starlings have landed, water is gurgling everywhere, there

is green grass already on thawed ground. The day stretches like
eternity. It feels like I'm living in Australia, at the edge of the world;
my state of mind is calm, contemplative and animal, in the sense that
I'm not worried about what happened yesterday and am not thinking
about tomorrow. From here, people seem very decent, and that is
natural, because when you move to the country you are hiding not
from people but from your own self-love, which can be inaccurate in
the town around people, and unreliable. Looking at the spring, I so
want there to be paradise on this earth. In a word, I sometimes feel so
good, that I have to pinch myself and remember my creditors, who
one day will drive me out of my well-acquired Australia.[53]

Chekhov was in expansive mood when he first moved to Melikhovo
and wrote these words to Suvorin. His sense of *joie de vivre* was not to
last, but the six and a half years he spent on his estate (six, if one bears
in mind the one winter spent in Nice) were to prove extraordinarily
fruitful. The bulk of his greatest short stories were written at
Melikhovo, as were *The Seagull* and *Uncle Vanya*. Although Chekhov
often felt tired, bored and lonely, as he had when living in Moscow,
there were enough moments of feeling ecstatically at one with nature
to reassure him of the wisdom of his decision to move. As he wrote to
his brother Alexander during his first autumn in Melikhovo, their
grandparents and great-grandparents had lived in the country, and he
felt he was going back to his roots. 'What a misfortune that we did not
have our own place when we were children,' he commented wistfully.[54]
The moments of epiphany Chekhov experienced outdoors provided the
fuel for his creative inspiration during the Melikhovo years. Take the
time in May 1894, after he left a meeting with zemtsvo doctors at an
old country estate ten miles away from home. The estate had been
turned into a psychiatric hospital, and Chekhov and seventy-four other
Moscow doctors had met to discuss medical issues:

I returned home late in the evening on my troika. I had to complete two-
thirds of the journey through the forest, by moonlight, and my state of
mind was extraordinary, such as I've not had for a long time; it was as
if I was returning from a tryst. I think that proximity to nature and
idleness represent the vital ingredients for happiness; without them it is
impossible.[55]

With the demands of a writing career, an estate to run, guests to entertain, people to see in Moscow and Petersburg, and several members of his family to provide for, not to mention various dogs and horses, one might have thought that was already a full life. But Chekhov was not living in the kind of rural idyll that Goncharov had so famously described in his novel *Oblomov*. His was no prelapsarian world of happy peasants, bountiful harvests and benevolent patriarchal values, in which a landowner could simply sleep his way through life, as the lovable Russian bear Oblomov does. Nor was it the kind of world where wisdom and truth were the exclusive preserve of the uneducated people who worked the land, such as Tolstoy presents in his novels. When Chekhov came to describe the world he inhabited in his story 'Peasants' (*Muzhiki*), written after he had been living at Melikhovo for several years, people were shocked. But precisely because what he saw around him was poverty, ignorance, misery, backwardness and disease, his strong ethical sense propelled him to do what he could to alleviate it.

The Russian intelligentsia were very good at identifying national problems, but there were a lot of Trofimovs out there – earnest young people like the eternal student in *The Cherry Orchard* – who were all talk and no action. Chekhov could take justifiable pride in what he had helped to achieve while he lived at Melikhovo. There was the opening of a post office, the building of a bridge over the river, the construction of a paved road from the station and the stopping at Lopasnya of fast trains; but of far greater significance were the three schools he built, the work he had carried out to contain cholera in the area, the role he played in conducting the national census and the medical care he gave to thousands of peasants who lived in the area. The vast majority of Chekhov's neighbours, of course, were peasants. As the grandson of a peasant himself, Chekhov was one of a growing number of Russian landowners who bought their property rather than inheriting it. Despite his humble origins, the local peasants in Melikhovo were as suspicious of Chekhov as they were of all newcomers: they knew nothing of his background, nor had they followed his literary career with avid interest; hardly any of them could read. What changed their opinion of him was the fact that he was a doctor, as he later explained in a letter:

I live peacefully with the muzhiks, they never steal anything from me and whenever I walk through the village the old women smile at me or cross themselves. I use the polite form of address with everyone except children, and never shout, but it was medicine which was the main thing which helped to create good relations.[56]

Once the peasants heard there was a doctor in the neighbourhood they came from far and wide to receive medical assistance (some from over fifteen miles away), particularly when they discovered that he would not charge them anything. From first light, there would be a queue of people waiting to see Dr Chekhov, in all seasons of the year. In the summer, Dr Chekhov would put up a red flag on the dacha in the garden to indicate he was receiving.

One of the reasons Chekhov did not charge for consultations (or for that matter for the medicines dispensed by Masha) is that he did not want to be seen as an official government doctor. When the cholera epidemic began spreading in 1892, a large number of superstitious peasants thought that it had been deliberately organized by the government, with doctors as their agents. One doctor was actually murdered. The cholera did seem to be following doctors, the peasants noticed; doctors were clearly burying the corpses of victims to hide the evidence! One mob of peasants invaded a cholera barracks to 'rescue' patients before burning it to the ground.[57]

It is hardly surprising there was such suspicion among the peasants. Until the introduction of a rudimentary national health service in the 1880s under the jurisdiction of local zemtsvos, medical care for peasants was wholly inadequate. No self-respecting doctor would want to live in a primitive village and earn next to nothing, when he could live in the town and charge fees. Peasants had to rely on the local *feldsher* (from the German word *Feldscher*, denoting an army surgeon). These medical orderlies often knew little more than the peasants themselves, and might be responsible for some 30,000 patients over a 65-mile radius.[58] Chekhov was very familiar with the work of these feldshers, as is evident from his description of the way the peasant Marfa Ivanova's illness is diagnosed in his story 'Rothschild's Violin':

Wrinkling his grey eyebrows and stroking his sideburns, the attendant started to examine the old woman, who was sitting hunched over on the stool. Emaciated and sharp-nosed, with her mouth open, she looked in profile like a bird wanting to drink.

'Hmm . . . I see,' said the orderly slowly. He sighed. 'Influenza, but maybe it is a fever. There is a lot of typhoid going round the town at the moment. Anyway, the old lady has done pretty well for herself, praise the Lord. How old is she?'

'A year off seventy, sir.'

'Well, then. She has done all right for herself . . . Time for her to say her farewells.'[59]

Medical care had not been included as a priority when the first zemstvos were set up in Russia as part of Alexander II's great reforms. The government's commitment in the 1860s and 1870s was to economic modernization. The young socialist-minded physicians who went to work as the first zemstvo doctors continually tried to exert pressure on the government to provide financial support for medical care where none had been forthcoming previously. Such activity was viewed as subversive, but slowly the doctors began to win the trust of peasants, whose lives they were transforming through the provision of free medical care, their remuneration coming from the zemstvo. Chekhov was a whole-hearted supporter of the progressive doctors who spearheaded the campaign. He was not politically active himself, but he developed close relationships with many local zemstvo doctors while living at Melikhovo, and immediately volunteered his services to help fight the cholera epidemic. He was allocated a district that included twenty-five villages, four factories, and the Davydovo-Pustyn Monastery. A month later, he wrote a long and breathless letter to Suvorin about what he had been up to as a medical sanitary inspector:

I spend my time organizing, getting quarantine shelters erected and so on, and I feel very lonely, because I find everything to do with cholera very alien. The work involves constant travelling, endless conversations and pettifogging details, and is exhausting. There is no time to write. Literature has long been abandoned, and I am poor and wretched because I thought it appropriate to my situation and supportive of my independence to decline the salary paid to the local doctors. I am tired of it all, but if you take a bird's eye view of cholera it has many interesting aspects. It's a shame you are out of Russia at the moment;

much good material for your regular columns is going to waste. There is more good than bad about the cholera epidemic, so it differs radically from what we saw with the famine last winter. Everyone is working this time, furiously hard. What is being done at the fair in Nizhny is a miracle, enough to make even Tolstoy have some respect for medicine and for cultured people's interference in life generally. It looks as though they've thrown a lasso around the cholera. Not only has the number of infections fallen, but the proportion of deaths is lower as well. In the whole enormous area of Moscow there are not more than 50 cases a week, whereas on the Don it claims 1,000 victims a day. That is a formidable difference. We district physicians are pretty well prepared: we have a solid action programme, so there is every reason to suppose that in our own areas we shall also succeed in reducing the proportion of deaths from cholera. We have no assistants, we are obliged to be both doctor and nurse at one and the same time. The peasants are coarse, dirty and suspicious; but the thought that our efforts will not be completely in vain stops one noticing any of this. Of all the Serpukhov doctors I am the most pathetic; my carriage and horses are run down, I don't know the roads, I can't see anything when evening falls, I've no money, I become exhausted very quickly, most of all, I can never forget that I ought to be writing, and I would really like to turn my back on the cholera and sit down and write. And I would like to to talk to you too. I feel utterly alone.[60]

Chekhov saw over a thousand patients between August and October 1892, when his unit ceased its work. The closest cholera came to his district were eleven cases twenty miles away, diagnosed just after his section was closed. He continued to see patients as well as the many visitors he constantly received at Melikhovo. One friend recalled:

He was not given a minute's peace in the literal sense of the word! From early morning there was some landowner who had come on a visit and sat for a very long time, then a zemstvo doctor came, then the village priest, then someone in military uniform . . . the Melikhovo police chief, most probably . . . And from the window in the little annexe where I was staying, I could see first a light carriage roll up to the porch of the modest one-storey Chekhov house, then an old-fashioned springless carriage . . . And in the small passage-way, near Chekhov's study, peasant men and women did not stop arriving – some had come on business, some for trifling reasons, some for medical care . . . And then to cap it all, a guest from Moscow turned up . . .[61]

To the end of his days Chekhov remained a passionate proselytizer for education. He was happy therefore to become trustee of a village school in the nearby village of Talezh at the end of 1894. He wrote to Suvorin to tell him about the young man in charge of the pupils:

> The teacher there earns 23 roubles a month, has a wife and four children, and hair that is already quite grey although he is only thirty years old. He is so ground down by poverty that whatever you talk to him about, he cannot prevent himself from bringing the conversation round to the subject of salaries. In his opinion, the only subject for poets and prose writers to write about should be salary increases; when the new Tsar appoints new ministers, teachers' salaries will probably be increased, etc.[62]

The experience of acting as trustee gave Chekhov the idea of building another school in the district. Work began in March 1896; the school opened later that year, in August. The following year, Chekhov returned as examiner, and was appointed assistant to the schools inspector. This involved him in visiting fifty-seven schools and preparing a report. Seeing the operation of village schools from all these different angles provided him with the raw material for 'In the Cart', one of his finest stories. He was to build two more schools in the Melikhovo area, the third one at the special pleading of the peasants themselves. They collected 300 roubles and the local zemstvo was prepared to put up 1,000 roubles, which left at least another 1,500 roubles for Chekhov to raise. The meagre proceeds of a theatrical performance he organized in Serpukhov, performed by excellent actors and attended by ladies in Parisian couture and diamonds, was dispiriting; the most affluent people also proved the most miserly with their donations. In the meantime, Chekhov had started sending regular parcels of books to Taganrog, to be donated to the library there.

In early 1897, Chekhov spent two months hitting his head on the low ceilings of peasant *izbas* in the course of his duties as the supervisor of fifteen census takers. Immediately this task was finished, he sat down to finish 'Peasants', the story with which, as he later told Suvorin, he exhausted Melikhovo as a literary source. It certainly represents the literary culmination of his years at Melikhovo. It may not be the best story he wrote in Melikhovo from an artistic point of view, but it was the most important. After a career as a waiter in a Moscow hotel, which ends when he famously drops a tray of ham and peas, the story's protagonist, the terminally ill Nikolai Chikildeyev, returns to his native village with his wife, Olga, and their daughter to die. We see the village and its inhabitants through Olga's shocked eyes as they try to adjust to the poverty and filth they encounter.

The Moscow censor S. Sokolov immediately had a lot of problems with the manuscript when it was submitted. The peasants were portrayed in very 'gloomy colours', he reported, always starving and drunk most of the time. The men physically abused their wives, and no peasant seemed to believe in religion. They lived in squalor. There was one particular page which the Moscow Censorship Committee decided had to go, resolving that the author be arrested if he refused to delete it. The page comes near the end of the story, at a point where another narrative voice seems to intrude into Olga's thoughts:

> During the course of the summer and the winter there had been hours and days when it seemed that these people lived worse than cattle, and living with them was frightening; they were rude, dishonest, dirty, drunk, and did not live peacefully but were always rowing, because they did not respect each other, were afraid and suspicious of each other. Who runs the tavern and makes them drink? The peasant. Who embezzles community, school and church money and spends it on drink? The peasant. Who steals from his neighbours, sets their house on fire and perjures himself for a bottle of vodka? The peasant. Who is the first to rail against the peasants at the zemtsvo and other meetings? The peasant.

This was bad enough: the Russian peasantry, post-emancipation, were not shown in a positive light in Chekhov's story. But what was infinitely worse, from the government's point of view, was the fact that Chekhov laid the blame squarely at its door, again seemingly taking over from his character Olga as the narrator in his story:

Yes, living with them was frightening, but they were still people, they suffered and cried like other people, and there was nothing in their life for which justification could not be found. Backbreaking work, from which their whole bodies ached at night, fierce winters, miserable harvests, cramped living space, and there was no help and nowhere to turn for help. Those who were richer and stronger than them could not help because they themselves were rude, dishonest, drunk and cursed in just as vile a way; the most lowly official or bailiff treated the peasants as if they were tramps, and even addressed village elders and church wardens as if they were peasants, believing they had a right to do so. And indeed, could there be any help or any good example set by people so self-serving, grasping, corrupt and lazy, who came to the village only to insult, rob and frighten people?[63]

Chekhov's story was published in the April issue of the Moscow journal *Russian Thought*, just after he suffered the massive lung haemorrhage that would turn him into an invalid for the rest of his life. It provoked a passionate debate in the press that went on for over a year, its intensity far exceeding the reaction to anything else he had ever written. Chekhov took no part in the discussion himself, considering his contribution was complete. A sentence he had jotted down in one of his notebooks seems to encapsulate the whole enterprise of writing for him: 'Man will only become better when you make him see what he is like.'[64] As with the landowner relishing his sour gooseberries, many educated Russian people simply did not want a mirror held up to their blemishes.

IV

Croquet on the Lawn

In the sitting room next door to my study there have been people playing the piano and singing romances all day, and so I am constantly in an elegiac mood.

Letter to Lidia Avilova, 1 March 1893

We played croquet and lawn-tennis, then when it grew dark, spent a long time over supper ...

The House with the Mezzanine

Not many people know about Chekhov's passion for croquet, an ideally democratic game of precision and latent aggression that, for good reasons, became most popular in England, the country with which it is still most strongly associated. By the time of the foundation of the All-England Croquet and Lawn Tennis Club in 1869, however, people were playing croquet all over the world – including in Russia. Obviously, in a country where there is winter for nine months and bad weather for three (as Voltaire famously put it),[65] opportunities for getting out one's mallet are not as abundant as in foggy Albion, as Russians still like to refer to England, but the game immediately became wildly popular after it was imported by expatriate Britons at the end of the nineteenth century. The extent of its popularity can be gauged by the fact that Soviet citizens were enthusiastically playing *kroket* well into the 1920s and 1930s: as many as 20,000 copies of Chesnokov's *Description and Rules of the Game* were printed in 1930. The notion of this decorous game being played against a background of collectivization and five-year plans does seem incongruous – until one studies the admonitions of a pre-revolutionary guide to croquet playing. The player must never forget that he is just a member of a team, exhorts the author: 'if every player only ever thinks about getting his ball through the hoops and hitting the post, never thinking about his comrades, croquet will become pointless and boring'.[66]

Chekhov's interest in croquet was therefore far from unusual. Indeed croquet was embraced by all sections of Russian society, from the imperial family and celebrities like the opera singer Chaliapin and the ballerina Anna Pavlova to the most humble dachnik. After moving to Melikhovo, Chekhov bought a croquet set in Moscow at the first opportunity, and the game was offered as an entertainment to his many house guests from the first summer there onwards. Chekhov started learning the technique of the *krokirovka* when he became a dachnik in the mid-1880s. He was apparently such an ardent player that he would insist on games continuing well after the sun had set. Sometimes it became so dark that he and his opponents would have to light matches in order to see the balls.[67] Sadly, we have no chronicle of historic croquet matches played at Melikhovo: this was an occupation that was far too frivolous to be recorded in Pavel Egorovich's annals. A single photograph of a game in progress suggests croquet was taken seriously, however.[68] It is safe to assume that it was *Russian* croquet which was played at Melikhovo. Like so many other cultural imports over the centuries, croquet was Russianized, with changes made to the layout of hoops (there was the 'Eagle' and the 'Andreyev Cross' style, for example), the number used (nine or ten), and the size of the court. Ironically, though, it is only in Russia where traditions of playing croquet with wooden balls have been preserved to this day at international level.

Chekhov was probably glad to have something with which to distract his guests. He was besieged by visitors at Melikhovo and it was often difficult for him to find time to write. 'If you only knew how worn out I was!' he wrote to Suvorin in December 1892. 'I'm unbelievably worn out. Visitors, visitors, visitors . . . My estate stands right on the highway to Kashira, and every passing educated person considers it necessary and obligatory to come and warm themselves up at my place, and sometimes even to stay the night. There's a whole legion of doctors alone! It's nice to be hospitable, of course, but there are limits. It was to get away from visitors that I left Moscow, after all.'[69] Like all human beings, Chekhov was a contradictory creature. He was miserable when no one came to visit him, and miserable when too many of his friends showed up. He both wanted and did not want to show off Melikhovo to Suvorin, his closest friend, who was one of the estate's very first visitors. Sensing that Suvorin would be expecting something much grander, Chekhov tried to lower his expectations, writing just after Easter in 1892:

> You won't like Melikhovo, at least not at first. Everything is in miniature here; the lime tree avenue is small, the pond is the size of an aquarium, the garden and the park are small, the trees are small, but after a while, when you look around again, the feeling of smallness disappears.[70]

Chekhov's misgivings were well founded. Suvorin did not like Melikhovo when he came that April, and only stayed two nights before going back to his life of comfort, where he could travel on proper roads in sprung carriages. He took care to meet up with Chekhov in Moscow after that, but he certainly did not see Melikhovo at its best. The trees had only started to come out, the snow had not completely melted and it was still cold.

March and April were, in fact, always the worst months of the year for people who lived in the country. As soon as the snows began to melt, effortless travel by troika gave way to agonizingly slow journeys plodding through deep mud. Russians refer to this brief but dreadful season as the *rasputitsa*, a glorious word conveying a sense of roads literally coming undone – and in autumn it would all begin again. Compared to many country estates, Melikhovo was relatively accessible. Several trains a day made the two- to three-hour journey from Moscow to the local station, but during the rasputitsa it often took far longer to travel the last few miles to the estate on the unpaved road. And to begin with the Chekhovs had to rely on the ancient Anna Petrovna as their only means of transport. Chekhov vividly conveyed what it was like to travel during the rasputitsa in his story 'In the Cart'. The local landowner in his four-horse carriage is being followed by the school teacher, travelling in a cart driven by the peasant Semyon:

> They turned off the highway on to the road leading to the village, Khanov in front and Semyon following behind. The four horses were moving along at a walking pace, straining to drag the heavy carriage through the mud. Semyon was trying to manoeuvre by going over hillocks and through the field in order to avoid the road, and he kept having to get off the cart to help the horses . . . Marya Vasilievna was still thinking about school and whether the exam would be difficult or easy . . . The road was getting worse and worse . . . They had entered a forest. There was nowhere to turn off here, the ruts were very deep and gurgling water was streaming along them. And prickly branches were hitting her face.[71]

When the mud hardened, journey times decreased, but comfort often did not. In November 1894, Chekhov complained to a friend that he had been jolted about so painfully the last time he had made the journey from the station that his heart had been torn out and he could no longer love.[72] Heavy rain meant having to travel through water so deep it might come up to the horse's belly. Whatever the weather, trips were made from Melikhovo to the station almost daily to pick up the mail and provisions, with the three farm dogs usually following the cart there and back. And horses would be sent along the tree-lined road to pick up guests, who would sit drinking cognac with the French waitress in the station buffet while they waited.

During the rasputitsa, Chekhov relied more than ever on being able to remain in contact with people by letter, particularly since there was no telephone at Melikhovo. The sheer volume of mail generated by his correspondence during the Melikhovo years with friends like Lika, Suvorin and the various literary editors, other writers and theatrical figures, as well as his numerous subscriptions to newspapers and periodicals, in fact, created a problem. In the six and a half years he lived at Melikhovo, Chekhov sent about 2,500 letters, but there was no post office at Lopasnya. The nearest post office was fifteen miles away, and anything other than ordinary letters sometimes incurred long delays before they were delivered. Chekhov depended on letters, so he renewed the appeal for a post office to be established at Lopasnya after he moved to Melikhovo, and then helped gather donations when permission was granted in 1894. When the post office opened, on 1 January 1896, next to the railway station, the station master was finally able to relinquish the task of keeping letters in his cupboard. In order to support its meagre income, Chekhov continued to buy stamps from the Lopasnya post office even after he left Melikhovo.

Generally speaking, the rasputitsa provided a respite from guests, since most people balked at the prospect of negotiating all that mud. The visiting period at Melikhovo peaked in the summer, when the weather was most clement and the roads at their most passable. Some of Chekhov's happiest hours with guests were spent fishing: he caught fifty-seven carp one June day in 1897 (the family had fish soup the next day), and he also spent happy hours sitting by the water's edge on his own. When one of his neighbours wondered why he did not want to go to the river where the fishing was superior, he was informed that the fishing was secondary; what Chekhov valued most of all was being able to sit and think without being disturbed.[73] In his euphoria at becoming a landowner for the first time, he succumbed to Leikin's incessant pleading and, in 1892, wrote a handful of humorous stories for *Fragments* under his old pseudonyms. One of them was clearly inspired by the population in his new pond (whom he joked he would have to give a constitution to). It was so close to the house he claimed that he could fish from the window.[74] For Chekhov fans who expect his mature stories to be unremittingly bleak, 'Fish Love' (written in the same year as 'Ward No. 6') might come as a bit of a shock. The story, all of a few pages long, is about a carp who falls in love with Sonya Mamochkina, a young lady who arrives to stay one summer at a general's dacha. The carp ogles Sonya when she comes to bathe every day, but is not optimistic:

> Of course there is no, absolutely no chance of reciprocation. Could such a beautiful woman fall in love with me, a carp? No, a thousand times no! Don't tempt yourself with dreams, you contemptible fish! Only one destiny awaits you – death! But how to die? There aren't any revolvers or phosphorous matches in the pond. There is only death open to carps and that is via the jaws of a pike. But where can I get hold of a pike? There was actually a pike in the pond at one point, but it died of boredom. Oh, how unfortunate I am!

The carp tries to commit suicide by getting itself caught by Sonya's fishing rod one evening, but succeeds only in getting his lower jaw ripped off, at which point he goes mad. Later mistaking a young poet

The guest annexe at Melikhovo, where Chekhov wrote The Seagull

called Ivan for his inamorata, he infects him with pessimism by kissing him tenderly on the back. Unbelievably, even a story as light-hearted as this one was held up by the censors for a couple of weeks. Perhaps they objected to Chekhov sending up Russian literature so effectively:

> The poet got out of the water, not suspecting anything untoward, and set off home, laughing wildly. In a few days he went to Petersburg: after visiting editorial offices, he infected all the poets there with pessimism too, and from that time onwards all our poets have been writing dark and gloomy poems.[75]

By the second summer at Melikhovo, Chekhov had already tired of the endless numbers of guests filling the small house, several to a room, with an overflow in the barn. In 1894 he commissioned his architect friend Franz Shekhtel to build an annexe in the garden, a clapboard cottage with a sloping roof and a balcony, consisting of all of two rooms. The Chekhovs now had their very own *Flügel*! It was originally intended as guest accommodation but usually ended up accommodating Chekhov himself, plus a writing desk. It was here that he famously wrote *The Seagull*, and where he sequestered himself when he needed to escape from all the people in the house. Iosif Braz, the Petersburg artist commissioned by the Tretyakov Gallery to paint Chekhov's portrait, came to stay for a month in June 1897. Even after all that time, he had got no nearer to capturing Chekhov's elusive nature on canvas. Both artist and subject were dissatisfied and agreed there should be another attempt.

Not all the guests at Melikhovo were unwelcome, of course. Before they fell out over Chekhov's indiscretions in 'The Grasshopper' (in particular a thinly disguised artist character, satirically portrayed), Levitan was someone Chekhov was glad to see. With the resumption of their friendly relations a few years later, Levitan's visits to Melikhovo also resumed. Among Chekhov's many female friends, most of whom were hopelessly in love with him, Lidia Mizinova continued to occupy a special place. She was, in fact, adored by all the Chekhovs, and particularly by Anton Pavlovich. 'The fair Lika', as she was known by everybody, made her first visit to Melikhovo early on in May 1892. At the end of March Chekhov had written her a long, typically playful letter, in which he used one of his own pet names for her, inspired by Sappho:

I've no money Melita. It's a bit smoky. We can't open any little windows.
Father has been burning incense. I've been stinking of turpentine. And
there are smells coming from the kitchen. My head aches. I don't have
any solitude. But worst of all – Melita is not here, and there is no chance
of seeing her in the next day or two . . . Yours from head to toe, with all
my soul and all my heart, to the gravestone, to oblivion, to stupefaction,
to insanity, Antoine Tchekhoff.[76]

Lika and Chekhov had become close at the beginning of the 1890s, just
before his trip to Sakhalin, and at Melikhovo they drew even closer. But
when it became clear that Chekhov was not ultimately going to
reciprocate Lika's feelings, she turned in despair to a mutual writer
friend, with whom she had an affair. Ignaty Potapenko was married,
and he refused to leave his wife and do the decent thing when Lika
became pregnant. He ended up abandoning her. Lika's relationship
with Chekhov was never quite the same afterwards, but she was
nevertheless one of the few people he wanted to see after the *Seagull*
fiasco. The letters she wrote to him over the course of their relationship
make sad reading, and Chekhov revealed his coldest, most callous side
in his prolonged silences. Lika was a talented musician (she would
accompany Potapenko when he sang Tchaikovsky songs during their
stays at Melikhovo), but she failed to become either an opera singer or
an actress. She was indirectly immortalized instead in the character of
Nina Zarechnaya in *The Seagull*. The magpie Chekhov also pilfered
from Lika's biography when he wrote his story 'Ariadna', about a young
woman whose affair with a married man leads to her being abandoned
in Europe. Written at roughly the same time as *The Seagull*, it is one of
his more misogynistic stories.

One of the very last visitors to Melikhovo was the actress Olga
Knipper, the woman who was finally able to capture Chekhov's heart.
They met briefly in the autumn of 1898, at a rehearsal in Moscow, just
before Chekhov headed off to spend his first winter in Yalta. Olga
Knipper's father was a German factory manager from Alsace who had
relocated to Russia as a young man, while her mother came from the
German-speaking Baltic provinces of the Russian Empire. Mr and Mrs
Knipper led Russian lives and brought up their three children,
Konstantin, Olga and Vladimir, as true Muscovites. Olga's father had
been as horrified by the idea of his only daughter becoming an actress

as the pious father in Chekhov's story 'Requiem'. But his unexpected
death in 1894 when Olga was twenty-five opened the way for her to
pursue her dreams. After three years of drama classes with Vladimir
Nemirovich-Danchenko at the Philharmonic School in Moscow, she
graduated in 1898, and was immediately taken on by her former
teacher and Konstantin Stanislavsky when they formed the Moscow Art
Theatre that autumn. One of the first plays they started rehearsing for
their inaugural season was *The Seagull*, and Olga was given the part of
Arkadina. On 9 September 1898, Olga's thirtieth birthday, Chekhov
came along for the first time to a rehearsal. Before heading off south to
Yalta he came along to two more rehearsals, by which time his head had
definitely been turned by the vivacious Miss Knipper.

The death of Pavel Egorovich during Chekhov's first winter in Yalta,
coupled with his illness which required long periods spent in a warm
climate, spelled the end of the Melikhovo period in the family's life.
The newly widowed Evgenia Yakovlevna had fled Melikhovo following
the unexpected death of her husband, and in time would relocate to
Yalta to live with her son. Chekhov came back to Melikhovo one last
time the following summer, in order to tie up loose ends before the
property was put on the market, and to complete the construction of
his last school. It was a sombre time, and Chekhov's mood was not
helped by the unseasonably cold weather and the demise of his beloved
dachshunds (probably suffering from rabies, Brom died in June 1899,[77]
and Quinine died a few weeks later probably also from rabies, having
been bitten by a yard dog).[78] The three days in May when Olga
Knipper came down from Moscow to stay at Melikhovo were an
exception, however. Although we have no record of how they spent
their time, it is safe to say that Olga Leonardovna and Anton Pavlovich
cemented their friendship during her stay; their correspondence began
soon after she left. A romance soon blossomed.

Chapter 8

A SEASON ON THE CÔTE D'AZUR

I

Nostalgia in Nice

I'd be sitting by an open window in the evening, you know, all on my own, and music would start playing and I'd suddenly get so homesick, and I think I would have given anything just to go home . . .

The Bishop

The severe haemorrhaging from his lungs, which occurred in March 1897, forced Chekhov to face up to the fact that he was definitely suffering from tuberculosis. Suvorin had come to Moscow from St Petersburg for a few days and Chekhov caught the train up from Melikhovo to join him for a Saturday night dinner at the Hermitage, which was still his favourite restaurant. But just after they had sat down at their table, blood suddenly started pouring out of Chekhov's mouth. All he had managed to order before being hurried away in a sleigh back to Suvorin's hotel was ice. Chekhov was understandably very scared. His brother and aunt had both died from tuberculosis in the last ten years, and he interpreted it as an ominous sign that he too was now bleeding from the right lung.

He was nevertheless still unwilling to give in to the idea of being seriously ill. He had been exceptionally busy since the beginning of the year, and early in the morning two days later he discharged himself from Suvorin's hotel before his friend was even up, saying he needed to deal with his correspondence and arrange meetings. But after another haemorrhage at six o'clock the next morning, he was taken by the doctor who had been summoned to his hotel to be treated in a specialist clinic, where he remained for over two weeks. The diagram by his bed showed his lungs shaded in blue, their upper parts coloured in red. It was in keeping with Chekhov's character to make light of the serious nature of his situation, but his frightened reaction to the news that the ice on the Moscow River had moved is revealing. Peasants he treated for tuberculosis would regularly tell him: 'It won't do any good. I'll go with the spring floods', and he clearly felt this was to be his fate too.

All around Moscow, the snow was indeed beginning to melt, and it had rained all night the day before Chekhov left Melikhovo. At first he was forbidden to talk but was soon besieged by visitors, who came in pairs and fired questions at him while telling him not to say anything. Tolstoy, who lived nearby, saved Chekhov's energy by doing most of the talking when he came to visit, but their prolonged discussion of immortality one evening provoked another haemorrhage at four in the morning. Eventually Chekhov was allowed to start walking about again, and in thundery weather on Maundy Thursday he was permitted to leave the clinic and return home to Melikhovo in time for Easter.[1] His father recorded in his diary on that day that they had eaten radishes and lettuces from the greenhouse. He also noted that ten poplar trees were planted in the garden on the day of his son's return, but made no mention of his illness (the gravity of which Chekhov was anxious to

The Hermitage restaurant, Moscow, where Chekhov
suffered a haemorrhage in 1897

conceal).[2] Chekhov now settled down to spend a quiet summer working in his garden, running away from guests, and posing for the portrait commissioned by the Tretyakov Gallery.

Along with the shock of confronting his mortality in this stark way came the awful realization that he would never be able to spend another winter in Moscow. Thus it was with a heavy heart that he set off for the south of France that autumn, dimly hoping that his health would benefit from the warm climate. Intending to stay abroad until the snow finally melted in Russia the following spring, he boarded the train for Paris at the beginning of September 1897, and a week later he was sitting in bright sunshine in fashionable Biarritz, surrounded by Spaniards, poodles, brightly coloured parasols, blind musicians – and lots of well-heeled Russians. The golf course which the British had built a decade earlier (the second oldest on the continent) did not exercise any attraction for Chekhov, but he did go on a couple of trips to the nearby Basque town of Bayonne, one of which was to hear a performance of *La Belle Hélène* at the casino there.[3] Offenbach's uproarious operetta was the work that had sparked Chekhov's lifelong interest in the theatre, and seeing it now in France must have taken him back to the tiny theatre in Taganrog, which he had first visited when he

The Grand Moscow Hotel, Chekhov's favourite place to stay during his visits from Melikhovo

was thirteen years old. After two weeks of sitting on the seafront reading newspapers and eating hearty meals, Chekhov abandoned the blustery Atlantic and its crashing waves for the gentler Mediterranean and moved to Nice, where he ended up staying for the next seven months. It was the longest period he ever spent abroad.

Nice had been officially ceded to France in a mutually advantageous deal struck between Napoleon III and Vittorio Emmanuele II of Savoy in 1860, the year of Chekhov's birth. Since then, with the horrors of the Crimean War quickly receding into the past, Russians had started flocking to Nice in greater numbers. The English had immortalized their presence on the French Riviera in the 1820s by building the famous Promenade des Anglais along the seafront so that they could indulge their penchant for taking bracing constitutionals,[4] and this was where Chekhov also took his daily walks. Once Nice was connected to Paris by rail, wealthy Russians threatened British supremacy on the Côte d'Azur. Alexander II and his retinue arrived just three days after the opening of the ornate Louis XIII-style station in 1865, pre-empting even Napoleon and the Empress Eugenie. Back then the journey took the best part of a day and some Russian aristocrats were known to order the trains to go more slowly so they could get a good night's sleep.[5] There were soon over a thousand people arriving each day during the high season.

There was already a sizeable Russian population living in Nice by the time Chekhov arrived in 1897, and the Dowager Empress Maria Fyodorovna felt the little church on the Rue de Longchamps was too small to accommodate the community's burgeoning spiritual needs. After returning home to Petersburg after her winter in Nice that spring, she petitioned her son, Nicholas II, to authorize the construction of a much larger place of worship. The Cathedral of St Nicholas continued to thrive while there were still hundreds of exiled Russian families living in Nice after the Revolution, and nowadays it is the new wave of wealthy visitors from Russia who have helped make the exotic-looking building become one of the most popular tourist attractions on the Riviera. Few visit the old church of Saints Nicholas and Alexandra, but the Russian library housed on the ground floor is open to visitors one day a week. Chekhov did not attend services regularly (if at all) while he was living in Nice, but he came to browse through the books in the library, some of which had been donated by its founder back in 1860. There was also a Russian

Prof. Ostroumov's clinic, Moscow, where Chekhov was a patient in 1897

bookshop nearby, and the editorial offices of the newspaper *Le Messager franco-russe*, which on 24 November 1897 belatedly reported the arrival of the 'celebrated young novelist' (*sic*) on the Côte d'Azur.[6]

It was around this time that Chekhov got to know Mordechai Rozanov, the endearing Jewish proprietor of the bookshop and the paper, and was soon treating his sick wife.[7] On the day that Chekhov's name appeared in the *Messager franco-russe*, he wrote to an old university friend commenting that the newspapers were full of gossip about the Dreyfus case, and the conversations he had with Rozanov and one of the Jewish Russian columnists for the *Messager franco-russe* undoubtedly fuelled his growing solidarity with those who supported the court-martialled officer against the anti-semitic French establishment. Shortly after Zola's famous letter *J'accuse!* was published in *L'Aurore* on 1 January 1898, at the height of the controversy, Chekhov wrote a long and vehement letter to Suvorin, whose newspaper had taken the side of the Establishment, in which he passionately defended Zola's crusade against the unjust treatment of Dreyfus. The continued anti-semitic bias of *New Times* appalled Chekhov. He was the only major Russian writer to take an active stand in the affair, and went out of his way to meet with Dreyfus's brother in Paris after leaving Nice the following April.[8]

Chekhov revelled in being able to walk about outside in a straw hat instead of being wrapped up in fur. He also liked the smell of the sea air, and was clearly reminded of the coastal port he had grown up in when he wrote to tell his cousin that Nice was about the same size as Taganrog.[9] Seeing some boys and a priest playing noisily with a ball near a school one day also reminded him of his home town, he told his brother Ivan in another letter. Chekhov was passionately fond of warm weather – he was from the south after all, and felt at home in the sun. But, unlike most other visitors, he had little enthusiasm for the precipitous and dramatic landscape of the Corniche with its umbrella pines, cypresses and olive trees. He told one correspondent that it left him cold, and to another described the local flora as 'decorative, just like an oleograph'. There was also no grass.[10] He had probably voiced some of his own sentiments in 'An Anonymous Story', which he had completed after his first visit to the city, in 1892. Above the shoreline, in the lilac mist, the narrator sees 'hills, gardens, towers and villas, all bathed in sunlight', but finds the vista 'alien, uninteresting, a strange kind of jumble'.[11]

This was the only occasion when Chekhov used Nice as a setting for his fictional writing. If anything, the local scenery appeared to arouse in him an intense nostalgia for the flat steppe landscapes of his childhood. How do we know this? Not from anything he said in the 200 odd letters he wrote during the long months that he spent in Nice, but from the fact that the first two short stories he wrote during his first winter there are set in a steppe landscape at the height of summer. The first of them, usually translated as 'At Home' (although its Russian title actually conveys the idea of being on one's 'home turf' or on one's native territory), stands out in particular for its lyrical description of the steppe. It was written in little more than a week and begun soon after Chekhov arrived in Nice in October 1897, when a brief spell of inclement weather had prompted him to go out and buy some paper and quills. The *papier écolier* he bought looked so appealing, and the buying of quills was such an enjoyable experience, that it was actually hard to restrain himself from writing, he explained to Vasily Sobolevsky, the editor of the newspaper *Russian Gazette*, who published the story a few weeks later.[12] The story's typically Chekhovian terse first sentence – 'The Don railway.' – locates us very precisely in the landscape directly north of Taganrog. Chekhov had travelled through it by train the previous summer on his way back to his native town. Twenty-three-year-old Vera is returning to her childhood home for the first time in ten years and we see the steppe through her eyes as she travels from the station in the family troika. She is mesmerized, after the long hours sitting in a stuffy train carriage, by the profusion of green, yellow, lilac and white flowering grasses around her and the smell of the warm earth:

> ... and little by little before you unfold landscapes endless and fascinating in their monotony, unlike any around Moscow. The steppe, the steppe and nothing else; an old kurgan or a windmill in the distance; oxen carrying coal ... Solitary birds fly low over the plain, and the rhythmical beating of their wings brings on drowsiness. It is hot. Another hour goes by and there is still nothing but the steppe, the steppe and a kurgan in the distance ...

The words 'The steppe, the steppe' are repeated three times in the space of a few paragraphs, as if to echo the call of the lonely birds which fly overhead. At the end of the story, disillusioned by the people she has come back to live among, Vera resolves that the only way for her to survive is to 'merge with the luxurious steppe and its flowers, kurgans and expanses, boundless and impartial like eternity'.[13] Chekhov was looking out on to a lush garden of palms, blooming oleanders and orange trees in his hotel as he wrote this.

The third story Chekhov wrote in Nice, 'On the Cart', one of his most poignant, is also set in surroundings far removed from the opulent French Riviera. It follows the thoughts of an impoverished young village school teacher travelling home by peasant cart one spring day after collecting her wages in town, her loneliness only reinforced by a casual encounter with the local bachelor landowner out in his carriage:

> 'Hold tight, Vasilievna!' said Semyon.
>
> The cart tilted heavily and almost keeled over; something heavy fell on to Marya Vasilievna's feet – it was her shopping. Now there was a steep climb up the hill through mud as thick as clay; noisy streams were running down the winding ditches, and it was as if the water had been eating away at the road – travelling round here was something else! The

horses were snorting. Khanov climbed out of his carriage and started walking along the edge of the road. He was hot.

'How do you like the road?' Khanov asked again with a laugh. 'My carriage is going to be wrecked at this rate.'

Glimpsing a woman on a passing train who resembles her deceased mother takes Marya Vasilievna back for a fraction of a second to the joyful surroundings of her family home in Moscow when she was growing up in more prosperous circumstances:

And for no apparent reason she burst into tears. Just at that moment Khanov drove up in his coach-and-four, and when she saw him she imagined the happiness she had never had and smiled at him, nodding her head as if she was a close acquaintance and his equal, and it felt to her as if her happiness, her exultation, was reflected in the sky, in all the windows and in the trees. No, her father and mother had never died, and she had never been a teacher; that was just a long, terrible, bizarre dream, and she had just woken up . . .[14]

But the train speeds off into the distance, taking with it her brief illusion of happiness. Marya Vasilievna is forced once again to confront the reality of her 'dull, difficult' existence, 'lacking in kindness, caring friends and interesting acquaintances', and reflected even in her dreams, which only ever seem to be about exams, peasants and snowdrifts. Chekhov found it easier to write from memory. In response to a commission from an international journal in St Petersburg for a suitably 'international' story set on the Côte d'Azur, he replied that he would only be able to write about his current surroundings when he was back in Russia. It was necessary for his memory to filter the subject first, he explained, so that only what was important or typical was left behind.[15]

After breakfast each day, Chekhov liked to walk down to the Promenade des Anglais and sit reading the newspapers or just gaze out to the soft blue sea in the curving Baie des Anges. Like the city's eucalyptus trees brought from Australia, the palm trees in whose shade he sat had actually been imported in the 1860s when Nice was first developed as a resort. Chekhov was something of a Russian newspaper fanatic, and confessed to being bored without them when he first arrived.[16] Soon he was receiving copies of *Russian Gazette* from the editor in Moscow, as well as *Russian Word*, *The Courier* and *New Times* from Petersburg, which he would then forward to his friend the Russian Vice-Consul. His father, meanwhile, started sending him regular bundles of issues of other newspapers, including the local Taganrog paper. When his French improved and the Dreyfus scandal was at its height, Chekhov also started devouring *Le Figaro*, *L'Aurore*, *La Parole libre* and other French newspapers. His other obsession was correspondence, and the friends who came to visit him could not help noticing that he received a lot of letters. Chekhov may have been a private and guarded person who kept people at arm's length, but he nevertheless needed to be able to keep them within reach. A week into his stay in Nice, a month after leaving Moscow, he was pining for letters from home, and said as much to Suvorin. In letter after letter written in his first weeks away, he carefully spelled out 'France, Nice, Pension Russe, à Monsieur Antoine Tchekhoff' to ensure that people knew his address and that envelopes addressed to him by his correspondents did not go astray. 'I'm going to be here a long time,' he wrote in one of his first letters, to his cousin Georgi in Taganrog; 'it's boring without letters, and if you keep your promise i.e. write and tell me what is going on in Taganrog, I'll be very grateful.'[17]

Eventually Chekhov began to receive replies to the many letters he was sending, and wrote back in ebullient form about his first impressions of Nice, the people he had met and his day trips by train up the coast: to Beaulieu to visit Maxim Kovalevsky, to Villefranche where there was an interesting Russian zoological station, and to Monte Carlo where there was the famous casino. And he had not coughed up blood once, he told his sister exultantly on 15 October, three weeks after his arrival; his friends were coughing much more than he was, and medical advice was that he could do anything but go to Paris in November when it was damp and snowy. He had seen the King of Siam, there was greenery all around, the chambermaid smiled at him all the time, he had discovered mosquito repellent so was sleeping better, the sky was always blue, and he had even started writing a new story.[18]

It is unlikely Chekhov would have wanted to go to the races or attend black tie dinners even if he had felt completely well (one senses that his excuse for refusing one such invitation on the grounds that he did not have a dinner jacket was a convenient one). The nearest he came to the world of high society was catching sight of Queen Victoria one spring day while out on his daily walk.[19] The doughty British sovereign had been enjoying visits to the French Riviera since 1882, and between 1895 and 1899 she made annual winter visits to Nice, which served to bring even more visitors to the area. In March 1897 she and her retinue of a hundred staff arrived to take over the entire west wing of the brand new Excelsior Hotel Regina, which had been specially built for her (the enormous *belle époque* edifice, up on the hill above the city in Cimiez, was where Matisse settled after the war). The Queen liked to go for afternoon drives in her carriage, and each year she was brought down to the Promenade des Anglais to view a parade of French soldiers. Perhaps Chekhov got hit by a carnation during the so-called 'Battle of the Flowers', which ensued when the Queen amused herself by throwing flowers at the young army officers.[20]

II

The Pension Russe

Yesterday I had blini at our Vice-Consul Yurasov's house.
Letter to Olga Knipper, Nice, 2 January 1901

Chekhov's residence in Nice was a spacious south-facing room with shutters, a grand Cleopatra-style bed and an *en suite* bathroom, on the top floor of the Pension Russe, a modest three-storey hotel set deep in a courtyard on the Rue Gounod and surrounded by a lush garden. There was a carpet and a fireplace in his room, but it was usually so warm he kept his windows wide open, and then found it difficult to work with the sun streaming in and the birds singing in the trees, enticing him outside.[21] Along with the problem of his faltering health, the copious meals every day also made him drowsy. He once told a friend that when he was writing he preferred to stick to a diet of coffee and bouillon: he disliked working on a full stomach. There was also the challenge of writing in a hotel room at an unfamiliar desk. He confided to his sister that it was sheer misery trying to work away from home – like sitting at someone else's sewing machine, or, worse, being hung from one leg upside down.[22] Eventually he came to the conclusion that Russians were constitutionally incapable of working unless the weather was bad. And the musicians who wandered into the courtyard with their mandolins, violins and guitars to give impromptu concerts under his windows every morning also provided a distraction, albeit sometimes a pleasant one. Chekhov decided that the street singers of Nice who performed arias for a handful of centimes were actually better than the stars at Moscow's second opera company, whose earnings ran into hundreds of roubles. He was becoming gradually convinced, he wrote to his sister, that Russians were not really born to be opera singers. Maybe they were capable of producing some great bass voices (the legacy of centuries of unaccompanied Orthodox chant), but he felt that they should stick to doing business, writing and tilling fields instead of going to Milan.[23]

The Pension Russe may have attracted more than its share of itinerant musicians in Nice, being located, as its street address suggests, in the bohemian musicians' quarter, which features, among others, a Rue J. Offenbach and a Rue Paganini (the great violinist died of tuberculosis in Nice in 1840). The Rue Gounod, which runs south towards the sea, was also in the heart of the Russian quarter of Nice: the Pension Russe was close to the Church of Saints Nicholas and Alexandra, and the Russian Consulate was around the corner on the Rue Rossini.[24] Located a few minutes' walk from the railway station, then still surrounded by gardens at the edge of the city, it was not the most salubrious part of town. Due to the soot and noise produced by the trains, the city's investors had been adamant that the railway station should not be built in close proximity to the main hotels and pedestrian areas; however, not everyone could afford to stay there. As one wag commented, to live in Nice it was no longer enough to be a consumptive – a *poitrinaire* – one had to be a *millionaire*.[25] In the 1890s at least, the Rue Gounod was a distinctly malodorous street, too narrow for carriages to drive down. Chekhov told one of his correspondents that respectable ladies refused to live there because they would be too ashamed to invite their friends to such a seedy part of town.[26]

The Pension Russe was certainly a far cry from the opulent Hotel Saint-Pétersbourg, the preferred residence for expatriate aristocrats, or the equally imposing Hotel Beau-Rivage on the seafront, where Chekhov had stayed on his first brief visits to Nice. After visiting the Beau-Rivage one day, he wrote to Suvorin to tell him that the enormous chandeliered dining room with its columns and ornately painted ceiling, and the reading room, were just as they had been when they had stayed there.[27] The Pension Russe, by contrast, was altogether more homely, but was something of a venerable institution for visiting Russians even before Chekhov's sojourns. The satirist Saltykov-Shchedrin spent a winter there in 1875, and Lenin was later to be a guest for a few days in the spring of 1909, as one of the plaques on the wall of the present-day Hotel L'Oasis attests.[28] In the concrete urban jungle of contemporary Nice, the quiet garden filled with palms, orange trees and twittering birds that still surrounds the hotel suggests its new name is entirely apt.

Cosmopolitan Nice drew visitors from all over the world, even from the remote Sandwich Islands, as Chekhov pointed out to his sister in one of the regular bulletins he sent back home to his family.[29] He, however, lived a decidedly Russian life in the midst of this Mediterranean setting, both in terms of where he was staying and the people he chose to spend time with. At the Pension Russe, not only the manager but also the cook was Russian. As well as sometimes serving cabbage soup and *borshch*, Evgenia provided the residents of the Pension Russe with something to talk about. She had not only thirty years experience of living in Nice, but a marriage to an African sailor behind her, and their daughter Sonia was to be seen on occasion returning home at night with different male escorts. Even Chekhov provoked a few raised eyebrows by receiving a female friend in his room rather than in the hotel's drawing room. To his great relief, the establishment's forty or so Russian residents seemed to have little idea who he was when he first arrived, although at one point he was amused to overhear a young couple from Kiev reading his stories aloud to each other in the room next door.[30]

The ordeal of having to dine with elderly widows, provincial officials and down-at-heel gentry every day was occasionally mitigated by the company of friends like the Moscow Art Theatre founder Vladimir Nemirovich-Danchenko, who came on short visits. And there was also some socializing at the Pension Russe with friends Chekhov made in Nice, all of them fellow countrymen, mostly scholarly types. There was the kindly Russian Vice-Consul Nikolai Yurasov, whose son worked round the corner from the hotel at the Credit Lyonnais where Chekhov did his financial transactions. He had people over to his house every

week for lunch *à la Russe*.[31] Then there was Professor Korotnev, a
zoologist who had also graduated in medicine from Moscow University
and shared Chekhov's passion for the landscapes of his friend Levitan,
Valerian Yakobi, a retired professor of art, also suffering from
tuberculosis, and Maxim Kovalevsky, a free-thinking former Moscow
University professor with a larger-than-life personality and his own villa
in nearby Beaulieu, twenty minutes away. Of all these people Chekhov
was friendliest with Kovalevsky, who was nine years his senior. As a
keen gardener, Chekhov admired the roses blooming in Kovalevsky's
garden, but decided that they were no better than the roses in Russia.
He hated to cut his own flowers, but was able to be less stringent in
Nice, where there were profusions of beautiful flowers everywhere on
sale very cheaply. His room at the Pension Russe was often filled with
the scent of flowers he had bought himself, or bouquets sent by
admirers,[32] and he clearly enjoyed walking in the mornings through the
open-air *marché aux fleurs* in the old part of the city.

Chekhov soon settled into the the Pension Russe's rhythm, generally
waking at seven, breakfasting on eggs, croissants and coffee at seven-
thirty, and having lunch at midday, followed by a cup of hot chocolate
at two-thirty. Dinner was served at six-thirty, and sometimes Chekhov
took tea and biscuits later on in his room with other guests, one of
whom, Dr Valter, was also a graduate of the Taganrog *gymnasium*, and
ensured Chekhov did not stay up too late with him reminiscing about
their childhood. Usually Chekhov went to bed at about 11 p.m., and
was then eaten alive by mosquitoes, which left him itching for days until
he eventually discovered citronella candles. He was relieved to report
to one friend that the mosquitoes seemed to have finally migrated to
Egypt by December.[33] French courtesy made a great impression on
Chekhov: he noticed that one could not leave a shop without saying at
least 'bonjour', and that even beggars had to be addressed as 'monsieur'
or 'madame'. The maid who greeted him with a radiant 'Bonjour
monsieur' and a large cup of coffee each morning, smiled continually
like a duchess in a play, he told his brother Ivan, even though the work
clearly exhausted her. In general, Chekhov had far more flattering
things to say about the 'kind and honest' French staff at the hotel than
about its Russian guests, who soon began to exercise his patience – the
female ones in particular.[34] Chekhov may have been mentally in Russia
while he was in Nice, but the long months he spent there gave him an

opportunity to learn French. He passed on some of the phrases he mastered in letters to his sister, in which he also remarked upon the bad pronunciation habits of expatriate Russians, and the contrast between the crude turns of phrase encountered in Russian and the unfailingly polite expressions used by the French.

During the *belle époque* no one went to the Côte d'Azur in the summer. Most hotels remained closed until the end of September, and so Chekhov arrived in Nice just as the high season was about to start. Between 1860 and 1911, the resort grew faster than any city in Europe, attracting over a hundred thousand foreign visitors annually.[35] But while affluent foreigners were pouring into Nice to attend glittering soirées, go yachting, play tennis, polo and, in the British case, cricket, Chekhov was receiving a chilling reminder of why he had come to the south of France in the first place: five days after boasting to his sister about the robust state of his health, he had started coughing up blood again. There was music in the municipal gardens every day except Monday from two-thirty to four in the afternoon, but in October thousands of musicians started arriving in Nice to take part in international competitions. To the accompaniment of laughter and dancing, whole orchestras strolled through the city, providing impromptu concerts lit by torchlight (electric light was only installed on the Promenade des Anglais in 1894).[36] Chekhov, meanwhile, was closeted indoors, far from all the gaiety, and forced while confronting his mortality to hear jubilant musicians out on the streets – as early as half-past seven one morning when he was writing to Maria, pretending bravely all was well.[37] Chekhov had pinned his hopes on Suvorin visiting him after learning that he was in Paris, and his spirits sank still further when he now heard that his friend was not going to come. 'Your letter was a bombshell. I was so looking forward to seeing you, I wanted to spend time with you, talk to you, and to be honest I really need you! I had prepared a whole basketful of things to talk to you about, I had conjured up some delightful hot weather and then suddenly this letter. I am terribly disappointed!' Suvorin was, of course, the first person he confided in about his worsening health, but he typically made light of his condition initially (and was anxious that his family should not find out). A few weeks later he confessed to Suvorin's wife, Anna, that he had been coughing blood continuously for three weeks:

I have had to submit to various privations because of it: I do not go outside after three o'clock in the afternoon, I do not drink at all or eat anything hot, I do not walk fast, and stick only to the streets, I am not living basically – I'm a vegetable. And it irritates me, I'm in low spirits, and it seems to me that the Russians at dinner just talk about trivialities and nonsense, and I have to make an effort not to be rude to them.[38]

Writing to his sister about his health two days later, he skilfully deflected discussion of what was really going on by giving her a French lesson:

Now about my health. Everything is fine. Je suis bien portant. In French healthy is 'sain', but that only relates to food, water, climate; people say about themselves 'bien portant' from 'se porter bien' – to carry oneself well, to be healthy. When you greet people you say 'Je suis charmé de vous voir bien portant' – I am delighted to see you looking well . . .[39]

It was not in Chekhov's nature to succumb to self-pity, and besides, Alexei Lyubimov, another doctor who he became friendly with in Nice, was suffering from pleurisy and inflammation of the heart. 'As for my health,' he informed Suvorin before he was struck by another bout of blood-spitting, 'my illness is proceeding *crescendo* and is obviously already incurable: I'm talking about laziness. Apart from that I am as strong as an ox.' Yet in order not to tire himself going up two flights of stairs, Chekhov now moved down to the middle floor of the Pension Russe, which meant once again having to get used to a new desk. He also found it difficult adapting to the new regime which confined him to barracks in the middle of the afternoon. 'Because of the blood I am sitting at home as if I was under arrest, and here I am writing to you and wondering what else to say,' he wrote to Suvorin in December. 'I am bored and lonely on my own'. A few weeks later Dr Lyubimov died, and Chekhov joined the mourners at his funeral in the Russian cemetery at Caucade on a hill five miles to the west of the city. Its views are now blighted by buildings and roads, but in 1898 it was a green and peaceful place with clean, sweet-smelling air. Chekhov loved it.[40] After the cemetery was founded in 1867, the bodies of Russians who had been buried in the English graveyard next door were transferred here, and a small Orthodox chapel erected.[41]

The pleasure that Chekhov took in being in the south of France palled when the symptoms of tuberculosis reappeared; he began feeling homesick for Russia and for proper winter weather. It rained continuously for three days at the end of November and he told his mother in a letter that he had bought a light silk umbrella for six francs. It is tempting to think he might have made his purchase at the little umbrella shop in the Rue Colonna d'Istria in the old city. With a sign proudly proclaiming *Maison fondée en 1850* above the door, and an interior that seems unchanged since those times, it was a venerable institution even by the time Chekhov was living in Nice, and still sells elegantly patterned parasols alongside more practical *parapluies*. Perhaps Chekhov went back there to buy the umbrellas requested by his mother and sister as well. Rain made him yearn for snow and crisp Russian winter days, and he wondered if his friend Alexandra Khotyaintseva in Paris was also hankering for snow. 'After all, like laikas, you and I don't feel quite normal without snow,' he wrote to her two days before the non-Russian residents of Nice celebrated Christmas.[42]

Chekhov missed his two laika puppies – he had had to leave them only weeks after they had arrived at Melikhovo, after all. Chekhov's father had written in September to tell him that the puppies had grown and that the first snow had fallen, and shortly afterwards Masha wrote to say that they had dug up all the tulips she had planted, and so she wished her brother had taken them with him to France.[43] Chekhov told her by return that the puppies needed disciplining, and asked his sister to take a photograph of them to send him, as people were always asking him what sort of dogs they were and were interested. He encountered all kinds of dogs when he went out for his walks every day, but toy breeds seemed to be more popular than Siberian hunting dogs in metropolitan Nice. They were usually in muzzles, he told his mother in a letter (describing to her one particular long-haired dachshund he had seen which he thought looked like a furry caterpillar), but even so they seemed very cultured to him somehow. 'Culture oozes out of every shop window, from every raffia basket,' he wrote to Suvorin's wife Anna; 'every dog smells of civilization.'[44] Sadly, before Masha could produce a photograph of Nansen and Laika, both puppies died at the hands of malicious boys from the village. The dogs had endeared themselves to the Chekhov household by coming home promptly for lunch and dinner after running round outside all day and even Masha was saddened by having to report the protracted death of Nansen in early January. It had ruined everybody's New Year festivities, she said. Then a few weeks later she had to write with the news that Laika too had fallen ill and died.[45]

Watching all those dogs being taken out for walks in Nice made Chekhov ponder a subject for a story which two years later would become 'The Lady with the Little Dog'. He made the following entry in his notebook around this time: 'Animals are always trying to sniff out secrets (find the lair), and that's why human beings are doing battle with their own animal instincts in respecting other people's secrets.'[46] In the story, this idea is recognizable in Gurov's thoughts as he walks his daughter to school on his way to a reunion with his beloved Anna:

> As he was talking, he was thinking about the fact that he was going to a rendezvous and that there was not one living soul who knew about it; probably no one ever would know about it. He had two lives: one was the public one, which was visible to everybody who needed to know about it, but was full of conditional truth and conditional deceit, just like the lives of his friends and acquaintances, while the other one was secret. And by some strange coincidence, perhaps it was just chance, but everything that was important, interesting and essential to him, in which he was sincere and did not deceive himself, and which made up the inner core of his life, was hidden from others, while everything that was false – the outer skin in which he hid in order to cover up the truth, like his work at the bank, for example, the arguments at the club, his 'lesser species', and going to receptions with his wife – all that was public. And he judged others to be like himself, not believing what he saw, and always supposing that each person's real and most interesting life took place beneath a shroud of secrecy, as if under the veil of night. Every individual existence is a mystery, and it is maybe partly for this reason that cultured people take such pains for their secrets to be respected.

'The Lady with the Little Dog' is set in Yalta, and was written in Yalta, but bearing in mind Chekhov's remark that he needed to write from memory, he may well also have been inspired by the dozens of chic ladies walking their poodles up and down the Promenade des Anglais in Nice when he composed its famous opening:

People were saying that someone new had appeared on the seafront: a
lady with a little dog. Dmitry Dmitrievich Gurov had been staying in
Yalta for two weeks now, and had settled into its rhythm, so he too had
begun to take an interest in new faces. As he was sitting in the pavilion
at Vernet's he watched the young lady walking along the seafront; she
was not very tall, fair-haired and she was wearing a beret; a white
Pomeranian dog scampered after her.[47]

Certainly all sorts of other details that partly inspired the story were
originally scribbled in Chekhov's notebook in Nice: first, a governor's
daughter sitting in the front row of the provincial theatre in a boa, then
an older woman falling for an interesting young man in Yalta, and,
finally, a young man falling for a much younger woman in a resort
town. Some of the features of a sick young Russian girl called Olga
Vasilieva, who became very attached to Chekhov after meeting him in
Nice, were probably also incorporated into the character of Anna.[48]

Chekhov was repelled by the self-indulgent indolence of most of the
Russians he was obliged to make conversation with at lunch and dinner
every day, and chafed at the enforced idleness imposed by his tubercular
condition. He managed to achieve a good deal for his home town while
he was in France, however. When he was in Paris, before arriving in
Nice, he had met expatriates from Taganrog to discuss building a library
and a museum there; and he continued to write regularly to Pavel
Iordanov, a doctor colleague in Taganrog who was supervising efforts
locally. Thinking of exhibits for the museum, he wrote to tell Iordanov
at the end of October 1897 that his aunt had an oil painting of the
unveiling of the statue of Alexander I and a picture depicting the British
attack on Taganrog during the Crimean War. In March 1898, shortly
before he left Nice, he wrote to say that he had bought all the French
classics to donate to the library (some 319 books by seventy authors)
and was having them shipped to Taganrog. The works of Molière,
Prévost and Pascal he had sent earlier by post; Voltaire he had kept back
for the time being to read himself.[49]

During the long months in Nice, Chekhov whiled away his hours
reading, writing a little, taking short walks, playing cards with his friend
Maxim Kovalevsky, going on day trips by train and eating. Cultural life
also provided some distraction. Nice during the *belle époque* was a
mecca for artistic celebrities and Chekhov was keen to see and hear the

great coloratura soprano Adelina Patti, the highest paid singer of her day. Her performances in Nice and Monte Carlo in 1897 were her last (she was by then fifty-four) and Chekhov wrote to ask for a press pass from the editor of the *Russian Gazette* with a view to getting a seat in the front row. He was also interested in seeing the celebrated French actress Sarah Bernhardt, despite having been scathing about her performances in Moscow in 1881. And he was extremely keen to see the superb Italian actress Eleonora Duse, who came to Nice to perform the lead in *La Dame aux camélias*, Alexandre Dumas's perennially popular play about a selfless courtesan who dies tragically of consumption. If Chekhov had described his bed at the Pension Russe to Suvorin as being like that of Cleopatra, it was because they had both gone to see Duse perform in *Antony and Cleopatra* during an Italian theatre tour to St Petersburg in March 1891, and he was clearly reminded of the set. Duse had been so compelling that Chekhov thought he understood every word of the Italian translation of Shakespeare's play, even though he had no knowledge of Italian, and now he tried to lure Suvorin again to Nice by telling him Duse would be appearing there.[50]

There was a magnificent opera house in Nice, and if Chekhov had come back to Nice the following winter, he would have been able to attend the French premiere of Glinka's *A Life for the Tsar* in February 1899. Russian society was at its most brilliant during this period, and by all accounts it was quite an event, attended by both the Russian and French beau monde. The critic of *La Vie mondaine* was deeply moved, not only by the sight of the quivering breasts of bare-shouldered French and Russian princesses in their glamorous décolletée gowns, dripping with diamonds, but by the intensity of the emotional outburst, and the unanimity of feeling experienced by the Niçois, Parisians and Russians alike – it was something quite unprecedented in the history of Nice's theatrical life. At the end of the patriotic peasant chorus which closes the third act, the whole audience had spontaneously cried out 'Vive la Russie!' and called for the national anthem amidst a fluttering of fans and waving of hats. With the entire audience and orchestra on their feet shouting 'Vive la Russie! Vive la France!' there was soon nothing to do but perform the 'Marseillaise' and 'God Save the Tsar', which were greeted with 'indescribable enthusiasm' and half an hour of wild applause.[51]

Many of Nice's theatrical and musical performances took place at the Casino Municipale. Casinos still only exercised a mild fascination for Chekhov, but everyone went to Monte Carlo, and he went along with his friends more out of idle curiosity than any desire to play the roulette table. He limited his gambling to placing a few bets on *le rouge et le noir*, as he put it, and sometimes brought home handfuls of francs. But he found it tiring having to stand for any length of time, and the casinos were invariably unpleasantly hot. As someone who preferred the outdoors, it is not surprising that Chekhov yearned to go off on adventures while he was in Nice. Even before he arrived, he was planning a trip to Algiers and Egypt, and he tried to persuade various friends to undertake the journey with him. Corsica was another destination he was interested in. He was thrilled when Maxim Kovalevsky agreed to accompany him to Africa after completing a lecture series in Paris, and he wrote jokingly to his sister that he would probably see Russian starlings there who might recognize him, but would not let on if they did. Chekhov started telling numerous correspondents of his impending trip, and told Kovalevsky he was dreaming of Africa 'day and night'. But first the departure date was pushed back and then Chekhov was crestfallen to receive a letter from Kovalevsky in Paris telling him he had fallen ill with rheumatism and could therefore not go. Chekhov did not want to go alone, and told Suvorin he would probably have to restrict himself to a short visit to Corsica, which was anyway very close to Nice. That journey did not take place either.[52]

All winter Chekhov bombarded Masha with requests that she run domestic and secretarial errands for him as she filled him in on what was going on at home. She received over fifty letters from him while he was away – far more than any other of his correspondents – and had to carry out her brother's commissions in between teaching at a school in Moscow and coming back to Melikhovo at weekends to keep an eye on their parents. There were no end of problems with the poplar saplings that had been ordered, for example, which first did not arrive and then were sent to the wrong address. 'If they send the poplars in October it might be difficult to plant them,' she wrote in September just as Chekhov was arriving in Nice. 'I've planted the narcissi,' she continued, 'and will plant the tulips today. I've got a huge amount of things to do, and it's difficult managing to do it all, but I will try to carry out all your orders accurately.'[53] The poplars were finally planted in November. In October Masha reported that a stove had now been installed in the little two-room hut in the garden where Chekhov had written *The Seagull* and where he escaped when there were too many guests. Seeking to supplement his meagre income, the village school teacher was going to do the wallpapering and paint the windows and the door.[54]

Masha kept her brother posted about who of his friends she had seen in Moscow and how much people had liked the stories he had written in Nice, now published, as well as filling him in on day-to-day life at Melikhovo. While he was still enjoying sunny weather at the end of October, she wrote to tell him that they had had to cut down trees in the forest to use as firewoood, and was worried there would not be enough wood to fuel the stoves all winter. Another day she wrote that Anna Petrovna, the old horse they had bought together with the estate, had died; meanwhile, their two remaining horses were no longer capable of working but were eating their valuable hay all the same. Masha also kept her brother informed about the money she was raising to build a village school in Melikhovo: she had put by money raised from selling that year's harvest of apples from their orchard, and Levitan had donated a couple of canvases to be auctioned. Chekhov himself donated a thousand roubles when he returned, and the school opened finally in 1899. In December Chekhov asked his sister to buy Christmas presents for the local schoolchildren, and she wrote back to tell him that she had bought calico to make shirts for the sixty boys and nice red scarves for the twenty girls.[55]

Chekhov did not only issue orders. He also spent time hunting out presents to send back to Russia for his family – French soap and perfume, gloves, umbrellas, Japanese teacups, pencils, scissors, ties, purses, and photographs of himself that he had taken in Nice. In his typically brief diary entry for 21 November, Chekhov's father noted receiving a purse from his son, but did not forget to add 'without money'. These items were all transported back to Moscow by Russians returning home from the Pension Russe. The time-honoured tradition of sending things to Russia with people travelling there is thus not merely a recent phenomenon, but it is – and was – sometimes a haphazard business, as emerges from a humorous letter Chekhov sent Masha in December:

Ma chère et bien aimable Marie, if you are brought or sent something completely worthless, don't express surprise and say that it was not worth sending such rubbish all those thousands of miles. The fact is that the chance to send things comes very suddenly; you usually find out that someone is going back to Russia by chance and so you send whatever you can manage to grab from the desk, like a magnifying glass or a cheap pen ... A certain Miss Zenzinova is going to get in touch with you next week, she is the young daughter of Zenzinov the tea merchant. She is going to bring you something, but please don't open the parcel in front of her because she will see that she has brought things which are not valuable all that way and will be offended. The Zenzinovs stayed in the Pension Russe and gave me tea in the evening ... Be friendly to the girl, i.e., thank her for the hospitality which I received from her parents in Nice, say a couple of nice things to her and her Papa will give you 1/4 pound of tea for your trouble.

Put the magnifying glass on my desk.[56]

By the end of March 1898, knowing that this was the time for his flowers to spring up again, Chekhov was longing to be back home looking after his garden. He wrote to Masha to ask her to put canes by the lilies and peonies so that they did not get trodden on. 'We've got two lilies,' he reminded her, 'one in front of your window and the other near the white rose, on the way to the narcissi.' He was also concerned about his roses. 'Don't prune the roses before I return,' he wrote a little later, 'just cut off the stems which have gone mouldy over the winter or aren't looking healthy; but be careful when you cut them, and bear in mind that some unhealthy-looking stems recover. The fruit trees need to be painted with lime. It wouldn't be a bad idea to put lime on the earth underneath the cherry trees either.'[57] It was already hot on the French Riviera in early April, but in Moscow there was still snow after a long, hard winter. 'We are still using sleighs,' Masha wrote back, 'the snow is melting slowly and today we had new snow falling for a good half of the day. There is frost in the morning, and you can walk on the ice on the pond behind the red gates. There is no way one could even begin to think about the roses and the lilies and you will probably have to do the pruning and put up the canes yourself; the snow has got to melt first and there is still a lot of it about.'[58]

Chekhov spent his last mornings in Nice in 1898, not entirely happily, in an artist's studio sitting in a green velvet chair wearing a black jacket and trousers and white tie, posing for a portrait that had been begun in Russia the previous summer. The 26-year-old painter Iosif Braz had come down to Nice to finish the painting for the Tretyakov Gallery in Moscow. Chekhov quipped that it was a good likeness of him and his tie, but he still thought the expression made him look as if he had been sniffing horseradish.[59] Just after a rainy Easter he left finally for Paris, longing now to be back home in Russia.

He returned to Nice for another prolonged visit in December 1900, again in pursuit of the chimerical dream of arresting the progress of his illness. This time he stayed for a month and a half rather than an entire winter, but was even less enthusiastic about the prospect of being abroad than before. A major factor now was his involvement, albeit mostly at a distance, with Olga Knipper. The success of their relationship was almost predicated on their living apart, but a large part of Chekhov's reluctance to return to Nice in December 1900 came from the thought of being so far away from Olga. Once again, Chekhov took a south-facing room with a balcony at the Pension Russe looking out into the garden, and immediately felt homesick. Even the large monkey puzzle tree which stood in front of his window reminded him of Olga, as she had one growing in front of her window in Moscow. Chekhov wrote twenty-two passionate love letters to her during the six weeks of his stay in Nice, and could not work out at first why he was not receiving any replies. He began wondering, with increasing indignation, why Olga had not been writing to him. 'Write to me, darling, don't be lazy,' he pleaded. 'You've got a pile of letters from me and I haven't had a single one from you. What have I done to make you angry?' A couple of weeks later the mystery was unravelled, when it turned out that Chekhov's life had inadvertently become entangled with that of a retired officer living in Nice. Andrei Chertkov had started receiving the love letters intended for Chekhov because their surnames were similar and the French postman had muddled them up. When the distinguished Russo–Turkish War veteran turned up one morning at the Pension Russe to hand the missing letters over to their rightful owner, Chekhov was relieved, but embarrassed that one had been opened. Chekhov reminded Olga of the need in future to spell out clearly *Monsieur Antoine Tchekhoff, 9 Rue Gounod*.[60]

When he returned to Nice for that last visit, he spent the first week of his stay putting the final touches to *Three Sisters*, already in rehearsal at the Moscow Art Theatre. The major changes he now made to the last act included the addition of Masha's last words: 'Oh, how the music plays! They are leaving us; one of them has gone for good, never to return, and we will be left alone to start our lives again. We have to live . . . We have to live . . .' Was Chekhov reminded, when he wrote these lines, of the miserable days spent sequestered in his room at the Pension Russe while itinerant musicians played underneath his window back in October 1897? Perhaps they were indeed in the back of his mind as he reworked the poignant last act of the play, which ends with the sisters stoically facing up to the bleak reality of their lives while listening to rousing merry tunes played by a military band offstage. It was such a potent image that he returned to it two years later when he was writing his story 'The Bishop'. As the bishop in the story enters the last days of his life, he remembers the years he spent working abroad earlier in his career. Apart from sounds of the warm sea, he particularly recalls the homesickness he felt when a blind beggar girl came to sing about love underneath his window every day, accompanying herself on the guitar.[61]

Chekhov had wanted to go to Africa back in 1898, and he refused to give up on the idea when those plans did not work out. When he returned to Nice in 1900, he started planning a trip to Egypt. That idea was dropped in early January, but he and his friend Kovalevsky started thinking about Algiers again. This time bad weather intervened: Kovalevsky thought the sea was too rough to make a safe crossing and refused to go. A few weeks later it seemed that Chekhov's dream of seeing the Sahara was at last to become a reality, but in fact it proved again to be a mirage. Kovalevsky's last-minute qualms about rough seas (or perhaps in truth he feared the effects of the journey on Chekhov's precarious health) meant that they actually got on a ship going east, towards Italy, rather than south, towards Algeria.[62] Like Dr Astrov in *Uncle Vanya*, Chekhov must have spent some time looking at a map and thinking about how hot it was in Africa at this time. The frequent references to his proposed journey to Africa in his letters home at this time are reminiscent of the way in which his three sisters repeatedly yearn to be in Moscow. One has the slight sense that Chekhov himself, deep down, doubted he would ever reach Africa, and that this exotic continent perhaps remained (like Moscow for Masha, Irina and Olga) an ideal, a symbol – something to focus on in the face of the depressing reality of his increasing infirmity. In other words, Africa was like an escapist fantasy which the 40-year-old Chekhov clung to as if to will away thoughts of the disease which he knew was slowly killing him. The time he spent on the French Riviera did not lead to any improvement in his condition.

Chapter 9

THE RUSSIAN RIVIERA

I

Yalta and the Romanovs

Nothing can be more charming than the sight of that white Yalta, seated at the head of a bay like a beautiful sultana bathing her feet in the sea, and sheltering her fair forehead from the sun under rocks festooned with verdure.

Travels in the Steppes of the Caspian Sea, the Crimea, the Caucasus, &c, Adèle and Ignace Xavier M. Hommaire de Hell, 1847

Chekhov first saw Yalta from the deck of the steamer that was carrying him from Sevastopol to Feodosia in July 1888. It was his first visit to the celebrated Crimean peninsula which Catherine the Great had regarded as the most precious jewel in her crown, and he had been looking forward with eager anticipation to seeing its exotic vistas with his own eyes. He was not impressed. The train carrying him from the heart of the lush Ukrainian countryside, where he was spending the summer with his family, first had to cross the steppe, and he was immediately overcome with disappointment as he sat looking out of the window. Chekhov was something of a connoisseur of the steppe, as we know, and he found the flat landscape on the way to Simferopol utterly dispiriting in its colourlessness and monotony. It was as bleak as the Siberian tundra and had none of the charm and loveliness of the steppe around Taganrog, in his opinion. After Simferopol the scenery became more attractive: hills covered with vineyards alternated with groves filled with poplars. But it was only when the train finally pulled into Sevastopol station late in the evening and he caught his first sight of the Black Sea that Chekhov's spirits soared: the water's extraordinary, indescribable colour reminded him somewhat of copper sulphate, he

wrote in a letter, and he would pillage his memories of the moonlit bay
four years later when he came to write the last pages of his story 'The
Black Monk'. Like Chekhov and thousands of other travellers, Kovrin,
the central character, spends the night in a hotel by the harbour in
Sevastopol prior to catching a steamer the next day:

> Kovrin went out on to the balcony; the weather was calm and mild and
> you could smell the sea. The glorious bay reflected the moon and the
> lights and had a colour that was difficult to pin down. It was a soft,
> gentle mixture of blue and green; in some parts the colour of the water
> was like copper sulphate, while in others it seemed that the moonlight
> had condensed and filled the bay instead of water; but what a harmony
> of colours in general; what a peaceful, calm and sublime mood![1]

The famous stone steps leading to the water's edge from the white-
columned pavilion of the 'Count's Landing Stage' afforded a fine view
of the sea, particularly on moonlit nights. As one English guidebook
commented at the time, '. . . the view is, if possible, even more splendid
on a dark and still night when the waters of the bay become beautifully
phosphorescent, and when every stroke of an oar produces a shower of
phosphoric sparks'.[2] The heat and the dust the following morning,
however, combined with the noise of the port, the brick-coloured,
sunburnt skin of the locals, and the putrid smell of old ropes produced
in Chekhov a feeling of deathly boredom.[3] And his mood did not really
change once they had weighed anchor. Perhaps he had impossibly high
expectations of the dramatic landscape of the Crimea's southern coast,
with its towering cliffs, cedars and cypresses, over which so many had
swooned. The numerous travel writers who helped to slake the sudden
British thirst for books on the Crimea in the 1850s (because of the war)
had certainly found plenty to praise, even taking into account the
national tendency towards understatement. 'Following the coast-line to
Yalta, one beautiful estate succeeds another, generally under high
cultivation,' one wrote, 'while thickly-wooded mountain declivities,
groups of fantastic rocks, fine views of the sea, attractive dwellings,
hedges of cypress and olive, pomegranate and myrtle, claim the
admiration of the traveller.'[4] When Levitan had made his first trip to
the region in 1886, he had burst out sobbing from the beauty of it all,[5]
and the dozens of sketches he had shown his friend on his return must

have played a role in fuelling Chekhov's imagination.[6] Seeing the Crimean shoreline from the ship, however, convinced Chekhov that its beauty had been exaggerated and made him understand why it had not inspired his fellow writers. He thought that the countryside surrounding the River Psyol where his dacha was located was far more varied and colourful. As for Yalta, where the ship made a stop before continuing east along the coast to Feodosia, it was a town with a European flavour which looked a bit like Nice, but he thought there was also something a bit common about it:

> Box-like hotels in which unfortunate consumptives are fading away, brazen Tatar mugs . . . the ugly mugs of the idle rich in search of cheap adventures, the smell of a perfumery instead of cedars and the ocean, a wretched grubby landing stage, sad lights in the sea far away, the chatter of ladies and their escorts who have flocked here to enjoy nature without understanding anything about it – all this in general produces such a thoroughly despondent impression that you start accusing yourself of bigotry and prejudice.[7]

It was not exactly an auspicious beginning to Chekhov's relationship with the town which would become his home for the last six years of his life. In an ironic twist of fate, a decade later he would himself, of course, join the ranks of unfortunate consumptives fading away in Yalta.

The circumstances of Chekhov's first proper visit to Yalta the following July were also far from propitious. His brother Nikolai had died his agonizing death from consumption in the middle of the family's summer holiday at the dacha, and Chekhov had simply fled in a haze of grief and guilt. He had intended to go abroad, but in his confusion and uncertainty he had ended up in Yalta instead, where he spent three weeks renting a room in a dacha near the seafront. Having made his debut in a literary journal that spring, Chekhov was now a Famous Writer and so was immediately besieged by pretentious young poets and budding writers wanting him to appraise their weighty manuscripts. He found this very tedious. There were a great many people earnestly writing away in Yalta, it seemed, but none of them had any talent as far as he could see. Chekhov may have grumbled about not getting much writing done himself while he was in Yalta, but in truth he was probably glad to make new acquaintances who could distract him with picnics in the nearby imperial parks at Massandra, Livadia and Oreanda. There were also invitations to take excursions further afield – along the coast to the village of Balaklava, scene of the famous Crimean War battle thirty years earlier, and over the forest-covered mountains inland to Bakhchiserai, the former Tatar capital. Chekhov was still unimpressed with the flora, which he condemned as pitiful, and he pointed out to his sister that the much lauded cypresses were in fact dark and dusty, and no taller than the poplar growing by the porch of the Lintvaryovs' house in Luka. He was also unimpressed with the fauna: women outnumbered the men twenty to one, but none of them were attractive in his opinion, and they smelt of ice-cream. Recent events had inevitably cast a pall over the summer, and his low spirits clearly only exacerbated his natural misanthropic tendencies. He enjoyed swimming in the sea every morning and going on sedate horse-rides, but told his sister that he spent much of the time sitting for hours on the seafront, listening to the waves breaking against the shore and imagining he was back with their friends at Luka. He certainly felt guilty at having abandoned his family in a state of despair and fear.[8]

Although one of Chekhov's friends nicknamed him 'Antoine Potemkin', this is not an indication that he had any interest in the Crimea's recent past. He actually had little in common with Catherine the Great's favourite, Grigory Potemkin, who in 1783 was put in charge of the newly conquered province of the Crimea, or Tauris as it was known in ancient times. It had been Potemkin, anointed Prince of the new province of Taurida, who organized Catherine's triumphant tour of the 'New Russian' realm four years later, erecting film-set villages along the way, according to the legend, and a spectacular show of fireworks in Sevastopol. It was the British who built the military harbour for Russia's Black Sea fleet and, ironically, it was the British who were responsible for its total decimation in the Crimean War some seventy years later when Sevastopol was almost 'wiped from the face of the earth', as an early Russian guide book put it.[9] The town was still recovering when Chekhov first visited it in the late 1880s, and then had a population of about 2,500. Yalta, on the other hand, universally regarded as the most attractive point on the coast, was already entering its most fashionable phase as a watering place, and its permanent population of 5,000 was swelled annually during the season by hordes of well-heeled holidaymakers thronging to take advantage of its gentle climate and picturesque situation. By the time Chekhov settled in Yalta in 1898 it was the top resort in Russia.

Like the British royal family's development of Brighton, the Russian imperial family played the most important role in the transformation of Yalta from a small fishing village, with just a handful of inhabitants, at the beginning of the nineteenth century into the most populated area in the Crimea a century later. But it was Count Vorontsov who championed it first: no Russian considered living on the southern Crimean coast before him. Catherine had handed out parcels of land to her favourites after conquering the Crimea, and among the palaces which sprang up along the coast in ensuing decades, Count Vorontsov's in Alupka and Massandra were by far the grandest. With an English education behind him (his father was appointed ambassador to London when he was three years old), a distinguished record in the Napoleonic wars (after which he was appointed head of the Russian occupying forces in Paris), and an immense fortune, Mikhail Vorontsov was one of the most prominent statesmen of his time. In 1823 he was appointed by Alexander I to be the governor of the new southern province of 'New Russia'. While he was officially based in Odessa, he chose the area around Yalta as the location for his private residence, and it was here that Alexander I came to visit in 1825 with his ailing wife. The Tsar was so taken with nearby Oreanda that he decided to acquire a plot of land and retire there. He managed to plant a vineyard and olive trees round the modest house that he had built, but his retirement plans were thwarted by his unexpected death in Taganrog later in the year.[10]

When Alexander's successor, Nicholas I, first visited the Crimea in 1837, he stayed in Vorontsov's new palace in Alupka, situated 150 feet above the sea. Its opulence aroused his envy. The enormous Gothic fantasy designed by Edward Blore, the British court architect who completed Buckingham Palace, was constructed by Blore's assistant, William Hunt, using stone hewn from an extinct volcano at the back of the property. Blore never set eyes on his whimsical creation, which mixed the Elizabethan and the Moorish, with a dash of mediaeval castle thrown in for good measure. Nor did he ever see the terraces, marble lions, fountains and rare plants in Vorontsov's immense park, which Winston Churchill was to enjoy during the Yalta Conference in 1945.

When he lived in Yalta, Chekhov made many visits to Alupka to admire the fine trees and subtropical plants in its sumptuous park (two cypresses had been planted by Potemkin), and on one occasion took a walk through the grounds with Tolstoy, who was staying nearby. He also attended the charity concerts that were held on the terrace in aid of the nearby sanatorium for children with tuberculosis.[11] His acquaintance with the Russian-Jewish pianist Semyon Samuelson, who was one of the regular performers, was probably helped along by their having a common friend in Rachmaninov, whom Chekhov had recently got to know in Yalta. Samuelson had graduated from the Moscow Conservatoire with the Gold Medal the year after Rachmaninov and was a frequent visitor to Yalta, not least because his brother owned a pharmacy down the road from Chekhov's house. An upright piano was one of Chekhov's first Yalta acquisitions for his house, and he must have been filled with nostalgic memories of listening to his brother Nikolai at the keyboard when Samuelson came and played Chopin nocturnes to him. Samuelson later related to Olga Knipper that Chekhov particularly liked 'Chopin's Nocturne in C Major', a probable transcription mistake which has been repeated in all subsequent Chekhov literature: Chopin never actually wrote a Nocturne in C Major. It is tempting to think that Samuelson was actually talking about Chopin's Nocturne in G Major (op. 37, no. 2),[12] whose straightforward simplicity and absence of dramatic effects, when compared to the others, could be described as Chekhovian qualities.

Due to Vorontsov's energetic ministrations, it was during Nicholas I's stay in Alupka in 1837 that Yalta was designated a town for the first time. It was then still a very small settlement, with around thirty households and an overall population of about 200.[13] The Austrian cartographer and travel writer Johann Kohl, who visited the Crimea the following year, was not persuaded that the mountains on the south coast were comparable to the Italian Alps or the French Pyrenees when viewed from the sea, but he was more impressed when he disembarked, and he particularly liked Yalta: 'The houses are all new, and the whole town has such a pretty toy-like appearance, that it looks just as if it were to be given for a plaything to a child at Christmas. There are three inns, a custom-house, a post-house, a little church, a little quay, a harbour about two ells long, two little streets and a little apothecary's shop.'[14]

It was also during Nicholas I's Crimean tour of 1837 that the first

Romanov palace on the coast was planned. Despite its low position close to the shore, overshadowed by trees and tall cliffs, the Empress Alexandra Fyodorovna had taken such a liking to Oreanda that her husband decided to give it to her, and the Berlin architect Karl Friedrich Schinkel was commissioned the following year to produce a design for a residence. In the end it was the leading St Petersburg architect Andrei Stakenschneider who took over the project, with William Hunt supervising the stonemasonry. The sumptuous neo-Greek palace and its landscaped English park (filled with specially imported stags and roebucks)[15] were completed in 1852 and the imperial family arrived that autumn for an extended stay.[16] It was to be Nicholas I's only visit to Oreanda. The Crimean War temporarily put a stop to recreational travel in the area, and after the Tsar himself died in February 1855, his widow felt little desire to return. Alexandra Fyodorovna in fact decided she would rather go to Nice, and the Oreanda palace received its first regular visitors only after her death in 1860 when it was bequeathed to her second son, Grand Duke Konstantin.

Oreanda became a beloved holiday destination for the members of his family and their entourage, but nothing remains today of the palace: it burned down not long after Konstantin's older brother, Alexander II, was assassinated in 1881. What stands in its stead is the small church the devout Grand Duke built in memory of his mother when it became clear that the costs of reconstructing the palace would be prohibitive. Grand Duke Konstantin was a man with refined artistic tastes, and he took the unusual step (for a Russian Orthodox Christian at any rate) of deciding to build his church in the Georgian Byzantine style. He felt this was the most suitable style for all small churches in that part of the world, since they were the first to be built in the southern Crimea since the original Greek churches of the early Byzantine period. For the interiors, Konstantin commissioned exquisite mosaic icons from Antonio Salviati, who was famous for reviving the Venetian glass industry in the second half of the nineteenth century. After sending the first couple of icons to Oreanda, the 74-year-old master even travelled himself to the Crimea in May 1886 to discuss the rest of the church's decoration with the Grand Duke.

Chekhov loved visiting Oreanda when he lived in Yalta. The park was open to the public and was an extremely popular destination with the locals: the Yalta branch of the Crimean Mountain Club organized

twice-weekly trips in its charabancs. Chekhov came here particularly
often during his first winter in Yalta, usually in the company of a young
lady called Nadezhda Ternovskaya, which set tongues in Yalta wagging.
Her father was the priest at the Church of St John Chrysostom, and
several people hoped a betrothal would follow. After a short carriage-
ride to the church, the two would sit on a bench just below it from
where they could look down at the sea and admire the unparalleled
view of the bay of Yalta. The 'Chekhov Bench', as it is now known, was,
of course, the setting for a famous passage in the celebrated story 'The
Lady with the Little Dog', in which Gurov and Anna take a dawn trip
up the coast to Oreanda at the beginning of their summer romance:

> They sat on a bench not far from the church at Oreanda, looking down
> at the sea and saying nothing. Yalta was barely visible through the
> morning mist, and white clouds stood motionless on the tops of the
> mountains. The leaves on the trees did not stir, the cicadas were
> chattering, and the monotonous, muffled noise of the sea coming up
> from down below spoke of rest and of the eternal sleep which awaits us.
> It had made that noise down below when neither Yalta nor Oreanda
> existed, it was making that noise now and would continue to make that
> noise in that same hushed and indifferent way when we are no longer
> here. And in that permanence, in that complete indifference to the life
> and death of each one of us, is perhaps concealed a guarantee of our
> eternal salvation, a guarantee of the endless movement of life on earth
> and endless perfection. Sitting tranquilly next to a young woman who
> seemed so beautiful in the dawn light, entranced by this magical setting –
> the sea, the mountains, the clouds, the vast sky, Gurov was thinking that
> when you really reflect on it, everything is beautiful on this earth,
> everything that is, except what we think and do, when we forget about
> the higher purpose of existence and about our human dignity.
>
> A person – most likely a night watchman – came up to them, peered
> at them and then went away. Even that detail seemed mysterious and
> beautiful too. You could see the steamer from Feodosia arriving, lit up by
> the dawn and already without lights.
>
> 'There is dew on the grass,' said Anna Sergeyevna, breaking the silence.
> 'Yes. Time to go back.'
>
> They returned to town.[17]

Chekhov must have sat on that bench at daybreak too, and when he wrote these lines he may have been thinking about a letter his friend Levitan had sent him back in 1886 from Yalta. Levitan had written to Chekhov to tell him about the day he had climbed a cliff to look down at the sea, describing the eternal beauty of the scene, and how insignificant the majestic Crimean landscape made him feel.[18] Levitan was by that time even more gravely ill than Chekhov, and in July 1900, at the age of forty, he died, having paid a final visit to the Crimea to see his friend in December the previous year, the month in which 'The Lady with the Little Dog' was published. The watchman mentioned in Chekhov's story was most likely modelled on the ex-Crimean War serviceman who had been first employed by Grand Duke Konstantin to guard the church.[19]

Of the two other imperial properties situated in the environs of Yalta, it was Livadia which provided the stimulus for the town's

The view from the bench by the church at Oreanda

development as a first-class resort, and thus directly impinged on Chekhov's decision to take up residence in 1898. Because it was actively used as an imperial residence at that time, it was not as accessible to the public as the other palaces and Chekhov visited only on rare occasions. The beautiful estate of Livadia (from the Greek word for 'meadow') stood next door to Oreanda, but without its precipitous cliffs. It was just a few miles up the coast from Yalta and conveniently came up for sale in 1860. The Empress Maria Alexandrovna suffered from tuberculosis, and Alexander II had been hoping to find a suitable dacha in the southern Crimea where his wife could recuperate from the ravages of dank St Petersburg winters and the strain of giving birth to eight children in quick succession. The spacious grounds of Livadia had already been extensively landscaped by Joachim Tascher (a relative of Napoleon's wife Joséphine, who had turned his back on his aristocratic background to pursue a career in gardening), and Maria Alexandrovna immediately fell in love with the place when the imperial retinue made their first visit in 1861. The author of *Murray's Handbook to Russia* also went into raptures when visiting the estate a few years later:

> The natural beauty of this retreat and the taste with which it is fitted up cannot be surpassed. On the terrace in front of the palace is a fountain, surrounded by the most exquisite flowers. From the pavilion which stands on a rock at the edge of the garden a most splendid view of Oreanda and Yalta is obtained, and nothing can be more beautiful or impressive than a sunset over the blue waters of the Euxine seen from this fairy spot.[20]

It became immediately clear, however, that the existing house and its adjoining buildings needed extensive remodelling and expansion, and while this work was being carried out by the court architect, the imperial family took their holidays in Nice. It was in Nice in 1865 that Nicholas, the heir to the throne, died from tuberculosis, and it would be tuberculosis which would later kill his mother. It was just at this time that the imperial physician Sergei Botkin became aware of the excellent climatic conditions in the southern Crimea and strongly advised Maria Alexandrovna to spend the autumn in Livadia. Botkin's advice was soon followed by hundreds of other consumptives, many of them (like Chekhov) doctors themselves, who started coming to Yalta in ever greater numbers in the hope of making a recovery. The connection of Sevastopol to central Russia by rail in 1873 also played a role in attracting invalids from the north, and by the time Chekhov first passed through Yalta in 1888, there were already so many tuberculosis sufferers living in the town that they were as distinctive a feature as the holidaymakers.

There was a brief hiatus in Yalta's expansion during the Russo–Turkish War of 1877–78; not only were there no visitors, but more than half the population left.[21] The gravely ill Maria Alexandrovna came back to her beloved Livadia for one last visit in 1879, and a little over a month after she died the following year, Alexander II married his mistress Princess Dolgorukaya; they already had three children. Their marriage was brief: Alexander was assassinated the following March, and his son, the new Tsar Alexander III, did not return with his family to Livadia until the autumn of 1884. Either his distaste in discovering his stepmother and her children living in his mother's rooms in the palace or a desire to make his own mark led to his search for another property in the Yalta area. In 1888 he settled on Massandra, which lay on the other side of the bay, about three miles from the town. This was another Vorontsov estate that incorporated extensive vineyards and beautiful gardens full of statues. Alexander never managed to move into the turreted Louis XIV-style château that was built for him, although he did spend a million roubles installing a fine wine-cellar;[22] he died unexpectedly while holidaying in Livadia in October 1894 at the age of forty-nine. Chekhov was taken to Massandra by new acquaintances when he made his second visit to Yalta in March 1894. The master of wines was so pleased to meet the famous writer when they visited the cellars, that he opened up some old bottles for them to taste which had been laid down in Vorontsov's time.[23]

Chekhov stayed at Yalta's largest and smartest hotel when he came for his second visit. Renowned for being 'replete with every comfort', the Rossiya had 150 rooms (many with a sea view), an elevator, a first-class restaurant staffed by waiters who spoke all the foreign languages, and a terrace where an orchestra played daily concerts throughout the peak season.[24] Chekhov, however, had come in the quieter (and cheaper) winter season, which was most popular with people convalescing from illness, particularly tuberculosis. Yalta had four distinct seasons – each with its own particular character and clientele –

and the winter season, lasting from the middle of October to Easter, was now beginning to vie with the fashionable 'velvet' season just before it, when people came to take the celebrated grape cure that had been developed by a local doctor. Chekhov had certainly come to Yalta this time for health reasons: he had been suffering from terrible headaches and an arrhythmic heartbeat (which on one alarming occasion made him think he was about to die), not to mention the haemorrhoids which perennially plagued him. But perhaps the most disquieting symptom was the persistent cough which continued throughout the month of his visit.

He spent two days travelling by train from Moscow, then completed the final leg of his journey to the Yalta harbour one foggy Friday evening in early March, with the ship's whistle on the steamer *Tsarevna* blowing almost continually in the poor visibility. Once installed in his room at the Rossiya, he resolved to stick to his abstention from smoking, and spent a fairly miserable month in continuing poor health, trying to rest but unable to avoid thinking about the need to keep writing, upon which his family's livelihood depended. Next door to him was a well-known Petersburg actress who made solicitous enquiries about his heart, and tried to lure him out on excursions, such as to the spectacular waterfall at Uchan-Su (Tatar for 'flying water'), a thousand feet above sea-level.

When he was not working or catching up with his sleep, Chekhov whiled away the time going for walks along the seafront with his new acquaintances, taking trips out of town, and dining out in the houses of the Yalta intelligentsia. He sold his fox-fur coat which had been moulting, and went along desultorily to rehearsals of Gounod's *Faust*. The worthy citizens of Yalta were organizing an amateur performance at the town's theatre in aid of the recently founded girls' *gymnasium*, and Chekhov enjoyed contemplating the different coloured heads of hair of the young ladies bobbing about. Everyone wanted to meet him, and he soon found the constant attention very tedious, even if there were some individuals he found interesting to talk to. Not only did everyone soon know that he was in town, but they were sometimes able to work out in advance exactly what his movements would be. The enthusiastic reception given by the capacity audience to a rather indifferent recital, given in late March at the Rossiya by a bass singer from Moscow who Chekhov had got to know, was attributed to the fact that most of the people there had actually bought a ticket in order to catch a glimpse of the debonair writer. And there was one young lady who knocked at the door of his hotel room one day, who finally overcame her nervousness to blurt out that she had just wanted to look at him, because she had never seen a writer before.[25]

Chekhov did not write much while he was in Yalta, but what he did produce more than made up in quality what it lacked in quantity. 'The Student', one of his slightest but most accomplished and lyrical stories, was published soon after his return to Moscow. It concerns a seminary student who has suffered a temporary lapse in faith on Good Friday, the bleakest day in the Russian Orthodox year, and compounds his sin by going woodcock shooting. He regains his sense of connection with the world by telling, as a form of confession, the story of Peter's betrayal of Jesus to two peasant women he meets on his way home. In doing so, he unconsciously uses a mixture of his own words with phrases from the Gospels, and the women's profound emotional reaction to the story, immediately comprehensible to them when not couched in the archaic biblical language of old Church Slavonic, translates to the student himself, so that he leaves them with a spring in his step, feeling reinvigorated and inspired.

According to his brother Ivan, Chekhov regarded this story (which is also a parable about the power of art) as his most polished work. It was also known to be his favourite story, its ending proving definitively, in his opinion, that he was not the cold-blooded, gloomy pessimist his critics made him out to be.[26] The last paragraph of the story is indeed one deliberately long sentence of exaltation:

And when he was crossing the river on the ferry, and then when he was walking up the hill, as he looked at his own village and to the west, where there was a narrow band of cold crimson sunset glowing, he realized that truth and beauty, which had guided human life there, in the garden and at the high priest's, had continued to do so without a break until the present day, and had clearly always constituted the most important elements in human life, and on earth in general; and a feeling of youth, health and strength – he was only twenty-two years old – and an inexpressibly sweet expectation of happiness, of unfathomable, mysterious happiness, gradually overcame him, and life seemed entrancing and miraculous to him, and full of sublime meaning.[27]

As with the stories he would write a few years later in Nice, Chekhov's imagination was sometimes fired by alien surroundings. Sensitive, as always, to the landscape, the 'cemetery-like' foliage of the Crimean riviera produced in him a deep nostalgia for the Russian north, which he considered infinitely superior to the south in spring time, despite the pleasant climate of the latter. As he wrote in a letter towards the end of his stay, 'Our Russian landscape is more melancholy, more lyrical, more Levitanesque, but here it's neither one thing nor the other – it's just like well-written, sonorous, but cold poetry.'[28] The reference to Levitan is telling – and touching. For the past two years the two friends had been incommunicado after Chekhov had sailed a little too close to the wind in his satirical portrait of an artist in the story 'The Grasshopper'. Perhaps he was thinking guiltily of Levitan when he wrote the opening of 'The Student', for if there was anyone Chekhov associated with shooting woodcock, it was Levitan, who was a passionate huntsman.

Chekhov had accompanied Levitan on his hunting trips when they were at Babkino (and even looked after his gun-dog at one point), but he was much keener on fishing, having by then lost the taste for shooting he had when he was younger. Nevertheless, soon after moving to Melikhovo, he had gone out several times into the fields with Levitan just after Easter in 1892, when the artist came down from Moscow for his first visit. The warm April weather had also suddenly given way to snow again that week, just as in the story. Levitan shot a woodcock in the wing, and after Chekhov picked it up from the puddle where it had landed, they both looked at its long thin beak, its beautiful plumage and the startled expression in its large black eyes. Levitan lacked the courage to kill the bird outright, and Chekhov was forced to overcome his distate and do the job for him. As he commented the next day in a letter to Suvorin, 'One beautiful loving creature was no longer alive; meanwhile two idiots went home and sat down to supper.'[29] The word 'Levitanesque' must have aroused mixed emotions in Chekhov's mind as he thought about the beauties of the Russian spring and conjured up that unseasonably cold Good Friday evening in 'The Student'. The incident later was also famously reflected in *The Seagull*.

Before his untimely death in 1894, Alexander III had made a serious contribution to the development of Yalta as a sophisticated world-class resort, although it cannot be said that he was motivated by altruistic considerations. Until 1891, travel to Yalta by steamship involved transferring to a small launch in the bay and being ferried to the landing stage. When the imperial family arrived for their annual visit in 1886 the sea was so rough that they had to stay overnight in their ship. Alexander promptly ordered the construction of a proper harbour so that vessels could dock right in the town. The increased access provided by the harbour made it possible to supply households in Yalta with running water and a proper sanitation system, and to equip the town's main streets with gas, and then electric, lighting. It was precisely these amenities that made Chekhov decide to live there when he became seriously ill.[30] New hotels, sanatoriums and shops began to spring up in profusion in Yalta, as well as churches, a theatre, a library and several schools.

It was not until 1898, the year that Chekhov moved down to Yalta permanently, that the new Tsar Nicholas II resumed imperial visits to the Crimea. He and the Empress Alexandra came to regard Massandra as a kind of dacha they could drive over to for brief sojourns while staying at their official residence at Livadia. Yalta was at the height of its popularity at this time, and Nicholas was scathing about the hordes of 'dull people' who crowded the streets whenever the imperial motorcade drove through the town. 'You'd think you were in some big foreign resort,' he complained to his mother in October 1900.[31] But that, of course, was exactly the idea. When he first developed Yalta in the 1830s, it seems that the ambitious Count Vorontsov had hoped that his resort would become 'the Cowes of the Crimea, as a station for the yachts of the nobles, and a fashionable bathing-place', as reported by the Rev. Thomas Milner in 1855. This was perhaps not surprising, bearing in mind Vorontsov's upper-class British upbringing, but at that point Milner was forced to conclude that 'the design has not prospered'.[32]

By the 1870s, however, Yalta had certainly taken off, although perhaps not in the direction which Vorontsov had intended. To the author of *Murray's Handbook for Travellers in Russia*, it seemed that the increasing number of Russian families going to Yalta to bathe 'bids fair to make Yalta the Russian Brighton'. The town's charming situation, excellent port, and proximity to fine scenery also made it seem like a miniature version of Naples.[33] But the most frequent comparisons were inevitably made with Nice.[34] Yalta's famous seafront promenade may have been a miniature version and pale imitation of the Promenade des Anglais, its clientele less international and its population far smaller, but with its elegant hotels, flowers blossoming in profusion through the winter, and the 'velvet' season drawing scores of princes and princesses, opera singers and actresses every autumn, everyone looked upon it as the Russian Nice. As we have seen, Chekhov also immediately thought of Nice when he first saw Yalta. After having spent protracted periods in both places, he formed the opinion that Yalta was more expensive and not as interesting, but he liked it more than the French Riviera,[35] not least because it was cleaner.[36]

Chekhov would never have been found in the crowds lining the streets to catch a glimpse of the imperial family during their visits to Yalta (his feelings for them were generally of contempt), but his mother was thrilled to see the Tsar at the consecration of the new Cathedral of St Alexander Nevsky in December 1902, which she attended by special ticket. Like the Church of the Saviour on the Spilled Blood in St Petersburg, also built in the pseudo-Russian style favoured by Alexander III, the Yalta cathedral was erected in memory of his murdered father. Chekhov was at that time so unwell that he had not been down to the centre of town for weeks, but he could hear the deep bass bells from his house, and they made him feel very homesick for Russia.[37]

II

Chekhov and the Tatars

A week after arriving in Yalta in 1898, Chekhov was taken to see a small red-roofed house that was for a sale in a Tatar village called Kuchuk-koy. The property was situated about twenty miles along the coast towards Balaklava, on a steep incline not far from the sea. It came with a small tobacco plantation, a vineyard, some wonderful old trees (including pomegranate, fig, olive, walnut) and a splendid sea view from the upstairs balcony. Dreaming of long days in which he would go and sit on the rocks and fish – he told his brother Ivan to bring hooks and a fishing line when he came to stay – in December he bought it, having already bought a plot of land to build a house on in Yalta itself. It seemed as wild as Africa.[38]

It was not surprising that Chekhov felt he was living in a foreign country when he was in the Crimea. He was. There was a mosque below the house he built, which was situated in a Tatar village, his first gardener was a Tatar called Mustafa, and both the men who came to dig up the old vines on his newly acquired plot wore red fezzes on their heads.[39] Even the English Gothic-style dacha he stayed in before his house was built was given a Tatar name – 'Omyur', meaning life.[40] Chekhov may have been slightly disparaging about the Tatars when he took in his first superficial view of Yalta as a young man back in 1888, but since then he had been to Sakhalin, had observed at close hand how contemptuously the indigenous population was treated there by the Russian colonists, and was now acutely conscious of a similar dynamic at work in the Crimea, where Tatars were often referred to as Turks, due to the similarity of the language they spoke.

Chekhov found these attitudes abhorrent, and he went out of his way to disassociate himself from the imperialist attitudes of most of his fellow countrymen. As his friend Bunin noted: 'There were many Turks and Caucasians working on the Black Sea coast. Knowing the hostility mingled with contempt which we have for other nationalities in Russia, he would never miss the opportunity of expressing his admiration at how honest and hardworking they were.'[41] After coming down to the harbour to meet his mother and sister and their old servant off the steamer *St Nikolai* in October 1899, Chekhov was horrified to see the assistant captain strike Mustafa in the face when he went to their cabin to pick up their luggage. The officer was appalled to see a Tatar mingling with the first-class passengers; Chekhov was appalled by the blatant racism.[42] The scandalous incident was even reported in the local Yalta newspaper.[43] As usual, it is the small details (revealed post-humously in memoirs) that give away feelings Chekhov largely kept to himself. During his visit to Yalta in 1894, he had become exasperated with a local journalist who had published a small book on 'Yalta and its Environs'. When Chekhov had encouraged him to write more, the journalist wondered what more there was to say about a place that was just one big station in the summer and a dead provincial town in the winter. Chekhov had suggested he write about the way of life of the Tatars, since he was so lucky to be in the Crimea all year round; he reckoned there must be an interesting legend to tell in each mountain village. It was a topic which had obviously never occurred to the journalist before, and he objected feebly that he did not know the language, to which Chekhov immediately retorted that their mutual acquaintance did, and could probably help, and that knowledge of the language was perhaps not a necessity anyway.[44]

When Chekhov moved to Yalta four years later, he was full of appreciation for its wonderful sanitation system, but at the same time he was acutely aware that it had been installed for the benefit of its Russian inhabitants, while the overwhelmingly Tatar villages beyond the town remained 'completely Asiatic'.[45] Beyond the exotic-sounding local place names, most Russians at that time did not stop to think about the fate of the Crimean Tatars, who had been emigrating to Turkey in large numbers ever since their land had been taken away from them to become part of the Russian Empire at the end of the eighteenth century. But Chekhov clearly did: all three of the properties he bought in the Crimea were in Tatar villages. He would have been horrified to have been alive in Stalinist Russia when the 200,000 remaining Tatars were taken away and callously deported to Central Asia. In November 1888 he had written to Suvorin: 'A propos Feodosia and the Tatars. The Tatars were swindled out of their land, yet no one spares a thought for their welfare. They need schools. You ought to write an article calling for the money the Ministry pours into that Dorpat University of Sausages for useless German students, to be spent instead on schools for Tatars, who can be valuable to Russia. I would write it myself, but I haven't the skill.'[46]

Over the centuries, the Crimean peninsula had been home to Cimmerians, Scythians, Tauri, Polovtsians, Khazars, Armenians and Byzantine Greeks (Yalta is derived from the Greek 'yalos', meaning shore), to name just some of the peoples who had passed through the territory, but it was the Tatars who could lay the strongest claim to its 10,000 or so hotly contested square miles. They were a distinct ethnic group, descended partly from the dominant group in the Mongol army which overran Europe in the thirteenth century under the leadership of Genghis Khan's grandson, and partly from the mixture of sedentary peoples who already inhabited the Crimea.[47] The most westerly settlement in the vast Mongol Empire was established by the Tatars in the Crimea at Bakhchiserai (meaning 'palace in a garden'), and in the fifteenth century it became the capital of one of several independent khanates formed when the newly Islamicized empire began to collapse. The Crimean Khanate, which was the only one to survive, soon became uncomfortably sandwiched between two emerging empires: the newly powerful Russians to the north, and the Turks to the south. With such close religious and linguistic ties, it was inevitable that an allegiance was formed with the Ottomans, who essentially ruled the Tatars for the next three centuries. This situation drastically changed when – to telescope many complex events – the Crimea (from the Tatar name *Arym* or *Grim*)[48] became a protectorate of the Russian Empire in 1772, and was finally absorbed into it in 1783 under Catherine the Great. Russia had finally acquired the access to the Mediterranean it had coveted for so long, along with the fertile lands of southern Ukraine and Russia along the Black and Azov Seas.

Once the Crimea belonged to Russia, it was subject to her laws. Only the nobility could own land, and the Tatars did not belong to the noble class. Therefore, went the argument, the land was not theirs to own. The Russian colonizers thus felt no compunction about seizing the territories, thereby restricting Tatar access to wells and the precious commodity of water, which led eventually to their complete impoverishment. To judge from the account of a British traveller who came to these parts in the 1830s and 1840s, the Russians performed a passable imitation – in reverse – of the Tatar invasion of the Russian lands in the twelfth century. 'Even now, although so many years have elapsed since Russia has established her rule in the Crimea,' he wrote, 'we hear these poor people enumerate the barbarities that were perpetrated upon their country by Potemkin and his host of rapacious agents, with as much vivacity and freshness of colouring as if these horrors had only occurred yesterday.'[49]

As the Tatars' traditional pastoral way of life collapsed, Catherine's aggressive Russification policies soon compelled them to start emigrating in large numbers, mostly to Turkey. By 1790, 80,000 had already fled, with a further 200,000 leaving after the Crimean War in 1860.[50] The last wave of emigration took place in 1902–1903, Chekhov's last years in the Crimea, when hundreds of Tatars left for Turkey daily.[51] From an initial population of about six million, their numbers had declined to less than a million by the beginning of the twentieth century.[52] This is the other side of Crimean life which Chekhov did not want to ignore. When the Russian colonization of the Crimea is viewed in this context, the decision in the 1860s to design much of the opulent new Romanov palace in Livadia in the 'style of a

Tatar cottage'[53] seems at best tasteless. However, this particular aesthetic had been subjected to 'ethnic cleansing' long before Roosevelt was billeted there for the 1945 Yalta Conference: the palace was remodelled more than once by its imperial inhabitants.

Although the vast majority of the overall population in the Yalta area was Tatar when Chekhov moved south, with Russians a small minority, the ratio was reversed in the town of Yalta itself. The ten per cent of the Tatar population in the Crimea who lived in towns resided in separate quarters and came into little contact with the Russian inhabitants. The rest had retreated into the mountains or deep into the steppe. An even smaller ethnic minority in the Crimea were the Turkic-speaking Karaim Jews, who numbered no more than 13,000 in the whole of Tsarist Russia. One of them became Chekhov's trusted friend. Isaak Sinani, who was someone he got to know when he first went to Yalta in 1889, was renowned as a bibliophile and an expert on the Crimea's ethnic groups. It is telling that Chekhov should specifically refer to him as 'the Karaim Sinani' when writing from Siberia to let his sister know she should pick up the telegram he had sent her at the bookshop where his friend worked.[54] By the time Chekhov moved to Yalta, Sinani had acquired his own bookshop.[55]

'I. A. Sinani's Russian Hut. Sale of Books and Newspapers' was located right in the middle of town on the seafront, and decorated like a traditional peasant log house. It immediately became a mecca for the writers, artists and theatrical personalities who came to Yalta. Sinani had placed a bench outside the *Russkaya izbushka*, and before he became too ill and too much of a local tourist attraction, Chekhov would come most days and sit there, sometimes to chat with other writers like Gorky and Bunin, and sometimes just to watch the world go by. He was such a celebrity by this time, though, that his visits to the shop usually had to be kept quite short because crowds of young female admirers would invariably try to follow him wherever he went – like dolphins behind a ship, as one Russian critic later put it.[56] The kind, learned Sinani was devoted to Chekhov, and soon introduced him to his wife, Anastasia, and their children, who lived above his shop. He was the person who would hear what properties were for sale, and it was he who took Chekhov to see the house at Kuchuk-koy, and the plot at Autka where he would build his house. It was Sinani who introduced him to Lev Shapovalov, the young architect who would design it, and he came along to the planning meeting with the contractor before building work started. He then went every day to check up on how the building was getting on, and later helped with planting trees in the garden. It was Sinani, too, who sold tickets for the Moscow Art Theatre tour in 1900, and who, following Chekhov's initiative, provided the reception point for charitable donations for the many invalids (mostly consumptives) who had come to Yalta without means. Chekhov picked up his telegrams from Sinani, and knew he could be relied on for all the latest Yalta gossip and any other information worth knowing. When Sinani delayed handing over the telegram about his father's unexpected death in October 1898, out of a reluctance to give him bad news, Chekhov was mortified that the whole of Yalta knew about it before he did.[57] Two years later, Chekhov had to break the news to Sinani that his student son had committed suicide in Moscow.[58]

As with his brother Nikolai's death, Chekhov felt guilty about being absent when his father died, but this time the feeling was deepened by the knowledge that he could have prevented it if he had been there. Pavel Egorovich had died three days after being taken to Moscow for an emergency operation, having made his last entry in his legendary diary on the evening of 8 October 1898. While Chekhov was still enjoying summery weather in Yalta, it had already started snowing in Moscow:

> Morning: −12°. The windows were frosted up like in winter. Sunrise was
> bright. It was cold in all the rooms in the house. The firewood has not
> been brought yet. Midday: 0°. Roman went on the sledge to Lopasnya.
> Tea, sugar and coffee has arrived from Vogau's. Evening: −2°.[59]

Chekhov's relationship with his father had always been difficult, but he was not prepared for his death, which shook him deeply, nor for its repercussions. Knowing that his mother would not want to continue living at Melikhovo on her own and that life there would not be the same without his father, he realized the estate would have to be sold. This meant taking up permanent residence in Yalta, rather than only spending winters there, as he had originally planned.

Autka, the Tatar village where Chekhov built his house was about twenty minutes walk uphill from the centre of town, near the Uchan-su River. It was certainly not everybody's first choice for an ideal location; the plot that Chekhov bought, with its withered old vineyard, was next to a Tatar cemetery and when his sister first saw it she burst into tears.

It was perhaps also not a good omen that a funeral was being held the day he first viewed the property. But it suited him. It had its own 'biblical' well, it was far enough from the town centre, he thought, to deter casual visitors and adoring fans (a vain hope: after he moved in, clusters of girls in floppy white hats would stand for hours by the garden railings, hoping to see him come outside), the air was better because of the higher altitude, there was a magnificent view of the Uchan-su River leading down to the sea, and, most importantly, there was room for a garden. Because few Russians wanted to live in a primitive Tatar village, far from the resort's amenities, the land was much cheaper in Autka (and Chekhov got it even cheaper because the vendor was a fan). Not that it was ever Chekhov's intention to go native: his house was the last word in what he referred to as 'American' mod cons, and was designed to his specification. It even had a telephone, which made it possible for him to call up Tolstoy for a chat when he was staying down the road in nearby Gaspra. And he told his brother Ivan jokingly that he was planning a fountain and a pond with goldfish.

His chief adviser, Masha, came down for a vist in November to talk everything over and draw up plans. Chekhov was soon inundated with frustrating offers from acquaintances of roses and trees for his new garden, but it was not possible to plant much in the early months when the plot was just a muddy building site. He had taken on a Tatar contractor whose employees were a little slow-witted, and he was nervous that everything would get trampled on. He also had a Tatar neighbour who always wanted to get into conversation with him whenever he came to see how things were getting on. The house was built directly into the sloping ground, to an asymmetric but simple design, with large south-facing windows and a first-floor terrace. There was a wonderful view of the bay from it.

III

The White Dacha

If I am Potemkin, then why am I in Yalta, and why is it so horribly boring here?

Letter to L. Avilova, 18 February 1899

While Chekhov was kept busy with the construction of his new house, and thinking about samovars, beds, and other necessary accoutrements for Kuchuk-koy, his spirits were quite buoyant. He had arrived in Yalta at the best time of year, after all, everything was new, there were lots of people in town, his health was bearing up, and he decided that he had never liked the Crimea as much as now. During the balmy autumn weather (it was warmer than it had been in Nice the previous year, he noted) he wrote four stories in quick succession and even found lots of mushrooms in the pine woods, which he knew would make his mother happy when she came to stay. But when he started spitting blood again – in November, just as he had in Nice the previous year – he began instantly to yearn for Moscow: for the company of friends, the theatre, restaurants. He could talk about writers in Yalta, but there was no one to talk to about writing, he complained miserably. Except for the people at the girls' *gymnasium*, whom he liked very much (they had immediately put him on their board of trustees), Chekhov had also tired of local society by the middle of December and was feeling like Dreyfus on Devil's Island.

His brother Ivan came down to visit over Christmas, but it had started snowing the day after he left, which brought the construction of the new

The seafront in Yalta, which the Lady with the little dog walks along

house to a halt. That is when Chekhov's nostalgia for Russia – particularly for the Moscow newspapers and the church bells he loved so much – really began. He was not accustomed to sitting still in one place for any length of time, and it was unbearable to see other people coming and going. By early January it seemed that everyone but the local tradespeople had left, and he felt he was in exile, a sensation that only deepened when the weather deteriorated. The main access to Yalta was via the sea, and when navigation stopped during storms, and the road to Sevastopol was impassable, there were no letters either. It really did feel as though the town was an island cut off from the world.[60] Meanwhile, Masha was writing to tell her brother that the snow was settling in Moscow, so it was at last possible to travel by sleigh (so much more pleasant than having to deal with carriages and slush on the streets). She also told him about the new flat she and their mother had just rented. It was very near the theatre where the Moscow Art Theatre was based, and their production of *The Seagull* was creating such a furore, she wrote, that she could still hear people talking enthusiastically about the play as they walked past their windows while she was lying in bed at one in the morning. Masha had been at the premiere and she wrote the next day to tell her brother how it had gone:

> People started calling for you after the first act, and when Nemirovich announced that you weren't there, everyone, particularly people in the stalls, started shouting out: 'We should send him a telegram then.' After the third act there was a lot of noise and ovations for the actors and calls for the author again. So Nemirovich said: 'I hope in that case that you will permit me to send the author a telegram.' The audience said: 'We do, we do.'

The three performances of the play were a complete sell-out.

Chekhov was alone at New Year. A family tradition from Taganrog days had been to bake pies and put a ten kopeck piece in each of them: Masha wrote to tell him that their brother Alexander had been given the slice with the 'treasure' in it on New Year's Eve, while on New Year's Day she had been the lucky one for the first time. Chekhov was also alone for his birthday on 17 January. Masha told him there had been so many guests at the party they held for him in Moscow that they had run out of cutlery and plates.[61] No wonder he grew homesick.

Chekhov spent the first winter in his 'warm Siberia' mostly reading newspapers and writing letters – so many that the joint on the middle finger of his right hand started aching. He would write even more letters as his health began to deteriorate and he was closeted indoors for longer and longer periods. Of the twelve volumes of letters in the Academy of Sciences edition of his collected works, half cover the last seven years of his life. Finally the warm weather returned, and he could stop playing cards and go out for carriage rides and walks again every day – to Oreanda and Massandra and into the hills. New people began appearing on the seafront, and soon the days were filled again with telephone calls and meetings. The great joy of spring was the profusion of white cherry blossom, pink almond blossom, and then peach blossom, which appeared everywhere. Once construction commenced again, his house also began taking shape, but Chekhov derived the greatest pleasure from being able to begin planting trees in his new garden. It was pure bliss, he told his sister, after he had planted twelve cherry trees, two almond trees and four pyramidal mulberry trees (planting 'pyramidal' trees that would grow vertically rather than

The Hotel Marino, Yalta, where Chekhov stayed in 1899

horizontally meant he would be able to plant more of them). A few days later an order went off to a horticultural establishment in Odessa, which included eight different kinds of bamboo, giant reeds, yuccas and two kinds of amaryllis. But all the tree planting could not mask the fact that he was not living in the full sense of the word, but merely passing the time in order to improve his health, and as he went for his walks along the seafront he said he felt like a spare priest.[62]

Chekhov was glad finally to escape to Moscow in April, where he would remain for most of the summer. He returned to Yalta for a couple of weeks in July, however, in the company of Olga Knipper. This was her first visit to Yalta, and she stayed at the home of Leonid Sredin, a family friend and, like Chekhov, another consumptive doctor. Chekhov, meanwhile, took a room nearby in an elegant hotel, the Marino, whose rooms stretched along the seafront, their balustraded balconies protected from the oppressive summer sun by long awnings. Showing Olga round Yalta in July 1899 may have given him the final stimulus to sit down and write 'The Lady with the Little Dog', which he finally completed that autumn after long rumination: Gurov and

The town park, where Gurov makes the acquaintance of Anna Sergeyevna

Anna begin their Yalta romance in high summer. Chekhov and Olga went for walks in the town garden, where Gurov and Anna have their first conversation at Vernet's patisserie, and they went to Oreanda and Massandra. They also went to see how building work on the house in Autka was progressing. On their way to catch the train back north, they took a romantic trip to Bakhchiserai. This was a whole day's journey in a horse and carriage, following winding mountain roads through the pine woods and up past the waterfall at Uchan-su to the peak at Ai-Petri – 4,000 feet above sea level with a spectacular view of the sea far below – and then down into the green valley, past the graves of thousands of Russian soldiers who had fought in the Crimean War, and past apricot orchards, sheep and goats. Nestled in a narrow gorge, the bustling old Tatar capital with its forest of minarets (Bakhchiserai once boasted over thirty mosques) provided a striking contrast to the new cities of Sevastopol and Simferopol on the plain, not least because no Russians lived there: Catherine II had magnanimously decreed that the Tatars should retain control of their former capital.

As Adèle and Ignace Xavier Hommaire de Hell found in the 1840s, Bakhchiserai was an atmospheric place:

> You would fancy yourself in the heart of the East, in walking through the narrow streets of the town, the mosques, shops and cemeteries which so much resemble those of the old quarters of Constantinople. But it is especially in the courts, gardens and kiosks of the harem of the old palace that the traveller may well believe himself transported into some delicious abode of Aleppo or Bagdad.[63]

The Khan's Palace had been sacked and then restored by Potemkin in preparation for the triumphant arrival of Catherine the Great in 1787, and Alexander I had also carried out renovation work. The intricate carvings and soft carpets of the palace's former harem, surrounded by quiet gardens and tinkling fountains (one of which famously inspired a poem by Pushkin), still exuded an Oriental mystique. Chekhov and Olga were certainly enraptured when they made their visit. When the train carrying him back down to Sevastopol at the end of August passed through Bakhchiserai, he thought wistfully about Olga and their recent trip.

The house at Autka was more or less ready for Chekhov to move

Крымъ. - Ялта. Отходъ парохода.

*The harbour in Yalta, where Gurov and Anna Sergeyevna come
to watch people disembarking from the steamer*

into when he finally returned to Yalta at the end of August. When it was
first built, it protruded so prominently from the naked hillside that
sailors on ships out in the bay claimed to be able to see through their
binoculars the green light on in his study on the first floor. And often
he had his binoculars trained on them.[64] The first-floor balcony gave
him a breathtaking panorama of the sea – a view that is now completely
obscured by the trees he planted in his garden, in particular cedars,
which are now very tall. Before the trees had a chance to cover the
house's newly plastered walls, the local cabbies and the Tatar villagers
christened it the 'White Dacha' and the name stuck. It was arranged
that Chekhov's mother would move permanently to Yalta now that the
house was ready. Masha would come down from Moscow during the
school vacations when she was not teaching.

In the days before Masha and Evgenia Yakovlevna arrived for the
first time that September, Chekhov busied himself with supervising the
last work on the house, installing a telephone, writing to his cousin in
Taganrog requesting him to send several hundred flowerpots for the
seedlings he wished to grow, and instructing Mustafa how to collect his
mail from the post office. But he had already started missing Olga,

saying in his first letter to her that autumn that he hardly went down to the town garden any more, but had been mostly staying at home, thinking about her:

> Dearest and most remarkable actress, wonderful woman, if you only knew how pleased I was to receive your letter. I bow down low before you, very low – so low that my forehead is touching the bottom of my well, which they have already dug to a depth of over fifty feet. I've got used to you and am missing you now, and I just cannot reconcile myself to the idea that I am not going to see you until Spring.[65]

The autumn continued busy as Chekhov started sorting out the new house once his mother and sister had arrived. Old Maryushka Dormidontovna, who had been the family's cook since 1884, had travelled down from Moscow with them, and was installed in the little *Flügel* next to the house, containing a room for her and the kitchen. Chekhov had thoughtfully planted a bay tree outside the kitchen window. Maryushka was already in her seventies by this time (nine years older than Chekhov's mother), and was living on in retirement as a member of the family, so Marfushka, a Cossack girl, was initially taken on to help out with cleaning and cooking.

Some precious items of furniture had arrived from Melikhovo, including the mahogany armoire that had been in the family since Taganrog days when Evgenia Yakovlevna used to keep sweets in it, out of view of her children. Chekhov was clearly remembering the reverent greetings they used to bestow on it as they walked past it when he came to write the first act of *The Cherry Orchard*, in which Gaev delivers a sentimental speech to the family bookcase. The armoire was placed in Chekhov's bedroom on the first floor, next to his study. Then there was the cherrywood dresser that Masha had designed, which had been made for the family by some peasants in Melikhovo. It was put next to the piano in the upstairs sitting room, where they took their meals while the ground floor of the house was being completed. The crystal glasses that had been part of Evgenia Yakovlevna's dowry made the journey, as did Pavel Egorovich's walking sticks, religious books, and the accomplished pen and ink drawing he had completed of St John the Baptist, which Chekhov hung in his study. Before the trees started growing, the south-facing room, which became Chekhov's study, was filled with so much light that it had to be toned down with coloured glass in the window, shutters and dark wallpaper (specially ordered from Odessa). This room was very much the heart of the house, where Chekhov again surrounded himself with beloved objects: paintings of Russian rural scenes by Levitan as well as canvases by his brother Nikolai and other friends, a huge painted wooden bowl acquired one summer in Luka, the Egyptian-style inkwell and candlesticks he had bought in Venice, the miniature carved elephants he had brought back from Ceylon (which also went on his desk), and many photographs of friends and contemporaries: Tolstoy, the actors at the Moscow Art Theatre, editors at the journals where he published.

Masha's bedroom up on the second floor of the house had been especially designed with lots of natural light so that she could paint in it. She would not settle permanently in Yalta until after Chekhov's death (she then lived in the large airy room for almost fifty years, until her death in 1957), but was to come for long visits in the school holidays. Evgenia Yakovlevna moved permanently to Yalta when they came down in the autumn of 1899, however, and settled, with the family icon and her needlework bags, into the room next door to her son. Her first impressions were positive, as Chekhov relayed to Ivan by letter: 'It's warm here, people don't swear at each other, you don't have to lock the doors, the house has turned out to be comfortable, the bread is good, and cheap, and only the milk is a problem still – it's expensive and not very nice.' Chekhov was relieved that there was a church down the road from the house for his mother to go to, and a cab driver who lived nearby who could take her.[66] It was at the Greek Orthodox Church of St Theodore Tyron (the fourth-century martyr) that the first memorial service to be held for Chekhov took place at eight in the evening the day after he died.

Before Masha returned to Moscow at the end of October, Chekhov took her and their mother to see his dacha at Kuchuk-koy. Once they had negotiated the terrifyingly steep track, they both liked it and looked forward to decamping to the seaside for the summer months. Chekhov wrote the day after Masha left to tell her that it had started raining, that he had dined alone with their mother, and that the Tatar builders had finally cleared away all the rubble left over from the construction. The Turkish carpenters were now no longer sleeping on the ground floor of the house (where the Chekhovs would later have their dining room and two guest rooms), but they were still finishing off the windows and the staircase, and there continued to be frequent calls to prayer. Chekhov also wondered if Masha had seen Kuchuk-koy from the deck of the ship as she was travelling round the coast to Sevastopol, and she replied that she had only just been able to make it out, because they had not sailed close to the coast.[67]

Unbeknownst to him, while Chekhov was writing that letter to his sister, the first night of *Uncle Vanya* at the Moscow Art Theatre was taking place. He had exchanged heartfelt telegrams with Stanislavsky and Nemirovich-Danchenko a few weeks earlier at the beginning of the the theatre's second season, but only found out the date of the *Uncle Vanya* premiere in a letter from Olga that arrived the following day. Later that evening he was woken up several times by the phone ringing, forcing him to get out of bed and pad barefoot across the cold floor to receive a series of congratulatory telegrams. It was the first time his own fame had prevented him from sleeping, he told Olga, and, of course, there were no telegrams the following night when he carefully put his dressing gown and slippers out by his bed in preparation. The cast had been very nervous on the first night, and Chekhov immediately perceived that all had not gone quite as well as the telegrams implied. Masha had been able to read about the first night in the newspapers on the train before arriving in Moscow at the end of her long journey from Sevastopol, but then wrote a long letter to tell her brother all about the second performance, which had been much more successful. She told Chekhov about everything else she had been up to, and who of their friends she had seen – she had lately become particularly close friends with her brother's inamorata, Olga Knipper. It was deeply frustrating and depressing for Chekhov to be stuck in Yalta at times like this:

> You write about the theatre, about the [Literary] circle and all sorts of other temptations, and it's as if you are teasing me, as if you don't know how boring and how oppressive it is going to bed at nine in the evening, to go to bed in a bad mood, knowing there is nowhere to go, no one to talk to and nothing to work for, since whatever happens, you know you're not going to get to see or hear your work. The piano and I are two objects in the house which are leading a silent existence, and at a loss to understand why we were put here when there is no one here to play us.[68]

It did not help that *Uncle Vanya* soon became a smash hit. Masha wrote

that even Grand Duke Sergei Aleksandrovich, the Governor of
Moscow, and his wife had been to see it, and had apparently liked the
play very much (but she had shrunk from being presented to them).
Tickets for the run had completely sold out, and Masha had been
handing out her visiting card right, left and centre to friends to take to
the theatre administration so that (in time-honoured Russian fashion)
they could get in to see the play via the back door.[69]

Chekhov tried sublimating his frustration by browsing through the
catalogues of Immer and Son, the Moscow horticultural firm. Ivan had
sent him a hundred tulip and twenty-five narcissus bulbs, which had
been promptly planted, as had ten cypress trees, and Mustafa had
finished making all the garden paths. The next task was to put up a
fence and some barbed wire between the garden and the Tatar
cemetery. At this point Mustafa decided to leave, and was replaced by
a quiet young man called Arseny, who was not only Russian, but a
devout Orthodox Christian who spent his free time reading the lives
of saints. This probably came as a relief to Chekhov's pious mother,
even if he was a little slow. Arseny had been employed at the Nikitsky
Imperial Botanical Gardens, which were located next to Massandra, a
few miles out of Yalta, and a place Chekhov was naturally very fond
of (its botanists were appointed to look after his garden after his
death). The Nikitsky Gardens had been founded in 1812. Among the
thousands of species cultivated in its spacious grounds was the largest
collection of vines in the world, which had been purchased by the
Russian government from an American merchant in France and
shipped all the way to the Crimea. Over the course of the autumn,
Chekhov continued to plant trees, shrubs and flowers in profusion:
fifty pyramidal acacias, a birch tree, a lemon tree, an orange tree, a
peach tree, oleanders, camellias, lilies, roses, magnolias, and they were
later joined by hyacinths, irises, rhododendrons, cedars, lilacs,
marigolds, stocks, and dozens and dozens of other trees and flowers.[70]
The bare ground in front of the new house was soon filled with
saplings and sprouting plants, and they clearly had an impact on
Chekhov's creativity, for he had begun writing again after almost a
year of silence. He sent off 'The Lady with the Little Dog' at the end
of October and immediately started work on 'In the Ravine' – a much
longer, bleaker work, more in keeping with the mordant satirical tone
of his earlier work.

On the surface Chekhov maintained a buoyant mood and continued to dash off witty letters, such as to his sister's friend Maria Malkiel, whom he had got to know in Moscow:

Dear Maria Samoilovna

I write to inform you that I have taken the Muslim faith and have already registered with the community in the Tatar village of Autka, near Yalta. Our laws do not permit us to enter into correspondence with such weak creatures as women, and if I am writing to you following the dictates of my heart, I am committing a major sin. I thank you for your letter and send warm greetings to you and your sister who is able to tell people's fortunes, and hope you both end up in the harem of a prominent gentleman, preferably someone handsome like Levitan.

Write again. Wishing you health and good fortune.

Osman Chekhov[71]

But no amount of his favourite pickled watermelons (specially sent over by his cousin in Taganrog) could mitigate his underlying gloom, accentuated by a cold northern wind in November which tore all the leaves off his newly planted camellia, and forced him to sleep in a nightcap and slippers under two blankets, just like his man in a case.[72] Chekhov livened up when the gravely ill Levitan came to visit in December 1899, but the two friends must have known they would never see each other again.

The White Dacha became a Yalta landmark as soon as it was built, and despite its relatively remote location, people began visiting in droves, which Chekhov mostly found very tedious. Masha had written to Olga during her first stay there that autumn and told her that a string of carriages lined up outside the house every day in the late afternoon, as if it was a theatre.[73] But among the people who turned up at Chekhov's door were supplicants he found hard to turn away, and it was the penniless consumptives who affected him most deeply – for obvious reasons. Seeing his own condition reflected in theirs can hardly have lightened his mood, and certainly made him feel guilty about the relative opulence of his own house. The increasing numbers of tuberculosis sufferers drawn to Yalta for its climate were creating a problem because the town was ill-equipped to deal with them, particularly if they were poor. Hotels only took in those who were suffering tuberculosis in its early stages, and charged handsomely for the privilege. Chekhov found it very disturbing, and expressed his disquiet in a letter:

> There are so many consumptives here! What poverty, and how difficult it is with them! The hotels and apartments won't take in those who are seriously ill, and so you can imagine the scenes one gets to witness here. People die from emaciation, from the poverty of their surroundings, from complete neglect, and that's in the celebrated Tauris. It makes you lose all appetite for the sun and for the sea.[74]

Until Chekhov resolved to do something about a situation he found nightmarish, those without means who were seriously ill had to depend on the slim resources of the Red Cross and the Yalta Charitable Society. Working with local charities, he launched a widespread appeal for funds, as a result of which it became possible to open the Yauzlar Sanatorium, located high up on the hill above Autka where the air was purest.

IV

Marx and the Meadow

> This contract now seems to me to be like a kennel which a shaggy old ferocious dog is peering out of.
> *Letter to I. Gorbunov-Posadov*, 27 January 1899

Much of Chekhov's time in early 1899 was taken up by protracted negotiations with his new publisher Adolf Marx – not the Adolf Marx who later became better known as Harpo (he was just eleven at the time), but the Adolf Marx who revolutionized the Russian publishing industry and put even Suvorin into the shade. Chekhov had not been at all surprised when, through intermediaries, Marx made it clear that he was interested in acquiring the rights to his works; he had long heard rumours that Marx wanted to 'buy him'. Apparently Tolstoy played a role in persuading Chekhov to give his agreement. On 1 January 1899,

Chekhov made it clear that he was equally well-disposed to the idea, but even he was surprised at the speed with which he became, as he put it, a Marxist (just over three weeks). 'It hit me like a flower-pot falling out of the window on to my head,' he said.[75] An old schoolfriend in Moscow stepped in to carry out the negotiations on his behalf, liaising between Marx in St Petersburg and Chekhov in Yalta. It was precisely because Chekhov was living in Yalta that he was keen to proceed. He had the building costs of a new house to pay for and was, as usual, running into debt. It was a tricky situation, because Suvorin's publishing company was supposed to be bringing out Chekhov's collected works and, just as he was drawing up the deal with Marx, he received the proofs of the projected first volume.[76] But he had long ago lost patience: Suvorin's editors had repeatedly lost his manuscripts and failed to answer his letters, and there was the souring of relations with Suvorin himself.

Meanwhile, he was aware that he had not much longer to live, and was anxious to put his works into final order before he became too incapacitated.[77] Suvorin rightly thought that Chekhov was worth more than the 75,000 roubles Marx was offering when news of the deal was relayed to him, but, pleading lack of sufficient funds and obligations to his children, he was not prepared to better that figure himself.[78] He did send Chekhov a long telegram, however, in which he warned against signing the contract, told him he deserved 50,000 roubles for just one issue of *The Meadow*'s literary supplement, and offered to lend him 20,000 roubles if that would ease his situation.[79] Immediately the deal was signed, on 26 January 1899, Chekhov wrote a conciliatory letter to Suvorin, explaining its terms and readily agreeing with his recent suggestion that they should meet.[80] In fact, it would be over three years before they saw each other again.

Chekhov was anxious to free himself from financial worries and get on quietly with his work, and this possibility was one of the main attractions of selling himself to Marx. Another was the prospect of seeing his works published well. When the contract was signed, he was initially euphoric, as if the Holy Synod had finally granted him a long awaited divorce. The sensation of having a lot of money for the first time in his life was also intoxicating, and so unfamiliar that he felt as if he had just married someone very rich: he told his friends he would now be able to eat caviar whenever he wanted and could at last play high stakes at the roulette table. He was also relieved at the thought of not having to deal with printers and bookshops any more, or spend time thinking about new titles for books, and about prices and formats.[81] But there were disadvantages too. Marx was indeed a shrewd businessman: 75,000 roubles was an unheard of sum in 1899, but it soon turned out that the deal was far more profitable for the publisher than for the writer. Chekhov had unwisely signed away the rights to all his works following their initial publication, and Marx made a profit on the deal in the first year alone.

Aggrieved at the patent injustice of the contract and its unprofitability for him, Chekhov's friends implored him to pay the penalty and break the contract, but he demurred, arguing that he should take responsibility for his actions.[82] Quite apart from the increasing bitterness with which Chekhov regarded the contract with Marx, the task of gathering together and preparing his collected works for publication proved extraordinarily burdensome. Hundreds of stories had first of all to be sought out in the ephemeral journals in which he had published in the early 1880s, and friends in Moscow and Petersburg had to be enlisted to help with this enormous undertaking. Marx had reckoned on Chekhov's collected works running to a few volumes; he was amazed by the sheer quantity of stories which were now unearthed, even after most of them had been discarded by their author as being of insufficiently high quality for inclusion. Then came revision of some works, and endless proof-reading.

Chekhov did not form a friendship with his new publisher, as he had with Suvorin, and their correspondence was restricted to business. On 11 June 1899, he met Marx for the first time when he travelled to St Petersburg to discuss how his plays should be published. The weather was vile, and he returned to Moscow the same day after having had his photograph taken. In May 1903, he made his final visit to the capital in order to try to remonstrate with his German jail-keeper. Although he was very sick, he proudly refused the offer of 5,000 roubles to pay for treatment abroad; all he came away with was 66 kilograms of beautifully bound books.[83]

Born into the family of a German clock maker, the fifth of nine children, Adolf Marx had developed a passion for books from a young age. He had moved from Berlin to St Petersburg when he was twenty-one (the year before Chekhov was born), thinking he would stay for a couple of years. However, he ended up settling into the 100,000-strong German community in St Petersburg, and remained in the Russian capital for the rest of his life. From lowly beginnings, his achievement was to build up a publishing empire that would transform the reading habits of most of the Russian population, founding both the publishing house of A. F. Marx and a spectacularly popular journal. When he died in Russia in October 1904 at the age of sixty-six, just a few months after Chekhov died in Germany, one obituary proclaimed that his name should be written in gold letters in the history of Russia's enlightenment. Since nearly everyone had at least one of his publications on their shelves at home, the obituarist declared that all Russian people should be sincerely grateful to him.[84] At the time of his death, by which time he had been elevated into the hereditary Russian nobility,[85] there were about a thousand people employed at his headquarters in Malaya Morskaya Street in downtown Petersburg and at his press a little further out on Izmailovsky Prospekt. Among the many novels published by A. F. Marx was Tolstoy's *Resurrection*.

Marx obtained permission to publish a journal in 1869, and it became the jewel in his crown. Although the Russian word *niva* simply implies a field that has been ploughed (with the stress on the first syllable – the opposite of the river *Neva* which flows through St Petersburg), the journal's name is usually translated as *The Cornfield* or *The Meadow*. It was nothing like a traditional Russian 'fat' journal. Modelled on a popular German journal called *The Summerhouse* (*Die Gartenlaube*), it had pictures, it came out weekly, and besides literature it included photo journalism, articles on scientific and medical subjects and features on world geography and historical events. *The Meadow* was also intended as family reading for Russia's burgeoning middle class and the provincial intelligentsia.[86] One cannot help but wonder, therefore, what readers made of the novella Chekhov published in its pages in the autumn of 1896, while he was undergoing his ordeal with the *The Seagull*. It was hardly reassuring reading: an educated young man living in a provincial town falls out with his domineering father over his disdain for middle-class values and goes to live as a labourer, experiencing a failed marriage and the collapse of his utopian ideals along the way. True to form, Chekhov challenged conventions with 'My Life', a story in which he enters into dialogue with Tolstoy's radical ideas about how people should live. Much to his chagrin, this tale of dysfunction and social apostasy was subjected to quite severe censorship. By the middle of the 1890s, publishing in a Petersburg journal had become a comparatively rare event for Chekhov, whose main allegiance was now with Moscow journals and newspapers. He did, however, publish one other story in *The Meadow* – another classic study in provincial unhappiness, written in 1898, entitled 'Ionych'.

Adolf Marx proved expert at marketing *The Meadow*; its circulation rose from under 10,000 in its first year of publication to over 200,000 by the time Chekhov's story appeared – a figure that was completely unheard of in Russia. The average circulation of most of the monthly literary journals, after all, was under 5,000. What made *The Meadow* so successful, apart from its low price (only religious journals were cheaper), was the free give-aways which Marx pioneered with special permission from the Ministry of the Interior in 1879. These included pictures, maps, photographs, calendars and, from 1894, the collected works of great Russian writers. To make this last venture economically viable, he merely raised the cost of the journal's annual subscription a little. In return, Russian readers got an incredible bargain, especially when Marx started issuing the collected works of Chekhov in 1903. The publishing house of A. F. Marx had already published a ten-volume edition of Chekhov's writings between 1899 and 1902, with a print-run of 20,000. At a cost of one and a half roubles per volume (or two roubles if you wanted the handsome calico binding), plus postage and packing, you could have books sent to wherever you lived in the empire. But it proved far cheaper simply to subscribe to *The Meadow* and pay the optional extra rouble for the literary supplement. Because of postal restrictions, the contents of this second edition of Chekhov's collected works were spread over sixteen volumes, beginning with the 20 January 1903 issue of *The Meadow*. It even included some stories omitted from the first edition for various reasons, so subscribers got an even better deal. No other publisher could have disseminated Chekhov's writings to such a wide audience. Chekhov's collected works were sent to 235,000 subscribers across the country.[87]

Chapter 10

A DREAM OF MOSCOW

I

Part-Time Resident

Chekhov never really settled back into Moscow life after he returned from Siberia in December 1890. Unable to afford the rent, his family had left the house on Sadovaya-Kudrinskaya soon after he departed for Sakhalin that spring, and he returned to live in the smaller flat they had rented on Malaya Dmitrovka Street instead. Malaya Dmitrovka was located more centrally than the house on Sadovaya-Kudrinskaya; and Chekhov joked that he had now become an aristocrat and so was obliged to live on an aristocratic street. After the endless open space of Siberia, living conditions seemed very cramped, and he was soon itching to leave again. Misha was now working in the town of Aleksin and had moved out, but Pavel Egorovich had moved in, having retired from his job, and the population of the Malaya Dmitrovka flat was further swelled by the animals Chekhov brought back with him from his travels: mongooses, one of which turned out to be a ferocious palm civet. The animals had predictably caused mayhem in the small flat, jumping up on tables and breaking china; the one that survived was donated a year later to the Moscow Zoo. Chekhov avoided having to spend too much time in the flat by first going on a long trip abroad with Suvorin, and then immediately departing for the family dacha. At the end of the summer, he began a serious search for a house in the countryside outside Moscow and the family moved to Melikhovo the following spring. However, he would later return to stay in the Malaya Dmitrovka area of Moscow when he was based in Yalta.

As soon as Chekhov was no longer living in Moscow, freed from

Chekhov photographed in St Petersburg after meeting Adolf Marx in 1899

worry about rent and the constant need to buy firewood during the cold winter months, he began to enjoy the time he spent there. During the Melikhovo years he only ever made visits to Moscow and preferred to stay at the Grand Moscow Hotel, which was located at the foot of Tverskaya, the city's central thoroughfare, a stone's throw from Red Square. He particularly enjoyed waking up in his favourite room, number five, when the bells were ringing in the churches on feast days. On 6 December 1895 – St Nicholas's Day – he wrote to Suvorin that he had woken up early, lit candles and started working, enjoying what he called the 'raspberry' sound of the bells outside.[1] In some respects the visits that Chekhov made during the six years that he was based at Melikhovo were his happiest times in the city: he had no ties or responsibilities now that his home and his main place of work were elsewhere, and so he was free to enjoy the bachelor lifestyle that had been denied him during the earlier years of penury when he had his parents to look after. There were numerous adoring women ready to throw themselves at his feet.

Although Chekhov's literary career had first taken off in St Petersburg, the pendulum swung back to Moscow in the 1890s. Starting with 'Ward No. 6', he began publishing many of his most important stories in the Moscow-based *Russian Thought*, while shorter stories were siphoned off to the main Moscow newspaper the *Russian Gazette*. Both had reputations for having a pronounced liberal bias. Chekhov's ability to form an alliance with these publications, while at the same time maintaining a close relationship with Suvorin, the proprietor of Russia's most right-wing newspaper, was a tribute to his ability to maintain independence and freedom in a suffocatingly small world dominated by narrow factions, but it did not go down well with *New Times*. The *Russian Gazette*, founded in 1863, was selling at least as many copies as *New Times* in the 1890s, and Chekhov enjoyed an easygoing friendship with its publisher, Vasily Sobolevsky; he liked the paper very much. By the time that 'Ward No. 6' was published in *Russian Thought*, Chekhov had patched up his differences with that journal's wealthy merchant owner, Vukol Lavrov, to whom he had fired off his impassioned refutation of the journal's allegation that he lacked principles, and he became particularly close at the end of his life to Viktor Goltsev, the journal's editor. Indeed, relations were to become so cordial that Chekhov later became part of the editorial team. His nostalgia for Moscow and the Russian winters grew acute when he was sur- rounded by Yalta's evergreen foliage during his final years of exile, and it was *Russian Thought* which published his most famous story, 'The Lady with the Little Dog', in 1899. In his description of Gurov's return to Moscow from his autumn trip to Yalta, Chekhov's prose was as autobiographical as it would ever be:

When the first snow falls, and when you climb back into a sleigh for the first time, how wonderful it is to see the ground and the rooftops all white; the air is all soft and lovely, and it makes you start remembering the time when you were young. When they are clothed in white rime, old lindens and birches have a good-natured sort of appearance; they seem far more endearing than cypresses and palms, and being near them dispels any desire to think of sea and mountains. Gurov was a Muscovite and he arrived back in Moscow on a wonderful frosty day; when he put on his fur coat and warm gloves and walked down Petrovka, and when he heard the church bells ringing on Saturday evening, his recent trip and the places he had visited completely lost their charm for him . . .[2]

'Petrovka', or Petrovskaya, was one of Moscow's most fashionable shopping streets, and very close to Malaya Dmitrovka, where Chekhov rented a flat in the summer of 1899.

If Chekhov pined for Moscow above all when he was in Yalta, it was because only in Moscow did he fire on all cylinders. It was where he had family and where most of his friends lived; it was where he received his medical training and subsequently practised; it was where his literary career started and was increasingly based in the 1890s, and it was where he had close ties with the theatre. Starting in 1898, when the Moscow Art Theatre first staged *The Seagull*, Chekhov even had a theatre that more or less understood what he was trying to achieve as a dramatist. Typically, this was just when he had to leave Moscow and relocate to the Crimea for the sake of his health. When he returned for the first time since moving to Yalta the following summer, a private command performance of *The Seagull* was put on specially for him on 1 May. A week later a photographer preserved for posterity the image of Chekhov reading *Uncle Vanya* to the assembled cast before it went into rehearsal. Seated close by the author was Olga Knipper, with whom he was about to embark on a romance.

II

The Art Theatre

A few months after Suvorin had brought his gravely ill friend back to his suite at the Slavyansky Bazaar Hotel after their abortive attempt to dine at the Hermitage in March 1897, Konstantin Stanislavsky and Vladimir Nemirovich-Danchenko sat down in one of its private dining rooms to have the famous lunch which launched the Moscow Art Theatre. The lunch turned into dinner and Stanislavsky suggested they leave the smoke-filled room and repair to his dacha just outside the city to continue the conversation. What resulted was a decision to found a new kind of theatre. The amateur actor and director, scion of one of the great merchant families in Moscow, made a good team with the drama teacher and playwright. The company they created in October 1898 finally injected the life into Russian theatre that it so badly needed. Picking up on the new approach to the stage that had begun with Wagner, Stanislavsky and Nemirovich-Danchenko elevated drama to high art, investing it with the capacity not only to uplift, but to transform and enlighten, its audiences.

Initially, the educational aspect of their activities was emphasized in the word 'accessible' being part of the company's original title, but the Moscow police objected to their early attempts to draw in audiences from the working classes and it had to be dropped.[3] The word 'artistic' (typically contracted in English to 'art') remained, however, serving as a reminder of the idealistic goals nurtured by the theatre's founders. Going to the theatre suddenly became a serious business: auditorium lights were no longer kept burning during performances so that audience members could inspect each other; they were dimmed, forcing spectators to concentrate from within the blackness on what was unfolding on stage. The décor of the auditorium was similarly austere – a marked change from the gilt and velvet of traditional theatres. Productions were properly rehearsed, and a production method pioneered which placed the emphasis on ensemble work. For the first time in the Russian theatre stagings were conceptual, their style and atmosphere determined by a director. The story of the Moscow Art Theatre is by now the stuff of legend.

Chekhov's *The Seagull*, first performed on 17 December 1898, was the Moscow Art Theatre's sixth production, but only the second to score a success. It saved the theatre from plummeting to financial disaster in its first season. After the scandalous first production of *The Seagull* by the Imperial Theatres in St Petersburg, Chekhov was reluctant to risk his play turning into a travesty a second time. In the end, he had no cause to regret giving his agreement after Nemirovich-Danchenko had pleaded with him twice, and his last two plays were written specifically with the Moscow Art Theatre in mind. Before *Three Sisters* and *The Cherry Orchard*, however, came *Uncle Vanya*, which had been written a few years earlier in Melikhovo and initially promised to the Maly Theatre. Chekhov was in Yalta when the premiere took place, and it was in Yalta that he first saw the Moscow Art Theatre production when the company came on tour in the spring of 1900. He was also in Yalta on 11 January 1902, when a special matinée performance of the play was given for the hundreds of Russian doctors who had gathered as delegates to the Eighth Pirogov Congress to discuss problems of national health care.

Dr Astrov in *Uncle Vanya*, perhaps Chekhov's most famous physician character, was partly inspired by his friend Pyotr Kurkin, a zemstvo doctor he had got to know during the Melikhovo years – Chekhov had borrowed his friend's maps for the actor playing Astrov to use in the Moscow Art Theatre production.[4] Dr Kurkin was responsible for correlating disease with geographical factors as part of his work as a zemstvo doctor, and it was only a short step from poring over maps to pondering the looming ecological crisis. 'Russian woods are groaning under the axe,' exclaims

Alexander Vishnevsky as Uncle Vanya in the first Moscow Art Theatre production, 1899

Astrov in the first act, 'millions of trees are dying, the dwellings of animals and birds are being ravaged, rivers are silting up and going dry, beautiful landscapes are disappearing for ever, and all because lazy human beings can't be bothered to bend over and pick up firewood from the ground.'[5]

Chekhov had also put a great deal of himself into Astrov and was extremely concerned that the play should make a good impression on his medical colleagues at the Pirogov Congress, as is evident from the increasingly anxious letters he sent to Stanislavsky and Olga Knipper in the days running up to the performance, containing instructions to the actors. Writing from Yalta on the day itself, cut off from his colleagues and friends, he complained to Olga that he felt as if he were exiled in Siberia. *Uncle Vanya* was a huge success with the doctors, of course; some of them even cried, and one woman had to be carried out in hysterics. Zemstvo doctors from the 'remotest corners of Russia' sent Chekhov a telegram afterwards to assure him that they would remember 11 January for the rest of their lives.[6]

It is ironic that tuberculosis was high on the agenda at the Eighth Pirogov Congress. In 1899, two years after Chekhov was officially diagnosed with the disease, a 'Pirogov Tuberculosis Commission' had been set up, chaired by Professor V. Shervinsky of the Moscow University medical school. In 1900 the fifteen members of the commission reported that about 350,000 people were dying from tuberculosis each year in Russia, and at the Eighth Congress it was advocated that their work be expanded to bring improvements in the living environments of the poor, among whom the disease mostly spread. After attending a tuberculosis conference in Berlin, Shervinsky organized a three-day conference in Moscow in May 1903.[7] It all came sadly too late for Chekhov, who had little more than a year to live at this point.

Visiting Moscow a year after Chekhov's death on his way to Manchuria, the English critic Maurice Baring was able to attend a performance of *Uncle Vanya*. He declared unequivocally that the Moscow Art Theatre was, after the services at the Kremlin's Assumption Cathedral and the Cathedral of Christ the Saviour, the most interesting place to visit. It was, he noted, almost the only thing in Russia which was organized. *Uncle Vanya* seemed to him to reflect 'the profound discontent of educated people with the manner in which they are governed', a discontent so 'hopeless and inconsistent as to lead to hysteria'. To this English visitor, who was vaguely

A. П. Чеховъ.   *„Дядя Ваня". д. IV.*

A scene during Act 4 of Uncle Vanya *in 1899*

reminded of Bernard Shaw minus the paradox and the extravagance, as he put it, the character Professor Serebryakov came across as a kind of Casaubon figure (from Eliot's *Middlemarch*), while his sultry wife Elena was 'a land mermaid, a middle class Pagan, not immoral but amoral, a passionless Cleopatra'. Chekhov had got heartily fed up with Stanislavsky's desire for his stagings to become hyper-realistic, but Bowra was impressed with the way Astrov killed flies on his cheek, and with other small details in the performance of *Uncle Vanya* that he attended, so that 'the sultry oppressiveness of the thundery day seems to reach us over from the footlights'. Baring also had some perceptive comments to make about Chekhov's dramatic technique, which he felt was important politically as well as artistically, 'even though politics are never directly mentioned':

> What he leaves unsaid, what he suggests is far more potent and effectual than any harangue or polemical discussion. He shows the Russian soul crying out in the desert, he shows the hopelessness, the straining after impossible ideals, the people who have been longing for the dawn, and condemned to the twilight chiefly owing to their own weakness.[8]

III

Part-Time Husband

On 25 May 1901 in Moscow came an event which most people had not expected: Chekhov's marriage. The seventeenth-century Church of the Exaltation of the Cross was chosen for the wedding ceremony, not only because it was small and out of the way, on a quiet back street in a rather nondescript part of town near the Moscow River where mostly merchants lived, but the priest, Father Nikolai, had officiated at the funeral of his father a year and a half earlier. For help with his wedding arrangements, Chekhov had turned to his brother Ivan as he always did where practical matters were concerned, and who knew Father Nikolai from the days when he taught at a school on the Arbat near to the church. Chekhov's sister had realized that marriage was on the cards. The day before the wedding, she had made clear her feelings in a letter sent from Yalta: 'Let me express my opinion about your marriage. I find the whole wedding process awful! And all that unnecessary stress wouldn't be good for you either . . . You'll always be able to get hitched . . . Tell that to your Knipschitz . . . You after all brought me up not to have prejudices!'[9]

The Church of the Exaltation of the Cross, Moscow, where
Chekhov married Olga Knipper, May 1901

By the time the letter arrived, however, it was too late. Despite avowals that he had lost his faith, Chekhov was unwilling to follow the route proposed by his sister and cohabit as his elder brother had done. All the same, he did not want to attract attention to the fact that he was getting married, so there was no reception or party after the service. There were no guests, just the four statutory witnesses, and Chekhov informed his mother of the event by telegram on the day itself. The honeymoon was a health cure undertaken, on the recommendation of a doctor in Moscow, in a remote sanatorium in Aksyonovo, in the foothills of the Ural mountains, where the prescribed treatment was large doses of fermented mare's milk. Meanwhile, with numerous papers publicizing the news as it leaked out and also printing portraits of the happy couple,[10] the hopes of numerous young women were crushed. Masha's painter friend Maria Drozdova wrote Chekhov an impassioned letter:

Dear, beloved Anton Pavlovich,
Goodness me, I was so disappointed by the news of your marriage. I was doing an oil painting at the time and my brushes and my palette went all over the place. I hadn't completely given up hope of marrying you, you know! I kept thinking that it was nothing serious with all the others, and that God would reward me for my modesty, but now my hopes have been dashed. How I hate Olga Leonardovna now! My jealousy has reached a state of frenzy. I cannot stomach seeing your dear, kind face, it's become so odious to me, and the thought of you and her together, for ever and ever, is just awful! The doors of your house are shut for me now. Oh, I am so unhappy! I am sobbing as I write these lines . . .[11]

Drozdova had been happy to meet Olga before, and written to Chekhov to tell him how much she had admired her black eyes, her slim figure and even her elegant little moustache, but that Chekhov had married her was insupportable.

Chekhov and Olga spent just over five weeks at the sanatorium in Aksyonovo before travelling together to Yalta. Six weeks later, in late August, Olga returned to Moscow to begin rehearsals for the next theatre season, and a month after that, Chekhov joined her. Nine months after its premiere, he finally saw *Three Sisters* for the first time. His presence in the theatre was electrifying for the actors performing before him, and when it became known to the audience as well, there were clamours for him to take a bow. He reluctantly appeared on stage at the end of the second act, to be greeted by a tumultuous ovation which was repeated at the end of the performance. Chekhov was pleased with the staging, and joked that it was better than the play. He stayed in Moscow for six weeks, but eventually, at the end of October, had to leave his weeping wife and return alone to Yalta. 'My wife, who I have got used to and grown attached to, will stay in Moscow on her own, and I am leaving and feeling lonely,' he wrote to a friend on the eve of his departure; 'she is crying, but I am not allowing her to give up the theatre. It's a mess, really.'[12]

After the happy summer spent at Bogimovo in 1891, Chekhov never rented another dacha: there was no need once he was living in the country all year round at Melikhovo. In his last two summers, however, he briefly became a dachnik again when he was invited to stay at the country properties owned by two friends from wealthy merchant backgrounds: Stanislavsky and Maria Yakunchikova. The invitation to stay in Stanislavsky's dacha at Lyubimovka came about because of Olga's illness in the summer of 1902: she had contracted peritonitis after an operation for a probable ectopic pregnancy. All this happened at the end of March during a Moscow Art Theatre tour to St Petersburg, and, although it was not openly discussed, Chekhov suspected with some justification that his wife was not pregnant by him.[13] He nursed Olga for two and half months, first in Yalta, then in Moscow, but by mid-June needed to escape for a few weeks. It had been wearing having to be at Olga's bedside all day, with occasional visits to see a very skilful juggler perform providing the only respite. Quite apart from the fact that he was not terribly well himself, Chekhov was simply not used to living with his wife.

Leaving Olga in the care of her German doctor, Chekhov accepted an invitation to travel some 800 miles east to the Urals, to visit the factory and estate of the great merchant patron Savva Morozov, the millionaire who underwrote the Moscow Art Theatre. It was not a particularly enjoyable trip, but the six weeks he spent with Olga at Lyubimovka on his return were invigorating for both of them. Stanislavsky's dacha, to the north-east of Moscow, was an attractive two-storey wooden villa with a spacious veranda, and stood next to a pine wood. In keeping with merchant style, the furniture was solid, comfortable and modest, and Chekhov felt very much at home.[14] What he delighted in most, though, was being able to fish in the deep waters of the River Klyazma while Olga recuperated. He had not spent a summer like this in ages, he told Stanislavsky: 'I fish every day, about five times a day, it's not been bad (yesterday there was fish soup from the ruff I caught), and I can't tell you how pleasant it is sitting on the river bank.'[15] Sitting with his fishing rod all day was liberty compared with Yalta, he wrote to his sister, and he gloried in the long grass and leafy trees, which could not be found anywhere in the Crimea.[16]

Chekhov mulled over ideas for *The Cherry Orchard* while he was staying at Lyubimovka (where there was, in fact, a cherry orchard), and Stanislavsky's old retainers and the English governess next door partly inspired some of the play's characters.[17] In mid-August, Chekhov returned to Yalta; when he came back for another six week stay in Moscow a month later, he went for the first time to the Moscow Art Theatre's new building on Kamergersky Lane, right in the centre of the city. With a 300,000 rouble investment from Savva Morozov, and leaving the façade largely unchanged, Franz Shekhtel had designed an austere Art Nouveau interior, whose simplicity well suited the aesthetic of Chekhov's untheatrical drama. *The Cherry Orchard* would be the first of his plays to be premiered there.

In 1903, during the summer months Chekhov spent in Moscow, he

The new Moscow Art Theatre building, designed by Fyodor Shekhtel, 1902

stayed for a few weeks in a *Flügel* on an estate which belonged to the artist Maria Yakunchikova, a niece of the railway tycoon and patron of the arts, Savva Mamontov. Nara was situated on the railway line running south-west from Moscow, and was an attractive location: there was a river with plenty of fish, lots of places to go for walks and an old chapel. Chekhov enjoyed the lovely weather, the blossom, and the birds singing in the garden; he even managed to do some work on *The Cherry Orchard*, sitting by the large window of the house.[18] The only down side seemed to be that the fish were not biting. He had still not caught even a tiddler after a week,[19] and lamented not having anyone to fish with.[20] Following the advice of Prof. Ostroumov, who now thought the climate in Yalta might not be ideal for Chekhov after all and was recommending that he spend his winters at a dacha outside Moscow, Chekhov also made two short trips with his wife to Zvenigorod and Voskresensk that summer to look at possible properties. He was delighted to have an excuse to stay up north, and immediately thought of buying a house in the area where he had enjoyed such happy times as a young man. In Voskresensk there were old friends to meet up with, and in Zvenigorod he visited the grave of the doctor he had replaced in 1884.[21] He wrote to tell Masha about the wonderful bells he had heard at St Savva's, and how lovely it was, but just too dusty and hot.[22] Although there was one charming property on the river bank behind the town church in Voskresensk, which would have suited his mother, the asking price was too high, and Chekhov returned to Yalta in July 1903 without having bought anything.

Rehearsals for *The Cherry Orchard* began in November 1903. When Stanislavsky started thinking about the 'dog on a lead' which Charlotta Ivanovna the governess enters with in the first act, Olga's dog, a black dachshund called Schnap, immediately presented himself as the obvious candidate and was summoned for an audition. It was undoubtedly Chekhov who had suggested, during his visit to Moscow the previous summer, that Olga get a dog. If she had a dog, he reasoned that it could keep her company in his absence, and in due course it could be taken to Yalta. Schnap had been duly delivered to Olga's apartment while she was seeing Chekhov off on to his train back to Sevastopol,[23] and she proudly announced to her husband that he was a pure pedigree. Masha was not so sure, and her doubts are borne out by the one extant photograph of Chekhov standing in his garden with Schnap and Sharik.

In his letters to Olga in Moscow, Chekhov wrote to say that he shook
his paw, and worried that when he got to Yalta he might torment the
two pet cranes who also were also part of the household.[24] Meanwhile
Schnap was being groomed for stardom. 'We rehearsed the second act
without Konstantin Sergeyevich [Stanislavsky] yesterday,' Olga wrote to
Chekhov in November 1903. 'I took Schnap along, so he had a chance
to walk about and look around the stage, and today we've got the first
act and he is going to have a go at acting. I'm worried that he's got too
much of a pedigree temperament, he isn't trained and he doesn't have
any discipline. We'll see. He was greeted with laughter yesterday.'[25]
Chekhov had got to know Schnap earlier that year and was alarmed at
the prospect of seeing him on stage. He immediately wrote back to tell

«ВИШНЕВЫЙ САДЪ» А. П. ЧЕХОВА.   Моск. Худож. Театръ.
Раневская—О. Л. Книпперъ.
Собств. изд. К. А. Фишеръ, Москва.

Olga Knipper as Ranevskaya in The Cherry Orchard, *1904*

Olga that what he actually had in mind for the play was a mangy, decrepit, shaggy little dog with a sour expression; short-haired Schnap would not do.[26]

A few weeks later, in December 1903, Chekhov came up to Moscow himself to attend the final rehearsals. The premiere of *The Cherry Orchard* took place on 17 January 1904, his birthday, and was accompanied by a celebration of the twenty-fifth anniversary of his activity as a writer. He was by this time very ill, and only arrived at the theatre during the third act, at the express request of Nemirovich-Danchenko. What happened next was torture for him. As soon as Chekhov appeared on stage during the interval, representatives of almost every newspaper, journal and literary organization in the country stood up to read their eulogies to him. Telegrams from all over the country were read out, too, to prolonged and vociferous applause from the audience. Quite apart from his hatred of self-promotion and being in the limelight, Chekhov could barely stand up. He felt like the bookcase to which Gaev delivers a maudlin speech in Act 1 of the play.

A few weeks later, he travelled back to Yalta for the last time, taking Schnap with him, as well as his mother and Nastya, the new cook. He sent a letter to Olga before the steamer left Sevastopol, giving her a bulletin on their progress: 'Schnap feels quite at home, he is adorable. In the train he also felt quite at home; he barked at the guards and amused everybody, and now he is sitting on deck with his legs stretched out behind him. He has clearly already forgotten about Moscow, however terrible that is to contemplate.'[27] It did not take Schnap long to settle in at the White Dacha. When he started barking a lot in a heavy bass, Chekhov felt he had successfully made the transition to mongrel,[28] but he was not always pleased when Schnap came and lay down in his study because he was always dirty from playing with the dogs in the yard.[29] Schnap soon had a routine which Olga was kept fully apprised of: Arseny took him to the market every day, and the rest of the time he spent walking round the garden, playing with the other dogs or sleeping downstairs by the warm ceramic stove, issuing the occasional groan. In the evenings he went upstairs to sleep in Chekhov's comfortable armchair by the fireplace and retired next door to Evgenia Yakovlevna's room at night.

Chapter 11

EXILE IN THE CRIMEA

I

The Gentleman with the Little Dog

Yalta is Siberia!
Letter to Leonid Sredin, 26 December 1900

Chekhov found his second winter in Yalta just as difficult as the first. His sister came to stay over New Year then left, and friends were few and far between. His mother was ill; Tolstoy was ill down the road in nearby Gaspra; Levitan was ill. And he was ill. So many organs in his body had become superfluous through lack of use, he joked, that he had sold them to a Turk. Nevertheless, he complained that he had to put up with guests who came for interminable visits. He felt as though he had been living in Yalta a million years. It was not a good start to the twentieth century. Meanwhile what he craved was intellectual stimulation, music and beautiful women, and he longed to go on an intrepid adventure to somewhere like Africa – which is exactly what he recommended his new friend, the young writer Maxim Gorky, should do. He unfortunately no longer had the strength for travelling to exotic climes. Chekhov typically played it down, but it was clearly more than 'annoying' for him at the age of forty to be suffering from breathlessness and 'all kinds of other rubbish' which prevented him from living properly, as he put it. He also longed for Russia. There was no snow in Yalta, and no sleighs, and therefore it seemed to him that there was no life. It was particularly painful to be so far away from Moscow. Even though he could have purchased identical items locally in Yalta, he studiously ordered writing paper, galoshes, sausage, and even lavatory paper from Moscow, in denial that he had moved.[1]

Bereft of stimulating company, and unable to do much in his garden over the winter, Chekhov found some consolation in the mongrels who had decided to settle in his yard and congregated round him whenever he stepped outside. There was the fierce, crooked-faced Tuzik who slept in the cellar (the Russian word for the ace in a pack of cards is 'tuz'). The yellow-eyed puppy who made its home under the ancient olive tree in the garden was christened Kashtanka, after Chekhov's famous early story about a dog who ends up as a circus performer (the name comes from the Russian word for 'chestnut'; Olga called him Ginger). Kashtanka would follow Tuzik's example and bark at people, but he was also prone to roll on to his stomach at the slightest opportunity, and acquired a reputation for laziness by sleeping all day on the wood chippings.[2] Chekhov pretended not to care very much about Kashtanka. All the same, when the dog was run over by a passing carriage out in the road and broke one of his back legs, Chekhov performed emergency surgery and tended to him solicitously. Then there was the afore-mentioned Schnap, Olga's dachshund (called Foma to begin with by Masha and Anton,[3] and Schwarz by Evgenia Yakovlevna[4]), whose arrival had been eagerly awaited by everyone at the White Dacha. 'Bring him to Yalta, or he won't have anyone to bark at,' Chekhov had written to Olga in November 1902, considering there would then be enough dogs in the household.

When two more mongrel puppies turned up the following February and barked furiously all night, they were finally bundled up and put in someone else's yard. But a doctor acquaintance in Yalta decided to take Kashtanka in the spring of 1903, and Masha wrote to her brother (then staying at the dacha in Nara) to tell him that their cook, Polya, was so upset she had been crying, and Tuzik had stopped barking. They both immediately decided to find another dog. Kashtanka had become so lazy and gluttonous that Chekhov was not all that sorry to see him go, and instructed Arseny the gardener to look out for a small male mongrel puppy. That puppy was Sharik ('little ball'), a small white Pomeranian-mix with black ears and very sharp teeth, who took a while to learn how to bark, and then made up for it by barking day and night. Masha loved the dogs as much as her brother did, and over the years he kept her up to date on how they were faring in her absence: Tuzik appeared ever more crooked-faced, and occasionally succumbed to pessimism[5] (maybe he had a presentiment that he would be poisoned

Chekhov with his dogs Schnap and Sharik, 1904

in the same year that Chekhov died), Kashtanka got fatter and was always asleep, Sharik felt that he was somehow a lower-class meshchanin kind of dog and so was rather timid about wagging his tail. The dogs seemed to have a pretty good life at the White Dacha all in all. Chekhov's Yalta doctor, Isaak Altschuller, felt the hours his patient spent in his garden surrounded by his dogs were among the happiest in his life.[6] 'Sobaka' – dog – and its many variations (Sobachka, Sobachonka, Pyos, Pyosik, even Fomka) was one of Chekhov's favourite terms of endearment for Olga. Sometimes he even wrote to her as though she *were* a dog, telling her he wanted to take her by the tail and wag it and stroke her fur gently. 'I love you and will love you even if you turn from a dog into a crocodile,' he once joked.[7]

The major event in the spring of 1900 was the Moscow Art Theatre's tour of the Crimea at Easter, a major undertaking in those

days. Olga arrived a few days early with Masha, and then joined her
colleagues in Sevastopol for the first performances. It was here that
Chekhov saw *Uncle Vanya* for the first time – and it was also the first
time he had seen the company perform before an audience. He also
attended performances of Hauptmann's *Lonely People* and Ibsen's
Hedda Gabler before his ill-health forced him back home to Yalta. Then
followed ten heady days over Easter when the company took up
residence in Yalta's brand new theatre. The dacha was suddenly full of
noisy actors, directors and writers, and it was a bit of a shock for
Chekhov now to have convivial lunches every day and stay up all hours
after his long, boring winter, but it was clear to his sister that he thrived
on the stimulating company. The Yalta Theatre had opened in 1896 and
was home to an operetta company, but never played to full houses.
Suddenly it was packed, and Chekhov was forced to endure ovation
after ovation. Two days before the Moscow Art Theatre left, members
of the company held a literary evening at the theatre whose proceeds
were donated to the charity that cared for people with tuberculosis and
other invalids who had travelled to Yalta without means of support. As
well as extracts from Sophocles, Maria Andreyeva, the beautiful young
actress playing Nina in *The Seagull*, read Chekhov's touching early
story 'Vanka'. It had been a great favourite with his fans ever since its
publication on Christmas Day 1886, and was one of his very best works
according to Tolstoy (who, conversely, had not long before gone to see
Uncle Vanya and found it exasperating). The orphaned young Vanka
(short for Ivan) has been sent from his village in the countryside to
become an apprentice shoemaker in Moscow. He is treated so badly by
his employers and the other apprentices, and is so lonely, that on
Christmas Eve he writes a letter to his grandfather, the only family he
has left, begging him to come and take him away. But it takes Vanka a
long time to write the letter because he keeps being distracted by
thoughts of home:

> Vanka trembled as he sighed and then again started staring at the window.
> He remembered that it was his grandfather who always went into the
> woods to get the master's Christmas tree and would take him along too.
> It was such fun! His grandfather would crackle, and the frost would
> crackle and Vanka would crackle too as he looked at them. His grandfather
> would smoke his pipe and stand there sniffing his tobacco for ages before

he cut the tree down, laughing at frozen-stiff little Vanyushka . . . The
young fir trees, all wrapped in frost, would stand without moving,
wondering which one of them would have to die. And then all of a
suddden a hare would shoot like an arrow over the snowdrifts . . .[8]

The nine-year-old Vanka thinks it is enough to address his letter to
'grandfather in the village' and put it in the nearest postbox for it to
reach him. The twenty-six-year-old Chekhov had already mastered the
art of ending his works on a tragi-comic note. Constant calls for the
author to take a bow had induced Chekhov to escape early from most
of the performances during the Moscow Art Theatre's tour to Yalta in
1900, but he stayed to hear all the readings on this particular evening.
Six months later the theatre burned down.

II

Pushkin, the Old Oak of Taganrog, and *Three Sisters*

Masha: A green oak by the curving shore, and on that oak a golden
chain . . .

Three Sisters, Act 1

Chekhov began the twentieth century thinking about Alexander
Pushkin. This was not only because he received news on 17 January
1900 (his birthday) that the august Academy of Sciences had elected him
to the new belles-lettres section it had recently inaugurated to mark the
centenary of Pushkin's birth. To old Maryushka this meant Chekhov was
now a 'general', but to him it was about the same as being made an
honorary citizen of a small provincial town. He knew the staid Imperial
Academy would never tolerate writers with any kind of a social
conscience having an active say in its affairs, still less writers who
actually lived in St Petersburg and could ask the distinguished professors
difficult questions at meetings.[9] It was not for nothing that his
appointment was only honorary. The Academy's president, after all, was
the poet K.R., otherwise the Grand Duke Konstantin Romanov (it was
his father who had built the church at Oreanda). That Chekhov and the

Grand Duke had shared a friend in Tchaikovsky made no difference and when Gorky's appointment was barred because of his subversive political activities two years later, Chekhov resigned. The rebellious Pushkin, the new section's *honorand*, would no doubt have looked on the affair with the same mixture of ironic detachment and disdain.

Chekhov had been thinking about Pushkin quite a lot lately. He had been an active member of the committee in Yalta which had planned events to celebrate the centenary, in 1899, of the poet's birth, but at the beginning of the new century he was thinking more about Pushkin in connection with the time the poet had spent in the Crimea in 1820. What interested him was that Pushkin was another Russian writer who had been exiled to the south, and who longed to return to his metropolitan literary life. On 15 January 1900, Chekhov wrote to his sister to tell her that he had bought a piece of the Crimean coast in the idyllic village of Gurzuf. It came with a secluded house located at the end of a path and the famous Pushkin Rock which stuck out of the sea in its own little bay. Chekhov had come to the conclusion that Kuchuk-koy was a little too far away, and a little too inconvenient for bathing (it was later sold), and he was hankering for a dacha closer to home that would be right on the sea.[10] Also, he needed to be able to escape from the endless stream of visitors who wore him down at his house in Yalta. Here he was successful, for almost no one ever found out about his new house. Part of Chekhov's motivation must have come from wanting to find somewhere he could be alone with Olga when she came down to stay; they had been exchanging increasingly affectionate letters for six months now, and it was not easy living under the watchful eye of his mother and sister, even though he had taken care when designing the White Dacha to ensure that the rooms would be well separated from each other. In November 1899, the month that he began thinking about *Three Sisters* for the first time,[11] Chekhov heard about a property that had come up for sale in Gurzuf, which was only about nine miles away from Yalta. Gurzuf boasted some of the most enchanting scenery along the coast, and the original Tatar village of whitewashed cottages, dominated by an enormous mosque (later destroyed in the earthquake of 1927), had already begun to give way to churches and smart Russian villas. The increasing exclusivity of the resort was reflected in the high price being asked by the vendor.

At the beginning of his southern exile, Pushkin had spent three

Olga as Masha in Three Sisters, *1901*

blissful weeks in Gurzuf in the autumn of 1820 during his extended
tour of the Caucasus and the Crimea with his new friends the Raevskys.
They had stayed in the large house built by the Duc de Richelieu when
he was Governor-General of New Russia in the early 1800s, on land
originally owned by Potemkin. When he was not wandering round the
beautiful park that Richelieu had created, Pushkin spent lazy days
eating grapes and swimming in the sea, hence the subsequent naming
of a large rock after him in one of the village's small bays. By chance it
was this very bay that had come up for sale, and Chekhov was excited
by the prospect of being able to tie up his own boat there and go
fishing. The house was a traditional Tatar *saklya* and rather decrepit –
just three tiny wooden rooms – but it had a red tiled roof, a veranda to
sit out in, and a short flight of steep steps leading down the cliff to the
pebbly beach below. It also had a garden in which there was all of one
tree: a mulberry. Why should this tree have reminded Chekhov of the
opening lines of Pushkin's *Ruslan and Lyudmila*, which he was to quote
in his new play *Three Sisters*, begun in spring 1900? Pushkin talks about

Stanislavsky as Vershinin in Three Sisters, *1901*

an oak, after all. The link between the mulberry tree and the oak tree in Pushkin's poem was Taganrog.

In the summer of 2002, botanists from the University of Rostov-on-Don were urgently summoned to Taganrog. They had been invited by local businessmen to inspect the remains of an enormous tree which had recently burned down. The businessmen were hoping it could somehow be resurrected.[12] This was no ordinary tree, of course, but the famous old oak of Taganrog which had supposedly inspired the opening lines of *Ruslan and Lyudmila*: 'A green oak by the curving shore / And on that oak a golden chain.' They are among Pushkin's best-known lines. They are also Masha's enigmatic opening lines in *Three Sisters*. Journalists descended on Taganrog when news first spread about the sudden demise of the 'Pushkin oak', but they unexpectedly ran into difficulties when trying to identify exactly which oak tree had inspired Russia's national poet. There were many venerable oak trees in

Taganrog, it turned out, the oldest dating from the early eighteenth
century (Peter the Great had given express orders to Count Apraksin
that acorns be planted after he founded the town in 1698). Some locals
maintained that the celebrated 'Pushkin oak' actually stood outside the
town; others were altogether more sceptical, aware of the existence of
dozens of 'Pushkin oaks' throughout Russia with equal claims to
authenticity.[13] It was not actually all that surprising that there were
difficulties identifying the 'Pushkin oak', because the oak, it turned out,
was a mulberry tree – a white mulberry, in fact, the kind used to
produce silk, of which there had traditionally been many in Taganrog.
Unlike Chekhov, who began to cultivate trees the minute he acquired
some land of his own and was later to advise the Taganrog town
authorities about which trees they should plant, Pushkin, it seems, was
less knowledgeable about such mundane things as tree species. But
people in Taganrog were generally willing to forgive the poet who
mistook a mulberry for an oak in their desire to claim their town as a
source of poetic inspiration. Pushkin had, after all, been infatuated at
the time with one of the young female members of his party, and was
not renowned as an expert in arboricultural matters.

The fabled mulberry tree had stood for 200 years in the grounds of
Taganrog's most historic landmark: the unassuming building on Greek
Street where Alexander I had mysteriously died in 1825. A one-storey
mansion built in the early nineteenth-century Russian classical style, it had
been initially acquired by General Pyotr Papkov, who wished to expand
his adjoining property. In 1816 it became the official residence of the
governor of Taganrog, Papkov's post from 1810 to 1822, but he preferred
to use it as accommodation for distinguished guests, while continuing to
reside in his old house next door. Alexander I and his retinue thus stayed
here during his tour of Russia in 1818, and Pushkin became a guest of
General Papkov while en route for the Caucasus with members of the
Raevsky family at the end of May 1820 – just a few months before his visit
to Gurzuf and the Crimea. The first edition of *Ruslan and Lyudmila* was
published that July, but the prologue, which begins with the famous lines
about the green oak and the curving shore, was written four years later.
There is indeed a fine view of the curving shoreline of the Azov Sea several
hundred feet below the high cliff on which Taganrog is situated, and the
mulberry tree in the garden of General Papkov's house would certainly
have been in full leaf at that time of year. 'And on that oak a golden chain'?

Before the tree was set on fire by vandals, locals claimed that it was still possible to see the marks left by the chains that had supposedly been fixed to its branches to encourage them to grow outwards rather than vertically.[14] As well as the water nymph sitting in the branches of his oak, Pushkin's poem also has a learned cat which walks round the tree, alternately singing a song when it turns right, and telling a story when it turns left. When the 'Palace of Alexander I' opened, shortly after the Tsar's untimely death, as Russia's first memorial museum, it was guarded by clean-shaven Cossacks with sabres, and legend has it that they maintained contact with each other precisely in this way when patrolling the perimeter of the palace grounds.

As we know, Chekhov was very familiar with the Palace of Alexander I and the 'Pushkin oak', having been made by his father to sing long services in the chapel there as a young boy, so the mulberry tree in his garden at Gurzuf, overlooking the Pushkin Rock, may well have reminded him of the mulberry tree in Taganrog when he began work on *Three Sisters*. Moreover, his new cottage in Gurzuf was also perched high above a curving shore and bathed in a warm, southerly climate, of course (as indeed was his house in Yalta: mulberries were among the first trees he had planted there even before he moved in). It is tempting to think that concealed within the quotation of Pushkin's lines are a series of complex personal associations to do with death, the difficult relationship Chekhov had with his father, his childhood, his enforced exile in the Crimea, and the complications of entering into a relationship with someone who lived far away. Chekhov had, after all, recently been to Taganrog (for the last time, as it turned out), where he had once been a pupil of numerous teachers like Masha's husband, Kulygin, at the classical *gymnasium* he attended. More significantly, news of the unexpected death of his father in October 1898 had set off a chain of events which resulted in him selling his beloved Melikhovo estate and moving permanently to Yalta. After handing over the Melikhovo keys to its new owner in July 1899, Chekhov had headed back south to the Crimea, stopping off in Taganrog on the way. He could not have failed to think about his childhood, his father, and his own mortality during that visit. The sister of one of his old school friends later recalled seeing a man standing alone on the shore staring out to sea as she drove by with her husband in a carriage one day. It was Chekhov.[15] *Three Sisters* begins with musings about the death of a father the previous year. Chekhov began thinking about *Three Sisters* just a little over a year after his own father died.

Pushkin's famous lines about the green oak tree by the seashore are symbolically invoked by Masha three times in the course of the play. The last occasion they are uttered comes when she has finally parted from Vershinin at the very end of the last act. Spring has given way to autumn, and the mood is one of loss as the three sisters must finally abandon the hopes and dreams they have cherished and confront the painful reality of their situation. 'Farewell trees!' exclaims Second Lieutenant Rode at the beginning of the last act. Just before his pointless death, Tuzenbakh becomes conscious of how potentially beautiful human life can be by perceiving the beauty of the trees in the Prozorovs' garden for the first time – the same fir trees, maples and birches which the destructive Natasha moments later peremptorily decides should be chopped down. As in *Uncle Vanya*, *The Cherry Orchard* and many of his short stories, trees are a favourite symbol of life and eternal renewal for Chekhov. 'In Yalta spring is already in full flood, all the trees are in blossom, although many have already stopped blossoming (including me),' he wrote to an acquaintance in March 1901,[16] during another bout of tree planting in his Yalta garden, perhaps thinking back to Tuzenbakh's identification with a dead tree swaying along with others in the wind.

Having written his last play about an enterprising young merchant who buys a beautiful old cherry orchard and then proceeds to chop down the trees with a view to future profits, Chekhov would no doubt have appreciated the irony of the destiny allotted to the charred stump of the 'Pushkin oak' by the modern-day Lopakhins of Taganrog who wish to raise it literally from the dead, but with no thought of making money from the enterprise. When the Taganrog Union of Businessmen declared its intention to pay scientists to clone the famous tree, believing it had a duty to protect its country's heritage, even the international media took an interest.[17] Funding this unusual project was not going to be a problem: it was in Taganrog, after all, that the first legal Russian millionaire was registered. Alexander Roginsky, the Rostov University botanist who visited Taganrog in June 2002, verified that the mulberry tree was indeed old enough to have inspired Pushkin, and declared that its remains contained enough living tissue for the tree to be reproduced using the latest cloning technology. Leonid

Matusevich, head of the Taganrog Union of Businessmen, and also a local government representative, told an *Izvestiya* correspondent that measures would be taken to protect the historic area in the Tsar's former garden (now otherwise asphalted over) from any kind of commercial enterprise[18] and later told the BBC that the tree's reappearance would herald a spiritual revival across the whole of Russia.[19] One wonders whether Chekhov's most famous scourge of Russia's deforestation, Dr Astrov, would have laughed or applauded.

The lonely mulberry in Chekhov's miniature walled garden at Gurzuf was soon joined by a fig tree, a palm, a cypress, and a bamboo – which came in very useful for making fishing rods. Chekhov brought Olga to Gurzuf when she came to stay in July 1900, and they spent many happy hours in quiet seclusion on their private beach, sometimes seeing dolphins in the bay. Olga went swimming and Chekhov sat on the rocks, fishing for mackerel and grey mullet, and perhaps also thinking about *Three Sisters*. As soon as Olga returned to Moscow (by which time they had become intimate and abandoned the formal manner of address with each other) he returned to work on the first act of the play at the new dacha, sitting at his desk in front of the window overlooking the sea. The yearning for Moscow, which pervades *Three Sisters*, reflects Chekhov's own yearning to be near his favourite actress. 'I'm dying for you to give me word that I can pack my bags and come to Moscow,' he wrote to her after they were married, but still living separate lives. 'Moscow, Moscow! These words are the refrain not of Three Sisters but One Husband!'[20]

Three Sisters was the first play Chekhov wrote with a particular company and even particular actors in mind. He created the character of Masha, the best part in the play, specifically for Olga. 'Oh, what a role there is for you in *Three Sisters*!' he wrote to her that autumn. 'What a role! If you give me ten roubles you can have it, otherwise I will give it to another actress.'[21] Masha was the Chekhovian character with whom Olga became indelibly associated, and the one she most strongly identified with. It became her signature role, and the quotation of Pushkin's verse about the oak tree by the shore her most famous lines. Thus, at the celebration held at the Moscow Art Theatre to honour her ninetieth birthday in October 1958, when some actors dressed in old-fashioned military uniform appeared on stage and one of them started acting Fedotik's part in *Three Sisters* as he presented her with a gift, Olga immediately followed the cue with the next lines in the script: 'A green oak by the curving shore, and on that oak a golden chain . . .' They were the last lines she spoke in the theatre.[22]

III

The Actress and the Bishop

> I am so bored without you that I feel that I have been shut up in a monastery.
>
> *Letter to Olga Knipper*, 31 August 1901

The Moscow Art Theatre residency in the spring of 1900 was a high point for Chekhov during the lonely Yalta years, as were the visits from Olga, who became his wife the following year. But in between were the long months of boredom and increasing ill-health. Chekhov had taken a particular pride in cultivating roses in his Yalta garden, since they were flowers he particularly loved. He planted by hand a hundred of what he called the most noble and cultured sort just after moving into his house in 1899, and there were soon fifty-seven varieties blooming among the peonies, which had been carefully uprooted from Melikhovo and brought down to Yalta. Each plant was entered into his gardening notebook, in Latin and in Russian. Then, in February 1902, Chekhov discovered that when he bent down to prune his roses he was soon out of breath and had to take a rest after each bush. This was a terrifying reminder of his frail condition, which was now beginning seriously to deteriorate. In truth, he had been so unwell in recent months that he had not been down to the centre of town for weeks. Coughing up blood every morning had confined him to bed, where he lay reading the vast numbers of newspapers he subscribed to.[23]

The situation was made worse by the unceasing interest shown in the state of his health by the very newspapers he so depended on. It was as if he was living in a goldfish bowl in Yalta. The minute he had arrived in the resort, reports about his health had appeared in the national press and the thought of such stories reaching his mother caused him a great deal of stress. The St Petersburg *News and Stock Exchange Paper*, for example, printed the following on 25 October 1898: 'The health of the

writer Chekhov, who has settled in Yalta, has worsened; he has a
constant cough, his temperature is fluctuating and he is spitting blood
intermittently.' Chekhov was mortified, and immediately wrote to his
brother Ivan:

> I'm writing to you again, dearest Ivan. There was a telegram from Yalta
> on 24 October printed in *The News* maintaining that my health has
> worsened, that I am coughing all the time, spitting blood etc. It's all a
> complete lie, an idiotic fabrication which could upset our nearest and
> dearest. I promise you, my temperature is normal, I don't even have any
> reason to take my temperature, I am not coughing any more than usual
> and I have not coughed blood once in Yalta. If the Moscow papers
> reprint the telegram it will be really dreadful; imagine if our mother read
> it. I swear to you again that the telegram is lying . . .[24]

The Petersburg newspaper had picked up a news item in *Odessa News*
the day before which spoke of Chekhov's worrying cough and blood-
spitting, and then several other papers had run with it, including
(unfortunately for Chekhov) the Moscow-based *Russian News*. A hack
for a local Crimean newspaper in Simferopol went for the
sensationalist angle by dressing the story up a little: 'There has been a
significant deterioration in recent days in the health of the famous
writer A. P. Chekhov, living in Yalta. He is tormented by a constant
cough and sometimes there is blood-spitting. These ominous
symptoms cause one to have serious fears for his life.' As it happens,
the editor of *Russian News* just then received a letter Chekhov had
sent earlier in which he professed to be in good health, so he swiftly
published a retraction, as did the local Yalta paper, the *Crimean
Courier*, at Chekhov's specific request – but not before he had, by his
own admission, spent five days panicking that his mother would find
out and start worrying about him; he found it all extremely
unpleasant.[25]

A few weeks later Chekhov actually met the editor of the *Crimean
Courier* (yet another native of Taganrog), and arranged for the paper to
be sent to Masha and Ivan in Moscow. Over the next few years, the
Crimean Courier would publish Chekhov's various appeals for
donations to charitable causes, including several to help peasant
children during the famine which followed the failure of the harvest in

Samara in 1898. Thanks to a group of village school teachers, doctors, priests and members of rural sections of the Red Cross, Chekhov reported that over 412,000 meals had been provided for more than 3,000 children in the 1891 famine. As a result of the new appeals (each person's donation was listed in the newspaper individually, from Olya and Vera T's five kopecks to Mrs M.M.'s twenty-five roubles), Chekhov was later able to report that over 24,000 children would be saved from starvation following the 1898 harvest failure. He also wrote about the appalling situation of the impoverished consumptives who flocked to Yalta in the winter months, with nowhere to live and no one to turn to.[26] Chekhov's name certainly helped both these causes. Meanwhile, the *Crimean Courier*'s readers were really more interested in reading about him, and the paper seized every opportunity to write about its most famous resident. The paper already published the names of those visiting Yalta as a matter of course – it had announced Chekhov's arrival on 20 September 1898[27] – and it was quick to announce that he had disembarked from the steamer from Novorossiisk, together with Olga, in July 1899. Their marriage was front page news two years later, and the *Courier* continued to follow the writer's every move, even publicizing his departure for Moscow in May 1904 and his subsequent journey to Badenweiler the following month. Such was the price of celebrity and Chekhov felt he had nowhere to hide. 'I'm fed up with the *Courier*,' he exclaimed in exasperation to Olga in August 1901, 'they write rubbish about me in almost every issue.'[28]

And so the notoriously reserved Chekhov was forced to endure the distasteful experience of watching the gradual extinguishing of his life being made public property, even as he took pains to minimize the seriousness of his condition to his family and, indeed, to himself. His health became noticeably worse in the autumn of 1901, right after his marriage, and not even the red blossom on his quince tree during the snowy days of February 1902 could distract him very long from thoughts of death. Ironically, this should have been a time of great personal happiness for Chekhov: he had recently married his beloved and, in so doing, had acquired the kind of part-time wife he had famously confided to Suvorin, back in 1895, was his ideal:

All right, I'll get married if you want. But these are my conditions: everything must be as before, i.e., she has to live in Moscow and I'll live

Yalta, seen from the east

in the country, and I'll go and visit her. I couldn't take the sort of round the clock happiness which goes on day after day. I get vicious when people talk to me about the same thing every day in the same tone of voice . . . I promise to be a wonderful husband, but give me a wife like the moon, who won't appear in my sky every day. NB: I won't start writing better if I am married.[29]

And yet the practicalities of marriage to a successful full-time actress in Moscow were not in the end very favourable to someone in Chekhov's tubercular condition. It is true that a man with his restless spirit found it hard to stay still in one place, but since moving to Yalta, where he was supposed to lead a quiet life, Chekhov had taken several trips to Moscow, had travelled to the Caucasus, and had gone all the way to France to spend a prolonged period in Nice. Olga heightened his desire to get away from Yalta even more, and the relationship was certainly beneficial in that it distracted him from his illness. 'Your letters are like medicine without which I can no longer exist,' he wrote to her in December 1901. But, conversely, the relationship probably also contributed to the advancement of his illness. There was the strain of being apart from Olga, and the strain of having to get used to being in each other's company again after their separations; and the Moscow Art Theatre productions of Chekhov's last four plays were also a source of intense emotional stress, following that disastrous first staging of *The Seagull* in 1896 in St Petersburg. The experience of seeing his plays staged well at last, and greeted with acclaim, ultimately brought Chekhov great happiness, but not before he had expended large amounts of nervous energy – the last thing someone in his delicate condition needed. Thus, in a way, Chekhov's last years became an example of the paradoxes of existence he had explored so masterfully in his fiction.

The potent mixture of love and death which pervaded Chekhov's last years found perhaps its greatest artistic expression in his penultimate story 'The Bishop', which was completed in February 1902. It is one of his most finely wrought pieces of prose, a highly lyrical work which was completed at great emotional cost. Due to his poor health, it took Chekhov longer to write this story than any other. He had been musing on the subject for about fifteen years, but first began it in December 1899. Work on the story continued in fits and starts for the next two years. It is hard to find much that is overtly joyful in the account of the rapid escalation of Bishop Pyotr's illness, from his initial feelings of infirmity on Palm Sunday to his untimely death from typhoid less than a week later on Easter Saturday. The story is exquisitely sad, and Chekhov poured into this sympathetic character all his own feelings of loneliness, alienation and fear experienced during his Yalta exile, where he considered his lifestyle so ascetic that he took to signing his letters 'Antony the monk'.[30] He too found his endless visitors debilitating; he too was weary of being treated with awe and reverence; he too longed for true companionship; he too could not but look back on his life with nostalgia as he confronted the prospect of it coming to its end; he too longed to get away from his provincial prison, and he also did not want to die. But the life-changing experience of love also filled his writing with a new warmth and a sense of peace:

> The monks' singing that evening was harmonious and inspired; there was a young monk with a black beard leading the service; and as he heard about the bridegroom who cometh at midnight, and about the bridal chamber being adorned, the bishop did not feel repentance for his sins, or sorrow, but a spiritual calm, a quietness, and he was carried away by thoughts of the distant past, of his childhood and youth, when they had

also sung about the bridegroom and the mansion, and now that past seemed vivid, beautiful and joyful, as it had probably never been. And maybe in our next life we will remember the distant past and our life here on earth with the same feeling. Who knows! The bishop was sitting by the altar where it was dark. Tears were running down his face. He was thinking that he had achieved everything possible for a man in his position, and he had faith, but still not everything was clear to him, something was missing, he did not want to die; it seemed to him that he was still missing something really important, something which he had dreamed about vaguely once long ago, and that same hope about the future stirred him now, as it had during his childhood, while he was at the academy and when he had been abroad.[31]

A few weeks after first setting eyes on Olga, and just before moving down to the Crimea in the autumn of 1898, Chekhov had given his younger brother Misha a lecture about marriage, telling him it was only ever worth marrying for love. 'Marrying a girl just because she is nice is the same as buying something you don't need in the bazaar just because it's pretty,' he wrote. 'In family life the most important element is love, sexual attraction, one flesh; everything else is just pointless and

Chekhov's house in Autka, 1901

boring, however cleverly we might pontificate about it.'[32] There was no question in Chekhov's mind as to why he married Olga. He was to write her hundreds of tender letters during the five years of their relationship. Sometimes the letters were ardent, as at the end of October 1901:

> My darling, angel, my dog, dear friend, I beg you, believe me, I love you, love you deeply; don't forget me, write and think about me more often. Whatever might happen, even if you suddenly turn into an old woman, I will still love you – for your soul and your good spirit. Write to me, little hound! Take good care of your health. If you fall ill, then come to Yalta and I will look after you. Don't wear yourself out my child . . . May God bless you. Don't forget me, I am your husband after all. I send you much, much love, hugs and more love. My bed seems lonely to me, as if I was a miserly, wicked old bachelor. Write!!
>
> Your Antoine
>
> Don't forget that I am your husband, write to me every day. Greetings to Masha. I am still eating the sweets your Mama gave me. Greetings to her too.[33]

And sometimes, despite his feeling completely wretched, Chekhov's letters were playful, as at the end of January 1902, just when he was putting the finishing touches to 'The Bishop'. Alluding to Olga's German origins, he wrote:

> And so, my wonderful, good, golden wife, may God preserve you, be healthy, be happy, remember your husband at least at night time when you are going to bed. The main thing is don't be down. Your husband is not a drunkard after all, nor a clod or a ruffian, but a totally German husband in his habits; I even wear warm underwear . . . I embrace you a hundred and one times, and kiss my wife endlessly.
>
> Your Antoine[34]

The sombre mood of 'The Bishop' is also infused with Chekhov's love for his mother, with whom he had lived almost his entire life and to whom he was very close. Bishop Pyotr's self-effacing mother unexpectedly comes to visit him in the story:

It was so stuffy, and so hot! Vespers had been going on for such a long time now! Bishop Pyotr was tired. His breathing was heavy and rapid, his mouth was dry, his shoulders ached with tiredness and his legs were shaking. And it was upsetting that there was a holy fool crying out occasionally from the gallery. And then suddenly, as if in a dream or a delirium, it seemed to His Reverence that his own mother Mariya Timofeyevna, whom he had not seen for nine years now, or an old woman who looked like his mother, had come up to him in the crowd and taken a branch of pussy willow from him, and then walked away, still beaming at him with a warm, joyful smile until she merged back into the crowd. Tears for some reason started pouring down his face. He was at peace in his heart, everything was fine, but he had his gaze fixed on the left *cleros* where the reading was taking place, and where you could no longer make out anyone in the evening darkness – and was crying. Tears glistened on his face and on his beard. Then someone near to him started crying, and another person further away as well, then more and more people started crying, until the whole church was full of quiet weeping. But after a little while, about five minutes later, the convent choir was singing, people had stopped crying and everything was as it had been before.[35]

Like Bishop Pyotr's mother, Evgenia Yakovlevna was a gentle, devout woman with little education but a kind and generous spirit. Having lived through the death of one son from tuberculosis, the state of her son Anton's health was her prime concern. Chekhov wrote to her punctiliously whenever they were apart – short, simple letters in which he never abandoned the formal form of address. She wrote back ungrammatical letters without much punctuation, usually in pencil, on whatever piece of paper she could find. Since Chekhov did not consider her large archaic-looking script suitable for the mail, he prepared cards for her to send to him while he was away, ready addressed to 'Anton Pavlovich Chekhov, Yalta'.[36]

Chekhov finished his story during the bleak early weeks of Lent in 1902, when not only his mother but also old Maryushka, the cook, the maid and the gardener were all fasting. In an odd kind of way, 'The Bishop' is also a veiled tribute to Chekhov's father, whose excessive piety may have caused his son to demur from attending church in adulthood, but left him nevertheless with a profound knowledge of the scriptures (which he certainly felt enriched by) and an interest in religious writing: Pavel Egorovich's spiritual books were all kept on the Yalta bookshelves. He had also left his son with a deep respect for people who had strong faith, religious or otherwise. Chekhov had known and been friendly with many priests and bishops during his life, and drew from that deep well of experience when creating the character of Bishop Pyotr. There was his contemporary Bishop Sergy, for example, who the Chekhov family had got to know back in the 1880s when he was a history student at Moscow University. He was made a bishop in 1899,[37] and exchanged several warm letters with Chekhov while he was living in Yalta. According to his friend Father Sergei Shchukin, who taught in the Yalta parish school, Chekhov also was inspired by a photograph he stumbled on in Yalta of Mikhail, Bishop of the Crimea, who had just died prematurely of tuberculosis. The photograph depicted him sitting with his head leaning sadly towards his old mother, who looked as if she was the widow of a village deacon, who had come to visit her son from deepest Tambov. Like the bishop in Chekhov's story, Bishop Mikhail had served abroad and had become known in clerical circles for founding a new kind of scholarly monasticism. Among the religious works Chekhov read during these years was Bishop Mikhail's book on the Gospel.[38]

Recalling an earlier conversation, the ailing, housebound Chekhov told Olga in September 1901 that he did indeed long to be able to go roaming round the world with just a knapsack on his back, 'breathing freely and wanting nothing'.[39] How poignant then that just before the lonely Bishop Pyotr dies in Chekhov's story, he has a vision of himself doing precisely that:

And he already could not say a single word nor understand what was happening and was imagining himself as a simple, ordinary person, walking briskly and happily through the fields, tapping his stick, while up above him was the huge sky, flooded with sunshine; he was as free as a bird now and could go wherever he wanted![40]

Chapter 12

WHITE DEATH IN THE BLACK FOREST

I

Badenweiler

Badenweiler is a nice little place, warm, easy to live in, and cheap, but in about two or three days I will probably be starting to think of where to run away from the boredom.

Letter to Dr P. Kurkin, 12 June 1904

Chekhov said his last goodbye to Moscow on 3 June 1904, when he was helped on to a train bound for Germany. He had arrived from Yalta exactly a month earlier, and had spent the intervening weeks taking his leave of the city. When he was well enough, what he most enjoyed was going for carriage rides with his wife along the city's leafy boulevards and basking in the spring sunshine; in early May the trees would have just come into leaf in Moscow. He had spent most of that time, however, bed-ridden and very ill, receiving daily visits from his wife's German doctor. Despite his condition, he still managed to check the final proofs of *The Cherry Orchard* before they were sent off to the printing press and read manuscript submissions in his capacity as literary editor of *Russian Thought*. He talked to actors from the Moscow Art Theatre about forthcoming productions, pulled strings on behalf of his acquaintance Deacon Lyubimov so that his son could be transferred to Moscow University, and met with his friend Pyotr Kurkin, who was now an important zemstvo doctor. Dr Taube, his German physician, recommended that Chekhov undertake a cure in the health resort of Badenweiler in the Black Forest. This meant a train journey from Moscow lasting several days, and when Chekhov was safely installed in his carriage, he must have known deep down that he would never return alive. En route came a stop in Berlin, where there was a consultation with the distinguished Dr Ewald who just threw up his hands, unable to conceal from his patient how hopeless his case was. Only the convivial and lighthearted company of the Berlin correspondent of the *Russian Gazette* could dispel Chekhov's overwhelming gloom. Then came a further day's train journey from Berlin in the north-east to Badenweiler in the south-west.

The Black Forest was a popular destination at the beginning of the twentieth century. Badenweiler, in particular, had become a fashionable resort to be seen in once it was made properly accessible by road in the 1850s, around the time when the first pump-room was built. Finally, in 1895, a narrow-gauge railway took over from the horse-drawn carriage in transporting people the four and a half miles from Müllheim on the main railway line. Winding through the hamlets of Niederweiler and Oberweiler, it carried scores of visitors up to Badenweiler, 700 feet above the Rhine. Chekhov and Olga probably made the gentle ascent on the steam train, perhaps even sitting in the open-air summer carriage for the thirty minutes of the journey's duration (three times quicker than going by horse-drawn carriage, and four times cheaper).[1] With its Arcadian setting, Badenweiler was a favoured summer watering place for the Grand Dukes of Baden, whose Grand-Ducal Palace faced the entrance to the Kurpark. The fairytale ruined castle on the conical hill above the Kurhaus had been built in the eleventh century by their ancestors, the first margraves of Baden, and destroyed in the eighteenth by Louis XIV.[2] Chekhov was so ill, he could not even contemplate climbing to the top to look out on the lush view of wooded mountains. It was here that the notorious 'white death' – so called because of the link of tuberculosis with childhood and purity, as well as its victims' anaemic pallor – was to claim another of its victims.

The thermal springs of Badenweiler's spa had been attracting visitors for almost 2,000 years when Chekhov and his wife finally arrived on 9 June 1904. Tucked into the soft green hills on the south-western edge of the Black Forest, near the French and Swiss borders, and sheltered by the fir-covered slopes of the Blauen mountain, Badenweiler was justly famous for the Roman baths which were established there towards the end of the first century. It is possible that their construction was commissioned by the Emperor Vespasian himself, having earlier commanded a legion in the area, as the Romans continued the relentless expansion of their empire north of the Alps into German lands. Bathing occupied such a hallowed place in Roman daily life that *thermae* were built wherever the army set up a fort. The sophisticated succession of hot and cold pools in the former Roman settlement of Aquae Villae were probably enjoyed by dusty centurions until the Alamannic invasion in the middle of the third century. Along with those at Bath and Pompeii, they are among the largest and best-preserved Roman baths in existence, and were first discovered in 1784 by accident in the middle of the Kurpark, just as Badenweiler was beginning to emerge as a spa resort. A distinguishing feature of the Roman baths at Badenweiler was the custom for men and women to bathe separately, as in Pompeii, and the tradition was initially continued in the vaulted spaces of the handsome late nineteenth-century Markgrafenbad, or Margravian Baths, built in imitation of the Roman style.

During the season, which lasted from March to October, Badenweiler's 700-odd permanent residents had to cope with the influx of some 6,000 visitors, each of whom would have their name recorded in twice-weekly Visitors' Lists and be made to pay a daily Visitors' Tax. Some of the grander resorts like nearby Baden-Baden (so named to avoid confusion with the municipalities of Baden in Switzerland and Austria) had come to be dominated by their smart hotels and casinos. Badenweiler, on the other hand, stayed true to the close-to-nature ideals of the original 'ville d'eau', established in the seventeenth century in the Belgian town of Spa. That resort, which in the twentieth century would acquire greater fame for the sound of screaming Formula One engines on its Grand Prix circuit, had also first been developed by the Romans. By the end of the nineteenth century, Badenweiler's gentle climate and invigorating air was attracting large numbers of visitors with cardiac and pulmonary complaints, along with those who simply came to take the waters. Chekhov, whose stay in Badenweiler provides the town's other main claim to fame, was one such visitor. The last hotel he stayed in was just across the road from the Markgrafenbad, but it was, sadly, too late for him to benefit from its amenities, so advanced had his tuberculosis become. Somewhat inconveniently for the spa management, who wished to promote Badenweiler primarily as a health resort rather than as a 'Magic Mountain' of sanatoria for emaciated consumptives, he died three weeks after he arrived.

Chekhov had always found the idea of going to a sanatorium abhorrent and only consented to the idea when Dr Taube in Moscow reassured him that it was possible to stay in a hotel or private apartment in Badenweiler. Taube particularly recommended Badenweiler because he revered Josef Schwoerer, who had been Grand-Ducal Baths doctor since 1900. The first two nights of Chekhov's stay were spent at Badenweiler's most prestigious hotel, the Römerbad. Located on the square at the end of the main street, the Kaiserstrasse, between the Grand-Ducal Palace and the Kurhaus, this was the preferred residence for certain wealthy Russian aristocrats who booked whole floors and brought their own chefs. This was not a milieu Chekhov had ever mixed with. The handsome Dr Schwoerer, whose scarred cheek bore the traces of student duels, was appalled that his new patient had been allowed to undertake such a long journey in his condition, but started coming three times a day to take his temperature, at eight, two, and six in the evening. He was thirty-five – nine years younger than Chekhov – and married to Elizaveta Zhivago, originally from Moscow. His best friend, also a doctor, was married to her sister and they travelled to Russia often, particularly for bear hunting in winter.[3]

When it turned out that the Römerbad would not accommodate people with lung diseases for fear of contagion (the emphasis was already changing from convalescence to leisure pursuits), the Chekhovs took a room in the much smaller Villa Friederike on the opposite side of the Kurpark. After being awakened each morning at seven by music being played in the garden and a cup of tea brought to his bed, Chekhov spent his days here lying on a chaise-longue in the sun, reading the Russian newspapers that were sent to him. Reading the issues of the *Russian Gazette* that his friend the editor sent him in Badenweiler was one of the few pleasures left to him during his last weeks alive. An inveterate newspaper reader to the very end, Chekhov wrote to Sobolevsky shortly before he died to tell him how grateful he was to receive the issues which had been arriving regularly since he arrived in the Black Forest; they warmed him, he said, like the sun.[4]

Chekhov also enjoyed simply gazing at the views of the undulating wooded mountains that surround Badenweiler. As an avid gardener, he was admiring of the horticultural display in the hotel garden, but found it difficult to acclimatize to the quiet orderliness of German village life, and almost immediately started straining to go to Italy. He would have been disgruntled therefore to read a poem written in 1851 by Justinus Kerner, eulogizing Badenweiler as a 'piece of Italy on German soil',[5] yet probably interested in the scientific discoveries of its late author who, like himself, had combined the careers of doctor and writer. It was Kerner who wrote the first clinical descriptions of botulism earlier in the century, suspecting a biological toxin was behind a spate of sausage poisoning in the Stuttgart area, known as 'Kerner's disease' because of his reports on the deaths it caused through muscle paralysis. These reports paved the way for the discovery of *Bacillus botulinus* (from the Latin 'botulus', meaning sausage) in 1897 by a Belgian bacteriologist. Kerner also first suggested the use of small amounts of this most lethal toxin in the treatment of nervous system disorders, which has led in recent times to the development of rejuvenating 'botox' injections to relax the muscles that cause wrinkles. Kerner had loved staying in Badenweiler, Chekhov did not.

Anxious to protect his mother to the end, however, he wrote his last heroically upbeat letter to her from the Villa Friederike a couple of weeks before he died:

> Dearest Mama, I send you greetings. My health is improving and I should think that I will be completely better in a week. I like it here. It's quiet and warm, there is a lot of sunshine, but it's not too hot. Olga bows to you and sends her love. My respects to Masha, Vanya and everyone else. I bow deeply before you and kiss your hand. I wrote to Masha yesterday.
>
> Your Anton[6]

On 22 June, after ten days at the Villa Friederike, Chekhov's restless spirit got the better of him and he and Olga moved again, this time to the imposing five-storey Hotel Sommer, where Josef Schwoerer was doctor-in-residence. Initially, because it was high season, the only room they could obtain overlooked the main road, but eventually they were able to move to a larger and quieter first-floor room with a balcony, on the side which looked out to the busy village post office and the Kurpark across the road. Chekhov was too ill to take the waters or go to hear the band play in the park, but he did manage brief walks in its magnificent arboretum, which had been cultivated since 1825. Alongside native trees, conifers, pines, laurels, yews and cedars of Lebanon, he would have enjoyed seeing fir trees from Chile and tulip trees from Japan. Grand Duke Friedrich I's Russian sister-in-law had even helped to bring two *Paulownia tomentosa* from north China. The giant Californian redwoods were planted at the time of Chekhov's stay in Badenweiler. Olga also took her husband out on carriage rides to neighbouring villages, where he delighted in seeing cherry trees, well-cared for fields and streams, and lilies and roses blooming in small gardens.[7] But then suddenly it became very hot, and Chekhov became even more uncomfortable. Apart from the breathlessness caused by his condition, he had no summer clothes, and on 29 June, three days before he died, Olga travelled to nearby Freiburg to order him some flannel suits (one white with a blue stripe and one blue with a white stripe). She took along for company Lev Rabenek, a young Russian student who had arrived in the hotel. Rabenek and his brother were Moscow University students, and were already acquainted with Chekhov and Olga through their friendship with Stanislavsky's family. They had been sent by their mother to Switzerland to attend lectures on French literature, but had detoured to Badenweiler when the younger brother fell ill. He was also put under the care of Dr Schwoerer.[8]

The next morning Chekhov almost collapsed in the hotel corridor and had to retreat back to bed, where Olga propped him up with five pillows to enable him to breathe more easily. Lev Rabenek had been coming to visit almost every day and now realized that Chekhov's sun-tanned face was a deceptive mask for the precarious state of his health. During his visits to Chekhov's room, he would read aloud from the Russian newspapers, and later recalled the writer's intense interest in everything going on in the Far East and his distress at hearing reports of the dismal progress of the Russo–Japanese War. When it had first begun, in February 1904, Chekhov had declared an intention to go to the Far East himself that summer and contribute to the war effort by working as a doctor. He now asked his wife to translate the articles in German newspapers about Russia's humiliating losses. Chekhov not only followed the events of the war closely because his wife's beloved Uncle Sasha was on active duty with his regiment (Olga's mother thought her brother was probably the prototype for Chebutykin, the army doctor in *Three Sisters*), but because of his own travels in the Far East; everything must have seemed particularly vivid to him. The Berlin correspondent of the *Russian Gazette*, to whom Olga recounted the events of Chekhov's last days alive, recorded that he started talking about a sailor and the Japanese in the last hours of delirium before he died.[9]

Chekhov spent his last day playing patience, and died in the early hours of a warm July night in the presence of his wife, Dr Schwoerer, and the student Lev Rabenek. It had been the first time he had actually asked for a doctor, and Olga had dispatched Rabenek to run down the road to Schwoerer's house and ask him to come. Events then moved rapidly and Chekhov died immediately after downing the glass of champagne prescribed by Schwoerer. It seems fitting that the self-effacing Chekhov died in this more modest resort, and not in the grander spas visited by the likes of Paganini, Queen Victoria, Bismarck, Wagner and Dostoevsky.[10]

Lev Rabenek was sent off to start writing telegrams. In the hours after Chekhov's death, with the smell of hay wafting in through the open window,[11] Olga was left alone to grieve with the body of her dead husband. At dawn the silence was broken by birdsong and then by the sound of the organ playing at the nearby church in preparation for the morning's services. Dmitry von Eichler, the Russian Consul to the state of Baden, who happened to be staying in Badenweiler at the time, arrived at the Hotel Sommer at seven, and was instrumental in cancelling official procedures and ensuring a minimum of fuss. It was agreed that Chekhov's body would remain at the Hotel Sommer for the duration of the next day, and then (in a faint echo of events following Pushkin's death) be removed under cover of darkness. Before being persuaded to move to the house of Dr Schwoerer and his Russian wife, Olga sat for a while on the balcony with Rabenek, and commented drily that the suits which had been made for her husband had turned out to be funeral shrouds. Towards evening later that day, Rabenek escorted Olga back to the hotel, where Chekhov's body now lay surrounded by flowers. Rabenek had earlier been involved in the unpleasant task of straightening out Chekhov's corpse (he had died on his side), and after nightfall was distressed to observe the undignified way in which it was put into a laundry basket that proved to be too small. He and his brother then accompanied the procession to the Catholic chapel a quarter of a mile down the road, with two people carrying lanterns to light the way.[12]

The next morning, Chekhov's widow and Dr Schwoerer's Russian wife did their best to create a Russian Orthodox atmosphere in the chapel by bringing their icons and setting them up on a stand by the coffin. Later in the day an Orthodox priest from Karlsruhe arrived to perform the first *panikhida*. The small congregation included Dmitry von Eichler, Grigory Iollos, the Berlin correspondent of the *Russian Gazette*, the two Rabenek brothers, and Olga's sister-in-law, who arrived from Dresden. Then began the long journey back to Berlin, Petersburg and finally Moscow. In Berlin, in a railway siding where the carriage bearing Chekhov's coffin sat waiting for permission to be coupled to a passenger train going to Russia, a second memorial service was conducted by the senior priest from the embassy church, Father Maltsev, whom Olga later recalled as a person of great depth, intelligence and humour. Russian staff from the embassy brought garlands of oak leaves, flowers and foliage to decorate the carriage. The panikhida was sung in hushed voices at the request of the German authorities, lending it a mysterious aura, and Olga was moved by Father Maltsev's oration, in which he praised her late husband's gentle, sad (and occasionally denunciatory) stories. They were distinguished, he said, by the desire to help people break loose from difficult situations by pouring warmth and light into their troubled souls.[13]

The train bearing Chekhov's body pulled into the Warsaw station in St Petersburg early in the morning on 7 July. Only one person was there to greet it – the temporary president of Russia's Literary Foundation, Semyon Vengerov – and he was as embarrassed by the fact that he was alone as Olga was shocked by the absence of other representatives of the Petersburg literary world. Masha soon arrived from Moscow, and the three of them sat down to wait for the train which would transfer Chekhov's coffin to the Nikolaevsky station, from which trains departed for Moscow. By midday they had been joined by Chekhov's brother Alexander and his family, his publisher Adolf Marx, and Suvorin. Despite their estrangement (the letter Suvorin wrote to Chekhov in February 1902 had been the first in three years), the manner in which the grief-stricken old man ran with his stick to greet Olga is revealing; it seemed to one witness to be more like that of a father struggling to cope with the death of his child.[14] A requiem was performed at the station.[15]

Exactly a month after arriving in Badenweiler, Chekhov was buried in Moscow's Novodevichy Cemetery, next to his father's grave.

II

The Russian Aftermath

The obituary in the *Times Literary Supplement*, published a week after his death, characterized Chekhov as the most Russian of contemporary Russian writers, and drew the equivocal conclusion that he 'may or may not have been a man of genius'.[16] Back in Russia there was no such doubt. The *Crimean Courier* in Yalta had followed Chekhov's every move from the time he went to live there, first recording his arrival in September 1898, and noting what proved to be his final departure for Moscow in May 1904. On 25 June the paper reported that Chekhov had arrived in Badenweiler. From 3 July 1904, the day after his death, there began a deluge in the Russian press as the nation began to grieve. Friends and relatives wrote memoirs, which were published next to poems inspired by the sad event, articles about the productions of his plays and information about the foundation of Chekhov societies and museums. Like every other newspaper, the *Crimean Courier* published a heartfelt obituary that day. It then reported a few days later that a huge congregation had gathered in the Greek Orthodox parish church in Upper Autka to attend the first requiem service to be held in Chekhov's memory the same evening. This was the church down the road from his house, which his mother attended. The family had got to know Father Vasily well since moving in, and he had visited them on occasion. The requiem service was attended by Chekhov's mother, with his sister and two younger brothers, who were in Yalta on holiday. A week later a requiem was held in Yalta's cathedral church as in the Autka church, and it was packed on each successive occasion when requiems were held, as per Orthodox tradition. When the cycle of requiem services ended, lectures and literary evenings were organized.[17]

Chekhov's body arrived in Moscow on 9 July, and thousands took part in the funeral procession as it wended its way slowly from the station in the north of the city, through the centre, past the Moscow Art Theatre building, where there was a temporary halt for prayers to be said, and then westwards to the cemetery at the Novodevichy Convent. In such volatile times, the police were extremely apprehensive that the crowds following the coffin might stage a demonstration, and stipulated that there should be no speeches at the funeral. But after the clergy and the grieving family had departed, and over 120 wreaths had been placed on his grave (did someone really count?), many mourners refused to leave. There were some impromptu speeches to which the police could no longer call a halt, and then it started to rain heavily.[18] The next day somebody placed a bunch of wild flowers on Chekhov's grave, with a slip of paper on which was scribbled a note in pencil which spoke of the great writer's ability to express the sad poverty of Russian life.[19] Telegrams arrived for weeks at the editorial offices of *Russian Thought* and *Russian Gazette*.

It is certain that Chekhov would have loathed all the eulogies. He once confessed to having 'autobiographophobia', and had always preferred to deflect attention away from himself, finding it boring to comment on his own work. 'I'm afraid of speeches,' he had said in 1899. 'As soon as someone starts giving a speech at a celebratory dinner, I become unhappy and want to crawl under the table.'[20] He could not even bear high-flown sentiment from his wife. When, in a rush of emotion, Olga had addressed him in November 1903 as her 'superman', he had immediately written back, signing himself as her 'superman who frequently has to run to the WC'.[21] He would have probably found the posthumous wrangles which appeared in the press about his deal with Adolf Marx as distasteful as the eulogies. They started the day after his death, when the writer Vlas Doroshevich devoted a whole section of his memorial article about Chekhov to deploring the unfairness of the contract. The following day, Suvorin produced an article along the same lines for *New Times*, which was then reprinted in numerous other Russian papers. It did not take long for the mud-slinging to start. One journalist pointed out that it was in very poor taste to argue over commercial matters when Chekhov had only just been buried, but no one appeared to take heed and eventually Marx was goaded into defending himself.[22] Chekhov might indeed have laughed had he known his body would be brought back to Russia in a refrigerated train carriage marked 'for oysters', but he would surely have despaired at this tawdry quarrel. He had once declared that seeing his name in the press made him feel as if he had eaten a woodlouse.[23]

EPILOGUE: CHEKHOV STREET

It was not long after Chekhov's death that his friends in Moscow began to raise the idea of founding a museum dedicated to his memory. Viktor Goltsev, the editor of *Russian Thought*, took the lead in 1906, but he died before the first very modest Chekhov museum opened in a room in Moscow's main research library six years later.[1] In the meantime, Chekhov's numerous correspondents had begun to donate letters he had written to them. The first edition of Chekhov letters, published in 1909, was a complete revelation to the thousands of his fans across Russia who had no conception either of the details of his private life, or the range and quality of his epistolary legacy, let alone its sheer quantity. It was not until much later that the house where the Chekhovs had lived during the 1880s on Sadovaya-Kudrinskaya was turned into a museum. First came the renaming of Malaya Dmitrovka as Chekhov Street to mark the fortieth anniversary of Chekhov's death, an event which was also accompanied by the erection of statues and plaques. The retiring Chekhov would no doubt have breathed a sigh of relief to know that the street named after him reverted to its old name of Malaya Dmitrovka after the collapse of Soviet power; the Chekhov metro station however, one of Moscow's newest, remains. The 'Chest of Drawers' finally opened to the Soviet public in 1954, and then underwent several years of *kapitalnyi remont* at the beginning of the twenty-first century in preparation for the next major anniversary: the centenary of Chekhov's death in July 2004. The trees that used to surround the house were all chopped down under Stalin, and it is nowadays difficult to imagine the vehicle-infested concrete jungle being the peaceful thoroughfare it was in the 1880s. The house now sits quaintly behind mostly stationary traffic, dwarfed by enormous buildings on either side.

The transformation of Melikhovo into a literary shrine took longer. The house was destroyed after the Revolution, and by the 1930s the estate had fallen into complete disrepair. The museum that opened in 1960, the centenary of Chekhov's birth, is a painstakingly built replica, on which work had begun two decades earlier. The village of Lopasnya was renamed Chekhov, and its old post office re-opened as the Museum of Chekhov's Letters. Another focus of literary pilgrimage for Chekhov fans in the Moscow region is the two-room exhibition about his time as a dachnik, housed in a pavilion in the grounds of the New Jerusalem Monastery (which was returned to the Orthodox Church in 1994, after seventy-six years of functioning as a regional museum). The exhibition has not weathered very well, but after looking at one of Chekhov's black ties, preserved for posterity behind dusty glass, at his brother Ivan's wedding pictures and his sister Maria's sketch book, visitors can retire to the café next door and sit among the potted plants, where a friendly old lady with her hair in a bun serves tea in spotted orange cups from a gleaming samovar, with a choice of cabbage or apple pies.

The cherry trees that now grow in the garden of Chekhov's birthplace in Taganrog are the descendants of saplings planted in 1928, in preparation for the opening of the house as a memorial museum. The 'Chekhov Cottage' has since become a major literary landmark in Taganrog, along with museums set up at Chekhov's former school and in the building where his father kept his grocer's shop. It was the first Chekhov museum to be opened in one of his former residences in Russia, and the street where it stands was the first in Russia to be renamed Chekhov Street in the writer's honour. One wonders what Chekhov would make of Taganrog in its post-Soviet incarnation. When Andrei Sedov, a reporter for the daily newspaper *Komsomolskaya pravda*, was sent from Moscow to investigate the murder of the city's mayor in November 2002, he decided that Chekhov's celebrated story 'Ward No. 6' was not only a devastating indictment of insanity and injustice in late imperial Russia, but prophetic of conditions in early twenty-first-century Taganrog. An *Izvestiya* journalist on the same beat noted that Mayor Shilo, who had been preparing to celebrate twelve years of office in the week he was murdered, had been an unlikely victor at the 2000 mayoral election. Investigations into his alleged involvement in cases of embezzlement and other scandals had led to a very low rating in the opinion polls, but support from Moscow via a presidential aide, a native of Taganrog serving in the State Duma, had clearly been very helpful.

'Ward No. 6' is set in the psychiatric ward of a run-down provincial hospital, whose brutal regime resembles that of a prison rather than a place of treatment. It is an asylum in which sane people are incarcerated if they start to question the status quo too closely. One such inmate is Ivan Gromov, a sensitive and impoverished young student in the Dostoevskian mould who, one day in the street, comes across a couple of shackled convicts being marched along by four police guards. Since violence is condoned almost as an act of mercy in the town in which Gromov lives, and the local authorities seem quite impervious to people's suffering, he comes to the reasonable conclusion that innocent citizens might easily be wrongly arrested, and then starts to develop a paranoia that he too might be clapped in irons. Judges, police and doctors, he reasons, have become so inured to corruption and injustice 'that they are no different to the peasant who slaughters sheep and cattle in the backyard and does not notice the blood'. When Gromov realizes there can be no justice in this 'filthy little town a hundred miles from the railway' he becomes increasingly disturbed. It is no surprise, therefore, when Andrei Ragin, the doctor called out to visit him before he is committed, merely prescribes some drops and declares that 'people should not be prevented from going mad'. But this, ironically, is the fate meted out to Ragin when his conscience is finally awakened by Ivan's unrelenting voice of protest during lengthy conversations they hold during his ward visits. Ragin exemplifies much of the pessimistic stoicism of the second-century Roman philosopher Marcus Aurelius, to whose writings Chekhov devoted much time. 'There is no logic or morality in the fact that I am a doctor and you are insane; it's just pure chance,' he tells Gromov one day. Soon he too is locked up and beaten by Nikita, the retired soldier employed as a guard, who uses violence to keep order in the ward. Ragin's own vigorous protest against his incarceration is an eloquent vindication of Gromov's belief that people should never just stand by when witness to human suffering; evil needs to be fought.[2]

Chekhov wrote 'Ward No. 6' when he was still under the strong impression of his visit to Sakhalin. When it was published in 1892, the story was immediately hailed by the liberal intelligentsia as allegorical of the corruption and stifling reaction of Russian society after ten years of Alexander III's rule. 'Ward No. 6 is everywhere. It's Russia!' exclaimed the writer Leskov. The young Lenin felt he had been shut up in 'Ward No. 6' himself when he finished reading the story. Readers in Taganrog, meanwhile, believed with some justification that Ward No. 6 was based on their own lunatic asylum. A hundred years later it seems that, apart from extending the trolleybus line to the cemetery, Sergei Shilo's main achievement as mayor of Taganrog was the building of a new maternity hospital. It was when he went to talk to Evgenia Konopliova, director of the Chekhov Museum located in the building of Taganrog's former *gymnasium*, that Andrei Sedov discovered that this maternity hospital had been built right opposite the asylum, which still stands to this day on the edge of town. Before the new hospital was built, he was told that mothers used to give birth in the asylum itself, so that the whole of Taganrog had actually gone through 'Ward No. 6' before even being born.[3]

Apart from gauging local opinion, Sedov's assignment in Taganrog was to investigate the circumstances surrounding the death of its late mayor, who was shot as he got out of his chauffeured car late one evening in October 2002 by a gunman using a converted stun gun fitted with a silencer. The first few hours of his visit were not exactly auspicious:

> I arrived in Taganrog an hour before the funeral of the former town boss. Instead of a city guide all I had rolling around in my bag was a volume of Chekhov's stories. 'To the high street!' I shouted at the taxi driver, fearing I would be late. He stepped on the accelerator and ... immediately drove into a pothole. The wheel of his little Zhiguli gave a mournful screech and fell off. The taxi driver slumped into a numbed silence. 'I hear your mayor was murdered,' I said in an attempt to distract him; 'why was that?' 'I would have murdered himself myself for roads like these. With my bare hands,' he snapped. Half the town had gathered to bid farewell to the mayor. One could sense the hand of a competent organizer. There were buses standing around with 'Shilo's funeral, such-and-such institute', 'Shilo's funeral, such-and-such factory'.

At the funeral, the governor of the Rostov-on-Don region shouted into the microphone that the murder was a shocking event in such a peaceful place. 'Villains have penetrated the quiet Don,' he declared, echoing the title of Sholokhov's famous novel set in the area of the slow-flowing river. The head of police, meanwhile, declared that the murder was shocking because Taganrog was the 'quietest and most stable city in Russia', with a crime detection rate of 90 per cent. After doing some research for his story, Sedov wondered whether the high incidence of reported suicides had anything to do with this high figure, despite the fact that many of this number seemed mysteriously to have been restrained before their deaths (as was the case with the president of the local arbitration tribunal). Sedov himself was somewhat alarmed when the concierge at his hotel warned him not to stray off the main street after nine o'clock in the evening.

The unveiling of a new statue to Alexander I had been one of the highlights of the three-hundredth anniversary of Taganrog in 1998 (zealous Bolsheviks had ordered the original to be melted down in the 1930s). In his speech, Mayor Shilo had particularly praised Alexander I for establishing a nineteenth-century version of a 'free economic zone' by supporting local merchants.[4] Mayor Shilo's great idea for Taganrog was also the creation of a 'free economic zone'. Certainly, it was a little disappointing for local officials to learn that the American bank they approached was not enthusiastic about their proposal that it loan the city a billion dollars against the value of its property. But the oligarchs who carved up former state-run concerns profited handsomely, even if they did have to start driving around in armoured jeeps. And a wealthy Greek Cypriot entrepreneur had been able to buy a bankrupt factory in Taganrog; so what if local officials had continued asking him for money when he thought he had already paid for everything? The paperwork for creating this free economic zone, it turns out, had necessitated the employment of 568 members of staff in the mayor's office; perhaps slightly excessive for a city with a population of 300,000. But at least Mayor Shilo could not be accused of lack of patriotism. When the Bank of Russia issued a 500-rouble note showing a statue of Peter the Great in Arkhangelsk that was identical to the one in Taganrog, he caused such a fuss that it made the news on national television. Why Arkhangelsk and not Taganrog? Peter had originally planned for Taganrog to be his new capital, after all. Many citizens of Taganrog still feel aggrieved that he changed his mind and chose St Petersburg instead.

A 500-rouble banknote issued in 1997, showing Antokolsky's statue of Peter the Great in Arkhangelsk

Despite his patriotism and professed love of Chekhov, Mayor Shilo had not felt it incumbent upon himself to support any of the museums dedicated to Taganrog's most illustrious native; the Chekhov museums are funded by regional money. As well as being able to boast the first legally registered millionaire in Russia, the city must certainly have some of the most loyal – and worst paid – employees anywhere in the country. But despite receiving a rouble salary equivalent to $25 a month, none of the staff at the town's three Chekhov museums was interested in becoming involved in the 'Adequate Pay' campaign in 2002, which had been driven by the harsh economic conditions of post-Soviet Russia. Evgenia Konopliova informed Andrei Sedov that elderly women should spend their time making cakes for their grandchildren instead of shouting their heads off at meetings. Ticket revenue certainly cannot bring much income for the Chekhov museums, but perhaps the friendly lady with the silver lamé shawl and orange lipstick who sits by the old ceramic stove in the ticket office at the 'Chekhov Cottage' does a roaring trade in the busts of Chekhov and Peter the Great, *matrioshka* dolls, and porcelain figurines of nude ladies and Father Christmas which are on sale with the scholarly monographs about Chekhov, their print-run in the low hundreds.

After visiting the Chekhov museums in Moscow and Taganrog, and perhaps even venturing as far as the Ukrainian town of Sumy where the family's dacha on the former Lintvaryov family estate stands, frozen in

time, the intrepid literary pilgrim might wish to retrace the steps of
Chekhov's Siberian odyssey and visit the little wooden house in the
town of Alexandrovsk on Sakhalin, which serves as the museum
commemorating his stay on the island. But a trip to the Crimea is more
inviting, especially in the spring when the air is fragrant with the scent
of lilac and acacia blossom. The preservation of the White Dacha in the
twentieth century was due to the tireless dedication of Chekhov's sister
Masha. She had been used to showing the house to curious admirers
even before Chekhov's death, and it became such a famous landmark
that it was featured on Yalta postcards.

Chekhov had bequeathed the White Dacha to his sister in his will,
and it was she who ensured the interior of the house was left precisely
as it was when her brother left it in May 1904, still hoping to return.
She could not bear to change anything, and moved permanently with
her elderly mother to Yalta after the Revolution. Evgenia Yakovlevna
died in 1919 and was buried in Yalta. Maria Pavlovna became the first
director of the memorial museum established in the White Dacha in
1921, and undertook a hazardous trip to Moscow that year in order to
secure the Chekhov archive, which she had left in a safe. The train
journey took her three weeks. Only by noticing a little boy reading
'Vanka' in the cramped compartment she was travelling in, and by
explaining who she was, did she save herself from being thrown off the
train as a bourgeois.[5] But these were difficult times. The house was
searched many times during the Civil War, and at one point an order
was even put out for Maria Pavlovna's arrest. Her younger brother
Misha later moved down to Yalta in order to help in preparing a
catalogue for the museum, and when he died in 1936 he was buried
next to their mother, as Masha herself would be in 1957, having lived
to the age of ninety-four. By the time of her death, the White Dacha
had survived an earthquake, two and a half years of Nazi occupation,
and damage caused by the final bomb raid which was the Luftwaffe's
parting gift in 1944. Faithful to the cause, Masha had refused to be
evacuated during the war; she put up pictures of the German dramatist
Hauptmann on the wall but refused point-blank to let a German officer
take up residence in her brother's rooms. As a result, nothing went
missing.[6]

Before the beginning of the Second World War, the museum had
received some 40,000 visitors, and was one of the first cultural

institutions in the Crimea to start functioning again when the Nazi occupation ended. It was attracting up to 2,000 visitors a day up until the early 1990s, but by the beginning of the twenty-first century, attendance was down to 25,000 a year. With the collapse of the Soviet Union, when the Crimea became part of an independent Ukraine, the fate of museums in the region which celebrated Russian cultural achievements was suddenly put in doubt. They had previously been the recipients of generous funding by the Soviet government, but who would be responsible now for their upkeep, and where would the money come from? The Chekhov Museum in Yalta now falls under the jurisdiction of the Ministry of Culture of the Crimean Autonomous Republic, whose budget is extremely limited. The seriousness of the problem may be gauged from the fact that in 1999 there simply were no longer any funds to pay for professional security services. The director of the museum, Gennadi Shalyugin, was forced at one point to invite the television cameras to film him patrolling the museum himself with his dog (a dachshund, of course).[7] This prompted the *Moscow News* reporter wittily to suggest a title for a new story: 'The Gentleman with the Little Dog'.[8] These were indeed black days for the White Dacha, as another journalist remarked.

When President Putin visited the White Dacha with Leonid Kuchma, the Ukrainian president, and their respective wives, during his state visit on 4 May 2003, it seemed that perhaps help was nigh: no Russian head of state had ever visited the museum before. Gorbachev, it is true, had thought about it once when he was holidaying down the road on the Crimean coast (which is where he was when power was wrested from him in August 1991). The museum's staff were instructed to make preparations and awaited his arrival all day, but in the end Mikhail Sergeyevich decided to take Raisa to Alupka instead.[9] Preparations for the presidential visit in 2003 involved the inevitable heightening of security measures in the area – a costly exercise – but the irony of this was clearly lost on Putin and Kuchma, who were presented with a personally addressed letter of appeal:

> Tolstoy called Chekhov, in whose veins flowed Ukrainian blood (his grandmother Efrosinia Shimko was Ukrainian), 'the most Russian writer'. Chekhov's work is the national property of both the Russian and Ukrainian peoples. Concern for the preservation of Chekhov's house in

Yalta is the cultural duty of both governments, but it is a duty that is not being fully carried out. Chekhov's 'White Dacha' is subject to various damaging processes. This is leading to the deterioration of the building, which is a hundred years old, to constant hydrological problems, and damage caused by leaks when it rains. During the winter period, the temperature in Chekhov's house does not rise above 10°, which in view of the high humidity is detrimental to the preservation of the exhibits. The building which houses the literary exhibition is in a state of collapse. For five months there has been no money to pay for security and the burglar alarm has had to be switched off because of debts. The museum's collection, which includes valuable canvases by Levitan worth tens of thousands of dollars, is being abandoned to the whim of fate . . .

Dear Vladimir Vladimirovich and Leonid Danilovich! 2004 will mark the centenary of the death of Russia and Ukraine's great son Chekhov. Resolving the urgent problems of the Chekhov Museum, albeit a hundred years after the writer's death, would be the best proof that your meetings in Yalta were truly of major significance.[10]

The presidents left fulsome thanks in the visitors' book – Putin even thoughtfully presented the museum with a book about national handicrafts and left his visiting card – but no money.[11]

In his will, Chekhov left the Gurzuf dacha to Olga, who continued to make annual summer visits until 1953. Maria Pavlovna was a regular guest, and she liked to sit and play patience on the veranda as her brother used to do. Olga had wanted to leave the dacha to the Moscow Art Theatre after her death,[12] but it was sold to a painter in 1956, and when he died ten years later the property was acquired by the Union of Artists for use as holiday accommodation by its members. Only in 1987 did it finally become a branch of the Chekhov Museum in Yalta, and was opened to the public for the first time in 1995. The exhibits include materials relating to the historic Moscow Art Theatre production of *Three Sisters* staged by Nemirovich-Danchenko in 1940, which remained in the repertoire for half a century.

Chekhov's houses are in a better state than the 450-seat Yalta Theatre, which once hosted the Moscow Art Theatre when it came on tour but was closed at the end of the 1990s due to its dangerous condition. Reconstruction was begun, but work was abandoned after partial demolition of its interior, and the theatre now stands in ruins behind a scruffy hoarding. To the *Moscow News* journalist who visited in June 2003, it looked as if it was a theatre in the bombed-out Chechen capital of Grozny, rather than in Yalta.[13] Alexander Kalyagin, an important figure in Russian theatre and a member of President Putin's Council for Culture, came on a tour of inspection in May 2003, just before Putin's visit, and declared that the ruined theatre was a source of pain for all of Russia. With his eye on UNESCO's proclamation of 2004 as the Year of Chekhov, he decided that it was time to revive the tradition of 'Chekhov Seasons' at the theatre. Meetings with the Ukrainian minister of culture and the mayor of Yalta resulted in the signing of a deal with a local firm: in return for paying for the restoration of the theatre, it would be given – this being the brave new world of post-Soviet Ukraine – premium land in Yalta to build a hotel.[14]

Chekhov once made a note about the Muslim custom of digging wells to save one's soul, adding: 'It would be good if each of us left a school or a well or something similar, so that our lives did not go by and disappear into eternity without trace.'[15] He took this custom to heart and built not one but three schools during his lifetime, and through his posthumous fame saved as many churches. The Autka church of St Theodore Tyron, where his mother worshipped, suffered an ignominious fate in the Soviet period, but nevertheless survived demolition thanks to the Chekhov connection. Clementine Churchill added her vociferous support when she met with the 82-year-old Maria Pavlovna during her visit to the Soviet Union in 1945, a few months after the famous Yalta conference. For most of the latter part of the twentieth century it was used as a gymnasium, but was returned to the Orthodox Church in the early 1990s, and has since been carefully renovated and reconsecrated. Services at the Oreanda church also ceased after the 1917 Revolution, and the building's survival seemed particularly doubtful when a large crack appeared in the altar following a major earthquake in the area in 1927. Between the end of the Second World War and 1992, when it was finally returned to the Orthodox Church, it was variously used as a workshop for the construction of a nearby sanatorium, and as a warehouse for storing building materials and vegetables. Although much of the delicate Venetian glass of its precious mosaics has been lost, either through being used as target practice by Young Pioneers wielding catapults, or simply through theft, careful restoration has transformed the church from its parlous state of neglect in the early 1990s. Nowadays there is an elderly black-robed nun living in a caravan instead of a night watch, but the church once again has its own priest.[16]

The Church of the Exaltation of the Cross in Moscow, where Chekhov married Olga, was also threatened with demolition on numerous occasions after the Revolution. It miraculously continued to hold services until 1930 because it was situated in what were then the suburbs of the city, but its degradation then proceeded rapidly. First its icons were stripped of the silver and gold decorations which had been donated by the wealthy merchants in the parish, then its cupola and belfry were destroyed. The priest was arrested and sent to the camps, and his former residence and the almshouse later turned into the Korean Embassy. Then the frescoes were painted over and the church was turned into a button factory, with a second floor added to provide accommodation for the employees. In the 1970s, production changed from buttons to men's shirts. When the Soviet authorities made a new proposal to pull the church down in the early 1990s, only the fact that Chekhov had been married there saved it.[17] The building was handed back to the Orthodox Church in 1992, and restoration proceeded in a typically Russian way, with the church's current spruce appearance owing a great deal to the personal intervention of the Russian minister of defence, who happened to be a local resident. Having seen the sorry state of the building as she walked past it every day, his wife persuaded her husband to help, and materials and labour were contributed to the restoration effort, which began in 1996. The building company next door then offered to help with the construction of a new cupola and belfry. With ten-storey apartment blocks for nouveau riche oligarchs springing up all around, Moscow seems set to remain a city of striking contrasts – one of the characteristics Chekhov had so loved about it.

Shrines to Chekhov continue to appear, and not only in Russia. The most recent Chekhov museum opened on the anniversary of his death in 1999 in the Grand Oriental Hotel in Colombo, where the writer had stayed during his journey back from Sakhalin (Sri Lankan actors staged a production of *The Cherry Orchard* in Singhalese the following year).[18] The previous year, a Chekhov museum opened in Badenweiler, to join the bronze bust, granite memorial and discreet plaque fixed to one of the first-floor balconies of the former Hotel Sommer which commemorate his connection with the resort. The bust of Chekhov unveiled on the wooded hill below the castle ruins in Badenweiler in 1908 appears to have been the first statue of the writer to be erected anywhere in the world, and probably the first of a Russian writer abroad. The idea of commissioning it had come from Stanislavsky, who visited Badenweiler in 1906 during a Moscow Art Theatre tour. Public commemoration of a foreign writer in Wilhelmine Germany was a political matter, however, necessitating the diplomatic assistance of the Russian consul and the official approval of Grand Duke Friedrich I and his government in Karlsrühe, capital of the state of Baden. After an additional delay caused by the official mourning following Friedrich I's death in 1907, funds were finally allocated, and the Russian deputy consul, a sculptor in his spare time, produced a bust showing Chekhov as if out for a walk in hat and overcoat. The unveiling ceremony was attended by several hundred people, and included a service of blessing led by the Russian Orthodox priest in Karlsrühe. Olga Knipper and others came from Russia to lay wreaths, and the festivities were marked by concerts and a performance of Chekhov's perennially popular one-act farce *The Bear*. During the First World War, however, the bust was melted down for munitions, and when Stanislavsky came to consult Dr Schwoerer in 1929 about his heart problems, not even the memorial plaque on the balcony outside Chekhov's room at the Hotel Sommer had been replaced.

In 1963 a simple rectangular granite memorial to Chekhov was unveiled under one of the giant sequoias in the park near to the Hotel Sommer. Political factors again delayed the execution of an idea first raised at the time of the fiftieth anniversary of Chekhov's death in 1954, although inevitably this time of a different kind, given postwar German–Soviet relations. The question of jeopardizing Badenweiler's reputation as a health resort by drawing attention to someone who had died there, furthermore, was still an issue for the town's local authorities, who were adamant that the new memorial should not in any way resemble a gravestone, although that is precisely what it looks like. When the plinth of the original bust of Chekhov was found under thick undergrowth in 1985, the energetic director of the Sakhalin Chekhov Museum commissioned a local sculptor to produce a replacement bust (this time Chekhov without a hat), and brought it all the way from Siberia in the back of his van.[19]

The 'Tschechow Salon' Literary Museum, which opened in 1998, prides itself on being the first dedicated to Chekhov 'in the western world'. It is located in the cultural centre built on the site of the original pump-room, where in former times gentlemen could repair to smoke cigars and play cards, or dance with the ladies (if they had removed their hats). One of the prize exhibits is a pair of Chekhov's pince-nez, an article the writer is associated with, although he only wore them in the last years of his life. The visitors' book in the museum is also something of an exhibit in itself. As well as heartfelt comments from numerous Russian Chekhov admirers who have made the pilgrimage to Badenweiler ('I am touched to the depths of my soul'), and the signatures of contemporary writers like Viktor Erofeev paying homage on the actual anniversary of Chekhov's death, the book contains the scrawls of several German teenagers ('I was here and found it dead boring'; 'I love you all!!!'), and some furious invective from a prim professor doctor from Moscow State University, outraged at the low cultural level of such people, 'who in my opinion should not be allowed to visit museums at all'. Clearly this high-minded Russian scholar had forgotten a humorous early publication by Chekhov, 'The Complaints Book' (1884), containing the following imaginative entries:

> *Your excellency! Just trying my pen!?*
> *While approaching this station and looking at the countryside through the*
> *window, my hat flew away. I. Yarmonkin*
> *Don't know who wrote this, but I am an idiot to read it.*
> *Nikandrov is a socialist!*
> *Katinka, I love you madly!*
> *Since I am being sacked for supposed drunkenness, may I declare that you*
> *are all scoundrels and thieves. Kozmodemyansky the telegraphist.*[20]

The complaints books at provincial railway stations used to make Chekhov laugh out loud,[21] and he would probably have chortled with delight to read the visitors' book at his own museum here.

ACKNOWLEDGEMENTS

The writing of this book has been informed throughout by the experience of translating Chekhov's stories and letters, and amongst the many people who have helped me both directly and indirectly, I should particularly like to thank:

Rebecca Abrams, Jonathan Aves, Laura Barber, Hilary and Paul Bartlett, Rachel Beckles-Willson, Erica Benner, Martin Bryant, Dmitry and Yaroslav Bykov, James Campbell, Peter Carson, Robert Chandler, Catherine Clarke, Richard Collins, Victoria Cooper, Gina Cowen, Mark Curtis, Yulia Dolgopolova, Jane Eagan, Nina Gerasimova-Persidskaya, Alla Golovacheva, Andrew Gordon, Barbara Graziosi, Alexandra Griffiths, Branka Grundy, Alex Harrington, Mariana Haseldine, Johannes Haubold, Alexander Hoare, Regula Hohl, Brook Horowitz, Robyn Karney, Vladimir Kataev, Laurence Kelly, Alevtina Kuzicheva, Andrew Lambert, Klaus Lauer, Nina Lobanov-Rostovsky, Andrew Louth, Stephen Lovell, Judith Luna, Alexei Pavlenko, Anthony Phillips, Cecily, Hannah, Marc, Naomi and Rachel Polonsky, Georgy Putnikov, Avril Pyman, Donald Rayfield, Irina Snitkova, Nicholas Stargardt, Elizabeth Stratford, Natasha Sutta, Marianna Taimanova, Vladimir Tarnopolsky, Tanya Tsaregradskaya, Lucy and Tom Walker, Elizabeth Zeschin, the staff of the Taylorian Slavonic Library in Oxford, and Russian National Library in Moscow. Thanks also to Mikhail Zolotaryov for supplying many of the photographs from Moscow.

An award from the K. Blundell Trust towards travel costs incurred during research for this book is gratefully acknowledged.

Part of an earlier version of chapter 11 first appeared as a feature article in the programme book accompanying the Guthrie Theater's production of *Three Sisters*, Minneapolis, April 2003.

Part of an earlier version of chapter 12 first appeared as a 'Letter from Badenweiler', in the *Times Literary Supplement*, 27 December 2002.

NOTES

All quotations from Chekhov's writings refer to the thirty-volume
Academy of Sciences edition of his complete collected works, published
in Moscow between 1974 and 1983: the works are published in
eighteen volumes and the letters in twelve volumes. Notes to the works
are preceded by 'W' and contain volume numbers followed by page
references; in the case of references to letters, volume numbers are
preceded by 'L'.

PREFACE

1 A. P. Kuzicheva, 'Chekhov o sebe i sovremenniki o Chekhove (Legko li
   byt' biografom Chekhova?)', *Chekhoviana: Chekhov i ego okruzhenie*, ed.
   V. B. Kataev et al., Moscow, 1996, 15–31.
2 Z. S. Papernyi, 'On ne s nami...', *Chekhoviana: Chekhov i ego
   okruzhenie*, 5.
3 A. P. Chekhov, *Polnoe sobranie sochinenii v tridtsati tomakh*, ed. N. F.
   Belchikov et al., Moscow, 1974–1983, *Pis'ma*, vol. 2, 30. See Leonard
   Shengold *Soul Murder: The Effects of Childhood Abuse and Deprivation*,
   New York, 1989, 225–27, for a psychoanalytic interpretation of this letter.

PROLOGUE

1 N. Gitovich, *Letopis' zhizni i tvorchestva A. P. Chekhova*, Moscow, 1955,
   809.
2 L. M. Leonidov, quoted in V. L'vov-Rogachevsky, *A. P. Chekhov v
   vospominaniyakh sovremennikov i ego pis'makh*, Moscow, 1923, 66.
3 See Y. Stepanov, *Konstanty: Slovar' russkoi kultury*, Moscow, 1997,
   650–55 for a more detailed comparison of Chekhov and Nansen.
4 L3, 132.
5 Cited in Michael Asher's obituary of Thesiger, *Guardian*, 27 August 2003,
   23.
6 Hugh S. Pyper, 'Desert', *The Oxford Companion to Christian Thought*,

ed. Adrian Hastings et al., Oxford, 2000, 161–162.
7   L5, 69.
8   L4, 114.
9   L9, 215.
10 L6, 15.
11 M. P. Gromova, ed., *Perepiska A. P. Chekhova v trekh tomakh*, 2nd rev. edn, vol. 1, Moscow, 1996, 206.

CHAPTER 1

1   L8, 18, 295; L9, 11.
2   L10, 232; see also L6, 39, 182, 330 and L7, 37.
3   Marianna Koromila, *The Greeks in the Black Sea*, Athens, 1991, 250–251.
4   Aleksandr Chekhov, 'V grecheskoi shkole', *Vokrug Chekhova*, ed. E. M. Sakharova, Moscow, 1990, 32–46.
5   W12–13, 112.
6   Aleksandr Chekhov, 'A. P. Chekhov – pevchii', *A. P. Chekhov v vospominaniyakh sovremennikov*, ed. N. I. Gitovich and I. V. Federov, Moscow, 1954, 60–61.
7   E. Stroiteleva, 'Gorod na dne. Mezhdunarodnaya ekspeditsiya budet iskat' sensatsiyu v Azovskom more', *Ivestiya*, 30 July 2002, 9.
8   L6, 8.
9   A. Vel'cheva, *Taganrog: Fotoal'bom*, Taganrog, 1999, 43.
10 Herodotus, *History of the Persian Wars*, IV: 20.
11 Neal Ascherson, *Black Sea*, London, 1996, 1.
12 Koromila, *The Greeks in the Black Sea*, 26, 143–144. See also John Boardman, *The Greeks Overseas*, 4th edn., London, 1990.
13 Victor Kopylov, 'Taganrog et la première colonisation grecque du littoral nord-est de la mer d'Azov', *Sur les traces des Argonautes*, ed. Otar Lordkipanidze and Pierre Lévêque, Paris, 1996, 327–334.
14 L2, 54.
15 Koromila, *The Greeks in the Black Sea*, 143.
16 Ascherson, *Black Sea*, 92.
17 N. M. Kleopatro, 'Istoriya zaseleniya Severo-Vostochnogo Priazov'ya s drevneishikh vremen do kontsa XVIII veka', *Taganrog: Sbornik statei*, ed. E. P. Konopleva and E. A. Kozhevnikova, Taganrog, 1997, 32–39.
18 S. Razuvaeva, 'Iz istorii Taganrogskogo gorodskogo parka', *Vekhi Taganroga*, 9, 2001, 5.
19 L7, 201.
20 O. P. Gavryushkin, *Vdol' po piterskoi*, Taganrog, 2000, 387–407.
21 Koromila, *The Greeks in the Black Sea*, 270.
22 Mariya Bondarenko, 'Dom, gde umiral imperator. Taganrog do sikh por khranit tainu konchiny Aleksandra I', *Nezavisimaya gazeta*, 20 May 2002, 16.

23 *Vokrug Chekhova*, 62–64.

24 L7, 90.

25 Andrew Lambert and Stephen Badsey, *The War Correspondents: The Crimean War*, Stroud, 1994, 202.

26 Andrew Lambert, *The Crimean War: British Grand Strategy Against Russia, 1853–1856*, Manchester, 1990, 230–231.

27 A. C. Dewar, ed., *Russian War, 1855: Black Sea Official Correspondence*, London, 1945, 179–182.

28 *Black Sea Official Correspondence*, 182.

29 A. G. Alfer'eva et al., *Taganrog i Chekhovy: materialy k biografii A. P. Chekhova*, Taganrog, 2003, 36.

30 L. A. Bodik, ed., *Taganrog: Istoriko-kravedcheskii ocherk*, Rostov-on-Don, 1977, 30.

31 S. Eardley-Wilmot, *Life of Vice-Admiral Edmund, Lord Lyons*, London, 1898, 317.

32 *Black Sea Official Correspondence*, 231, 233.

33 *Black Sea Official Correspondence*, 264.

34 *Vokrug Chekhova*, 164.

35 *Black Sea Official Correspondence*, 297–321.

36 *Black Sea Official Correspondence*, 297, 323.

37 *Vokrug Chekhova*, 168.

CHAPTER 2

1 V. D. Sedegov, ed., *A. P. Chekhov: Sbornik statei i materialov*, Rostov-on-Don, 1959, 369.

2 O. P. Gavryushkin, *Mari Val'iano i drugie (khronika obyvatel'skoi zhizni)*, Taganrog, 2001, 382–389.

3 Alfereva et al., *Taganrog i Chekhovy*, 53.

4 A. M. Linin, ed., *A. P. Chekhov i nash krai. K 75-letiyu so dnya rozhdeniya*, Rostov-on-Don, 1935, 25–32.

5 L. D. Gromova-Opul'skaya and N. I. Gitovich, *Letopis' zhizni i tvorchestva A. P. Chekhova. Tom Pervyi. 1860–1888*, Moscow, 2000, 1–17.

6 *Vokrug Chekhova*, 162–163.

7 Sedegov, *A. P. Chekhov: Sbornik statei i materialov*, 337.

8 Gavryushkin, *Mari Val'iano i drugie*, 417–419.

9 *Vokrug Chekhova*, 163.

10 A. Sedoi [Aleksandr Chekhov], 'Nevadnee proshloe azovskogo poberezh'ya', *Istoricheskii vestnik*, 10, 1904, 244–247.

11 O. Gavryushkin, *Gulyaet staryi Taganrog*, Taganrog, 1997, 7–31; *Vdol' po piterskoi*, 56–61.

12 *A. P. Chekhov i nash krai*, 33–34.

13 Gitovich, *Chekhov v vospominanyakh sovremennikov*, 42–46.

14 Sedegov, L, A. P. *Chekhov: Sbornik statei i materialov*, 339.

15 L4, 162.

16 M. Semenov and N. Tulupov, eds., *Chekhovskii yubileinyi sbornik*, Moscow, 1910, 482.

17 W16, 506.

18 P. P. Filevsky, *Istoriya goroda Taganroga*, Moscow, 1898, 262.

19 V. Bandakov, *Prostye i kratkie poucheniya protoireya Vas. Bandakova*, 5th edn., Moscow, 1900, 25, 52.

20 W16, 245.

21 Alfereva et al., *Taganrog i Chekhovy*, 62.

22 Alfereva et al., *Taganrog i Chekhovy*, 83.

23 A. P. Kuzicheva, 'Chekhov o sebe i sovremenniki o Chekhove (Legko li byt' biografom Chekhova?)', *Chekhoviana: Chekhov i ego okruzhenie*, 18.

24 W9, 39.

25 W2, 251.

26 See Alfred J. Rieber, *Merchants and Entrepreneurs in Imperial Russia*, Chapel Hill, 1982 and Edith W. Clowes, Samuel D. Kassow and James L. West, eds., *Between Tsar and People: Educated Society and the Quest for Public Identity in Late Imperial Russia*, Princeton, 1991.

27 See James L. West and Y. A. Petrov, eds., *Merchant Moscow: Images of Russia's Vanished Bourgeoisie*, Princeton, 1997.

28 Gromova-Opul'skaya and Gitovich, *Letopis' zhizni i tvorchestva*, 12.

29 W8, 303.

30 Alfereva et al., *Taganrog i Chekhovy*, 184–185.

31 Semenov and Tulupov, *Chekhovskii yubileinyi sbornik*, 347.

32 Y. Simkin, *Sem' let iz zhizni A. P. Chekhova*, Rostov-on-Don, 1987, 49.

33 L2, 28.

34 L2, 56.

35 L2, 71.

36 L2, 73–74.

37 A. K. Vaganova, 'Chekhovskaya step' kak natsional'nyi obraz', *Chekhovskie chteniya*, ed. L. P. Vaganova et al., Taganrog, 2001, 54.

38 H. D. Seymour, *Russia on the Black Sea and Sea of Azov*, London, 1855, 20–21.

39 L7, 230–231.

40 L8, 13.

41 E. A. Shapochka, '. . . Fantasticheskii krai' Chekhovskogo Priazov'ya', *Chekhoviana: Chekhov i ego okruzhenie*, 280–290.

42 L2, 219.

43 W6, 216.

44 W6, 217.

45 L2, 219.

46 W6, 666.

47 *Vokrug Chekhova*, 55–109.
48 L2, 79.
49 L2, 75–76.
50 L3, 11.
51 *Vokrug Chekhova*, 176.
52 L2, 185.
53 L2, 178.
54 W7, 46.
55 L7, 231.
56 L2, 190.
57 W13, 224.
58 W6, 215.

CHAPTER 3

1   See D. Merezhkovsky, 'Brat chelovecheskii', *Chekhovskii yubileinyi sbornik*, 207.
2   Cited in Kuzicheva, 'Chekhov o sebe i sovremenniki o Chekhove (Legko li byt' biografom Chekhova?)', 16.
3   L1, 22–23.
4   L1, 27.
5   Kuzicheva, 'Chekhov o sebe i sovremenniki o Chekhove (Legko li byt' biografom Chekhova?)', 16.
6   Cited in A. B. Kulikovskaya, 'Otets Chekhova', *Chekhoviana: Chekhov i ego okruzhenie*, 65.
7   Rossiiskaya Gosudarstvennaya Biblioteka, fond 331.81.20, folio 1.
8   Rossiiskaya Gosudarstvennaya Biblioteka, fond 331.81.20, folio 4.
9   *Vokrug Chekhova*, 177–178.
10 L2, 520.
11 W1, 245.
12 W1, 247.
13 Donald Rayfield, *Anton Chekhov: A Life*, London, 1997, 64.
14 Mikhail Gromov, *Chekhov*, Moscow, 1993, 62–63.
15 Gromova-Opul'skaya and Gitovich, *Letopis' zhizni i tvorchestva*, 75.
16 L1, 40.
17 W1, 103.
18 L1, 42.
19 Gromova-Opul'skaya and Gitovich, *Letopis' zhizni i tvorchestva*, 88.
20 W9, 65–66.
21 G. F. Shcheboleva, 'Pushkinskie torzhestva 1880 g. v Moskve glazami khudozhnika Nikolaya Chekhova', *Chekhoviana: Chekhov i Pushkin*, ed. V. Kataev et al., Moscow, 1998, 264–272.
22 L1, 81.
23 W3, 590.

24 N. I. Gitovich and I. V. Federov, eds., *A. P. Chekhov v vospominaniyakh sovremennikov*, Moscow, 1960, 117.

25 M. P. Gromova, ed., *Perepiska A. P. Chekhova*, 2nd rev. edn, vol. 1, Moscow, 1996, 290.

26 L1, 216.

27 L1, 234.

28 L1, 231.

29 L1 137.

30 L1 136.

31 W16, 271.

32 M. B. Mirsky, *Doktor Chekhov*, Moscow, 2003, 13.

33 Nancy Mandelker-Frieden, *Russian Physicians in an Era of Reform and Revolution, 1856–1905*, Princeton, 1981, 126.

34 John Coope, *Doctor Chekhov: A Study in Literature and Medicine*, Chale, 1997, 19.

35 L1, 116–117.

36 L3, 184.

37 Pushkin, *Evgeny Onegin*, ch. 5, stanza IV.

38 Vladimir Nemirovich-Danchenko, *Rozhdenie teatra: Vospominaniya, stat'i, zametki, pis'ma*, Moscow, 1989, 60.

39 L4, 73.

40 E. A. Zvyagintsev, *Moskva: Putevoditel'*, Moscow, 1915, 112.

41 L3, 281.

42 L2, 131.

43 L2, 330.

44 L2, 138.

45 Gromova-Opul'skaya and Gitovich, *Letopis'*, 352.

46 L4, 54–57.

CHAPTER 4

1 For further details, see Stephen Lovell, *Summerfolk: A History of the Dacha, 1710–2000*, Ithaca, 2003.

2 Gromova-Opul'skaya and Gitovich, *Letopis'*, 74.

3 *Vokrug Chekhova*, 82.

4 *Vokrug Chekhova*, 86.

5 *Chekhov v vospominaniyakh sovremennikov*, Moscow, 1954, 77.

6 Arkhiepiskop Tikhon, ed., *Russkaya pravoslavnaya tserkov'. Monastyry: entsiklopedicheskii slovar'*, Moscow, 2000, 43.

7 L1, 73.

8 L1, 114.

9 L1, 152.

10 L1, 118.

11 Gromova-Opul'skaya and Gitovich, *Letopis'*, 164.

12 L1, 149.
13 L1, 153–154.
14 L1, 156–157.
15 Gromova-Opul'skaya and Gitovich, *Letopis'*, 122.
16 N. I. Gitovich, ed., *A. P. Chekhov v vospominaniyakh sovremennikov*, Moscow, 1986, 591.
17 W2, 195.
18 *Chekhov v vospominaniyakh sovremennikov*, Moscow, 1954, 78.
19 *Vokrug Chekhova*, 95.
20 W4, 84–87.
21 W4, 37–39.
22 Leonid Sabaneev, *Zhizn' i lovlya presnovodnykh ryb* (reprint of *Ryby Rossii*, 1911), Moscow, 1991, 215–219.
23 'Strazha pod strazhei', *Peterburgskya gazeta*, 17 June 1885, 4, 20–23.
24 L2, 167–176.
25 L2, 508.
26 L2, 509.
27 Sabaneev, *Zhizn' i lovlya*, 9.
28 W1, 117–121.
29 W1, 67–79.
30 W1, 566.
31 W1, 572.
32 Sabaneev, *Zhizn' i lovlya*, 9.
33 W16, 101–102.
34 N. V. Turkin, Introduction to Sabaneev, *Zhizn' i lovlya*, 5–14.
35 L2, 508.
36 L1, 157.
37 W4, 375–586.
38 W6, 92–96.
39 *Chekhov v vospominaniyakh sovremennikov*, 76.
40 Gromova-Opul'skaya and Gitovich, *Letopis'*, 191.
41 W4, 79–83.
42 W4, 476.
43 L1, 218.
44 L1, 246.
45 L1, 255.
46 L2, 94.
47 *A. P. Chekhov v vospominanyiakh sovremennikov*, 80.
48 *Vokrug Chekhova*, 110.
49 L2, 266.
50 L2, 268.
51 W2, 267.
52 L2, 269–270.
53 L2, 268–269.

54 L2, 277.

55 L2, 271–272, 293.

56 Hymn sung standing in honour of the Blessed Virgin Mary on the Saturday of the fifth week of Lent in the Orthodox Church, consisting of 24 stanzas, alternately long and short, each beginning with one of the letters of the Greek alphabet.

57 L2, 278.

58 Rayfield, *Anton Chekhov: A Life*, 171.

59 L2, 278–279.

60 L2, 280.

61 L2, 293.

62 L2, 286–287.

63 L2, 288.

64 L2, 291.

65 Chekhov could never be accused of anti-semitism; the pejorative 'zhid' that he uses here was unfortunately widespread.

66 L2, 290.

67 L2, 292.

68 L2, 308.

69 L2, 325.

70 L2, 313.

71 L2, 321.

72 L3, 201.

73 L3, 221–223.

74 L3, 227.

75 N. I. Gitovich, *Letopis' zhizni i tvorchestva A. P. Chekhova*, 233.

76 A. S. Melkova, 'Khudozhnik Nikolai Chekhov. Sud'ba i konchina', *Chekhovskie chteniya v Yalte*, ed. V. A. Bogdanov, Moscow, 1997, 213–214.

77 L3, 233.

78 L3, 235.

79 L4, 224–225.

80 L4, 227.

81 L4, 232.

82 *Chekhov v vospominanyiakh sovremennikov*, 87.

83 W9, 174–175.

84 L4, 242.

85 L4, 240.

86 L4, 246.

87 L4, 250.

88 L4, 255.

CHAPTER 5

1   L9, 527.

2   L9, 223.

3   L1, 175.

4   L1, 166.

5   Rayfield, *Anton Chekhov: A Life*, 504.

6   W1, 17.

7   Louise McReynolds, *The News Under Russia's Old Regime*, Princeton, 1991, 68.

8   W2, 14.

9   W2, 43.

10 L1, 108.

11 E. A. Dinershtein, *Chekhov i ego izdateli*, Moscow, 1990, 48.

12 L1, 122.

13 L1, 166.

14 L1, 233.

15 Marvin Lyons, *Russia in Original Photographs*, London, 1977, 34.

16 Old Believers did not win the right to worship publicly until 1906, but the Edinoverie (Single Faith) sect reached a compromise with the Russian Orthodox Church. Built by A. I. Melnikov in 1820–26, the cube-shaped building has housed the Museum of the Arctic and Antarctic since 1937. Nikolaevskaya Street was named after Robespierre's fellow conspirator Jean-Paul Marat in 1918.

17 http://www.palkin.ru/rus/history.htm

18 L1, 399.

19 L1, 175, 177.

20 W4, 326.

21 Gitovich, *Letopis'*, 216.

22 McReynolds, *The News Under Russia's Old Regime*, 74.

23 L1, 201–202. We unfortunately will never know what Suvorin's suggestions were: soon after Chekhov's death he destroyed all the letters he had ever written to him, after exchanging with Maria Pavlovna all the letters Chekhov had written to him.

24 W4, 355.

25 L1, 193.

26 L1, 238–239.

27 Dinershtein, *Chekhov i ego izdateli*, 93.

28 L2, 322.

29 L1, 204.

30 A. S. Suvorin, *Pis'ma A. S. Suvorina, k v.v. Rozanovu*, St Petersburg, 1913, 4–5.

31 L2, 213.

32 L2, 178.

33 For further details, see Andrew Durkin, 'Chekhov and the journals of his time', *Literary Journals in Imperial Russia*, ed. Deborah A. Martinsen, 338–245.

34 L2, 134–136.

35 L2, 16.

36 Gromova-Opul'skaya and Gitovich, *Letopis'*, 252.

37 L2, 183. This is a slightly loose translation: what Chekhov says literally is that *partiinost* 'does not love' freedom and the grand scale.

38 L2, 159.

39 *Perepiska A. P. Chekhova*, vol. 1, 87.

40 L2, 35.

41 *Perepiska A. P. Chekhova*, vol. 1, 80.

42 L2, 115.

43 W12, 341.

44 Yury Bychkov and Marina Orlova, *Chekhovy v Melikhove: Semeinyi al'bom*, Moscow, 2000, 46.

45 W11, 430.

46 L3, 439.

47 L3, 238.

48 V. L'vov Rogachevsky, *A. P. Chekhov v vospominaniyakh sovremennikov i ego pis'makh*, 55.

49 *Oskolki*, 45, 4 November 1889, 1.

50 A. Izmailov, *Chekhov, 1860–1904: Biograficheskii ocherk*, 417.

51 L6, 498.

52 W12–13, 361–364.

53 *A. P. Chekhov v vospominaniyakh sovremennikov*, 338.

54 L6, 181.

55 L6, 183.

56 Gitovich, *Letopis'*, 429.

57 L6, 211.

58 W17, 223.

59 W13, 371–372.

60 *Oskolki*, 43, 26 October 1896, 1.

61 L6, 555.

62 L6, 231.

63 *Dnevnik Alekseya Sergeyevicha Suvorina*, ed. D. Rayfield and O. Makarova, Moscow, 1999, 302.

64 L6, 415.

CHAPTER 6

1 V. P. Dunaeva, 'Plavanie A. P. Chekhova na parakhode "Peterburga" (Po materialam fonda "Dobrovol'nogo Flota")', *Literaturnoe nasledstvo 87*, ed. V. R. Shcherbina, Moscow, 1977, 299.

2 See David Schimmelpenninck van der Oye, *Toward the Rising Sun: Russian Ideologies of Empire and the Path to War with Japan*, De Kalb, Illinois, 2001, 16. All information about Nicholas' 1890–1891 Grand Tour comes from this source.
3 W14–15, 748.
4 L6, 253.
5 L5, 132–133.
6 L3, 204.
7 W16, 236–237.
8 Gromov, 'Chekhov i Przhevalskii', *Tvorchestvo A. P. Chekhova*, 7.
9 Again I am indebted to David Schimmelpenninck van der Oye: see his chapter 'Conquistador imperialism: Nikolai Przhevalskii', *Toward the Rising Sun*, 24–41.
10 W6, 426.
11 Fridtjof Nansen, *Through Siberia: The Land of the Future*, London, 1914.
12 W4, 31–33.
13 W14–15, 745–748.
14 Ch. Darvin, *Puteshestvie naturalista na korable 'Bigl'*, St Petersburg, 1865; cited in N. E. Razumova, *Tvorchestvo A. P. Chekhova v aspekte prostranstva*, Tomsk, 2001, 35.
15 L4, 65–68.
16 George Kennan, *Siberia and the Exile System*, London, 1891, vol. 1, 77.
17 L4, 69–97.
18 L4, 99.
19 W2, 17.
20 W4, 101–102.
21 L4, 117.
22 L4, 126–127.
23 See Mark Bassin, *Imperial Visions: Nationalist Imagination and Geographical Expansion in the Russian Far East, 1840–1865*, Cambridge, 1999.
24 W14–15, 45.
25 W14–15, 54.
26 W14–15, 65.
27 John Stephan, *Sakhalin: A History*, Oxford, 1971, 43.
28 W1, 116.
29 W14–15, 163.
30 W14–15, 124.
31 See T. G. Miromanov, 'Ieromonakh Iraklyi', *Chekhoviana: Chekhov i ego okruzhenie*, 89–95.
32 W14–15, 795.
33 W14–15, 26.
34 W4, 140.

35 Benson Bobrick, *East of the Sun: The Conquest and Settlement of Siberia*, London, 1992, 370.

36 George Lensen, *The Russian Push Towards Japan: Russo–Japanese Relations, 1697–1875*, Princeton, 1959, 464.

37 Izmailov, *Chekhov, 1860–1904. Biograficheskii ocherk*, 258.

38 Stephan, *Sakhalin*, vol.1, 81.

39 L4, 140.

40 W7, 339.

41 L4, 199–200.

42 L4, 202.

43 L4, 203–212.

44 L4, 217.

45 Raymond de Ponfilly, *Guide des russes en France*, Paris, 1990, 391.

46 Conversation with M. Kourdukov, administrator of the Church of Sts Nicholas and Alexandra, February 2003.

47 L4, 220.

48 L5, 317–326.

49 Article in *New Times*, 4 July 1904, cited in Rayfield, *Anton Chekhov: A Life*, 244.

CHAPTER 7

1 L11, 142.

2 L5, 67.

3 L7, 21.

4 A. I. Kuzicheva and E. M. Sakharova, eds., *Melikhovskii letopisets*, Moscow, 1995, 242.

5 L7, 14.

6 L5, 88.

7 W13, 481–482.

8 L3, 250.

9 L1, 167.

10 L4, 367.

11 Y. Bychkov, ed., *Al'manakh Melikhovo*, Tula, 1999, 116.

12 W13, 69.

13 L5, 42.

14 L5, 60, 76.

15 W10, 58.

16 Y. Avdeev, *V Chekhovskom Melikhove*, 3rd rev. edn, Moscow, 1972, 95.

17 L. Z. Abramenkova, 'Sosed Chekhovykh V. N. Semenkovich', *Chekhoviana: Melikhovskie trudy i dny*, ed. V. Lakshin et al., Moscow, 1995, 264–271.

18 L5, 70.

19 Bychkov and Orlova, *Semeinyi al'bom*, 41.

20 L5, 19.

21   *Vokrug Chekhova*, 139.
22   L5, 29.
23   *Vokrug Chekhova*, 138.
24   *Vokrug Chekhova*, 146.
25   Kuzicheva and Sakharova, *Melikhovskii letopisets*, 220.
26   L5, 193.
27   Kuzicheva and Sakharova, *Melikhovskii letopisets*, 162.
28   Kuzicheva and Sakharova, *Melikhovskii letopisets*, 180.
29   Kuzicheva and Sakharova, *Melikhovskii letopisets*, 47.
30   Kuzicheva and Sakharova, *Melikhovskii letopisets*, 121.
31   W17, 30, 37, 46–47, 76, 84, 160.
32   L8, 271.
33   L8, 296.
34   Kuzicheva and Sakharova, *Melikhovskii letopisets*, 238–239.
35   *Vokrug Chekhova*, 293.
36   L5, 196.
37   L6, 68.
38   *A. P. Chekhov v vospominaniyakh sovremennikov*, 370.
39   L8, 226–227.
40   L5, 40.
41   L5, 201.
42   L6, 78.
43   L6, 50.
44   L6, 71; L. Z. Abramenkova, 'Sosed Chekhovykh V. N. Semenkovich', 268.
45   I. S. Ezhov, ed., *Pis'ma A. P. Chekhovu ego brata Aleksandra Chekhova*,
     Moscow, 1939, 290, 320, 324.
46   L7, 7.
47   L6, 296. On the eve of the 1917 Revolution one of Brom and Quinine's
     offspring was apparently acquired by the Nabokov family in St Petersburg
     and named Box II. This dachshund accompanied the Nabokovs into exile
     and spent his last years in a suburb of Prague. As late as 1930, Nabokov tells
     us in *Speak, Memory*, (London, 1969), 40) 'he could be still seen going for
     reluctant walks with his mistress, waddling far behind in a huff,
     tremendously old and furious with his long Czech muzzle of wire – an
     émigré dog in a patched and ill-fitting coat.' Was Nabokov right in claiming
     that Box II was the grandson of Brom and Quinine? Perhaps he meant great-
     grandson, or even great-great-grandson. We do not know whether Saltpetre
     ever had puppies (let alone with another dachshund), whether Quinine
     produced any more pedigree puppies, or whether any of them made the
     journey to Petersburg. It is unlikely even Quinine's grandchildren were still
     producing puppies in 1916; Saltpetre, for example, would have been
     twenty-one. Perhaps Box II was in fact a descendant of Alexander's Saltpetre,
     if she came from Leikin, as Brom and Quinine had? We shall probably never
     know the answer to any of these pressing questions.

48 Kuzicheva and Sakharova, *Melikhovskii letopisets*, 173.
49 L6, 298.
50 Kuzicheva and Sakharova, *Melikhovskii letopisets*, 176.
51 L6, 339.
52 L6, 33.
53 L5, 25.
54 L5, 120.
55 L5, 296.
56 L8, 121.
57 Coope, *Doctor Chekhov*, 103.
58 This was the case in Vyatka in 1883. See Coope, *Doctor Chekhov*, 119.
59 L8, 299–300.
60 L5, 100.
61 A. P. *Chekhov v vospominaniyakh sovremennikov*, 79.
62 L5, 339.
63 L9, 311–312.
64 W17, 90.
65 Chekhov cites this famous declaration in a letter sent from Melikhovo on 11 May 1892, in which he proudly announces that he will be offering possibilities for croquet that summer: L5, 60.
66 M. Vol'f, *Kroket: Obshchie pravila igry*, Petrograd, 1916.
67 A. P. *Chekhov v vospominaniyakh sovremennikov*, 118.
68 Bychkov and Orlova, *Semeinyi al'bom*, 35.
69 L5, 139.
70 L5, 46.
71 L9, 336–337.
72 L5, 341.
73 V. Feider, *A. P. Chekhov: Literaturnyi byt i tvorchestvo po memuarnym materialam*, Leningrad, 1928, 210.
74 L5, 19.
75 L8, 51.
76 L5, 38–39.
77 L8, 201.
78 M. P. Chekhova, *Pis'ma k bratu A. P. Chekhovu*, Moscow, 1954, 124.

CHAPTER 8

1 L6, 313–327.
2 Kuzicheva and Sakharova, *Melikhovskii letopisets*, 180.
3 L7, 46–55.
4 See Patrick Howarth, *When the Riviera was Ours*, London, 1977.
5 See Mary Blume, *Côte d'Azur: Inventing the French Riviera*, London, 1992.
6 Ludmila Nalegatskaia, 'Tchekov à Nice', *Revue des deux mondes*, November 1973, 342.

7 L7, 147.
8 See V. B. Kataev, 'Chekhov i Frantsiya', *Chekhoviana: Chekhov i Frantsiya*, Moscow, 1991, 8–19.
9 L7, 64, 109.
10 L7, 98, 177.
11 L8, 203.
12 L7, 76.
13 W9, 313–314, 324.
14 W9, 337–338, 342.
15 L7, 123.
16 L7, 63.
17 L7, 58.
18 L7, 76.
19 L7, 193.
20 See Michael Nelson, *Queen Victoria and the Discovery of the Riviera*, London, 2001.
21 L7, 123.
22 L7, 106.
23 L7, 75.
24 See pages on Nice in Baedeker, *France Sud-Est*, Paris, 1897.
25 Robert Kanigel, *High Season in Nice: How One French Town Has Seduced Travellers for 2000 Years*, London, 2002, 98, 101.
26 L7, 115.
27 L9, 157.
28 The plaque commemorating Lenin's stay dates the year erroneously as 1911. According to documents in the file on 'Tcheklov' (*sic*) in the Archives Municipales de Nice, the Chekhov plaque was affixed in 1963 by the city of Nice, following the lobbying of the local 'poète, artiste and cinéaste' W. J. Zapp-Kamensky, to commemorate the centenary of his birth in 1960; See also *L'Esprit*, 24 June 1963.
29 L7, 91.
30 A. P. *Chekhov v vospominaniyakh sovremennikov*, 367.
31 A. P. *Chekhov v vospominaniyakh sovremennikov*, 314.
32 L7, 121, 140, 172, 177.
33 L7, 112.
34 L7, 64, 76, 115, 121.
35 See Kanigel, *High Season in Nice*, 137.
36 Michel Bourrier and Gerard Colletta, *Chronologie illustrée de l'histoire du Comte de Nice*, Nice, 2000, 198.
37 L7, 96.
38 L7, 83, 95–96, 97, 100.
39 L7, 99.
40 L7, 112, 120, 125, 161.
41 *Guide des Russes en France*, 407.

42 L7, 105, 117, 193.
43 M. P. Chekhova, *Pis'ma k bratu*, 41.
44 L7, 65, 98.
45 M. P. Chekhova, *Pis'ma k bratu*, 63.
46 W17, 51.
47 W10, 141, 128.
48 W10, 419–423.
49 L7, 181–182.
50 L7, 168.
51 Leroy Ellis, *Les Russes sur la Côte d'Azur: La colonie russe dans les Alpes-Maritimes des origines à 1939*, Nice, 1988, 161.
52 L7, 49, 53, 113, 117, 134–139, 160.
53 M. P. Chekhova, *Pis'ma k bratu*, 39.
54 M. P. Chekhova, *Pis'ma k bratu*, 44.
55 M. P. Chekhova, *Pis'ma k bratu*, 39, 44, 49, 52, 54–55.
56 L7, 111.
57 L7, 195.
58 M. P. Chekhova, *Pis'ma k bratu*, 70.
59 L7, 191.
60 L9, 151, 153, 166.
61 W10, 193.
62 L9, 154, 178, 182, 190, 192.

CHAPTER 9

1 W8, 254.
2 *Murray's Handbook for Travellers to Russia*, London, 1875, 354.
3 L2, 294–295.
4 T. Milner, *The Crimea*, London, 1855, 321.
5 A. Fedorov-Davydov, ed., *Levitan: Pis'ma, dokumenty*, Moscow, 1956, 27.
6 G. Shalyugin, ed., *Krymskie penaty: A. P. Chekhov i krym*, Simferopol, 1998, 10.
7 L2, 296.
8 L3, 232–234.
9 G. Moskvich, *Illyustrirovannyi prakticheskii putevoditel' po Krymu*, Odessa, 1908, 24.
10 M. Zemlyanichenko and N. Kalinin, *Romanovy i Krym*, Moscow, 1993, 12.
11 L10, 428.
12 A. P. Derman, ed., *Perepiska A. P. Chekhova i O. L. Knipper*, vol. 2, Moscow, 1936, 11.
13 *Krym: Putevoditel'*, Simferopol, 1914, 482.
14 J. G. Kohl, *Russia: St Petersburg, Moscow ... and the Interior of the Empire*, London, 1842, 450.

15 Thos. Milner, *The Crimea, its Ancient and Modern History: The Khans, the Sultans, and the Czars with Notices of its Scenery and Population*, London, 1855, 321.

16 Zemlyanichenko and Kalinin, *Romanovy i krym*, 17–18.

17 W10, 133–134.

18 *Levitan: Pis'ma*, 27.

19 Conversation with Vladimir Evdokimov, May 2003.

20 *Murray's Handbook*, 372.

21 *Krym: Putevoditel'*, 482.

22 Zemlyanichenko and Kalinin, *Romanovy i krym*, 58.

23 A. P. Chekhov *v vospominaniyakh sovremennikov*, 269.

24 Karl Baedeker, *Russia, with Teheran, Port Arthur and Peking: Handbook for Travellers*, London, 1914, 416.

25 L5, 275, 281–282, 532; A. P. Chekhov *v vospominaniyakh sovremennikov*, 265.

26 W8, 506–507.

27 W8, 309.

28 L5, 280, 282.

29 L5, 44, 49; Kuzicheva and Sakharova, *Melikhovskii letopisets*, 19.

30 L7, 289.

31 Zemlyanichenko and Kalinin, *Romanovy i krym*, 57, 77.

32 Milner, *The Crimea*, 322.

33 *Murray's Handbook*, 373.

34 Moskvich, *Illustrirovannyi prakticheskii putevoditel'*, 144, 170.

35 L7, 286, 289.

36 L8, 13.

37 L11, 77, 79.

38 L7, 278, 357–358, 361, 364.

39 A. G. Golovacheva, ed., *Chekhovskie chteniya v Yalte*, Moscow, 1983, 134.

40 *Krymskie penaty*, 48.

41 Gitovich, A. P. Chekhov *v vospominaniyakh sovremennikov*, 496.

42 Gitovich, A. P. Chekhov *v vospominaniyakh sovremennikov*, 512.

43 L8, 544; Rayfield, *Anton Chekhov: A Life*, 497.

44 Gitovich, A. P. Chekhov *v vospominaniyakh sovremennikov*, 263.

45 L7, 289.

46 L3, 79.

47 See Brian Glyn Williams, *The Crimean Tatars. The Diaspora Experience and the Forging of a Nation*, Leiden, 2001.

48 Entry for Crimea in *Encyclopaedia Britannica*, vol. 7., 1910.

49 Capt. Spencer, *Turkey, Russia, the Black Sea and Circassia*, London, 1855, 266.

50 See Mubeyyin Batu Altan, 'A Brief History of the Crimean Tatar National Movement', *Crimean Review*, 1995.

51 *Krym: putevoditel'*, 288.

52 Following the difficult process of repatriation which began in the late 1980s, there are now about 300,000 Tatars living in the Crimea today (about 12 per cent of the total population), with approximately another 300,000 living in Central Asia, following their deportation under Stalin. About 5 million Tatars live in Turkey. See Greta Lynn Uehling, 'The Crimean Tatars' in *Encyclopaedia of the Minorities*, Chicago, 2002.

53 *Romanovy i krym*, 37.

54 L4, 115.

55 I. Losievsky, 'Nesravnennyi Sinani', *Chekhovskie chteniya v Yalte: Chekhov segodnya*, ed. V. I. Kuleshov, Moscow, 1987, 126–131.

56 N. Sysoev, *Chekhov v krymu*, Simferopol, 1954, 60.

57 L7, 348, 295.

58 L9, 148.

59 Kuzicheva and Sakharova, *Melikhovskii letopisets*, 258.

60 L7, 305–358.

61 M. P. Chekhova, *Pis'ma k bratu*, 88, 95, 97.

62 L8, 87, 126–127, 143.

63 Adèle Hommaire de Hell's account in Ignace Xavier M. Hommaire de Hell, *Travels in the Steppes of the Caspian Sea, the Crimea, the Caucasus, &c*, 359.

64 L8, 257.

65 L8, 257.

66 L8, 257, 273, 281, 310, 330.

67 L8, 286, 289; M. P. Chekhova, *Pis'ma k bratu*, 128.

68 L8, 300.

69 M. P. Chekhova, *Pis'ma k bratu*, 126–129, 138; L8, 300.

70 L8, 285, 299, 305, 309, 311, 323, 325, 331.

71 L8, 299.

72 L8, 305.

73 A. G. Golovacheva, ed., *Chekhovskie chteniya v Yalte. Chekhov: Vzglyad iz 1980-kh godov*, Moscow, 1990, 181.

74 L9, 71.

75 L8, 8, 49, 54.

76 I. P. Viduetskaya, *Chekhov i ego izdatel' A. F. Marks*, Moscow, 1977, 7.

77 L9, 36.

78 Dinershtein, *Chekhov i ego izdateli*, 171–173.

79 Viduetskaya, *Chekhov i ego izdatel' A. F. Marks*, 25.

80 L8, 51–52.

81 Gitovich, A. P. *Chekhov v vospominaniyakh sovremennikov*, 472.

82 Viduetskaya, *Chekhov i ego izdatel'* 8–9.

83 L11, 219.

84 Viduetskaya, *Chekhov i ego izdatel'*, 150.

85 Dinershtein, *Chekhov i ego izdateli*, 173.

86 Viduetskaya, *Chekhov i ego izdatel'*, 149.

87 Dinershtein, *Chekhov i ego izdateli*, 186.

CHAPTER 10

1 L6, 107.
2 W10, 135–136.
3 Eugene Swift, *Popular Theater and Society in Tsarist Russia*, Berkeley, 2002, 1.
4 Mandelker-Frieden, *Russian Physicians in an Era of Reform and Revolution*, 93.
5 L13, 72.
6 Gitovich, *Letopis'*, 692–693.
7 Mandelker-Frieden, *Russian Physicians in an Era of Reform and Revolution*, 234.
8 Maurice Baring, *With the Russians in Manchuria*, London, 1905, 4–9.
9 Anatoly and Natalya Vasilenko, 'Lyudi i gody: Moskovskii khram Vozdvizheniya Chestnogo i Zhivotvoryashchego Kresta, chto na Vrazhkakh', *Moskva*, 8, 1994, 191.
10 Simkin, *Sem' let v zhizni A. P. Chekhova*, 124.
11 RGB, fond, 331.46, cited in Simkin, *Sem' let v zhizni A. P. Chekhova*, 149.
12 L10, 94.
13 Rayfield, *Anton Chekhov: A Life*, 557.
14 Nemirovich-Danchenko, *Rozhdenie teatra*, 90.
15 L11, 11.
16 L11, 12–13.
17 Rayfield, *Anton Chekhov: A Life*, 562.
18 L11, 217.
19 L11, 221.
20 L11, 225.
21 L11, 223. Uspensky had died in 1896.
22 L11, 223.
23 V. A. Vilenkin, ed., *Ol'ga Leonardovna Knipper-Chekhova*, vol. 1, Moscow, 1972, 128.
24 L11, 86.
25 Vilenkin, *Ol'ga Leonardovna Knipper-Chekhova*, vol. 1, 340, 343.
26 L11, 316–317.
27 L12, 37–38.
28 L12, 41.
29 L12, 49.

CHAPTER 11

1 Drossi-Steiger, 'Yunyi Chekhov': *Chekhov*, ed. V. V. Vinogradov, Moscow, 1960, 690.
2 Gitovich, *A. P. Chekhov v vospominaniyakh sovremennikov*, 511.
3 *Vokrug Chekhova*, 366.

4 L12, 52.
5 L11, 78, 147, 249, 258, 313; M. P. Chekhova, *Pis'ma k bratu*, 217.
6 Rayfield, *Anton Chekhov: A Life*, 601; A. P. *Chekhov v vospominaniyakh sovremennikov*, 541; L12, 95.
7 L10, 210; L11, 118, 128.
8 W5, 480.
9 L9, 62.
10 L8, 295.
11 L8, 308–309.
12 Elena Stroiteleva, 'Pushkinskii dub kloniruyut', *Izvestiya*, 27 June 2002, 3.
13 Maksim Federov, 'U lukomor'ya dub spalili', *Novye izvestiya*, 11 July 2002, 1.
14 Stroiteleva, 'Pushkinskii dub kloniruyut'.
15 Drossi-Steiger, 'Yunyi Chekhov', 541.
16 L9, 234.
17 Steve Rosenberg, 'Russians to clone legendary tree', BBC, 11 July 2002.
18 Stroiteleva, 'Pushkinskii dub kloniruyut'.
19 Rosenberg, 'Russians to clone legendary tree'.
20 L11, 311.
21 L9, 125.
22 M. Turovskaya, *Ol'ga Leonardovna Knipper-Chekhova, 1868–1959*, Moscow, 1959, cited in Harvey Pitcher, *Chekhov's Leading Lady: A Portrait of the Actress Olga Knipper*, London, 1979, 271.
23 L8, 309; L10, 136, 188; A. P. *Chekhov v vospominaniyakh sovremennikov*, 546.
24 L7, 648, 312–313.
25 L7, 336, 648–649.
26 W16, 363, 368–369, 372–376.
27 A. S. Melkova, 'Dni pamyati Chekhova v Yalte v 1904 godu', *Krymskie penaty*, 72.
28 Drossi-Steiger, 'Yunyi Chekhov', 693; L10, 68.
29 L6, 40.
30 L10, 193, 208, 210.
31 L10, 195.
32 L7, 311.
33 L10, 99.
34 L10, 175.
35 W10, 186.
36 Simkin, *Sem' let iz zhizni A. P. Chekhova*, 129.
37 L8, 22.
38 *A.P. Chekhov v vospominaniyakh sovremennikov*, 544–545.
39 L10, 73, 459.
40 W10, 200.

CHAPTER 12

1 Karl Baedeker, *The Rhine from Rotterdam to Constance: A Handbook for Travellers*, 16th rev. edn, Leipzig, 1906. See also Stefan Kirner, *Die Lokalbahn Mühlheim-Badenweiter*, Nordhorn, 2000.

2 Gustav Faber, *Badenweiler: Ein Stück Italien auf deutschem Grund*, Badenweiler, 1990, 52.

3 See Rolf-Dieter Kluge, *Anton Tschechow in Badenweiler*, Marbach am Neckar, 1990, 52.

4 L12, 120.

5 See Faber, *Badenweiler*, 5.

6 L12, 123.

7 Vilenkin, *Ol'ga Leonardovna Knipper-Chekhova*, vol. 1, 63.

8 See Lev Rabenek, 'Poslednie minuty Chekhova', *Vozrozhdenie*, 85, 1958, 28–35.

9 G. B. Iollos, cited in V. L'vov-Rogachevsky, ed., *A. P. Chekhov v vospominaniyakh sovremennikov i ego pis'makh*, Moscow, 1923, 78.

10 He was not the first writer to die of tuberculosis in Badenweiler. That place belongs to the American Stephen Crane, who died almost immediately upon arrival four years earlier in 1900, at the age of twenty-nine. Crane did not know Chekhov's work, but shared his deep veneration for Tolstoy and an impressionistic approach to the writing of short fiction which has certain similarities with Chekhov's style. Both began their writing careers working for the press.

11 I. N. Sukhikh, ed., *A. P. Chekhov: Pro et Contra*, St Petersburg, 2002, 892.

12 Rabenek, 'Poslednie minuty Chekhova', 34.

13 See Vilenkin, *Ol'ga Leonardovna Knipper-Chekhova*, vol. 1, 67.

14 Suvorin, *Pis'ma A. S. Suvorina k V. V. Rozanovu*, 10.

15 S. A. Vengerov, cited in L'vov-Rogachevsky, *A. P. Chekhov*, 79–80.

16 Victor Emeljanow, *Chekhov: The Critical Heritage*, London, 1981, 73.

17 Melkova, 'Dni pamyati Chekhova v Yalte v 1904 godu', 74–76.

18 A. Derman, *Moskva v zhizni i tvorchestve Chekhova*, Moscow, 1948, 190–192.

19 L'vov-Rogachevsky, *A. P. Chekhov*, 80.

20 L8, 196.

21 L11, 302.

22 Viduetskaya, *A. P. Chekhov i ego izdatel'*, 10–18.

23 L6, 161.

EPILOGUE

1 Derman, *Moskva v zhizni i tvorchestve Chekhova*, 196.

2 W8, 72–126.

3 Andrei Sedov, *Komsomolskaya pravda*, 20 November 2002.

4 Gavryushkin, *Mari Val'iano i drugie*, 266.

5 Pitcher, *Chekhov's Leading Lady*, 231.

6 M. P. Chekhova, *Dom-muzei A. P. Chekhova v Yalte*, Moscow, 1958.

7 Yury Guller, 'V Yalte, u Chekhova', *Vechernyaya moskva*, 24 August 2001, 1.

8 Yulia Larina, 'Chitatel', dama, sobachka, Yalta', *Moskovskie novosti*, 17 June 2003, 27.

9 Larisa Lysova, 'Na fone Chekhova snimalis' prezidenty', *Yuzhnaya guberniya*, 24 May 2003, 16.

10 'Dozhili . . . Na proizvol sud'by broshen dom-muzei A. P. Chekhova v Yalte', *Literaturnaya gazeta*, 18 June 2003, 13.

11 Donations may be made to account number 2600731472001 at the Ukrainian Savings Bank in Yalta, MF0 32470, bank code OKPO 02174017. For further information write to: info@yalta-chekhov.org

12 Vilenkin, *Ol'ga Leonardovna Knipper-Chekhova*, vol. 2, 233.

13 Larina, 'Chitatel', dama, sobachka, Yalta'.

14 Elena Nikityuk, 'Aleksandr Kalyagin vykhodit na yaltinskuyu tsenu', *Yuzhnaya guberniya*, 29 May 2003, 8.

15 W17, 171.

16 V. M. Evdokimov, *Khram Pokrova Presvyatoi Bogoroditsy v Nizhnei Oreande (Bol'shaya Yalta)*, Simferopol, 2002.

17 Petr Palamarchuk, *Sorok sorokov*, vol. 3, Moscow, 1995, 143–144.

18 Yuliya Sedova, 'Istoriya s geografiei. "Doktor Chekhov" na Tseilone', *Literaturnaya gazeta*, 5 September 2001, 13.

19 Kluge, *Anton Tschechow in Badenweiler*, 15.

20 W2, 358.

21 W2, 549.

BIBLIOGRAPHY

Abramenkova, L. Z., 'Sosed Chekhovykh V. N. Semenkovich', *Chekhoviana: Melikhovskie trudy i dny*, ed. V. Lakshin et al., Moscow, 1995

Alfer'eva, A. G., et al., eds., *Taganrog i Chekhovy. Materialy k biografii A. P. Chekhova*, Taganrog, 2003

Altan, Mubeyyin Batu, 'A Brief History of the Crimean Tatar National Movement', *Crimean Review*, 1995

Ascherson, Neal, *Black Sea*, London, 1996

Avdeev, Y., *V Chekhovskom Melikhove*, 3rd rev. edn, Moscow, 1972

Baedeker, Karl, *France Sud-Est*, Paris, 1897

Baedeker, Karl, *The Rhine from Rotterdam to Constance: A Handbook for Travellers*, 16th rev. edn, Leipzig, 1906

Baedeker, Karl, *Russia, with Teheran, Port Arthur and Peking: Handbook for Travellers*, London, 1914

Bandakov, V., *Prostye i kratkie poucheniya protoireya Vas. Bandakova*, 5th edn, Moscow, 1900

Baring, Maurice, *With the Russians in Manchuria*, London, 1905

Bassin, Mark, *Imperial Visions: Nationalist Imagination and Geographical Expansion in the Russian Far East, 1840–1865*, Cambridge, 1999

Blume, Mary, *Côte d'Azur: Inventing the French Riviera*, London, 1992

Boardman, John, *The Greeks Overseas*, 4th edn, London, 1990

Bobrick, Benson, *East of the Sun: The Conquest and Settlement of Siberia*, London, 1992

Bodik, L. A., ed., *Taganrog: Istoriko-kravedcheskii ocherk*, Rostov-on-Don, 1977

Bourrier, Michel and Gerard Colletta, *Chronologie illustrée de l'histoire du Comte de Nice*, Nice, 2000

Bychkov, Yury, ed., *Al'manakh Melikhovo*, Tula, 1999

Bychkov, Yury and Marina Orlova, eds., *Chekhovy v Melikhove: Semeinyi al'bom*, Moscow, 2000

Chekhov, A. P., *Polnoe sobranie sochinenii i pisem v tridsati tomakh*, ed. N. F. Belchikov et al., Moscow, 1974–83

Chekhov, A. P., *About Love and Other Stories*, ed. and tr. Rosamund Bartlett, Oxford, 2004

Chekhov, A. P., *Chekhov: A Life in Letters*, ed. Rosamund Bartlett, tr. R. Bartlett and A. Phillips, London, 2004

Chekhov, Aleksandr, 'A. P. Chekhov – pevchii', *A. P. Chekhov v vospominaniyakh sovremennikov*, ed. N. I. Gitovich, Moscow, 1954

Chekhov, Aleksandr, 'V grecheskoi shkole', *Vokrug Chekhova*, ed. E. M. Sakharova, Moscow, 1990

Chekhova, M. P., *Pis'ma k bratu A. P. Chekhovu*, Moscow, 1954

Chekhova, M. P., *Dom-muzei A. P. Chekhova v Yalte*, Moscow, 1958

Chudakov, A. P., "Neprilichnye slova' i oblik klassika', *Novoe literaturnoe obozrenie*, 11, 1991, 54–56

Clowes, Edith W., Samuel D. Kassow and James L. West, eds., *Between Tsar and People: Educated Society and the Quest for Public Identity in Late Imperial Russia*, Princeton, 1991

Coope, John, *Doctor Chekhov: A Study in Literature and Medicine*, Chale, 1997

Derman, A. P., ed., *Perepiska A. P. Chekhova i O. L. Knipper*, 2 vols, Moscow, 1936

Derman, A. P., *Moskva v zhizni i tvorchestve Chekhova*, Moscow, 1948

Dewar, A. C., ed., *Russian War, 1855: Black Sea Official Correspondence*, London, 1945

Dinershtein, E. A., *Chekhov i ego izdateli*, Moscow, 1990

Drossi-Steiger, M. D., 'Yunyi Chekhov', *Literaturnoe nasledstvo 68: Chekhov*, ed. V. V. Vinogradov, Moscow, 1960, 538–541

Dunaeva, V. P., 'Plavanie A. P. Chekhova na parakhode "Peterburga" (po materialam fonda "Dobrovol'nogo flota")', *Literaturnoe nasledstvo 87: Iz istorii russkoi literatury i obshchestvennoi mysli, 1860–1890*, ed. V. R. Shcherbina, Moscow, 1977, 294–300

Durkin, Andrew, 'Chekhov and the journals of his time', *Literary Journals in Imperial Russia*, ed. Deborah A. Martinsen, Cambridge, 1997

Eardley-Wilmot, S., *Life of Vice-Admiral Edmund, Lord Lyons*, London, 1898

Ellis, Leroy, *Les Russes sur la Côte d'Azur: La colonie russe dans les Alpes-Maritimes des origines à 1939*, Nice, 1988

Emeljanow, Victor, *Chekhov: The Critical Heritage*, London, 1981

Evdokimov, V. M., *Khram Pokrova Presvyatoi Bogoroditsy v Nizhnei Oreande (Bol'shaya Yalta)*, Simferopol, 2002

Ezhov, I. S., ed., *Pis'ma A. P. Chekhovu ego brata Aleksandra Chekhova*, Moscow, 1939

Faber, Gustav, *Badenweiler: Ein Stück Italien auf deutschem Grund*, Badenweiler, 1990

Fedorov-Davydov, A., ed., *Levitan: Pis'ma, dokumenty*, Moscow, 1956

Feider, V., *A. P. Chekhov: Literaturnyi byt i tvorchestvo po memuarnym materialam*, Leningrad, 1928

Filevsky, P. P., *Istoriya goroda Taganroga*, Moscow, 1898

Gavryushkin, O. P., *Gulyaet staryi Taganrog*, Taganrog, 1997

Gavryushkin, O. P., *Vdol' po piterskoi*, Taganrog, 2000

Gavryushkin, O. P., *Mari Val'iano i drugie (khronika obyvatel'skoi zhizni)*, Taganrog, 2001

Gitovich, N. I. and Federov, I. V., eds., *A. P. Chekhov v vospominaniyakh sovremennikov*, Moscow, 1954

Gitovich, N. I. and Federov, I. V., eds., *A. P. Chekhov v vospominaniyakh sovremennikov*, Moscow, 1960

Gitovich, N. I., *A. P. Chekhov v vospominaniyakh sovremennikov*, Moscow, 1986

Gitovich, N. I., *Letopis' zhizni i tvorchestva A. P. Chekhova*, Moscow, 1955

Golovacheva, A. G., ed., *Chekhovskie chteniya v Yalte. Chekhov: Vzglyad iz 1980-kh godov*, Moscow, 1990

Gromov, L. P., 'Chekhov i Przhevalskii', *Tvorchestvo A. P. Chekhova: Sbornik statei*, ed. L. P. Gromov, Rostov-on-Don, 1977

Gromov, M., *Chekhov*, Moscow, 1993

Gromova, M. P., ed., *Perepiska A. P. Chekhova*, 2nd rev. edn, 3 vols., Moscow, 1996

Gromova-Opul'skaya, L. D. and N. I. Gitovich, eds., *Letopis' zhizni i tvorchestva A. P. Chekhova. Tom Pervyi. 1860–1888*, Moscow, 2000

Henderson, E., *Biblical Researches and Travels in Russia*, London, 1826

Herodotus, *The Histories*, tr. Robin Waterfield, Oxford, 1998

Hingley, Ronald, *A New Life of Anton Chekhov*, London, 1976

Hommaire de Hell, Ignace Xavier M., *Travels in the Steppes of the Caspian Sea, the Crimea, the Caucasus, &c*, London, 1847

Howarth, Patrick, *When the Riviera was Ours*, London, 1977

Izmailov, A., *Chekhov, 1860–1904: Biograficheskii ocherk*, Moscow, 1916

Kandidov, A. V., *Chekhov v Bogimove*, Kaluga, 1991

Kanigel, Robert, *High Season in Nice: How One French Town Has Seduced Travellers for 2000 Years*, London, 2002

Karlinsky, Simon, ed. and intr., *Anton Chekhov's Life and Thought: Selected Letters and Commentary*, tr. Michael Henry Heim in collaboration with Simon Karlinsky, New York, 1973

Kataev, V. B., 'Chekhov i Frantsiya', *Chekhoviana: Chekhov i Frantsiya*, ed. G. I. Romanova, Moscow, 1991, 8–18

Kennan, George, *Siberia and the Exile System*, 2 vols., London, 1891

Kirner, Stefan, *Die Lokalbahn Müllheim-Badenweiler*, Nordhorn, 2000

Kleopatro, N. M., 'Istoriya zaseleniya Severo-Vostochnogo Priazov'ya s drevneishikh vremen do kontsa XVIII veka', *Taganrog: Sbornik statei*, ed. E. P. Konopleva and E. A. Kozhevnikova, Taganrog, 1997

Kluge, Rolf-Dieter, *Anton Tschechow in Badenweiler*, Marbach am Neckar, 1990

Kohl, J. G., *Russia: St. Petersburg, Moscow . . . and the Interior of the Empire*, London, 1842

Kopylov, Victor, 'Taganrog et la première colonisation grecque du littoral nord-est de la mer d'Azov', *Sur les traces des Argonautes*, ed. Otar Lordkipanidze and Pierre Lévêque, Paris, 1996

Koromila, Marianna, *The Greeks in the Black Sea*, Athens, 1991

Krym: Putevoditel', Simferopol, 1914

Kulikovskaya, A. B., 'Otets Chekhova', *Chekhoviana: Chekhov i ego okruzhenie*, ed. V. B. Kataev et al., Moscow, 1996

Kuzicheva, A. I., *Vash A. Chekhov*, Moscow, 1994

Kuzicheva, A. I., 'Chekhov o sebe i sovremenniki o Chekhov (legko li byt' biografom Chekhova?)', *Chekhoviana: Chekhov i ego okruzhenie*, ed. V. B. Kataev et al., Moscow, 1996

Kuzicheva, A. I. and E. M. Sakharova, eds., *Melikhovskii letopisets*, Moscow, 1995

Lambert, Andrew, *The Crimean War: British Grand Strategy Against Russia, 1853–1856*, Manchester, 1990

Lambert, Andrew, and Stephen Badsey, *The War Correspondents: The Crimean War*, Stroud, 1994

Lensen, George, *The Russian Push Towards Japan: Russo–Japanese Relations, 1697–1875*, Princeton, 1959

Linin, A. M., ed., *A. P. Chekhov i nash krai. K 75-letiyu so dnya rozhdeniya*, Rostov-on-Don, 1935

Losievsky, I., 'Nesravnennyi Sinani', *Chekhovskie chteniya v Yalte: Chekhov segodnya*, ed. V. I. Kuleshov, Moscow, 1987

Lovell, Stephen, *Summerfolk: A History of the Dacha, 1710–2000*, Ithaca, 2003

L'vov-Rogachevsky, V., ed., *A. P. Chekhov v vospominaniyakh sovremennikov i ego pis'makh*, Moscow, 1923

Lyons, Marvin, *Russia in Original Photographs*, London, 1977

Malcolm, Janet, *Reading Chekhov*, London, 2003

Mandelker-Frieden, Nancy, *Russian Physicians in an Era of Reform and Revolution, 1856–1905*, Princeton, 1981

McReynolds, Louise, *The News Under Russia's Old Regime*, Princeton, 1991

Melkova, A. S., 'Khudozhnik Nikolai Chekhov. Sud'ba i konchina', *Chekhovskie chteniya v Yalte*, ed. V. A. Bogdanov, Moscow, 1997

Melkova, A. S., 'Dni pamyati Chekhova v Yalte v 1904 godu', *Krymskie penaty*, ed. G. Shalyugin, Simferopol, 1998, 72–77

Milner, Thos., *The Crimea, its Ancient and Modern History: The Khans, the Sultans, and the Czars with Notices of its Scenery and Population*, London, 1855

Miromanov, T. G., 'Ieromonakh Iraklyi', *Chekhoviana: Chekhov i ego okruzhenie*, ed. V. B. Kataev et al., Moscow, 1996

Mirsky, M. B., *Doktor Chekhov*, Moscow, 2003

Moskvich, G., *Illyustrirovannyi prakticheskii putevoditel' po Krymu*, Odessa, 1908

Murray's Handbook for Travellers to Russia, London, 1875

Nabokov, Vladimir, *Speak, Memory*, London, 1969

Nalegatskaia, Ludmila, 'Tchekov à Nice: 1', *Revue des deux mondes*, November, 1973, 340–350

Nalegatskaia, Ludmila, 'Tchekov à Nice: 2', *Revue des deux mondes*, December 1973, 578–589

Nansen, Fridtjof, *Through Siberia*, London, 1914

Nelson, Michael, *Queen Victoria and the Discovery of the Riviera*, London, 2001

Nemirovich-Danchenko, Vladimir, *Rozhdenie teatra: Vospominaniya, stat'i, zametki, pis'ma*, Moscow, 1989

Palamarchuk, Petr, *Sorok sorokov*, 3 vols., Moscow, 1995

Papernyi, Z. S., 'On ne s nami . . .', *Chekhoviana: Chekhov i ego okruzhenie*, ed. V. B. Kataev et al., Moscow, 1996

Pitcher, Harvey, *Chekhov's Leading Lady: A Portrait of the Actress Olga Knipper*, London, 1979

Ponfilly, Raymond de, *Guide des russes en France*, Paris, 1990

Pritchett, V. S., *Chekhov: A Spirit Set Free*, New York, 1988

Rabenek, Lev, 'Poslednie minuty Chekhova', *Vozrozhdenie*, 84, 1958, 28–35

Rabenek, Lev, 'Serdtse Chekhova', *Vozrozhdenie*, 92, 1959, 117–122

Rayfield, Donald, *Anton Chekhov: A Life*, London, 1997

Rayfield, Donald, *Understanding Chekhov*, London, 1998

Razumova, N. E., *Tvorchestvo A. P. Chekhova v aspekte prostranstva*, Tomsk, 2001

Razuvaeva, S., 'Iz istorii Taganrogskogo gorodskogo parka', *Vekhi Taganroga*, 9, 2001

Rieber, Alfred J., *Merchants and Entrepreneurs in Imperial Russia*, Chapel Hill, 1982

Sabaneev, Leonid, *Zhizn' i lovlya presnovodnykh ryb* (reprint of *Ryby Rossii*, 1911), Moscow, 1991

Sakharova, E. M., ed., *Vokrug Chekhova*, Moscow, 1990

Schimmelpenninck van der Oye, David, *Toward the Rising Sun: Russian Ideologies of Empire and the Path to War with Japan*, De Kalb, Illinois, 2001

Sedegov, V. D., ed., *A. P. Chekhov: Sbornik statei i materialov*, Rostov-on-Don, 1959

Sedoi, A. [Aleksandr Chekhov], 'Nedavnee proshloe azovskogo poberezh'ya', *Istoricheskii vestnik*, 10, 1904

Semenov, M. and Tulupov, N., eds., *Chekhovskii yubileinyi sbornik*, Moscow, 1910

Seymour, H. D., *Russia on the Black Sea and Sea of Azov*, London, 1855

Shalyugin, G., ed., *Krymskie penaty: A. P. Chekhov i krym*, Simferopol, 1998

Shapochka, E. A., '. . . Fantasticheskii krai' Chekhovskogo Priazov'ya', *Chekhoviana: Chekhov i ego okruzhenie*, ed. V. B. Kataev et al., Moscow, 1996

Shcheboleva, G. F., 'Pushkinskie torzhestva 1880 g. v Moskve glazami khudozhnika Nikolaya Chekhova', *Chekhoviana: Chekhov i Pushkin*, ed. V. B. Kataev et al., Moscow, 1998

Simkin, Y., *Sem' let iz zhizni A. P. Chekhova*, Rostov-on-Don, 1987

Simmons, Ernest J., *Chekhov: A Biography*, Boston, 1962

Spencer, Capt., *Turkey, Russia, the Black Sea and Circassia*, London, 1855

Stepanov, Y., *Konstanty: Slovar' russkoi kul'tury*, Moscow, 1997

Stephan, John, *Sakhalin: A History*, Oxford, 1971

Sukhikh, I. N., ed., *A. P. Chekhov: Pro et Contra*, St Petersburg, 2002

Suvorin, A. S., *Pis'ma A. S. Suvorina k V. V. Rozanovu*, St Petersburg, 1913

Suvorin, A. S., *Dnevnik Alekseya Sergeyevicha Suvorina*, ed. D. Rayfield and O. Makarova, Moscow/London, 1999

Swift, Eugene A. S., *Popular Theater and Society in Tsarist Russia*, Berkeley, 2002

Tikhon, Arkhiepiskop, ed., *Russkaya pravoslavnaya tserkov'. Monastyry: entsiklopedicheskii slovar'*, Moscow, 2000

Turovskaya, M., *Ol'ga Leonardovna Knipper-Chekhova, 1868–1959*, Moscow, 1959

Uehling, Greta Lynn, 'The Crimean Tatars' in *Encyclopaedia of the Minorities*, Chicago, 2002

Vaganova, A. K., 'Chekhovskaya step' kak natsional'nyi obraz', *Chekhovskie chteniya*, ed. L. P. Vaganova et al., Taganrog, 2001

Vel'cheva, A., *Taganrog: Fotoal'bom*, Taganrog, 1999

Viduetskaya, I. P., *Chekhov i ego izdatel' A. F. Marks*, Moscow, 1977

Vilenkin, V. Y., ed., *Ol'ga Leonardovna Knipper-Chekhova*, 2 vols., Moscow, 1972

Vol'f, M., *Kroket: obshchie pravila igry*, Petrograd, 1916

West, James L. and Y. A. Petrov, eds., *Merchant Moscow: Images of Russia's Vanished Bourgeoisie*, Princeton, 1997

Williams, Brian Glyn, *The Crimean Tatars. The Diaspora Experience and the Forging of a Nation*, Leiden, 2001

Zemlyanichenko, M. and N. Kalinin, *Romanovy i Krym*, Moscow, 1993

Zvyagintsev, E. A., *Moskva: Putevoditel'*, Moscow, 1915

INDEX

Page numbers in italics denote illustration.